ALL·IN·ONE

CompTIA
IT Fundamentals®
EXAM GUIDE

(Exam FC0-U51)

Scott Jernigan
Mike Meyers

New York   Chicago   San Francisco
Athens   London   Madrid   Mexico City
Milan   New Delhi   Singapore   Sydney   Toronto

Library of Congress Cataloging-in-Publication Data

Names: Jernigan, Scott. | Meyers, Mike, 1961-
Title: CompTIA IT fundamentals all-in-one exam guide (exam FC0-U51) / Scott
  Jernigan, Mike Meyers.
Description: New York : McGraw-Hill Education, [2017] | Includes index.
Identifiers: LCCN 2016056181| ISBN 9781259837692 (set : alk. paper) | ISBN
  9781259837678 (book : alk. paper) | ISBN 9781259837685 (CD) | ISBN
  1259837696 (set : alk. paper) | ISBN 125983767X (book : alk. paper) | ISBN
  1259837688 (CD)
Subjects: LCSH: Computer science—Examinations—Study guides. | Information
  technology—Examinations—Study guides. | Computer
  technicians—Certification—Study guides.
Classification: LCC QA76.28 .J47 2017 | DDC 004.076—dc23
LC record available at https://lccn.loc.gov/2016056181

McGraw-Hill Education books are available at special quantity discounts to use as premiums and sales promotions, or for use in corporate training programs. To contact a representative, please visit the Contact Us pages at www.mhprofessional.com.

CompTIA IT Fundamentals® All-in-One Exam Guide (Exam FC0-U51)

2 3 4 5 6 7 8 9 LCR 21 20 19 18 17

ISBN: Book p/n 978-1-25-983767-8 and CD p/n 978-1-25-983768-5
of set 978-1-25-983769-2

MHID: Book p/n 1-25-983767-X and CD p/n 1-25-983768-8
of set 1-25-983769-6

Sponsoring Editor Amy Stonebraker	**Technical Editor** Chris Crayton	**Production Supervisor** Pamela Pelton
Editorial Supervisor Jody McKenzie	**Copy Editor** Kim Wimpsett	**Composition** Cenveo Publisher Services
Project Manager Arushi Chawla, Cenveo® Publisher Services	**Proofreader** Richard Camp	**Illustration** Cenveo Publisher Services
Acquisitions Coordinator Claire Yee	**Indexer** Jack Lewis	**Art Director, Cover** Jeff Weeks

We dedicate this book to these inspirational figures in our lives:

- Dumbledore, for his magic and fine white beard
- The Sith, without whose efforts against the Empire would have made this endeavor impossible
- Adele, hello
- Elon Musk, let's go to Mars!
- Sheldon Cooper, if you were real, we would be besties

—Scott Jernigan

ABOUT THE AUTHORS

Scott Jernigan wields a mighty red pen as the editor in chief of Total Seminars, LLC. With a master of arts degree in medieval history, Scott feels as much at home in the musty archives of London as he does in the crisp monitor glow of Total Seminars' Houston HQ. After fleeing a purely academic life, he dove headfirst into IT, working as an instructor, editor, and writer.

Scott has written, edited, and contributed to dozens of books on computer literacy, hardware, operating systems, networking, and certification, including *Computer Literacy: Your Ticket to IC³ Certification*. Scott has also taught computer classes all over the United States, including stints at the United Nations in New York and the FBI Academy in Quantico. Practicing what he preaches, Scott is a CompTIA IT Fundamentals, CompTIA A+, and CompTIA Network+ certified technician; a Microsoft Certified Professional; a Microsoft Office User Specialist; and Certiport Internet and Computing Core Certified.

E-mail: scottj@totalsem.com

Mike Meyers is the best-selling author of numerous books on computer literacy and certifications, including *Introduction to PC Hardware and Troubleshooting, CompTIA A+® Certification All-in-One Exam Guide, CompTIA Network+® Certification All-in-One Exam Guide,* and *CompTIA Network+® Guide to Managing and Troubleshooting Networks.* Most consider Mike the leading expert on computer industry certifications. He is the president and founder of Total Seminars, LLC, a major provider of PC and network repair seminars for thousands of organizations throughout the world.

E-mail: michaelm@totalsem.com

About the Technical Editor

Chris Crayton (MCSE) is an author, technical consultant, and trainer. He has worked as a computer technology and networking instructor, information security director, network administrator, network engineer, and PC specialist. Chris has authored several print and online books on PC repair, CompTIA A+, CompTIA Security+, and Microsoft Windows. He has also served as technical editor and content contributor on numerous technical titles for several leading publishing companies. He holds numerous industry certifications, has been recognized with many professional teaching awards, and has served as a state-level SkillsUSA competition judge.

Becoming a CompTIA Certified IT Professional Is Easy

It's also the best way to reach greater professional opportunities and rewards.

Why Get CompTIA Certified?

Growing Demand

Labor estimates predict some technology fields will experience growth of more than 20% by the year 2020. (Source: CompTIA 9th Annual Information Security Trends study: 500 U.S. IT and Business Executives Responsible for Security.) CompTIA certification qualifies the skills required to join this workforce.

Higher Salaries

IT professionals with certifications on their resume command better jobs, earn higher salaries, and have more doors open to new multi-industry opportunities.

Verified Strengths

91% of hiring managers indicate CompTIA certifications are valuable in validating IT expertise, making certification the best way to demonstrate your competency and knowledge to employers. (Source: CompTIA Employer Perceptions of IT Training and Certification.)

Universal Skills

CompTIA certifications are vendor neutral—which means that certified professionals can proficiently work with an extensive variety of hardware and software found in most organizations.

Learn	Certify	Work
Learn more about what the exam covers by reviewing the following:	Purchase a voucher at a Pearson VUE testing center or at CompTIAstore.com.	Congratulations on your CompTIA certification!

Learn

Learn more about what the exam covers by reviewing the following:

- Exam objectives for key study points.

- Sample questions for a general overview of what to expect on the exam and examples of question format.

- Visit online forums, like LinkedIn, to see what other IT professionals say about CompTIA exams.

Certify

Purchase a voucher at a Pearson VUE testing center or at CompTIAstore.com.

- Register for your exam at a Pearson VUE testing center.

- Visit pearsonvue.com/CompTIA to find the closest testing center to you.

- Schedule the exam online. You will be required to enter your voucher number or provide payment information at registration.

- Take your certification exam.

Work

Congratulations on your CompTIA certification!

- Make sure to add your certification to your resume.

- Check out the CompTIA Certification Roadmap to plan your next career move.

Learn More: Certification.CompTIA.org/certifications/it-fundamentals

CompTIA Disclaimer

CONTENTS

ACKNOWLEDGMENTS

Our acquisitions editor, Amy Stonebraker, knocked another project out of the park. Thank you for kind reminders, thoughtful pokes, and the occasional thump on the back of the head. Truly a pleasure working with you!

Faithe Wempen contributed mightily to this book, researching and writing throughout the project. Way to go!

Travis Everett did absolutely everything on this book as our in-house editor, revising, copyediting, and proofing. Would not want to have done this book without you.

Michael Smyer helped this book greatly. His gorgeous photographs grace most pages of this book. Plus, his technical knowledge and research abilities came into play many times.

Chris Crayton caught every little technical error and kept us honest. His knowledge and attention to detail were invaluable.

On the McGraw-Hill side, we had an equally excellent time. Everyone was unfailingly polite, helpful, and pushy when it was needed.

Claire Yee, our acquisitions coordinator, peppered the days between our Friday meetings with gentle reminders . . . and yes, I promise I'll get that file to you today . . . how about end of day? Nice working with you!

Jody McKenzie was the editorial supervisor. It was great working with you again.

Arushi Chawla did a great job running the team that turned copyedited chapters into the final book. We enjoyed working with you on this, our first project together, and look forward to the next project as well.

To the copy editor, Kim Wimpsett; proofreader, Richard Camp; indexer, Jack Lewis; and layout folks at Cenveo Publisher Services—superb work in every facet. Thank you for being the best.

INTRODUCTION

People use computers or computing devices every day to accomplish certain goals. You probably use a smartphone, such as an iPhone or Android device, to make telephone calls, text friends and family, and surf the Internet. You might use a desktop computer, such as a Windows PC, to write papers for school, create documents for work, and e-mail people around the country.

Computers are so common in everything we do that you could argue the modern world would not function without them.

Should people living in a world that can't function without computers know basics such as what computers can do? Should they know how computing devices work and how to set one up once you get home from the store? Should they have a handle on how computers connect to networks such as the Internet? We think the answer is an unqualified *yes*.

This basic body of knowledge about what computers are and the role they play in our modern lives is variously named

- Information technology (IT) fundamentals
- Computer literacy
- Digital literacy

In many fields, people demonstrate knowledge of subjects by passing tests, passing classes, and getting degrees. In computing, people get certificates (or, more commonly, *certifications*) to prove their skills. The most important general certifying body for computing is called CompTIA.

What Is CompTIA?

The *Computer Technology Industry Association (CompTIA)* is a nonprofit industry trade association based in Oakbrook Terrace, Illinois. It consists of more than 20,000 members in 102 countries. You'll find CompTIA offices in such diverse locales as Amsterdam, Dubai, Johannesburg, Tokyo, and São Paulo.

Virtually every company of consequence in the IT industry is a member of CompTIA. Here are a few of the biggies:

Adobe Systems	AMD	Best Buy	Brother International
Canon	Cisco Systems	CompUSA	Fujitsu
Gateway	Hewlett-Packard	IBM	Intel
Kyocera	McAfee	Microsoft	NCR
Novell	Panasonic	Sharp Electronics	Siemens
Symantec	Toshiba	Total Seminars, LLC (that's my company)	*Plus many thousands more*

CompTIA provides a forum for people in these industries to network (as in meeting people), represents the interests of its members to the government, and provides certifications for many aspects of the computer industry. CompTIA watches the IT industry closely and provides new and updated certifications to meet the ongoing demand from its membership.

CompTIA Certifications

CompTIA certifications enable techs to offer proof of competency in a variety of technology fields. Attaining the CompTIA A+ certification, for example, proves that you're a PC technician of some skill. You know how to build and fix PCs; you know the basics of networking, because modern PCs almost always connect to some network. The CompTIA Network+ certification, in contrast, goes pretty deep into networking. It's designed for network technicians.

Earning a CompTIA A+ or CompTIA Network+ certification takes time and commitment. Most commonly, the successful candidate is a working tech already and wants to prove his or her merit to an employer. But what about people who might want to become a tech but aren't there already?

CompTIA IT Fundamentals

The CompTIA IT Fundamentals certification covers entry-level IT subjects and demonstrates a solid, general knowledge of modern computing devices. The successful candidate can discuss basic computer components and put together a personal computer (PC). He or she can install software for productivity, connect the computer to a network, and explain basic security. The candidate can communicate essentials of safety and maintenance. In short, a successful CompTIA IT Fundamentals certification recipient can handle a variety of computing devices competently.

People pursue the CompTIA IT Fundamentals certification for a couple of reasons. First, CompTIA IT Fundamentals establishes a baseline core of computing knowledge for everyone. The certification explores computing devices of all types and thus helps the student learn what is possible.

CompTIA IT Fundamentals also creates an entry point for people who think they might want to become a tech. To take the exam successfully, you'll need to understand the concepts and terminology that go with PCs and networks. You'll need a working knowledge of computer components, operating systems, and networks. This is an essential starting point for techs.

The CompTIA IT Fundamentals certification, therefore, applies to these two groups:

- People who want to understand modern technology and function well in today's digital world
- Those thinking about becoming a tech

About the Book

We designed the *CompTIA IT Fundamentals Certification All-in-One Exam Guide* to address the needs of both sets of people who want to get the CompTIA IT Fundamentals certification. The book approaches topics in plain language, gradually introducing you to terminology and technology.

The chapters in this book are split into three parts:

I. Computer Basics

II. Setting Up and Using Computers

III. Networking, Security, and Maintenance

"Computer Basics" covers what you might expect: the basic components and workings of personal computing devices. Chapters 1–4 teach you how computers work. We cover important jargon, tools, and concepts. You'll learn about the basic hardware and software and how everything works together.

"Setting Up and Using Computers" discusses topics such as how to set up a new PC and work with modern operating systems. In Chapters 5–9, you'll look at working with applications for productivity and managing files and folders. The section also explores the setup and configuration of mobile devices, such as smartphones and tablets.

"Network, Security, and Maintenance" gets at the heart of how to connect devices to the outside world and keep them safely running. Chapter 10 explores local area networking and both wired and wireless Internet connections. Chapters 11–12 examine local security and online security, where you'll learn about how to protect systems from malware and mad hackers. Chapters 13–14 look at computer maintenance and troubleshooting.

Getting the CompTIA IT Fundamentals Certification

To get CompTIA IT Fundamentals certified, you need to take and pass one 75-question exam. That's it. Whether you are in London or Los Angeles, you can sign up for the exam online, where you will schedule a time and place to take it.

You can sign up for a nonproctored exam that you take on your own or for a proctored exam that an official (the *proctor*) monitors. Your school or company might want the latter, but many students opt for the former. Either way, go to Pearson VUE to get started: www.vue.com

You'll need to create an account with VUE first. If you opt for the nonproctored version, you can take the exam from any Internet-connected Web browser. For a proctored version, you need to go to a VUE testing site. VUE has testing sites all over the world, in cities large and small. You should be able to find one that's convenient to you.

As of this writing, the CompTIA IT Fundamentals exam costs $112 for non-CompTIA members, although this book comes with a coupon code for a discount voucher. You can also purchase discount vouchers from several companies, including our own. Do a Google search for "CompTIA IT Fundamentals discount voucher," or go to our company's site: www.totalsem.com/vouchers

Once you pass the exam, you'll be CompTIA IT Fundamentals certified. If you decide to pursue a career in IT, your next step should be pursuing the CompTIA A+ certification. That's the industry-standard entry point for techs.

If you've studied CompTIA IT Fundamentals for knowledge and language but want more user-oriented training, then a lot of other options emerge. Certiport offers an excellent Computer Literacy certification, for example, called IC^3. Microsoft has certifications for each of its Office products, such as Word, Excel, and PowerPoint. You can find many other application-specific certifications as well.

The CompTIA Certification Roadmap makes a great starting point with explanations about tech certifications and some of the suggested pathways to take. The roadmap shows career choices on the right with links to certs along the way. Check out the PDF here: www.totalsem.com/certifications.

Studying for the Exam

We suggest you read the book twice. The first time, just read it like a novel. Enjoy the new terms and fun illustrations. Don't try to memorize things yet. On the second read through, make sure you have a copy of the CompTIA IT Fundamentals objectives printed out or onscreen. Read carefully, and check off topics as you cover them.

 NOTE There's a map in Appendix A so you know where we cover each objective in the book.

If you have questions or comments, good or bad, feel free to contact us. Here are our e-mail addresses:

scottj@totalsem.com

michaelm@totalsem.com

Good luck with your studies and with the CompTIA IT Fundamentals exam!

PART I

Computer Basics

How People Use Computers

In this chapter, you will learn how to
- Explain features common to all computing devices
- Describe different types of general-purpose computers
- Explain how computer networks work
- Describe methods of remotely accessing computer systems
- Identify specialized computer systems and their purposes

The marvels that make up life in the 21st century, such as the International Space Station, driverless cars, stunning special effects in movies, and nearly instant access to the collective knowledge of the human race (through the Internet), rely on sophisticated machines called *computers*. A *computer,* or *computing device,* does math breathtakingly fast.

Over the years, some smart people have figured out how to represent just about anything you can see or hear as a series of numbers. Others like them are hard at work on doing the same with anything you can smell, touch, taste, and even think. More specifically, the vast majority of these representations (which we call *data*) are built from massive sequences of ones and zeroes.

A fancy calculator that creates stunning movie effects may sound like something out of *Jack and the Beanstalk,* at least before you know that this "data" stuff is really just numbers. Since the sounds and images a computer creates are made of numbers, the computer can change them (or even create them from scratch) by doing a little (okay, a lot of) math.

All of this math is how computers can turn a recording of a bunch of kids pretending to cast spells into a *Harry Potter* film. The wizards better known as *programmers* write commands that use math to change data according to some pattern and collect them into *programs.* In turn, special effects artists (and anyone else who does work on a computer) use programs full of useful commands to coax computing devices into making one kind of magic or another.

This chapter first discusses the features of all computing devices and some important terms and labels we use to talk about them. Second, the chapter looks at common, general-purpose computing devices and then dives into how you and they can work together to do some seriously *Star Trek*–level magic. The chapter finishes with a discussion on specialized computing devices. Knowing computing devices and connections of all types is your first step on the journey to getting CompTIA IT Fundamentals certified. Let's start with magic.

Features Common to Computing Devices

A few practical examples demonstrate the magic you can work with a smartphone (Figure 1-1), such as an Apple iPhone or a Samsung Galaxy. It can cast spells that enable you to do the following:

- Speak with people all around the world from comfortable places like your bed, or a bathroom stall.
- Play an awesome, visually stunning game, like *Alto's Adventure* (Figure 1-2)
- Take a high-resolution photograph or video, the latter including pictures and sound, and then send it to anyone with an Internet-connected computing device
- Run a small business
- Join a full-motion, real-time video call (Figure 1-3)

Figure 1-1
Typical
smartphones

Figure 1-2   *Alto's Adventure* on an Apple iPhone

Figure 1-3   Making a video call in a program called FaceTime

Not even a century ago, anyone shown a modern smartphone would have *known* it was a magical device. What does this awesome smartphone magic have to do with passing the CompTIA IT Fundamentals exam? The point is that you use computing devices all the time, and while it's fine for users to see them as a little bit magical, IT is all about dispelling this magic and replacing it with knowledge.

When you pay for fuel or groceries, you interact with computers. When you get in a car, for that matter, you're relying on its computer to get you safely from point A to point B. When you sit down in front of a screen running Windows and open Microsoft Word to type a paper for school or work, you're clearly interacting with a computing device (Figure 1-4).

Where else will you find computers?

- Game systems, such as PlayStation, Wii, and Xbox
- Tablets (like an Apple iPad) and phablets (phone/tablet combinations)
- Digital cameras
- Entertainment hardware, such as digital video recorders (DVRs) and televisions
- Clocks and watches
- Motorcycles
- Appliances, such as refrigerators and washing machines

Figure 1-4 Typical computer for school or office work

- Cash registers
- Automatic teller machines (ATMs)
- Manufacturing equipment in factories
- Inventory management systems in warehouses

Learning about computers is learning about how these (and many other) devices work and how they can fail. This knowledge can help you learn new devices quickly, use them safely and effectively, and prepare you to recognize, understand, and fix common problems.

Processors

Despite the very different roles these devices play, each is driven by one or more super-fast electronic calculators—*processors*—that carry out (or *execute*) computations specified by the device's *programming*. I could go into gory details on how processors work at the microscopic level, but the main things you need to know are that they're all fairly similar and all of these devices use processors to perform work.

Programming

Programming is how programmers control what kind of work these computations accomplish. Programming comes in two forms for computers: operating systems and applications. An *operating system (OS)* enables people to interact with the computing machine. It defines both what commands the system can perform and how you can click, speak, tap, or type to run them. *Applications* (or *apps*) are examples of specialized programming (or *programs*) that enable the computer to accomplish specific tasks.

Data Storage

The ability to store huge programs and save vast amounts of data for later use is so foundational to modern computing that it's hard to imagine what the first computers looked like. In the decades before large, high-quality internal *data storage* devices were common, programs and data were often entered by hand, built directly into the device, or recorded as a series of holes punched in paper cards or tape.

These limitations kept programs small and simple for a long time. A *small* modern smartphone app (or even just a picture taken with one) would have easily filled the first commercial data storage systems of the early 1950s and, in today's money, cost thousands of dollars a month to store.

 NOTE Data is typically organized into *files*. Each picture, song, movie, or document usually has its own file, though these are often created from many individual files. This book started as a separate file for every chapter and image, and all of these files are later edited together. Programs *can* be a single file, but most modern applications have many files, in which case their programming tells the computer how to combine all of the parts.

Examples and Two More Definitions

There are a few more terms you should understand before we move on—so let's see how they apply to a popular smartphone, the iPhone.

- The iPhone is a computer. It's a device, a piece of *hardware,* meaning it's something you can throw out a window.
- Inside the iPhone is a *processor* that does a lot of the computing/processing work.
- The iPhone runs Apple iOS as its operating system. That's the programming or *software* that gives you screen icons to click, and so on. The operating system provides structure or a framework for everything else.
- FaceTime is an *app,* a program that enables you to accomplish a specific task.

I realize I've already thrown a zillion terms at you, but at least you have a handy reference going forward. Refer to this section as needed until the terms *hardware, software, processing, processor, programs, programming, computing,* and *computing device* have crystallized in your mind. Let's go on.

Common General-Purpose Computing Devices

General-purpose computing devices (those that enable you to do a whole bunch of different things) come in many shapes and sizes. This section looks at multi-user computers and dedicated computers and then goes into detail on the variations among dedicated computers. We'll examine operating systems and mobile variations as well.

Multi-user Computers

A *multi-user computer* can serve more than one person at a time. Mainframes, minicomputers, and supercomputers all fall into this category. Most people use dedicated computing devices these days, but multi-user computers are still useful. All the computerized cash registers in a large retail store, for example, typically connect to a multi-user computer that records transactions and adjusts the store's inventory database so individual registers can't get out of sync.

From their introduction in the 1940s into the 1970s, powerful computers called *mainframes* were widely used in the academic, banking, industrial, and scientific fields. Figure 1-5 shows a military mainframe from the 1960s. Mainframes specialize in multitasking, supporting dozens or even thousands of user sessions (each with its own programs and files) at the same time. Smaller versions of mainframes called *minicomputers* were also popular with businesses that didn't need the full power (and expense) of a mainframe. Mainframes and minicomputers aren't as popular these days because there are cheaper, smaller options available.

Supercomputers focus the power of a mainframe computer on a single task, making them arguably the most powerful computers on the planet. Most supercomputers are

Figure 1-5   Military mainframe computer from the 1960s

single large machines with hundreds or thousands of processors working in tandem. Supercomputers tackle big-brained tasks like the following:

- Tallying census results
- Compiling geothermal imaging data
- Determining the answer to life, the universe, and everything

Supercomputers also handle other *essential* processing chores, such as rendering the sophisticated *computer generated imagery (CGI)* effects for movies. CGI enables dinosaurs to roam Jurassic Park, and Spiderman to soar through the skyscrapers of Manhattan using nothing more than webs and spider-enhanced muscle. Like I said, *essential* processing.

Dedicated Computers

For decades, multi-user computers enabled users to perform computing chores from the simple, such as composing documents, to the complex. Starting in the 1970s, *dedicated computers*—those meant for one user at a time—gradually replaced multi-user computers for just about every computing task. The most common dedicated computer these days is called a PC.

Figure 1-6
Typical PC with a
few peripherals

A typical *personal computer (PC)* runs the Microsoft Windows operating system, for example, and comes with certain *peripherals*—devices that enable you to interact with the machine, such as a keyboard, mouse, and monitor (Figure 1-6). PCs have their own computing power and storage capabilities, so you can do work without connecting to any other computing device. Even though a PC is dedicated computer, multiple users can certainly take turns.

NOTE PCs are sometimes referred to as *microcomputers* because they're so much smaller than mainframes and minicomputers.

Personal computers can be linked together in a computer *network* that enables them to communicate and share resources. In a network environment, processing power is still in the hands of each networked device, but data storage can be centralized on a single computer that all the other computers can access called a *file server,* making it easier for each PC to manage and back up data files.

PCs vary according to capabilities, but also in their level of portability. This relates to both the size and the ease with which the entire computer can be packed up and transported.

Desktop and Laptop Computers

PCs that aren't easily transportable are known as *desktop computers* or *desktops PCs,* and PCs that are transportable are called *laptops* (or *notebooks*). A desktop computer typically has a separate display (though some have built-in monitors), with its own power cord and separate keyboard and mouse components. You can also connect other devices (or *peripherals*) such as a printer, a webcam, or a scanner.

Figure 1-7
Regular PC

Desktop PCs come in many shapes and sizes, from the metal box you've seen in offices, schools, and homes (see Figure 1-7) to exotic-looking creations with blinking lights, transparent cases, custom paint jobs, and other stylistic touches (see Figure 1-8).

Figure 1-8
Fancy PC

A *laptop* computer typically has all essential components built into a single package. The laptop monitor, for example, folds down to cover the keyboard for transport. Instead of a mouse, most laptops have a touchpad or some other built-in pointing device. Some of them also have a touch-sensitive screen (a *touchscreen*) that enables users to control the device with their fingertips. Laptops PCs are often called *notebooks* because they approximate the size and shape of a paper notebook.

There are many related terms for variations on this theme. Small laptop PCs are sometimes called *subnotebooks,* for example, and thin, powerful, high-quality laptop PCs are called *ultrabooks*. Figure 1-9 shows a standard-sized laptop, and Figure 1-10 shows an ultrabook.

Chapters 2, 3, and 4 cover specific hardware components in desktop and laptop PCs, and Chapter 5 explains how to set up and configure desktop and laptop PCs.

Figure 1-9
Laptop

Figure 1-10
Ultrabook

Operating Systems for Desktop and Laptop PCs

A computer's OS runs the device, supports its applications, and defines how users can interact with it. You can think about an OS as a *software foundation,* the piece of the computing device upon which everything else builds. With more than 90 percent of the market, the most popular OS for desktop and laptop PCs is by far Microsoft Windows. You can find several other operating systems in the market that offer contrasting strengths.

EXAM TIP   Objective 1.1 of the CompTIA IT Fundamentals exam refers to an OS for a desktop or laptop as a *workstation operating system,* in contrast to a *mobile operating system* used in smaller mobile devices such as tablets and smartphones.

Hardware Platform   Your choice of OS depends on the capabilities of your computer's hardware; not every PC can run every operating system. The hardware on which an OS runs is known as the *platform* (though the term *platform* applies to more than just hardware).

The standard platform that runs the Windows OS has a lot of nicknames: *IBM-compatible platform, IBM platform,* or *Intel platform.* IBM was the company that made the first popular personal computers (that used a text-based operating system called MS-DOS). Intel provided the processors for the platform. This platform today can also run a free OS known as Linux or a small and efficient variant of it called Google Chrome OS.

Apple makes both the hardware and the OS for the *Macintosh platform.* Early Macs had proprietary hardware that would run only Apple's OS, but today most Macs use the same Intel-manufactured CPUs as Intel-platform PCs. As a consequence, most Macs can also use a utility called Boot Camp to run Windows.

EXAM TIP   Objective 1.2 of the CompTIA IT Fundamentals exam refers to the *platform* (desktop, mobile, or Web-based) that programmers design an application to use. The term is tricky because its meaning changes in different contexts. Think of the platform as all of something's features, requirements, and limitations.

Building an app for a generic *mobile platform* means (among other things) building it to take advantage of common mobile device sensors and interfaces and to run well on more modest mobile hardware. Building an app for the iPhone platform means something more specific—designing an app explicitly for the features and limitations of the iPhone and iOS.

GUI vs. Command Line   Most common operating systems have both a *graphical user interface (GUI)* and a *command-line interface (CLI).* A graphical user interface displays pictures on a monitor, and the user interacts with the pictures by moving a mouse or other pointing device. GUIs are popular because they are easy to use and require little training or memorization of commands. Users interact with a CLI by typing commands at a text-based onscreen prompt.

In operating systems where both interfaces are available, the CLI appears in a window within the GUI. Figure 1-11 shows command prompt windows in Windows (top) and Linux (bottom). The commands used to perform the same actions differ between Linux and Windows, although you can accomplish the same tasks in each OS.

 NOTE macOS has a command-line interface that uses the same basic command set as Linux.

The following sections introduce the major operating systems available today. Chapter 6 looks at them in more detail.

Microsoft Windows The Microsoft Windows OS, shown in Figure 1-12, runs on both desktops and laptops. Microsoft makes Windows editions for smaller devices such as tablets and smartphones; these are "Windows" in name, but they differ a lot from the desktop versions (we'll look at them later in the chapter).

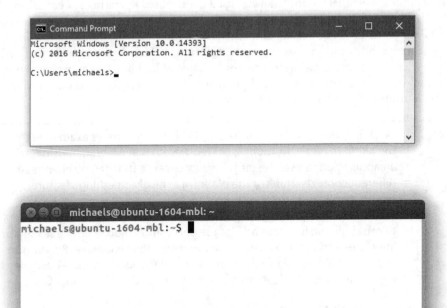

Figure 1-11 Windows (top) and Linux (bottom) command-line interfaces

Figure 1-12   Microsoft Windows 10

Windows enables you to connect to the Internet and other networks, run applications, manage files, and do just about anything you might want to do with a computer. The current version is Windows 10, but you may encounter other, older versions as well, including Windows Vista, Windows 7, and Windows 8.1.

Apple macOS   The *Apple Mac* (formerly *Macintosh*) computer offers an alternative to Windows-based computers. Figure 1-13 shows a typical Apple Mac. Macs use Apple's own operating system, which Apple renamed from *OS X* (see Figure 1-14) to *macOS* in 2016. Macs can tackle the same tasks as PCs but are more common in creative fields such as music, video, and the graphic arts.

EXAM TIP   Apple changed the name from *OS X* (as in the Roman numeral, pronounced "oh-ess ten") to *macOS* while we were working on this book, but because the OS X name was used from 2001 to 2016, be prepared to encounter either name on the exam and in other resources.

Macs require macOS-specific software. You can't run (or even install) an app designed for Windows in macOS. Programming companies often make apps for both platforms; you need to install the compatible version. Figure 1-15 shows OS-specific versions of an application.

Linux   Linux is a variant of a much older operating system, UNIX, which started as a command-line operating system used on servers. It is a free, *open source* operating

Figure 1-13
Apple iMac

system, meaning that anyone can download and modify the source code (assuming you know how to program). You can find versions of Linux tailored for just about any kind of computer system.

EXAM TIP Open source software is usually free (you may have to pay to license some software for business use), but the important part is that anyone can make changes and release this new version to the public. In contrast, commercial software like Windows is owned by a company or individual who retains all rights to make, modify, and sell it.

A version of Linux packaged with add-ons and utilities suitable for a particular purpose is called a distribution, or *distro*. Different distros have their own user interface known as a *desktop environment (DE)*. One of the most popular distros for personal computers is Ubuntu Linux; you can download it for free online. Figure 1-16 shows the Ubuntu Linux graphical interface. Other popular operating systems such as Chrome OS are based on Linux, but these typically come with their own unique interface and many other modifications.

Figure 1-14
OS X desktop

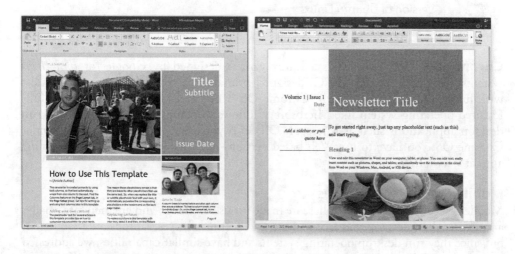

Figure 1-15 Microsoft Word comes in both Windows and macOS versions

Figure 1-16 The Ubuntu Linux GUI

NOTE Check out Ubuntu's Web site (www.ubuntu.com) to download a free version of Ubuntu Linux.

Chrome OS Chrome OS is a Linux variant designed by Google for *thin client* systems (minimally equipped PCs designed primarily for Internet usage, in contrast with fully equipped *thick clients*). Chrome OS is not a viable replacement for a full-featured operating system like Microsoft Windows, because it lacks the ability to run desktop applications such as Microsoft Office. If you want to run applications under Chrome OS, you have to use Web-based versions of them, such as the Office Online apps at www.office.com.

Mobile Computing Devices

Mobile devices, as the name implies, are made for use on the go and are therefore smaller and lighter than desktop and laptop systems. (Technically, yes, laptops are mobile too, but since they run desktop operating systems and have similar capabilities, we addressed them earlier in the chapter along with desktops.)

Handheld devices have a small touch-sensitive screen that acts as both an input and output device. Modern devices often have touchscreens with virtual keyboards that pop up onscreen when needed, though a few devices (such as the BlackBerry in Figure 1-17) still use integrated hardware keyboards.

Figure 1-17
BlackBerry

The two major types of mobile device available today are smartphones and tablets. Other kinds of device (such as digital music players, e-book readers, and personal organizers) have been popular in the past, but their popularity faded when smartphones and tablets got good enough at their jobs.

Smartphones   Smartphones are not just mobile phones; they're tiny computers that help you stay connected by enabling you to access the Internet on the go. They also help you stay organized by giving you a way to copy and carry around data that you'd normally store on your PC, such as your address book, calendar, task lists, and so on.

Most smartphones have enough processing power to allow you to play games, edit text documents and spreadsheets, read books, listen to music, and do many other computing tasks on the go. The most common way to categorize smartphones is by OS (more on each in a moment), leaving us with iPhones (iOS), Androids, and Windows Phones. Figure 1-18 shows an iPhone.

Tablets   A *tablet* is a digital slate with a touchscreen (see Figure 1-19). It resembles an extra-large smartphone, but most don't have cell phone functionality. (A tablet that does have cell phone capability is called a *phablet*.) A tablet fills a niche between the pocket-size portability of a smartphone and the computing power of a laptop. The iPad is the world's most popular tablet, using the same iOS operating system as the iPhone; other alternatives include a variety of tablets that use the Android operating system, such as the Samsung Galaxy Tab.

Figure 1-18
Apple iPhone

NOTE Microsoft's Surface and Surface Pro tablets feature a detachable keyboard, blurring the line between laptop and tablet (inspiring some to call them *laplets*). These still use the full workstation (desktop and laptop) version of Windows, so it's best to think of them as laptops that can pass as tablets.

Specialty Mobile Devices   The trick with specialty mobile devices is that they tend to be popular for some specific task until the hardware and apps on generic mobile devices like smartphones or tablets get *good enough* for the average user to prefer the app over carrying another device.

E-book readers (such as Amazon Kindle or Barnes & Noble Nook), which are basically tablets specialized for reading e-books, enable you to carry the equivalent of a small library in your pocket. They have nice touches like long battery life and screens that cause less eye strain and don't wash out in sunlight.

If number crunching is your thing, a modern *scientific calculator* puts more raw processing power into an index card–sized shell than the first mainframes could boast. Calculators are available with video screens that enable you to graph complex equations, but so can a smartphone app.

Figure 1-19   Apple iPad

Devices with *global positioning system (GPS)* receivers enable you to pinpoint your physical location and help you find your way around. Many smartphones and automobiles now offer GPS capabilities, so having a separate GPS device has become less desirable for navigating roads and cities on foot or by car. Some separate GPS devices have features that make them essential for activities such as sailing or extended backpacking trips.

Operating Systems for Mobile Devices

Many companies make smartphones and tablets, but almost all models use one of four operating systems optimized for mobile use: Apple iOS, Android, Windows Phone, and BlackBerry OS.

Whereas most desktop and laptop operating system interfaces have icons, menus, and windows that you access with a mouse, most mobile operating system interfaces have icons and full-screen applications that you access by tapping the touch-sensitive screen.

Operating systems are built into mobile devices, stored in *nonvolatile memory* (memory that retains its content when the computer is off). A mobile device ships with a dedicated OS and you cannot change to a different OS, although you can install updates.

Apple iOS   Apple iOS (shown in Figure 1-20) works the same way across the iPhone and iPad, even though the screen sizes differ. iOS is available only on Apple hardware; it does not run on any third-party devices.

Android   Google designed the Android OS—a variant of Linux—for mobile devices. Many lower-cost phones and tablets employ the free and open source Android OS. Android works on the same basic interface design as iOS, with icons arranged on a home screen. Most apps available for iOS are also available in Android versions. Figure 1-21 shows the Android OS on a smartphone.

Figure 1-20   The Apple iOS operating system on an iPad

Figure 1-21
The Android
operating system

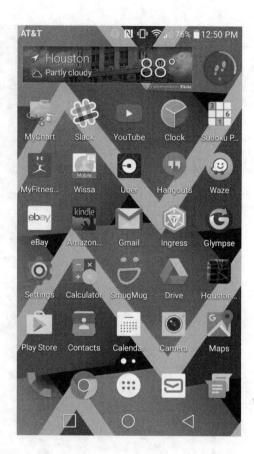

Windows Phone Microsoft produces Windows Phone (see Figure 1-22) as a mobile-device version of Microsoft Windows. The Windows Phone main screen features resizable rectangular tiles, and you can make the tiles larger for applications you use most. Windows Phone has not been as widely adopted as iOS or Android; thus, fewer developers create versions of their apps for it. Microsoft licenses the Windows Phone OS to several different hardware manufacturers, so you'll find it on a variety of smartphones. A tablet version called Windows RT was available for a time, but it has been discontinued; current Windows-based tablets use Windows 10 Mobile, a mobile-friendly version of Windows 10 (note the name change to "Mobile" from "Phone").

Figure 1-22
The Windows
Phone operating
system

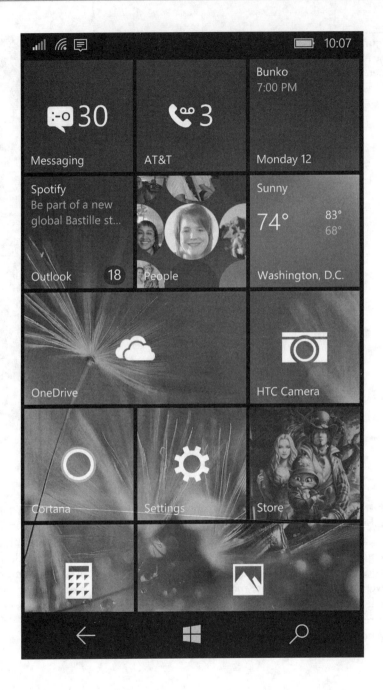

Figure 1-22 The Windows Phone operating system

BlackBerry The BlackBerry OS is a proprietary OS used only on BlackBerry smartphone hardware. Its parent company has recently announced that it will release only limited updates to the BlackBerry OS; BlackBerry has lost its market share in recent years and is not expected to be further developed. You'll likely encounter BlackBerry today only on exams.

Networks: Hooking It All Together

Whenever two or more computers communicate, a *network* occurs. This section covers some basic concepts about networks; we'll get to more details in Chapter 10.

Networks come in a couple of flavors, named to describe their location and scope.

- A *local area network (LAN)* connects computers in a single physical location, such as a school, office, or home.
- Two or more LANs connect to form a *wide area network (WAN)*.

Computers in a wired LAN connect through network cabling and connection boxes called *switches* (see Figure 1-23). Wireless LANs use radio waves instead of physical *network cables* to connect PCs. Computers on wireless networks connect through a special wireless connection box called a *wireless access point (WAP)*. Some types of switch enable the computers to also communicate with other networks beyond the local one; these are called *routers*. A typical *small office/home office (SOHO)* network uses a SOHO router to enable the local computers to communicate with one another and to share a single Internet connection among them.

WANs are generally a collection of LANs in multiple buildings or multiple cities, which is why you'll occasionally hear them described as *remote networks*. The best example of a remote network is the *Internet*—a worldwide network of remote networks connected by a series of high-speed communication lines (see Figure 1-24). Other examples of remote networks are school or office networks that enable you to connect to them from home or on the road.

Figure 1-23
Typical LAN

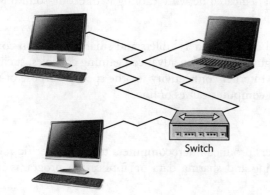

Switch

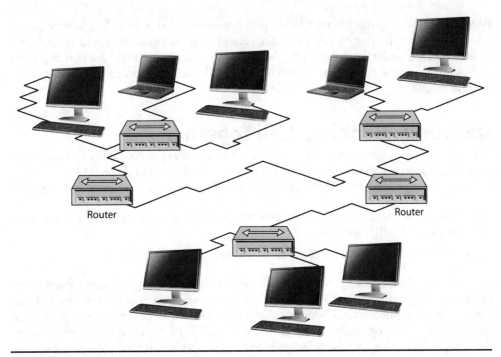

Figure 1-24   Typical WAN

Single computers and LANs connect to WANs such as the Internet through wired or wireless hardware devices called *routers*. Routers send network communications out through the following:

- Regular telephone lines
- Digital subscriber line (DSL) connections
- Cable television lines
- Special dedicated network cabling with exotic-sounding names like ISDN, T1, and T3

Handheld devices such as tablets and smartphones can connect to the Internet wirelessly (see Figure 1-25). Even advanced gaming consoles, such as Xbox One and PlayStation 4, offer Internet connectivity for the special purpose of smacking your friends and neighbors in computer games online.

Servers

Manufacturers produce microcomputers to fulfill specific roles on computer networks, such as storing and sharing data or application programs from a central location, or

Figure 1-25
Apple iPhone
surfing the Net

providing network services such as e-mail and printing. We usually label these special-ized systems—called *servers*—based on what they serve: file servers, application servers, mail servers, print servers, and so on. PCs that receive services from server systems are called *clients*. A well-equipped desktop PC can act as a server, provided you install server software on it; servers can also be much more powerful than a desktop PC, and groups of servers can work together to handle the computing tasks of businesses or Web sites.

Resource Sharing

Decentralized networks enable computers to share storage space, printers, scanners, application programs, and in special cases, even processing power. Sharing one printer is much cheaper than installing ten separate printers on ten separate computers. All modern operating systems enable you to share resources with a few clicks (see Figure 1-26). You'll learn how to share files and printers on a network in Chapter 10.

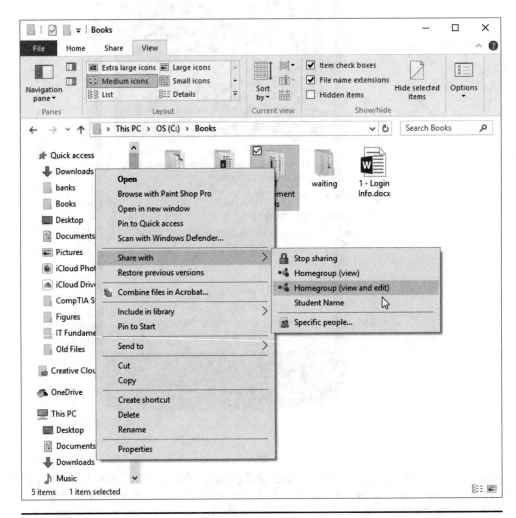

Figure 1-26   Sharing a folder in Windows

Remotely Accessed Computer Systems

Earlier in the chapter you learned about mainframes, which users accessed via *dumb terminals*—a keyboard and monitor connected to a device that had no processing power, just connection points. The mainframe did the processing, in other words, and the terminal simply provided the input and output devices for the user and the communication medium to access the mainframe. This same principle is at work in modern remotely accessed systems. A big, high-capability computer exists somewhere (the *server*), and other computers (the *clients*) located elsewhere access it through the Internet or a private network.

Clients access servers for a variety of reasons. At the simplest level, a client accesses a file server to share files; the server functions like an external *hard drive* (a device for storing data). Remote access can be much more than that, however, as you will learn in the following sections.

Mobile Apps

Mobile apps are simple applications that run on smartphones and tablets. Mobile apps come from online stores maintained by the same company that makes the operating system (Apple Store for Apple devices, Windows Store for Windows devices, and so on). Having all apps come from a single store helps ensure they are virus-free and compatible with the OS.

Some mobile apps run alone on the device, but most connect to servers on the Internet. The app itself provides a basic user interface through which the user can interact with data from the server. For example, a smartphone weather app, like the one in Figure 1-27, retrieves current local weather data from a server and drops it into placeholders on the app screen. Although the app itself resides on the phone, it is useless without a connection to the server.

Streaming Media

When you *download* a music or video clip, the file transfers permanently to your local computing device, and you can play it back even when your device isn't connected to the Internet. *Streaming*, on the other hand, is when your system plays the clip back immediately as the data transfers without bothering to save it for later. Streaming is popular with subscription-based music services (such as Pandora or Spotify) where users pay a monthly fee to stream as much music as they like (using a specific app) but lose access if they cancel their subscription.

Web Apps

Whereas mobile apps and music-streaming services simply access online databases of content, Web apps take remote access a step further. With a Web app, you run an application directly from the Internet via a Web browser. You don't have to download or install an app; the app remains on the remote server, and you access it from there, as you would a Web page.

Figure 1-27
This weather app formats and displays weather data from an online server.

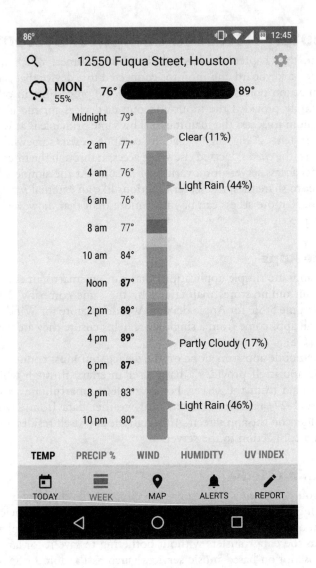

Microsoft produces Microsoft Office Online (www.office.com), a popular set of Web apps that enable anyone with a Web browser to use free, simplified versions of their Microsoft Office applications online. Figure 1-28 shows the Word Online Web app in action. The applications work only when the computer is connected to the Internet. Documents are stored in Microsoft's free online file storage service, OneDrive, and can be downloaded to the user's local hard drive as needed.

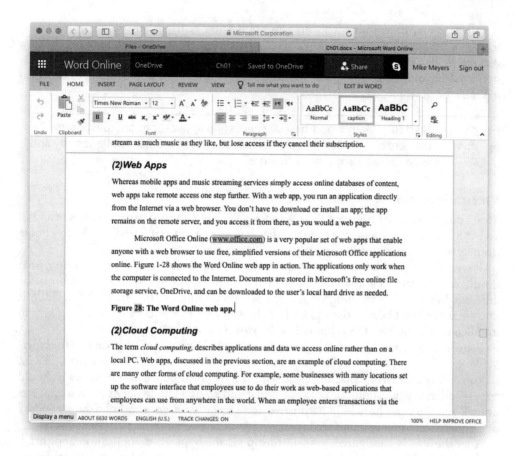

Figure 1-28   The Word Online Web app

Cloud Computing

Cloud computing describes applications and data you access online rather than on a local PC. Web apps are an example of cloud computing. Cloud computing comes in many other varieties. Businesses with several different office locations, for example, can set up a software interface that employees use to do their work via Web-based applications from anywhere in the world. When an employee enters transactions via the online application, the data is saved to the company's server.

Cloud computing has become a popular means of software distribution in some industries. Rather than an individual purchasing an application once and owning it forever, the user will buy a subscription to the application and access it online as needed. Whereas a retail version of an application might cost hundreds of dollars, a subscription might cost less than $10 a month.

Furthermore, if an individual buys an application outright and then the company releases a new version, the individual would have to shell out *more* money for the new version. With a subscription to an online application, the developer makes the latest version available online. Using online applications also saves local disk space because nothing must be downloaded or installed.

 EXAM TIP Many cloud-based services and applications are *collaborative*—they enable multiple people to work on the same data simultaneously and instantly see each other's changes.

Virtualization

Most computers have only one OS (a Windows PC has Windows 10; a Mac has macOS). You can also set up a *multiboot* system that has more than one installed OS to choose from at startup, but you still run only one OS at a time.

Virtualization enables one computer to run an application (called a *hypervisor*) that simulates a "virtual" computer. This virtual computer has its own OS, which can be different from the OS running on the real system (Figure 1-29). The PC's "real" OS is known as the *host OS,* and the PC itself is the *host PC*. The secondary operating system installed inside the host OS is known as the *guest OS*.

Popular hypervisors include VMware, Oracle VM VirtualBox, and Microsoft Hyper-V. We call the computer simulations that the hypervisor creates *virtual machines (VMs)*. As you configure a virtual machine, you tell the hypervisor how much memory it should appear to have, what input and output ports, and so on. The hypervisor even allocates unused space on the host PC's hard drive as a *virtual hard drive* to hold the secondary operating system and its associated files.

After the VM is configured, you start it up via the hypervisor application and install an OS into it. When that task is complete, you can run that secondary operating system

Figure 1-29
Virtualization in
action

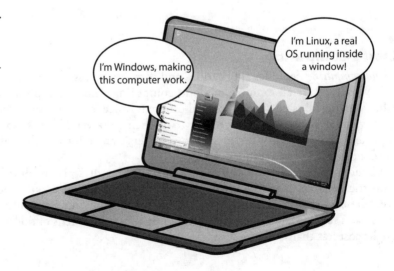

Figure 1-30   Linux running in a VM on Windows 10

in a window on the host PC any time. (You can also run it full-screen so it appears to be the primary OS on the PC, if you like.) We used virtualization when writing this book to check the steps for performing various tasks in different operating systems, including several versions of Microsoft Windows, Linux, and macOS. Figure 1-30 shows Linux running in a window on a Windows 10 PC.

Virtualization is handy for individual users on client PCs, but its primary use is on large networked servers. Virtualization enables one of these powerful systems to run many virtual machines containing different kinds of server software, saving companies a lot of money on not only initial hardware purchases but also hardware repair and maintenance.

Specialized Computer Systems

As we said at the beginning of the chapter, computers are everywhere. In addition to the desktops, laptops, and smartphones we all recognize as computers, there are hundreds of special-purpose computer systems permeating every aspect of modern life. You need to know the following for the CompTIA IT Fundamentals exam:

- Point-of-sale terminals
- ATMs
- GPS
- Voice over IP/telepresence

Point-of-Sale Terminals

Point-of-sale (PoS) terminals process purchase transactions. When you pump your own gas and pay with a credit card at a gas pump, for example, you interact with a PoS terminal like the one in Figure 1-31. These computing devices contain a display screen, user input controls, and enough memory and processing power to collect user data and transmit it to a central computer (perhaps located inside the gas station or in the business's office).

ATMs

An *automated teller machine* is a variation of a PoS terminal, designed for banking transactions. Banking customers have access to their money 24/7 by visiting an ATM terminal and inserting their ATM card.

Because theft is such an issue when money is involved, users authenticate their identities using *multifactor authentication*—in other words, by using more than one method of verifying ID. ID verification can be based on either what you have or what you know. An ATM requires you to have something (a valid ATM card) and also know something (your personal identification number, or PIN) to prove your identity.

GPS

The global positioning system is a series of satellites that orbit Earth at an altitude of about 12,400 miles (20,000 kilometers). GPS satellites constantly transmit signals to Earth. Every location on Earth has access to at least four of these satellites at any given time. A GPS receiver unit requires data from at least three satellites to function. It calculates how far away it is from each satellite by determining how long it took for the signal (traveling at the speed of light) to arrive. Based on that data, it calculates a 2D position of longitude and latitude, accurate to within a few feet.

Figure 1-31
A point-of-sale computer in a gasoline pump

The original GPS units were stand-alone devices, but today's smartphones and cars integrate GPS receivers with navigation applications that have become wildly popular with everyday consumers, changing the way people give directions and making standard paper maps nearly obsolete.

VoIP/Telepresence

Voice over IP (VoIP) is a means of using the Internet as a conduit for telephone calls, rather than using the standard telephone lines owned by a phone company. VoIP translates audio data into digital packets that can be sent on computer networks, just like any other kind of network traffic. VoIP phone services such as Vonage and Skype beat the offerings of many more traditional telephone providers in quality, price, and additional features such as teleconferencing and telepresence.

Teleconferencing means having a conference (meeting) via telephone, but the term has come to mean having a video-enabled remote business meeting. Teleconferencing uses a video camera and microphone at each end of the conversation, with VoIP service software to facilitate the connection.

Telepresence is a step up from teleconferencing; it uses sophisticated, high-quality video-conferencing equipment to create an immersive environment where the remote user feels almost *present* at the meeting. The remote user might use local controls, such as a virtual reality headset that enables the operator to look around the robot's environment from hundreds of miles away.

Chapter Review

Whew! What a first chapter, right? Let's do a quick review.

In this chapter, you started with features common to all computing devices, such as processors, programming, and data storage. You learned about many different kinds of computers in the modern world. A multi-user computer serves more than one person at the same time, as opposed to a dedicated computer. Dedicated computers include desktops, laptops, and mobile computers such as smartphones and tablets.

The type of operating system a computer runs depends on the computer's hardware. PCs and many portables use Windows or macOS, for the most part, although you'll see Linux and Chrome OS out in the wild. Mobile devices run iOS, Android, or Windows Phone. (BlackBerry OS is an afterthought today.)

You also learned how LAN and WAN networks tie computers together. We went through some of the basic hardware devices that make connectivity happen, such as routers, servers, and clients.

Various programs enable remote connectivity, such as mobile apps, streaming media, and Web apps. You learned about cloud computing concepts and touched on virtualization, running an operating system within another operating system.

Finally, the chapter discussed how specialty devices such as point-of-sale terminals and ATMs help consumers accomplish their daily tasks.

Questions

1. What type of computer, also called a notebook, has a monitor that folds down to cover the keyboard for transport?

   A. Server

   B. Laptop

   C. GPS

   D. Mainframe

2. What would be an appropriate use for a supercomputer?

   A. Playing online games

   B. Running a high-volume Web site

   C. Tallying census results

   D. Managing a large business's accounting department

3. Which of these is a workstation operating system?

   A. iOS

   B. Windows Phone

   C. Windows

   D. Android

4. Which of these operating systems *cannot* run on a desktop PC with an Intel processor?

   A. Linux

   B. iOS

   C. Google Chrome OS

   D. Windows

5. What kind of OS enables users to interact with it using a pointer and graphics?

   A. Command line

   B. GUI

   C. Decentralized

   D. Centralized

6. A version of Linux packaged with add-ons and utilities for a particular purpose is known as a:

   A. Distro

   B. GUI

   C. Version

   D. Service Pack

7. A BlackBerry is a type of smartphone known for what distinctive feature that most other modern smartphones lack?

   A. Graphical screen

   B. Internet connectivity

   C. Touchscreen

   D. Hardware keyboard

8. What operating system is used on an iPad?

   A. macOS

   B. Windows

   C. Android

   D. iOS

9. What kind of network is used to connect individual computers in a single physical location?

   A. WAN

   B. LAN

   C. Internet

   D. Remote

10. Listening to music using an online service like Spotify is an example of what?

    A. Cloud computing

    B. Virtualization

    C. Streaming media

    D. Telepresence

Answers

1. **A**. A laptop is a portable computer that folds up for transport, with the monitor covering the keyboard. A server is a specialized computer accessed by multiple other computers. A GPS is a single-user computing device that provides the current geographical location. A mainframe is a large single computer that multiple users access.

2. **C**. Supercomputers are for the most intensive computing applications. They are so expensive that it would be a waste to do any of the other listed activities with one.

3. **B**. Windows is a workstation OS (that is, one designed for desktops and laptops). iOS, Windows Phone, and Android are all mobile operating systems.

4. **B**. iOS is an operating system for portable Apple devices such as the iPad and iPhone. All the other operating systems listed here will run on a desktop PC with an Intel processor.

5. **B**. A graphical user interface (GUI) uses a pointer and graphics. A command-line interface uses text. Decentralized and centralized processing have no relationship to whether there are graphics and a pointer.

6. **A**. Distro is correct, short for distribution. A GUI is a graphical user interface. A version is a release of an OS at a particular point in time, usually numbered, like Windows 10. A Service Pack is an update to a certain version.

7. **D**. A traditional BlackBerry has a hardware keyboard, unlike most other smartphones. All other choices are features that all smartphones have.

8. **D**. iOS is used on an iPad. macOS is by Apple but used on Mac desktops and laptops. Windows and Android are not Apple operating systems.

9. **B**. A local area network (LAN) connects computers in the same location. A wide area network (WAN) connects computers far away from one another. The Internet and a remote network are both examples of WANs.

10. **C**. Streaming media allows you to watch and listen to video and audio clips from online sources without downloading them. Cloud computing involves running applications and accessing storage online. Virtualization runs different operating systems on a host OS. Telepresence creates an immersive remote environment.

System Hardware

In this chapter, you will learn how to

- Differentiate among CPUs in terms of speed and features
- Explain the types and technologies of memory in a PC
- Describe motherboard form factors and features
- Identify the purpose and functions of a power supply

Knowing how all computing devices work enables you to accomplish several goals. First, you can understand the importance of various components and know when a computer has the right stuff for the job. Second, you can gauge the efficiency of the computing process. Third, you can troubleshoot when something goes wrong.

As you know from Chapter 1, computers consist of two elements, hardware and software, with software further divided into operating systems and programs/apps. Both elements work together to make the computing process happen. This chapter starts the discussion, focusing on hardware. Later chapters cover the software in more detail. Let's look briefly at the process and then get to the meat of the chapter.

Data flows through a computer in this three-step process:

- **Input** The computer accepts incoming data. This could be the user clicking the mouse, typing something, or starting a program that loads instructions.

- **Processing** The computer performs operations (math) on data to transform it. For example, data of 2 + 2 would be processed as 4.

- **Output** The result of the calculation is delivered to the appropriate recipient. This result might go back to an application that requested it, for example, and the application might then display the result on a screen or print it on a printer.

 NOTE An important part of the computing process is *data storage*, where you save stuff to work on later. We address storage in Chapter 4.

With the computing process firmly in mind, let's turn now to the core hardware involved. We'll start with a discussion of the processors and then turn to memory. The chapter examines motherboards and wraps up with a discussion about power supplies.

Figure 2-1
An Intel Core i7
CPU

CPUs

The *central processing unit (CPU),* sometimes called the *microprocessor* or the *processor,* handles most of the math processing in any computing device. Physically, processors are thin, fragile wafers of silicon and tiny transistors packaged in a robust shell (see Figure 2-1).

Intel and *Advanced Micro Devices (AMD)* make most of the CPUs in today's laptops and desktops. Intel has a much larger market share; AMD is the scrappy underdog.

EXAM TIP   ARM Holdings designs the vast majority of CPUs used in mobile devices, such as smartphones and tablets. ARM licenses its CPU designs to many manufacturers that produce the physical chips. Despite the overwhelming presence of ARM-based processors in modern computing devices, ARM does not show up on the CompTIA IT Fundamentals exam.

CPUs (and just about every other component in a computer) plug into a circuit board called a *motherboard* (Figure 2-2). The motherboard enables all the components to communicate. We'll tackle the specifics about motherboards a little later in the chapter.

All processor manufacturers work hard to make each generation of CPUs better than the one before. To make CPUs better, processor makers have focused on optimizing for speed, features, and efficiency.

Speed

The basic measurement of a CPU is its speed, or how many things it can do in one second under perfect conditions. Each thing is a *cycle,* and one cycle per second is expressed

Figure 2-2   CPU plugged into a motherboard

as 1 *hertz (Hz)*. In the 1980s and 1990s we measured CPU speed in millions of cycles per second, or *megahertz (MHz)*, but we measure today's CPUs in billions of cycles per second, or *gigahertz (GHz)*.

EXAM TIP   Megahertz and gigahertz are measures of the speeds at which things happen. In contrast, megabytes (MB) and gigabytes (GB) are measures of storage capacity.

To get a sense of what these numbers mean, add 2 to 3. How long did it take you? What about 323 + 718? A typical CPU in a modern PC can add or subtract more than three *billion* such equations every second. That amazing speed translates into what seems like magic, as we discussed in Chapter 1—a glorified calculator that can generate full-motion pictures or play fabulous games.

A CPU works directly with the motherboard to achieve the proper speed. Similar to CPUs, motherboards run at a specific clock speed (called the *bus speed*), again measured in hertz. CPUs run at some multiple (such as 10× or 25×) of that bus speed. If the motherboard runs at 100 MHz and the CPU has a 25× multiplier, the CPU runs at 2500 MHz (or 2.5 GHz).

Features

CPU clock speeds hit a wall around 4 GHz, so CPU makers needed to find new ways to continue increasing processing power. Many of these improvements go beyond a CompTIA IT Fundamentals discussion, but let's look at four relevant methods:

- 64-bit computing
- Multicore CPUs
- Program handling
- Cache

64-Bit Computing

For more than a decade, CPUs in personal computers had a *32-bit architecture*, meaning the CPU could handle data that was 32 bits in complexity. If you know your binary math (and who doesn't?), a 32-bit CPU could work with numbers up to about 4 billion and could handle an operating system or application with an equal number of lines of code.

Today, most desktop and full-size laptop CPUs are 64-bit. In binary math, doubling the potential size of a value requires just one more bit. Each bit added, therefore, doubles the complexity. A 33-bit value can be twice as large as a 32-bit one. Double that again and it's 34 bits. You get the idea. A 64-bit CPU can easily handle numbers up to 18,446,744,073,709,551,615. Moving to 64-bit computing has enabled programmers to increase the complexity and awesomeness of their applications.

Multicore CPUs

Both Intel and AMD decided at virtually the same time to combine two CPUs into a single chip, creating a *dual-core architecture*. This architecture increases both processing capability and efficiency because each core can pick up the slack when the other core gets too busy. Prior to dual-core CPUs, all CPUs were *single-core*.

Today, CPU makers offer CPUs with two (dual-core), four (quad-core), six (hexa-core), and even eight cores (octa-core) on a single chip. These are known collectively as *multicore* processors.

Handling Programs

CPUs have a preset list of commands they understand called the *codebook* or *instruction set*. Programmers write applications in different computer languages that are translated into code understood by the CPU's instruction set. The processor then works through the code and outputs commands to various parts of the computer.

Every CPU works with incoming commands and data differently. Two different CPUs with the same clock speed won't necessarily process the same image in a complex application like Adobe Photoshop in the same amount of time. The CPU that processes the image faster might even come in last at copying a huge file from one drive to another. These improvements typically mean a previous-generation processor with a fast clock speed may be outperformed by a current-generation CPU with a slower clock speed. It's all about the efficiency of processing (along with other features).

Cache

When you launch an application, it's loaded into the PC's memory, and it operates from there while the application is open. The application sends data to the CPU for processing and receives the processed data back.

Every time the CPU needs data it doesn't already have, it must fetch it from random access memory (RAM). The pathway between memory and the CPU (the *system bus*) is fast, but it's still subject to the physical limitations of the motherboard's *traces* (electrically conductive metal pathways embedded into the circuit board).

Another way to speed up CPU performance is by embedding small amounts of superfast RAM, called a *cache,* in the CPU chip itself. When the CPU grabs data from RAM, it also copies it into the cache. When the CPU needs the same data again, it first checks the cache. If the data is there, the CPU uses that copy to save time.

Today's CPUs have several levels of cache. Level 1 (L1), the smallest and fastest, is checked first; each subsequent level (L2 and L3) is larger and slower. Different multicore CPU designs will have shared or separate caches for each core, which can influence cost and performance.

Power and Heat Management

When trying to produce better processors, CPU makers need to overcome the fact that faster CPUs require more electricity and thus generate more heat that can damage components.

CPU makers discovered while working on processors for portable computers that if you make the components of the CPU very tiny, you can get the same performance with less electricity. Further, if you refine the way the CPU processes its instruction set, the CPU can perform better with even less electricity. Taking design cues from those portable processors, CPU makers have transformed current CPUs into leaner, greener processors.

Even today's lower-powered CPUs still run hot enough to burn you. Other components in the PC (such as chips on the motherboard and hard drives) also generate heat. When a chip overheats, it may malfunction or even stop working until it cools down, and repeated overheating can shorten a chip's life span. Therefore, it's important to have effective cooling systems in many computing devices.

Passive Cooling

Passive cooling does not use power or mechanical parts, meaning it can't keep hotter components cool. The most common type uses a *heat sink* (shown in Figure 2-3), which is a block of heat-conductive metal such as aluminum affixed to a chip with some heat-conductive *thermal paste*. The heat sink has spikes or baffles that increase its surface area. Heat wicks away from the chip into the heat sink and dissipates into the air. Case fans then circulate the hot air out of the case (more on those in a moment).

Figure 2-3   A passive heat sink is made of metal that conducts heat away from the CPU.

Figure 2-4
A CPU fan is an
active cooling
device that keeps
the CPU from
overheating.

Active Cooling

Active cooling uses electrically powered mechanical parts. In most PCs, a fan is strapped
to the CPU's heat sink in an attempt to circulate air through the heat sink and away from
the CPU to keep it cool. The fan typically has its own two-wire cable to draw the small
amount of power it needs from the motherboard. Figure 2-4 shows a simple CPU fan
and heat sink.

In addition to the CPU fan, a desktop or laptop typically also has one or more *case fans*
that cool off the entire interior of the computer, not just the CPU. Figure 2-5 shows a
case fan. On a desktop PC, the power supply (discussed later in the chapter) has its own
fan that pulls in air from the outside of the case, and there may be extra fans and air vents
in the sides of the case, or fans that blow directly onto other hot components.

Figure 2-5
A case fan
circulates air
in the case in
general.

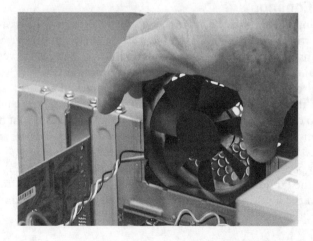

Figure 2-6
Liquid cooling systems circulate liquid among multiple heat sinks placed in key locations in a PC case, wicking away heat from each chip.

Liquid Cooling

Combining liquids with electronics is normally a recipe for disaster because liquids conduct electricity very efficiently and can cause short-circuiting. Some high-end gamers and enthusiasts run that risk and use *liquid cooling* systems for very effective active cooling. (Liquid is a more efficient conductor of heat than air.)

Liquid cooling systems attach heat sinks (sometimes called *water blocks*) to each of the chips that get hot in the PC, including the CPU and key chips on the motherboard and video card (Figure 2-6). (The video card has a processor that helps the CPU produce images on the screen.) The liquid flows through sealed tubing and channels inside the heat sinks, so it doesn't directly touch any of the electronics.

A pump circulates liquid from a reservoir through the tubing, from hot chip to hot chip. As the liquid reaches a chip, it picks up some of the heat from the chip and carries it back to the liquid reservoir (which may itself be a fan-cooled radiator to dissipate the heat).

EXAM TIP Be sure you are familiar with system cooling methods, including case fans, CPU fans, and liquid cooling.

RAM

Generically, *memory* is solid-state storage that stores the binary translation (ones and zeroes) of some data. (*Solid state* in this case implies no moving parts.) There are many kinds of memory, but if someone mentions PC memory, they probably mean *system RAM*. The word *system* means the memory generally serves the computer as a whole, not one particular component. It's called *random access memory (RAM)* because data can be read from any section of memory. It does not need to be accessed sequentially. A table keeps track of what's stored where.

There are different kinds of RAM, but the kind used for system RAM is *dynamic RAM (DRAM)*, which must be constantly refreshed because it can retain data only while powered. When the computer is powered down, whatever was in system RAM vanishes.

EXAM TIP Computers come with other types of memory, including *read-only memory (ROM)*. The ROM stores important pieces of information for how the computer works. ROM is not volatile, so it retains information when the power goes off.

Identifying RAM in a Computer

If you look at a desktop PC's motherboard, you'll see some long, thin circuit boards (these may be encased in a heat spreader in high-performance systems) slotted perpendicular to the mainboard. This is RAM. Those circuit boards are called *dual inline memory modules (DIMMs)*. Figure 2-7 shows performance DIMMs (with heat spreaders) on a desktop motherboard.

Laptop PCs use space-saving *small outline DIMMs (SODIMMs)* instead. They typically install almost parallel to the motherboard, at a slight angle. Figure 2-8 compares SODIMMs to regular DIMMs. RAM circuit boards are commonly called *sticks*.

The metal tabs across the bottom of a DIMM or SODIMM are called *pins*. Different types of RAM have different numbers of pins so that they fit into certain types of slots. These types are not just physically different but differ in terms of how they operate. See "RAM Technologies and Speeds," later in this chapter.

NOTE The RAM in this section is for desktop and laptop computers. In mobile devices like smartphones and tablets, the RAM is built in, and you can't see it without disassembling (and probably ruining) the device, so just take my word for it; it's there.

Figure 2-7   RAM installed inside a desktop PC

RAM Capacity

RAM sticks vary in capacity, with higher-capacity sticks naturally costing more than lower-capacity sticks. A DIMM might have a capacity ranging from 1 GB to 16 GB in a typical desktop system, for example. A particular computer's motherboard will support only a limited range of RAM capacities, so you must be careful when replacing and upgrading RAM in a computer to buy the right capacity, as well as the right type.

Figure 2-8
SODIMM (top)
and DIMM
(bottom)

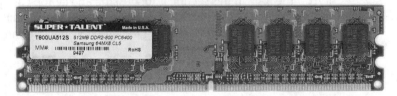

RAM Technologies and Speeds

Single data rate (SDR) RAM, now mostly obsolete, is synchronized with the motherboard's system timer so that it performs one operation per tick of that timer. (That timer isn't a literal time clock but more like a very fast metronome, ticking millions of times per second.) SDR RAM had 168 pins on a DIMM.

 NOTE You can't mix RAM stick types or technologies. RAM sticks are keyed so that they only fit in the motherboard designed for that technology.

Double data rate (DDR) RAM can send or receive data twice for each clock tick on the motherboard. DDR RAM has 184 pins on a DIMM and fits into a different kind of slot than SDR RAM, so there's no way to accidentally mix them up.

In addition to capacity, RAM also has a speed rating that describes how fast it can transfer data. There are four different speed technologies: DDR, DDR2, DDR3, and DDR4. Each is faster and more efficient than the technology that preceded it. Figure 2-9 shows DDR2 and DDR3 with their pins lined up so you can see the difference.

There are a few other changes between generations aside from the improvements in speed and efficiency.

- DDR2 uses a 240-pin DIMM that, like with the other types, fits into only its own type of slot.

- DDR3 uses a 240-pin DIMM (same number of pins as DDR2), but there is a notch in a different position on DDR3 RAM so it won't fit in a DDR2 slot, or *vice versa*.

 EXAM TIP The CompTIA IT Fundamentals acronym list includes both terms, but DDR RAM and DDR SDRAM are synonymous. The *S* in SDRAM means synchronous, and there is no such thing as nonsynchronous DDR RAM.

- DDR4 uses a 288-pin DIMM. DDR4 is relatively new as of this writing, so you can expect to see the earlier generations for some time. The CompTIA IT Fundamentals exam objectives don't cover DDR4.

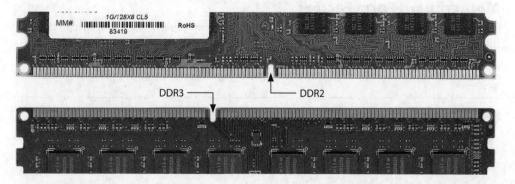

Figure 2-9 DDR2 and DDR3—you can't mix and match because of the position of the spacer.

Figure 2-10
The motherboard provides connectivity among all the pieces.

Motherboards

Everything in a computer plugs directly or indirectly into the motherboard (Figure 2-10). The motherboard, therefore, is an essential component in the computing process.

The motherboard provides pathways (buses) between the memory slots, CPU socket, input and output ports, and built-in devices like network adapters and sound adapters. It's not just a dumb highway system; the motherboard has its own intelligent controller (the *chipset*) that manages the traffic and tells the various buses how fast they can run.

Motherboard Form Factors

Motherboards come in different sizes and shapes (*form factors*), each one fitting into a different kind of case. Figure 2-11 shows three different form factors from left to right: an ATX (a full-size motherboard for large desktops), a microATX (a motherboard for smaller systems), and a Mini-ITX (a tiny motherboard for even smaller or specialty systems).

EXAM TIP The purpose of the motherboard/mainboard is to connect computer components. Know that they come in different sizes called *form factors*.

Figure 2-11   Three motherboards: ATX, microATX, and Mini-ITX (left to right)

Motherboard Features

Motherboards vary widely in price, mostly based on the following features:

- **CPUs supported**   Each motherboard supports only a narrow range of CPUs, based on specific physical chip attributes, such as the number of pins. Motherboards only support chips from Intel or AMD; they're never interchangeable.

- **RAM supported**   Each motherboard supports only a certain kind of RAM, such as DDR3 or DDR4, with a certain minimum and maximum capacity.

- **Built-in components**   Some motherboards have built-in capabilities such as audio, video, and network support. You will probably want these in any computer, so having them built in saves you from having to buy and install separate expansion cards. High-end users who are choosy about these components often find the built-in ones lacking.

- **Expansion slots**   A motherboard will have several slots into which you can place expansion cards (circuit boards that add capabilities beyond the basics). There are different technologies for these slots, but the most common kind today is PCI Express (PCIe). Chapter 3 explains these slots in more detail.

- **Firmware**   Each motherboard has a setup program stored on a chip on the motherboard; this chip is its *firmware*. Contemporary systems should come with Unified Extensible Firmware Interface (UEFI) firmware, but you'll probably still encounter older systems with Basic Input Output System (BIOS) firmware.

- **Special features**   Higher-quality motherboards include controllers for special types of storage, extra security measures, hardware assistance for virtualization, and more. Know your needs and shop accordingly.

Power Supplies

The *power supply unit (PSU)* in a desktop PC is a big metal box (Figure 2-12) mounted in one corner of the case. It has a bouquet of multicolored wire bundles coming out of it; these wires and connectors provide power to multiple individual components inside the case, including the motherboard and the disk drives. It's often referred to as just the *power supply,* and that's how we refer to it here as well, but keep in mind that you may see the acronym PSU on the exam.

A power supply converts the alternating current (AC) power from the wall outlet to the direct current (DC) power that computer components require, and it steps down the voltage of the incoming power to the exact amounts that each component requires. The step-down is dramatic: wall-outlet power comes in at 110 volts (V), and components require somewhere between +2 and +12 V.

EXAM TIP When we talk about DC current, there is a positive or negative symbol associated with it because direct current stays at a certain polarity, either positive or negative. In contrast, AC switches continuously between positive and negative.

Figure 2-12
A typical
computer power
supply

The largest connector on the power supply (20- or 24-wire) connects to the motherboard, which in turn parcels out small amounts of power to each of the built-in components and to the CPU and RAM slots. This connector is commonly known as the *P1* or *ATX* connector. Some systems have an extra 12-volt connector with four pins that attaches elsewhere on the motherboard; this is the *P4* connector. Figure 2-13 shows these attached to a motherboard.

NOTE Higher-end motherboards require an eight-wire additional power connector, rather than the four-wire P4.

Each wire color is significant; red wires provide +5 V power, white wires provide −5 V, yellow wires provide +12 V, orange wires provide +3.3 V, and black wires are for grounding. (I'm just telling you the voltages for each color because it's interesting; you don't have to memorize them for the exam.) The small connectors from the power supply each have different purposes. Some are for drives, while others connect directly to different spots on the motherboard or on certain kinds of expansion cards.

A laptop doesn't have a power supply inside the case that converts power. Instead, it has a power cord with a transformer block on it (sometimes called a *brick*) like the one in Figure 2-14. This block converts the power to DC and steps down the voltage for the system, but then the motherboard passes power on to each component as needed.

Figure 2-13
A power supply
connected to a
motherboard

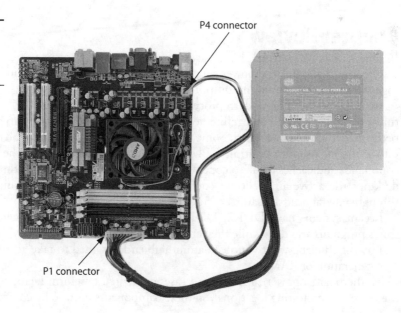

P4 connector

P1 connector

Figure 2-14　A laptop's power cord includes a transformer block that converts power.

Chapter Review

In this chapter, you learned about the essential system components (CPU, RAM, cooling system, motherboard, and power supply) inside a personal computer and how they work together to process inputs and outputs.

Because the speed of modern processors has run into a wall around 4 GHz, manufacturers work hard to add and refine new features with each generation to achieve greater performance at the same speed. Some of these improvements include the move to 64-bit CPUs, the inclusion of multiple CPU cores, and refinements to how the CPU executes commands and caches data. To cope with the heat produced by these components, most desktops use active air or liquid cooling systems that push air or liquid, respectively, through a metal heat sink attached to the CPU.

Recent systems have DDR2, DDR3, or DDR4 RAM, which is where the system stores programs and data while they are in use. Each generation of RAM improves speed and power efficiency, but you need a motherboard designed to take advantage of a specific generation of RAM.

Motherboards, power supplies, and cases come in a few form factors (a standard for their size and mounting locations), so these components need to be compatible with the same form factor. The motherboard provides a foundation for the system and the buses (pathways) between components, so it affects what CPUs, RAM, expansion slots, and other features the system can use. The PSU converts AC current from a wall outlet to appropriate DC current for the system; some components receive this power through direct connections to the PSU, and others receive it through the motherboard.

Questions

1. Which of these is *not* part of the data processing sequence?
   A. Networking
   B. Processing
   C. Output
   D. Input

2. What is another name for a CPU?
   A. Microprocessor
   B. Intel
   C. System memory
   D. Chipset

3. Which of these is *not* a feature of a CPU?
   A. Multicore
   B. 64-bit processing
   C. L1 cache
   D. DDR

4. Why is passive cooling not usually used for a CPU?
   A. Draws too much power
   B. Not effective enough
   C. Moving parts break down
   D. Uses too much RAM

5. What is the main advantage of liquid cooling over air cooling?
   A. Less expensive
   B. Safer
   C. More effective
   D. Uses less power

6. In what type of computer is SODIMM memory used?

    A. Laptop

    B. Desktop

    C. Server

    D. Smartphone

7. In what two ways are DDR3 DIMMs better than DDR2 DIMMs? (Choose two.)

    A. Less expensive

    B. More reliable

    C. Uses less power

    D. Faster

8. What manages and controls the speed of a motherboard's buses?

    A. RAM

    B. CPU

    C. Chipset

    D. L1 cache

9. What are the two functions of a desktop PC's power supply? (Choose two.)

    A. Steps down the voltage

    B. Increases the voltage

    C. Converts AC to DC

    D. Converts DC to AC

10. What is the reason for different color wires on a power supply?

    A. The wire color determines the appropriate component for the connector.

    B. Each wire color represents a different voltage.

    C. Certain color wires deliver AC power and certain ones DC power.

    D. Certain color wires deliver higher-quality power than others.

Answers

    1. A. Input, processing, and output are the three steps in the data processing sequence.

    2. A. Microprocessor is another name for the central processing unit (CPU). Intel is a company that makes CPUs. System memory is RAM. The chipset is a controller for the motherboard.

    3. D. DDR is a type of memory. All the others are CPU features.

    4. B. Passive cooling is not effective enough to cool most CPUs. Passive cooling draws no power, has no moving parts, and uses no RAM.

5. **C.** Liquid cooling is more effective than air cooling. It is more expensive and less safe (because of the risk of leaks) and uses more power.

6. **A.** SODIMM is a small-outline DIMM used in a laptop PC. Desktops and servers use regular DIMMs. A smartphone has built-in memory.

7. **C, D.** DDR3 uses less power and is faster than DDR2. It is not more reliable or less expensive.

8. **C.** The chipset manages the motherboard. RAM and CPU are items installed on the motherboard. The L1 cache is a memory cache inside the CPU.

9. **A, C.** A desktop power supply converts 110 V AC current from the wall to DC current in the range of +3.3 V to +12 V.

10. **B.** Each wire color is a different voltage. All wires deliver DC power of the same quality level.

Input and Output Ports and Peripherals

In this chapter, you will learn how to
- Differentiate among expansion card and slot types
- Identify the common ports and connectors on a PC
- Describe the types, technologies, and connectors for monitors
- Explain standard input devices
- Describe other common I/O devices

In Chapter 2 you learned about the essential processing components of a computer: the central processing unit (CPU), memory, motherboard, and power supply. Without any one of those, a computer doesn't function.

This chapter explores ways to expand the capabilities of a computing device through expansion slots and common ports. We'll look at monitors, the primary output device for most computers, and examine standard input devices such as the keyboard and mouse. The chapter wraps up with a survey of other input/output (I/O) devices you'll see in the wild.

Expansion Cards and Slots

As you learned in the "Motherboards" section of Chapter 2, motherboards have expansion slots, into which you can install *expansion cards* that add capabilities to the computer. You could add a video adapter (to replace a built-in adapter or to use in addition to it), for example, or you could add a type of port the motherboard doesn't natively support, such as FireWire or eSATA (which you'll see later in this chapter).

Expansion Cards

Expansion cards have a row of metal tabs (pins) along one edge (shown in Figure 3-1) that fit into expansion slots on the motherboard. The position and number of pins depend on what kind of slot the card is designed to fit into. An adjacent edge has a metal *backplate* that fits into an opening in the back of a desktop PC so you can access the expansion card's port (or ports).

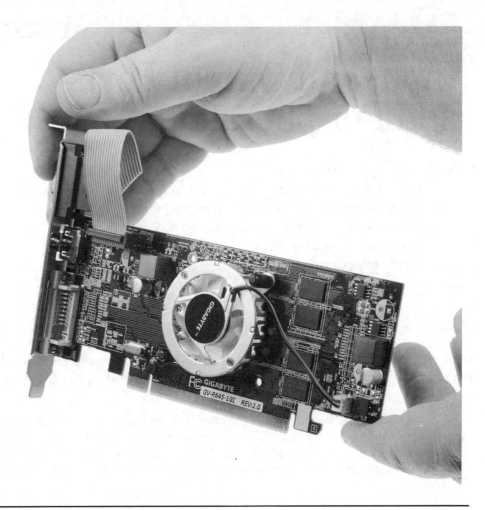

Figure 3-1 An expansion card for a desktop PC

There are many types of expansion cards providing different capabilities, and you can also find motherboards with the most common types built in. You need to know these four for the CompTIA IT Fundamentals exam:

- **Video card**   Also called a *display adapter,* a *video card* provides ports to connect to an external display and acts as a graphics processor interface between the operating system and the monitor. Monitor types and connections are covered later in this chapter. Video cards work hard, so it's best to use the fastest interface available.

- **Audio (sound) card**   A *sound card* provides ports to connect speakers, headphones, microphones, and other digital audio input and output devices. Most of sound ports are round 3.5-mm connectors.

- **Network card** Also called a *network interface card (NIC)*, a *network card* enables you to connect to a local area network. A network card can be wired or wireless. If wired, it has an *RJ-45* port (covered later in this chapter). If wireless, it may have a small antenna.

EXAM TIP Network adapters are often referred to as NICs even when built into the motherboard. The term *NIC* has come to refer to the adapter's functionality, rather than the physical card.

- **Modem** A *modem* enables you to connect to the Internet or some other network using a regular telephone land line. A modem expansion card will have two *RJ-11* (telephone) ports on it, side by side. Figure 3-2 shows the similar RJ-45 and RJ-11 ports.

Expansion Slot Types

Computer manufacturers have used many different expansion slot types over the years; currently *PCI Express (PCIe)* dominates the market. The term applies to both the slot and the bus that carries data from the slot to the system bus. Each slot has between 1 and 32 independent lanes that carry data, and a slot has a numeric designation (such as ×1, ×4, ×8, or ×16) to describe how many lanes it has.

Lower-capacity slots can be used for expansion cards that do not carry a lot of data at once, like network cards. A motherboard typically has several ×1 slots. Higher-capacity slots, like ×16, are reserved for expansion cards that carry a lot of data, such as video adapters. A motherboard typically has only one or two ×16 slots.

Figure 3-2 Expansion cards with one RJ-45 port (top) and two RJ-11 ports (bottom)

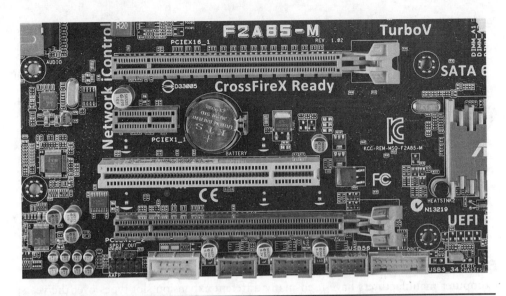

Figure 3-3   From top to bottom: PCIe ×16, PCIe ×1, PCI, and a black PCIe ×16 that operates at ×8 speed

Many motherboards sport an older general-purpose slot type, *Peripheral Component Interconnect (PCI)*. Figure 3-3 compares a standard PCI slot with several PCIe slots (if you look closely, you can see labels near the slots).

Some laptop PCs have *mini-PCIe* slots that accept smaller versions of the same kinds of expansion cards that desktop PCs use. Older laptops, as you might expect, had *mini-PCI* slots. Figure 3-4 shows a mini-PCIe slot and card.

Figure 3-4
A mini-PCIe slot
and card in a
laptop PC

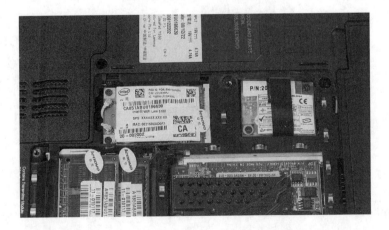

EXAM TIP The exam's acronym list includes PCI, PCIe, and PCI-X. You know the first two from this section, but PCI-X is a 32-bit version of PCI that was used on some high-end servers and workstations before PCIe replaced it.

Common Ports and Connectors

Different types of peripherals connect to computers in different ways, so a computer will typically have multiple port types, each with its own connector size, shape, and specifications. You should be able to identify many of these connectors on sight and tell what kinds of devices they may work with. We'll look at ports for monitors and other video devices later in the chapter, so for now we'll turn to ports and connectors for other peripherals.

USB

The *universal serial bus (USB)* enables you to add a remarkable variety of peripherals to computers. USB is an industry-standard connector; you'll find them on many brands and models of many computing devices. USB can carry both data and power, so a USB cable is sometimes used to connect small electronics to computers (or to alternating current [AC] power outlets, with the appropriate adapter) to charge them.

USB Generations and Speeds

USB comes in several flavors, such as USB 2.0, USB 3.0, and USB 3.1. USB 2.0 has two standards, USB and Hi-Speed USB. For the most part, their ports are all physically interchangeable and backward compatible.

USB 2.0   Regular *USB*—often mistakenly called USB 1.1—transfers data at up to 1.5 megabits per second (Mbps) at low speed or 12 Mbps at full speed. On a system that color-codes different speeds of USB port, these are typically white.

   Hi-Speed USB transfers data at up to 480 Mbps. Hi-Speed USB ports are sometimes color-coded black to differentiate them from the slower regular USB ports, and the little tabs inside the cable connectors may also be black rather than white.

USB 3.x   USB 3.0 (also called *SuperSpeed USB*) transfers data at up to 5 gigabits per second (Gbps). On systems that use color-coding, USB 3.0 is usually bright blue. When USB 3.1 was released, USB 3.0 was confusingly renamed *USB 3.1 Gen 1*. USB 3.1 (or more correctly USB 3.1 Gen 2 and sometimes SuperSpeed USB 10 Gbps) increases the speed to 10 Gbps.

USB Connector Types

There are a number of USB connector and port formats that you might see. Here's a little about each of the connectors shown in Figure 3-5.

- **Type-A**   The "standard" rectangular USB ports on most desktop and laptop PCs and on one end of most USB cables.

- **Type-B**   A near-square connector used most for full-size peripherals such as printers.

Type-A   Type-B   Mini-B   Micro-B   Type-C

Figure 3-5   Common USB connectors

- **Mini-B**   A smaller peripheral connector for smartphones, digital cameras, MP3 players, and so on. Mini-B is less durable than Micro-B, so it has become rare because few new devices use it.

- **Micro-B**   Also for smaller peripherals and devices. The original Micro-B is more compact than Mini-B, though USB 3.x updates the Micro-B connector to add another part. The old Micro-B cables will fit into the new USB 3.x Micro-B ports (without using the new part), but the new part prevents the new 3.x Micro-B cables from using the older ports.

- **Type-C**   A compact connector for both larger and smaller devices introduced alongside (but separate from) USB 3.1. To eliminate the problem of trying to insert a USB connector upside down, Type-C can be inserted in two orientations. Type-C connectors will eventually replace all previous USB connectors.

Other Peripheral Ports and Connectors

You should know how to spot a few more common ports that aren't USB, and the CompTIA IT Fundamentals objectives also expect you to be able to identify some legacy ports that are rarely used anymore.

- **Thunderbolt**   Like USB, Thunderbolt supports a variety of peripherals. Thunderbolt enables you to daisy-chain up to six devices, which means you can plug a Thunderbolt external storage drive into a Thunderbolt monitor, into another Thunderbolt monitor, and so on. Thunderbolt uses connectors adopted for earlier technologies and in turn supports those technologies. The version 1 and version 2 Thunderbolt ports (shown in Figure 3-6) used primarily on Macs for connecting monitors use a Mini DisplayPort connector. Thunderbolt 3 uses the same connector as USB 3.1 Type-C ports. That means you can plug a USB Type-C device into a Thunderbolt 3 port, for example, and the device will function. (The reverse is not true.)

  - Thunderbolt 1 runs at 10 Gbps.

  - Thunderbolt 2 runs at 20 Gbps.

  - Thunderbolt 3 runs at 40 Gbps.

Figure 3-6 Thunderbolt version 1 and 2 connectors (right) on a MacBook Air

- **FireWire** Also known as IEEE 1394 (for the standard that defines it). This is used primarily with digital cameras, media devices, and external hard drives. It is generally a viable but less popular alternative to USB.
  - FireWire 400 runs at 400 Mbps.
  - FireWire 800 runs at 800 Mbps.
- **eSATA** Used exclusively for external SATA storage devices, such as external hard drives. These ports and connectors resemble USB and plain SATA, but they are *not* interchangeable with either.
  - The various eSATA standards run at 1.5, 3, or 6 Gbps.

EXAM TIP I've listed the speeds of USB, Thunderbolt, FireWire, and eSATA so that you can rank them clearly. You don't need to memorize the numbers; just rank the standards from fastest to slowest—Thunderbolt, USB, FireWire, and then eSATA.

- **RJ-45** Ethernet networking connector. The port has visible metal pins inside; the rectangular plastic connector is transparent (with wires visible inside) and has a small release tab on top.
- **3.5-mm audio** The same connector as a small headphone jack, used for microphones, headphones, and speakers. These are color-coded on most systems.
- **PS/2** Round plugs for connecting older mice and keyboards (color-coded green and purple, respectively). This has been mostly replaced by USB.
- **RJ-11** Used for modems and landline telephones. Both the port and connector look like smaller versions of the RJ-45 connector. This is becoming very rare as dial-up Internet connections all but vanish.
- **Legacy parallel** Old printers. This uses a 25-pin D-shaped connector and has mostly been replaced by USB.
- **Legacy serial** Very old low-speed devices of many kinds. This uses a 9-pin D-shaped connector. It has been mostly replaced by USB.

Figure 3-7 shows each of these common connectors.

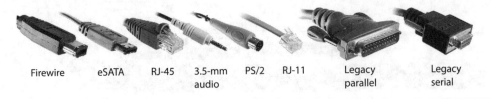

Firewire   eSATA   RJ-45   3.5-mm   PS/2   RJ-11   Legacy   Legacy
                              audio   parallel   serial

Figure 3-7   Common connectors

EXAM TIP   Take the time to study the appearance and purpose of each of these connectors and think through how to tell them apart from the other connectors in this chapter and how to spot the corresponding port on a device.

Monitors

The *monitor* is the primary output device for the computer. It displays the results of input and the computer's processing. This could be anything from moving through a level of an intense action game to moving your mouse across the desktop. When most people think about their interactions with a computer, they are probably thinking about what happens on the monitor.

Every monitor, while distinct, has the same basic components. The back of the monitor has connections for receiving a video signal from the computer and power from a wall outlet. The most important part is, of course, the display itself (see Figure 3-8).

You can power the display on and off and adjust other settings using a set of buttons usually found on an edge of the monitor. Pressing the Menu button opens an onscreen menu that enables you to adjust the brightness, contrast, color balance, size, and position of the display (see Figure 3-9). Most monitors also have a button that will automatically choose the best settings for you.

Monitor Types

There are two main computer monitor types: flat-panel displays (of various kinds) and the now-obsolete cathode ray tube (CRT). Computers can also hook up to external projectors. Let's look at the basics of how they work.

LCD and Other Flat-Panel Displays

A *flat-panel display (FPD)* is very thin (many are thinner than a half-inch), is lightweight, and very little power.

The most common FPD is the *liquid crystal display (LCD),* which has a backlit layer of liquid crystal molecules (called *subpixels*) sandwiched between polarizing filters. The older backlights are efficient, long-lasting *cold cathode fluorescent lamps (CCFLs).* Newer *light-emitting diode (LED)* backlights use a grid of many tiny lightbulbs. When power is applied to the diodes, the bulbs glow.

Figure 3-8
Front of monitor

Screen

Menu buttons

Figure 3-9
Onscreen menu
options

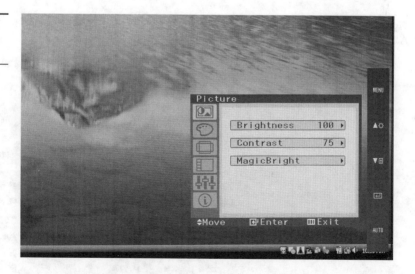

A very efficient variant of LED called *organic light-emitting diode (OLED)* has grown popular on devices such as high-end smartphones and televisions, but as of early 2016 it was finally beginning to show up on laptops and monitors. OLED uses organic compounds that naturally produce (colored) light rather than needing a backlight.

Plasma display technology is mostly for televisions, but you can of course connect a computer to it. Plasma TV sizes begin at around 32 inches because of the large pixel size. Plasma displays have their own method of lighting the screen with phosphorous cells instead of liquid crystals, and the phosphors do not require backlighting. Plasma displays are unfortunately thicker, require more power than LCDs, and suffer burn-in from screen elements that never move (such as elements on a computer desktop). One upside is a wide viewing angle.

Instead of being nearly square like old televisions (a 4:3 *aspect ratio* of width to height), most modern FPDs use a 16:9 or 16:10 *widescreen* aspect ratio. This ratio is great for looking at two documents side by side (or, of course, watching movies).

CRTs

A *CRT monitor* (see Figure 3-10) is bulky because it contains a large cathode ray tube. It uses electron guns to activate phosphors behind the screen, causing each pixel on the monitor to generate red, green, or blue. CRT monitors are obsolete, though you might see them in a CompTIA IT Fundamentals question. CRTs have extremely-high-voltage capacitors inside, so don't open one for any reason. If a CRT is malfunctioning, dispose of it.

Figure 3-10
A CRT monitor

CRT monitors are heavy and use a lot of electricity, though they do have the same sharp, crisp image at any display resolution. LCD monitors only look crisp at their native (highest) resolution.

EXAM TIP   CRTs contain an assortment of hazardous materials, including lead, phosphorus, and mercury, so don't throw them out with the trash! Instead, contact a computer recycling company near you. They will dispose of old computer components for you.

Projectors

Projectors shoot an image out the front and onto a screen. Front-view projectors (see Figure 3-11) connected to computers running Microsoft PowerPoint have been the cornerstone of almost every meeting since the Clinton administration. The qualities that matter most are brightness (in lumens—larger rooms need higher-lumen projectors) and throw (in image size at a given distance from the screen).

All projectors have a recommended minimum and maximum *throw* distance. Manufacturers create short and long throw projectors. A high-end short throw projector can create a 100-inch diagonal image from ~4 feet away. A long throw projector would need 10+ feet to accomplish the same thing. Pick a projector based on the space (and price).

Projector lamps work hard to generate a tremendous amount of light, and a lot of heat is a byproduct, so projectors come with a fan to keep the lamp from overheating. Replacement lamps are costly.

Monitor Ports and Connectors

Monitors come with at least one port to connect to computers (which seems pretty obvious). Many offer several types of connectors to give you options. Let's dig into what you might find.

Figure 3-11
Front-view
projector
(photo courtesy
of Dell, Inc.)

Figure 3-12
A DVI cable and
connector

Digital Visual Interface (DVI)

A typical monitor sports one *Digital Visual Interface* port (shown in Figure 3-12). Despite the name, this connector does not always carry a digital signal. There are actually three connector types: DVI-D (digital), DVI-A (analog), and DVI-I (integrates digital and analog).

High Definition Multimedia Interface (HDMI)

The *High Definition Multimedia Interface* is the current standard for television and home theater equipment connections and is increasingly common on computer monitors. HDMI handles both video and audio signals (in contrast to video-only DVI). Figure 3-13 shows the full-size Type-A connector. You will also see a smaller, mini connector (called a Type-C) on a lot of portable devices.

Figure 3-13
An HDMI
connector

Video Graphics Array (VGA)

The oldest type of video connector still in use today is *Video Graphics Array,* shown in Figure 3-14. It has 15 pins, laid out in three rows of five. This is an analog connector, meaning it sends an analog (not digital) signal to a monitor. Use VGA when DVI and HDMI are not available.

Composite Video

A *composite* video connector (see Figure 3-15) is a round, yellow RCA connector. The figure also shows an RCA port (on an adapter), which is color-coded to match the connector. Many composite cables are joined to red and white RCA connectors (for stereo audio). Composite video is not a great interface for PC use and doesn't support high resolutions.

S-Video

S-Video (short for *separate video*) is an interface for standard-definition video. It is a round plug with four pins (as shown in Figure 3-16). It provides better image quality than composite video but is not as good as component video (discussed next). S-Video carries audio as well as video signals, like HDMI, but with lower resolution video.

Component (RGB) Video

Component video is an analog video signal where the three main video components (one for black and white and two for color information) are separated into their own channels. As shown in Figure 3-17, it uses three RCA cables (color-coded red, green,

Figure 3-14
A VGA connector

Figure 3-15
The composite
(RCA) video port
and connector
are color-coded
yellow.

and blue). Although some monitors support it, few computer display adapters do, so it's not a popular interface for PC monitors. It's more common on TVs and home theater components.

 EXAM TIP Some people assume the red, green, and blue (RGB) cables carry corresponding (red, green, and blue) signals as in the RGB color scheme, but in this case RGB just indicates the connector colors.

Figure 3-16 S-Video cable and connector

Figure 3-17
Component
video

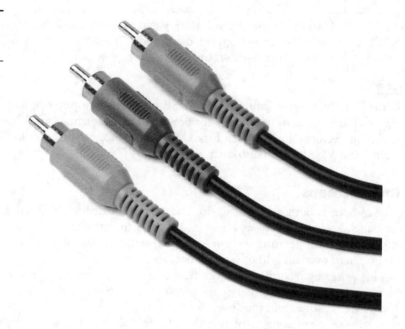

DisplayPort, Mini DisplayPort, and Thunderbolt

DisplayPort, Mini DisplayPort, and Thunderbolt are found primarily on Macintosh computers. DisplayPort was meant to be a replacement for VGA on all platforms, but it has failed to catch on, probably because of the growing popularity of the HDMI interface.

Thunderbolt and the older Mini DisplayPort are physically identical and can both be used to connect monitors. Thunderbolt ports can also accommodate other types of devices.

Thunderbolt and DisplayPort support both high-definition video and audio, just like HDMI.

The full-size DisplayPort connector is roughly the size and shape of a USB connector, but it has a keyed corner to differentiate it. Figure 3-18 compares the Thunderbolt, DisplayPort, and USB ports.

Figure 3-18   From left to right: Thunderbolt port, DisplayPort, and USB

EXAM TIP Keep track of which video connections carry only video signals and which carry both video and audio. The latter group includes HDMI, S-Video, Thunderbolt, and DisplayPort.

USB

With the right adapter, you can use a USB port on a computer to connect to a monitor. You'll find these in use mainly for projectors and presentations. I have no idea what kind of projectors I'll meet when I travel to teach. Since my presentation laptop only has HDMI and VGA ports, I also carry a USB-to-DVI adapter.

Touchscreens

A *touchscreen* is both an input device and an output device. It functions like a regular flat-panel display in every way, but it also has a touch-sensitive surface you can use to interact with the operating system. The touch-sensitive part of the screen, the *digitizer*, is a transparent overlaid grid of sensors that record your touch.

This works by recording how the flow of electricity through the sensor grid changes when you touch the screen. The most common variants used in consumer computing devices are resistive and capacitive.

A *resistive screen* consists of two thin, flexible sheets of plastic, with a gap between them. When you touch the surface of one sheet, that sheet presses down onto the sheet below it, creating an electrical signal. A resistive screen works no matter what is pressing on it—a finger, a gloved finger, or a stylus.

A *capacitive screen* uses the electrical properties of the human body to alter the capacitance of an electrostatic field on the screen. This type of screen is made of glass, so it is more durable than the plastic resistive touchscreen. The main drawback is that it doesn't usually work with gloved fingers or with styluses not designed for capacitive screens.

Standard Input Devices

Almost all desktop and portable computers feature two input devices, a keyboard for typing and a mouse or other pointing device for moving a cursor across the monitor screen. This section looks at both input device types in some detail.

Keyboards

The keyboard is the primary input device for many computing devices. Keyboards enable you to input text and to issue commands by pressing key combinations (called *keyboard shortcuts*).

Over the years, manufacturers have added extra keys to the standard keyboard, but most standard keyboards in English-speaking countries have the same QWERTY layout (see Figure 3-19). The *QWERTY* name comes from the first six letters on the top alphabetic row; there's typically a row of numbers above this row and a row of function keys

Figure 3-19   A QWERTY keyboard

above that. *Function keys* can change a lot depending on the program, but F1 is almost always Help.

NOTE   Not every language uses the same alphabet. There are keyboard layouts available for most languages in the world. This is called *regionalization.* A keyboard for Spanish adds accented characters such as *é* and Spanish-only characters such as *ñ.*

Other keys you'll find on a Windows-based keyboard are ESC, TAB, CAPS LOCK, SHIFT, CTRL, ALT, and WINDOWS. On every keyboard you'll find keys such as HOME, END, BACK-SPACE, DELETE, and so on. Keyboards for Macs have CONTROL, OPTION, and COMMAND keys instead of CTRL, WINDOWS, and ALT keys.

At the right side of all full-size keyboards is the *numeric keypad,* or *number pad.* The number pad lays out the numbers 0–9 along with various math symbols (plus, minus, and so on) like a calculator. Some keyboards, such as those on portable computers, leave off the number pad, but you can buy a stand-alone number pad peripheral if needed.

Most keyboards (even wireless ones) use a USB Type-A connector to connect to the computer. Very old keyboards used a PS/2 connector.

Modern wireless keyboards require two components. A wireless receiver plugs into a USB port and then communicates via radio frequency (RF) with a wireless keyboard. You may find much older wireless peripherals that communicate with short-range infra-red (IR) light that requires an unbroken line of sight between the sending and receiving devices.

NOTE Wired keyboards and mice don't need a separate power connection. Their power is provided by the PS/2 or USB port. A wireless RF receiver plugs into (and is powered by) the USB port, but the keyboard or mouse needs battery power.

Pointing Devices

Mice and other pointing devices such as trackballs and touchpads are input devices that enable you to move a cursor around the screen and click things (Figure 3-20). Mice designed for Windows computers traditionally have two buttons, and this standard has evolved to include a scroll wheel in the center that enables you to move up and down in a window, as if you were clicking the scroll bar. They use the same Type-A USB or PS/2 connectors as keyboards.

 NOTE Mice for Apple Mac computers traditionally had only one button, but modern Mac mice have two buttons and a scroll area in the middle.

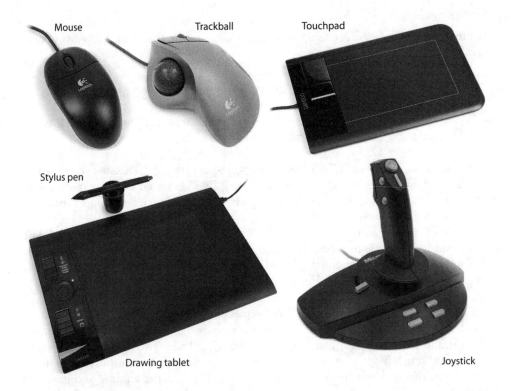

Mouse Trackball Touchpad

Stylus pen

Drawing tablet Joystick

Figure 3-20 Various pointing devices

Mice originally came with a rubber ball on the bottom. When you move the mouse around, sensors inside track the ball's rotation and translate it to the screen. These *ball mice* collect dust and grime on the sensors and must be cleaned periodically. Modern *optical mice* use an LED or laser to track their movement.

Mice aren't the only game in town. A *trackball* is like a ball mouse but with the ball atop the device where you can manipulate it with a finger to move the cursor. Trackballs are great if you don't have a good surface or have wrist problems. You can also drag your fingers across a touch-sensitive *touchpad* to move the pointer (and tap it to click). Most laptops have a built-in touchpads, and you can find stand-alone versions for desktops.

A variant of a touchpad, called a *drawing tablet,* uses an inkless *stylus pen.* Where the pen touches the drawing tablet, it changes the electrical flow through a grid of underlying wires to send data to the computer. Drawing tablets are used by professional artists, drafters, and engineers to create computer graphics, blueprints, and designs.

A joystick is a fun input device that many gaming enthusiasts use to play certain kinds of games, like flight simulators. It's an upright vertical "stick" mounted in a base that allows it to tilt in any direction, and it typically has buttons or triggers on the stick to allow for selecting (or, as the case may be, firing missiles at alien invaders).

Other Common I/O Devices

Computing devices offer a phenomenal amount of adaptability to various tasks. Plug in the correct device and you can turn a simple portable computer into DJ-jamming sonic experience. The only thing missing will be the disco ball. Plug in different devices and turn the same machine into a miniature office, complete with printing and faxing capabilities.

This section explores the typical devices used today to extend the capabilities of computing devices. We'll look at audio devices, imaging peripherals, and printers and fax machines.

Audio Devices

Audio controllers enable the computer to play and record sound. All modern computers come with sound controllers built into the motherboard, but older systems needed add-on sound cards. The simplest sound controllers have three 3.5-mm audio ports (jacks), while more complex sound controllers have five or six jacks (see Figure 3-21). Each jack

Figure 3-21
3.5-mm audio
jacks on an add-
on sound card

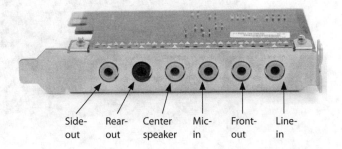

Side-out   Rear-out   Center speaker   Mic-in   Front-out   Line-in

Table 3-1
Names and Color
Codes for 3.5-mm
Audio Jacks

Connector	Color	Purpose
Line-out	Green	Main speakers or headphones
Microphone	Pink	Recording sounds
Line-in	Blue	Sound input from an audio device
Subwoofer	Orange	Thumping bass with a subwoofer attached
Rear surround sound	Black	Rear speakers
Middle surround sound	Gray	Extra speakers in a 7.1 sound setup

traditionally handles a specific audio input or output, although manufacturers use auto-sensing controllers on many portables. Most manufacturers use the color-coding scheme in Table 3-1.

EXAM TIP If you've connected a pair of headphones to a cell phone or portable media (cassette, CD, MP3, DVD) player in the past few decades, you've almost inevitably used one of these audio jacks. These are smaller than the full-size headphone jacks used in higher-quality home audio equipment (don't worry—the full-size version isn't on the exam). If you aren't familiar with the 3.5-mm connector, flip back to Figure 3-7.

Sound Output

A computer uses the sound processor and audio software to play music and sounds through speakers or headphones. Better motherboards offer high-definition audio processors.

Many users replace cheap bundled speakers with higher-quality systems, like the 2.1 system shown in Figure 3-22. In any *x*.1 speaker set, the *x* refers to the number of stereo speakers or satellites, and the 1 refers to the subwoofer (which provides the bass).

Figure 3-22
Klipsch ProMedia
2.1 speakers

NOTE You can create a surround-sound experience in a media room with 5.1 or 7.1 speaker sets. These have a single subwoofer and multiple satellites for *surrounding* the listener.

Sound Input

A computer can also use the sound processor, the audio software, and a microphone or other audio device to record sound. All operating systems come with some (often limited) recording capability. Most desktops have at least a microphone (or mic) port, though portable computers may only have a built-in mic (don't despair—you can find excellent USB audio peripherals). Still, recording a great song or podcast may require more robust software, microphones, and other hardware.

Imaging Peripherals

Manufacturers create many computing devices dedicated to capturing and digitizing visual information, but the CompTIA IT Fundamentals exam focuses on two such peripherals: scanners and webcams. There's an argument for including fax machines here, but we'll look at those alongside printers and multifunction devices. Most modern imaging devices connect via USB.

Scanners

Scanners make digital copies of existing paper photos, documents, drawings, and other items. Some can copy directly from a photographic negative or slide, providing images of stunning visual quality (if the original was decent).

These days, traditional *flatbed* consumer-grade scanners are usually combined with a printer to make a multifunction device. You can also find scan-only devices for various purposes. A camera-based *document* or *book scanner* combines a digital camera with some hardware for positioning it squarely above a book or document, and sheet-fed document scanners can be found in desktop or travel-friendly formats for scanning full-size documents, receipts, business cards, and so on.

Digital Cameras

Not that I have anything against your smartphone and selfie stick, but a dedicated digital camera or camcorder can offer higher quality, features tuned to the task at hand, and more room for creativity. While cameras and camcorders are converging and can each shoot still photos and video, consumer cameras are designed around shooting photos, and camcorders are designed for comfortable continuous recording.

The only digital cameras in the CompTIA IT Fundamentals objectives, *webcams,* tend to have modest, bandwidth-friendly resolutions that serve their primary mission: video calling and chatting over the Internet. You may already be familiar with this concept if you have a smartphone with rear and front-facing cameras; the high-quality camera on the back of the phone functions as a traditional digital camera for taking pretty pictures, and the lower-quality front-facing camera functions as a webcam for video chat, messaging, and so on.

Webcams often come built into portable computers, all-in-one desktop computers (where the computer and monitor are integrated), and even some stand-alone monitors, but you can also buy stand-alone USB models. The webcam in Figure 3-23 includes a microphone, a typical feature. You can also use a separate stand-alone mic or headset.

Printers and Fax Machines

Printers, as you probably know, output data (such as text and images) to paper. There are even printers capable of outputting three-dimensional objects made of plastic, metal, concrete, and chocolate—but the exam focuses on the more mundane two-dimensional kind. You don't see many stand-alone fax machines anymore, but fax technology is often included in all-in-one (multifunction) printers.

Let's look first at printer technologies and then examine costs associated with consumables. The next sections look at fax technologies and multifunction devices. The final part is about setting up printers and multifunction devices.

Figure 3-23
A stand-alone
HD Pro Webcam
C920 (courtesy
of Logitech)

Printer Technologies

Manufacturers have created many types of printing devices over the years and have incorporated various technologies to get text and images from the monitor to the physical object. You need to know four printing technologies for the exam: impact, inkjet, laser, and thermal.

Impact Printers   *Impact* printers create an image by physically striking an *ink ribbon* against the paper's surface, which makes them relatively slow and noisy. Impact printers are largely gone from our homes, but one kind—the *dot-matrix* printer—is still common in businesses because they can print to multipart forms. *Point-of-sale (POS)* machines, for example, use special *impact paper* that can print two or more copies of a receipt. Dot-matrix printers (see Figure 3-24) have a *printhead* that holds the pins or *printwires* that strike the inked ribbon, and many use tiny sprockets to advance *tractor-feed impact paper*.

Inkjet Printers   *Inkjet* printers squirt ink out of special cartridges and combine ink colors to create a wide range of hues suitable for printing text and images. Inkjet printers use liquid ink cartridges. The process starts with a *friction feed* mechanism in which small rollers press down on paper stacked in the tray and pull a sheet through the printer. On its way through, most liquid inkjet printers use heat to eject ink through hundreds of tiny nozzles on the printhead (see Figure 3-25) and onto the paper. The other type uses pressure to move the ink through the printhead.

Laser and LED Printers   Laser printers (such as the one in Figure 3-26) rely on certain organic compounds that conduct electricity when exposed to light. Lasers can do this precisely, though some cheaper "laser" printers do a lower-quality job with LEDs.

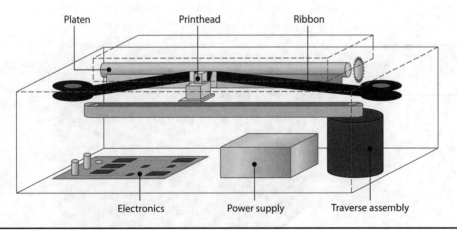

Figure 3-24   Inside a dot-matrix printer

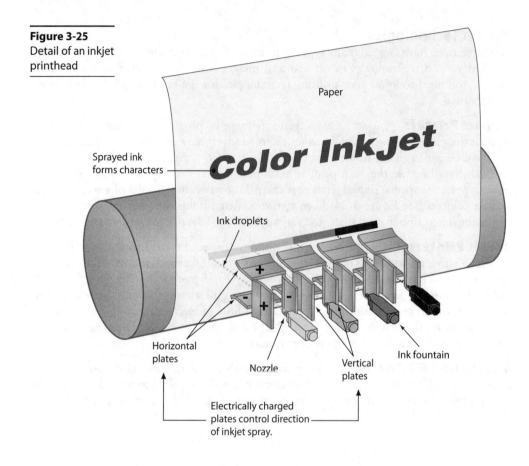

Figure 3-25
Detail of an inkjet printhead

Paper

Color InkJet

Sprayed ink forms characters

Ink droplets

Horizontal plates

Nozzle

Vertical plates

Ink fountain

Electrically charged plates control direction of inkjet spray.

Figure 3-26
A typical laser printer

NOTE Printer resolution is measured in dots per inch (dpi) and speed in pages per minute (ppm). Higher is better.

Inside a laser printer, a spinning drum gets magnetized and demagnetized by the laser, and other components, which are tiny iron particles wrapped in plastic (called *toner*), jump to the drum. The printer transfers the toner to the paper and then melts it in place. That's why paper coming fresh from a laser printer feels a little warm to the touch. Toner is essentially the laser printer's ink.

Color laser printers, just like color inkjets, need multiple types of toner to match the primary colors. Color laser printers used to be very expensive but have become much more affordable in the past couple of years. Snatch one up!

Thermal Printers   *Direct thermal printers* selectively heat specially coated paper so that the heated areas turn black. Common uses are receipt printers and stand-alone fax machines. They don't print pretty pictures since they can't do gray, but they are simple, durable, and cheap to run.

Thermal transfer printing uses a heat-sensitive film ribbon instead of heat-sensitive paper and can even print in color with a wax-based film ink that melts onto the paper.

Printer Consumables

Printers, like all other good pets, cost more to feed and maintain than to buy; there's also a *cost per page* that accounts for ink/toner, paper, and parts that eventually wear out and must be replaced (such as the drums on laser printers). If you print often, don't let a low purchase price trick you into getting taken for a ride over the long term.

Inkjet printers are cheap, but ink cartridges are very expensive per page. Laser printers cost more to buy, but toner is cheaper per page than ink. Over time, therefore, inkjet printers cost more to operate than laser printers. If you can live with their limitations, direct thermal printers are the cheapest to operate, requiring only thermal paper.

 EXAM TIP   Printers tend to generate a lot of waste paper and cartridges, the latter containing chemicals we don't want in our food, water, or air. At minimum, check with the local sanitation department or disposal service company before throwing away components. But really, recycle everything you can. Cartridges often come with a mailer to return them for reuse, and some companies will pay good money for used toner cartridges.

Fax Machines

Fax machines predate personal computers. A fax machine is both an input device and an output device; it scans a hard copy and then converts it to digital data and transmits it across telephone lines using a built-in modem to another fax machine. At the receiving end, a fax machine functions as a printer, re-creating the original hard copy.

The original fax machines included direct thermal printers. As a result, they required special thermal paper, and they printed only black and white (no gray shading). Today's fax machines, however, use laser or inkjet technology, so they can receive faxes in grayscale or in color.

While stand-alone fax machines are still sold, it is much more common to find faxing built into a multifunction printer.

Multifunction Devices (MFD)

A *multifunction device* (also called a *multifunction printer* or *all-in-one printer*) is a printer with one or more other devices rolled in. The typical MFD combines a printer, copy machine, scanner, and fax machine in one unit.

MFDs don't cost much more than regular printers, so you can make out like a bandit if you need the additional functions. Figure 3-27 shows a typical multifunction device with a feed tray for the scanner and copier portion and a variety of slots for memory cards on the lower right.

Setting Up Printers and MFDs

After you unpack a new printer or MFD, you have a couple of steps to take before you can use the device. Essentially you plug it into the computer and install software to support the device. Printers and MFDs bring a couple of wrinkles to the process, though, so you need to read the documentation thoroughly. Some devices require you to start installing the software and plug the device in during that process.

Printers today connect in one of three ways: through USB directly to a computer, plugged into a switch, or connected wirelessly for availability to all network devices. FireWire printers were a thing for a very short period of time. Much older printers

Figure 3-27
A multifunction
device

connected to one of two now-extinct ports, the parallel and serial ports. Parallel ports were 25-pin ports; serial were 9-pin. Both used a D-shaped format appropriately called a *D-shell*.

 EXAM TIP FireWire, parallel, and serial printer connections went away a long time ago. For some reason, though, questions involving them show up on the CompTIA IT Fundamentals exam. Be prepared.

Installing software for a printer is pretty straightforward. Place the installation media—usually a CD that came with the printer—and follow the instructions on the screen.

Installing software for an MFD, on the other hand, can get tricky. You're essentially installing four or five different devices, after all, so you need to follow the manufacturer's instructions carefully.

Note that you need to install software for every computer that will use the printer or MFD. This can trip up newer computer users, especially if they move a printer from one computer and plug it into another one. Even a known-good printer won't work without the software installed.

Chapter Review

In this chapter, we looked at many of the devices you can connect to a computer and the slots and connectors you use to do so. Most contemporary expansion cards use PCIe, with intensive cards such as video adapters typically using a 16-lane (×16) slot and less-demanding cards using ×1, ×4, or ×8 slots. USB is the predominant external expansion port, though it's important to recognize the many USB versions and connector types for compatibility and performance reasons. Other important connectors include Thunderbolt, FireWire, eSATA, RJ-45, and 3.5-mm audio, as well as older (rare) connectors such as PS/2, RJ-11, legacy parallel, and legacy serial.

Flat-screen displays (including LCD, LED, and OLED) are ubiquitous these days, but you may also encounter CRT and projector displays. There are tons of ports and connectors that can carry video signals, though only a few (DVI, HDMI, DisplayPort/Thunderbolt, and USB 3.*x*) can handle modern high-definition video; you should be able to recognize other connectors such as VGA, composite video, S-Video, component (RGB) video, and older generations of USB, but use them only as a last resort. Some recent displays are also integrated with touchscreen technology, which enables them to double as both an input and output device.

The ports introduced early in the chapter enable us to connect common input and output peripherals such as keyboards, pointing devices (mice, trackballs, touchpads, drawing tablets, joysticks), and devices for inputting and outputting sound, images, and video. Finally, we examined a few key printer technologies such as inkjet, laser, and thermal printers, including how to manage the "consumables" such as paper and ink.

As you finish studying the material in this chapter, make sure that given a device, you can say whether it is for input, output, or both. Here's a list of the device types to know:

Input	Output	Both Input and Output
Keyboards	Printers (laser, inkjet, thermal)	Fax machines
Pointing devices (mouse, touchpad, joystick, stylus pen, trackball)	Displays (flat screen, CRT, projector)	External storage devices (covered in Chapter 4, includes flash drives, external hard drives, optical drives, network attached storage, memory cards, mobile media players, and smartphones)
Scanners	Speakers	
Microphones		Touchscreen displays
Webcams		

Questions

1. A video card on a modern motherboard would run best in which type of slot?

   A. PCI

   B. PCIe

   C. VGA

   D. DVI

2. Which port is used exclusively for external hard drives?

   A. FireWire

   B. USB

   C. eSATA

   D. PS/2

3. Which of these external ports is *not* obsolete?

   A. FireWire

   B. Legacy parallel

   C. Legacy serial

   D. PS/2

4. What type of connector does a modem use?

   A. PS/2

   B. RJ-45

   C. 3.5 mm

   D. RJ-11

5. The USB connector that plugs into a full-size printer is:

    A. Type-A

    B. Type-B

    C. Mini-B

    D. Micro-B

6. Which of these is *not* a flat-panel display?

    A. OLED

    B. LCD

    C. Plasma

    D. CRT

7. Which of these ports are physically identical?

    A. USB Type-A and USB Type-B

    B. Thunderbolt and Mini DisplayPort

    C. DisplayPort and FireWire

    D. DVI and VGA

8. What is the purpose of a wheel on a mouse?

    A. Scrolling the display

    B. Greater precision of pointer movement

    C. Right-clicking alternative

    D. Locating the pointer

9. A video camera that works only when connected to a computer is a:

    A. Scanner

    B. Digital video camera

    C. Megapixel camera

    D. Webcam

10. A receipt printer on a cash register is likely to be what kind of printer?

    A. Inkjet

    B. Laser

    C. LED

    D. Thermal

Answers

1. **B**. PCIe is correct. PCI is an older type of slot that is slower and less desirable for video cards. VGA and DVI are not slot types.

2. **C**. eSATA is correct. FireWire and USB can be used for external hard drives, but they also have other uses. PS/2 is an old port used for keyboards and mice, not hard drives.

3. **A**. FireWire is correct. All the others are obsolete.

4. **D**. RJ-11 is correct. PS/2 is an old port used for keyboards and mice. RJ-45 is used for wired Ethernet networking. The 3.5-mm connector is used for audio ports.

5. **B**. Type-B is correct. Type-A is the standard full-size USB connector on a PC. Mini-B and Micro-B plug into smaller devices.

6. **D**. CRT is correct. All the other types are flat-panel displays.

7. **B**. Thunderbolt and Mini DisplayPort are correct. The other pairs are not identical.

8. **A**. Scrolling the display is correct. The other actions are not controlled by the mouse wheel.

9. **D**. Webcam is correct. A scanner is not a video camera. A digital video camera can be removed from a computer and used independently. A megapixel camera is a still camera that supports at least 1 million pixels in resolution.

10. **D**. Thermal printing is common on cash registers because of the low cost of consumables. The other answer choices are types of printers but not the most likely choice for a cash register.

Data Storage and Sharing

In this chapter, you will learn how to
- Differentiate among types of storage
- Choose appropriate storage locations

This chapter reviews the current storage and file-sharing landscape. We'll start with three common storage technologies: magnetic, optical, and solid state. Then we'll evaluate the available options for local, network, and online storage.

Storage Technologies

Modern computers can store enormous programs, documents, and media files on spacious storage devices. An understanding of how we measure the size of these devices is important for comparing them. Let's start there.

In computing, files are measured in *bytes*. One byte is 8 binary digits (*bits*). Storage devices are available in different capacities measured in some multiple of bytes. Most files are measured in kilobytes or megabytes, but storage drives are currently measured in gigabytes and terabytes. Refer to Table 4-1 for a summary of capacity measurements.

 EXAM TIP The list of CompTIA IT Fundamentals acronyms includes *kilobit (Kb)*, *megabit (Mb)*, and *gigabit (Gb)*. Note the lowercase *b*, which indicates bits, not bytes. (Recall that a byte is 8 bits.) Storage is described in bytes, such as 100 GB. Data transfer rates are usually described as a certain number of bits per second, as in 1 Gbps.

Don't confuse bits or bytes with *hertz*, as in megahertz (MHz) and gigahertz (GHz), describing a certain number of processing cycles per second for a central processing unit (CPU).

These days, most data is stored on magnetic, optical, and solid-state storage devices. Most storage devices are internal (they mount inside the computer case), but you'll also see some external storage devices that connect via an external port and may have an additional source of power. Let's take a look at the different mechanisms these devices use to read and write data.

Unit	Exact Amount	Notes
Kilobyte (KB)	1,024 bits	Approximately 1 thousand bits
Megabyte (MB)	1,024 kilobytes	Approximately 1 million bytes
Gigabyte (GB)	1,024 megabytes	Approximately 1 billion bytes
Terabyte (TB)	1,024 gigabytes	Approximately 1 trillion bytes

Table 4-1 Storage Capacity Measurements

NOTE The section "Storage Locations" examines the different interfaces that internal and external drives use.

Magnetic Storage

Magnetic storage encodes data in patterns of positive and negative magnetic polarity on some magnetic medium. In previous decades, there were different kinds of magnetic storage such as floppy disks or zip disks, but the only ones left standing are hard disks and magnetic tapes. You won't see magnetic tape on the exam, but it is cost effective in large archival systems where it may well soldier on for years or decades after most hard disks are retired.

A *hard disk drive (HDD)* is a sealed metal cartridge with a stack of metal platters inside (Figure 4-1). Modern consumer HDDs range from 500 GB to 10 TB, but you may see older systems with smaller disks.

Figure 4-1 Inside a hard disk drive

The platters are coated with iron dust, and each side of each platter has a separate read/write head. The platters spin under the read/write head, which uses an actuator arm to access data from the outside to the center. The drive's *integrated drive electronics (IDE)*, a controller that translates requests from the PC into action, tells the heads where to read or write.

NOTE The terms *hard disk drive, hard disk,* and *hard drive* are all synonymous because the disk and drive can't be separated without destroying the unit. In contrast, optical media (such as CDs, DVDs, and BDs) are separate from the drives that read them.

Once HDD platters spin up, they spin at a constant *rotation speed*; the most common speeds are 5,400; 7,200; and 10,000 revolutions per minute (rpm). Higher rotation speeds result in more noise, faster transfers, more power consumption, and greater cost. Modern drives have a small RAM cache to help get data to and from the drive faster. Standard cache sizes are 16, 32, 64, and 128 MB (see Figure 4-2).

Optical Storage

Optical discs (note the spelling of *disc* versus *disk*) store data in reflectivity patterns on a shiny surface. Common optical discs include CDs, DVDs, and BDs. Unlike with HDDs, optical discs are removable from the drives that read them, so the *optical disc* and *optical drive* are two different things. The optical drive (which may be internal or external) measures how much laser light the disc reflects.

You should be familiar with these generations of optical media in use, all of which you can find in single or double-sided varieties:

- The *compact disc (CD)* initially became popular for distributing music but later became the standard for distributing computer programs and data.

- The *digital versatile disc (DVD)* was developed to distribute standard-definition movies, but software distribution followed for programs too large to fit on a CD. DVDs can also be single-layer or double-layer (the drive uses a different laser angle to read each layer). Double-layer discs have a -DL suffix, as in *DVD-DL*.

Figure 4-2
Hard drive package advertising rotation speed and cache size (photo courtesy of Western Digital)

- The *Blu-ray Disc (BD)* was designed for high-definition movies. The name comes from the blue laser these drives use (rather than the red laser used in CD and DVD drives). Blu-ray Discs are also available in triple-layer and quadruple-layer versions, called *Blu-ray Disc XL (BDXL)*.

The combination of these various features means there are a number of potential capacities (summarized in Table 4-2) for each disc technology. The drives are backward compatible, so a Blu-ray Disc drive can read both DVDs and CDs, and a DVD drive can also read CDs.

 EXAM TIP The list of CompTIA IT Fundamentals acronyms includes *DVD-RAM*, which is a different type of writeable DVD disc that is used primarily in camcorders and personal video recorders. DVD-RAM discs typically come in insertable cartridges. Most modern computer operating systems support DVD-RAM, but not all optical drives support DVD-RAM discs.

Optical drives have a maximum rate at which they can read or write to a disc expressed in multiples of the technologies' base rate (for example, 1×, 48×, or 150×), and more is better. Each generation has a faster base rate (but you don't need to know these for the exam). Early optical drives were read-only, but modern ones can also write (and rewrite) to a variety of optical discs. In this case, you'll typically see multiple speeds for reading, writing, and rewriting.

Discs that cannot be written to have a *ROM* suffix, as in CD-ROM, DVD-ROM, and BD-ROM.

Some writeable discs can be written only once; these typically end in *R* (as in CD-R, DVD-R, and BD-R). Once the disc surface has been changed, it can't be redone. Discs that end in *RW* or *RE* (as in CD-RW, DVD-RW, and BD-RE) have a different kind of metal surface; the drive can write at one temperature and erase at another.

 NOTE Writeable DVDs have two different standards referred to as *plus* and *minus*. For single-write DVDs, you'll find DVD+R and DVD-R discs; most drives support both, but make sure.

Table 4-2	Disc Type	Layers	Capacity (Per Side)
Optical Disc	CD	1	700 MB
Capacity	DVD	1	4.7 GB
	DVD	2	8.5 GB
	BD	1	25 GB
	BD	2	50 GB
	BDXL	3	100 GB
	BDXL	4	128 GB

Solid-State Storage

Instead of disks (or discs), solid-state storage uses nonvolatile (*flash*) memory that can retain data when powered down. This technology has no moving parts. Solid-state storage is more expensive per gigabyte than disk-based storage, but it is also lighter, faster, quieter, and more efficient. Because there isn't a disk, flash media can take many creative forms. Here are the most common:

- A USB *flash drive* (Figure 4-3) is a stick of highly portable storage that plugs into a USB port.

- Flash *memory cards* are used in devices such as digital cameras, smartphones, and navigation devices. A prolific photographer will carry several, swapping out full cards for empty ones. You can transfer images off the camera with a cable or just pop the card out and insert it in a memory *card reader* (see Figure 4-4). Either way, the computer treats it like a drive. The most common formats are CompactFlash, Secure Digital (SD), MemoryStick, and MicroSD.

- Hard drives made with flash memory, called *solid-state drives (SSDs),* are more expensive per gigabyte but have quickly matured to the point where drives large enough to support the average user are affordable. Tablets and smartphones have an *embedded multimedia controller (eMMC)* containing flash memory permanently built into the device.

Figure 4-3
Inexpensive USB flash drives easily fit in a pocket or backpack.

Figure 4-4
Memory cards
fit into built-in
or separate card
readers.

EXAM TIP Objective 2.1 of the CompTIA IT Fundamentals exam mentions *mobile media players* as a type of external storage. Mobile media players, such as iPods, store music and videos on built-in solid-state storage, similar to the storage in a USB flash drive. You can connect one to a computer to transfer media clips to and from the device's storage. However, as you will learn in Chapter 6, these media players are not very popular anymore since smartphones and tablets can store and play media just as easily.

Storage Locations

Local storage is physically connected to the individual computer accessing it. It is always available on that device, fast (because it doesn't have to travel far), and convenient. The catch is that it's available *only* on that device. *Network storage* is connected to a local area network (LAN) to share files with other devices on the same LAN. Businesses use network storage extensively to make sure all employees have access to important data and applications. A computer can access network storage only as long as it remains connected to the network.

But what if the devices aren't on the same network? That's when you turn to *online storage,* where files are available anywhere in the world via the Internet. Let's look at these locations in more detail.

Figure 4-5
A SATA power
cable

Local Storage

Local storage, also called *direct attached storage,* has a direct internal or external connection
to the device accessing it. Internal storage devices are physically located inside the main
case of the computer, share its power supply, are harder to steal quickly, and don't take
up desk space. On almost all systems, the primary hard drive is internal. Internal drive
interfaces have historically been faster than external ones, but modern interfaces such as
eSATA, USB 3.1, and Thunderbolt are just as fast (or faster).

Modern internal hard drives connect with *serial ATA (SATA)* connections, including a
five-wire SATA connector from the power supply (see Figure 4-5) and a seven-wire SATA
data cable from the motherboard (see Figure 4-6). Both connectors are keyed so you can't
plug them in incorrectly.

Figure 4-6
A SATA data
cable

Figure 4-7
An 80-wire
ribbon cable

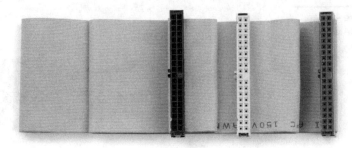

The older (now-obsolete) *parallel ATA (PATA)* drives used a wide 80-wire ribbon cable for data (Figure 4-7) and a 4-wire Molex connector for power (Figure 4-8). You might occasionally see these in an older desktop PC, particularly with an internal optical drive.

External Storage

External storage connects to external ports. Some drives will draw all of their power from the port, but others may need an additional alternating current (AC) adapter.

The most common interfaces (shown in Figure 4-9) for external storage are as follows:

- **USB** Hi Speed USB 2.0 and USB 3.0/3.1 are fast enough for nearly any external storage device.
- **Thunderbolt** Thunderbolt connections are also a good candidate for external storage, but Thunderbolt comes with a higher price tag than USB.

Figure 4-8
A Molex
connector

Figure 4-9   From left to right: USB, Thunderbolt, FireWire, and eSATA

- **FireWire (IEEE 1394)**   FireWire offered a viable alternative to USB but has faded in use. Some drives support both USB and FireWire, which can be nice if your USB ports are full.
- **External SATA (eSATA)**   eSATA is specifically for connecting external SATA drives to the internal SATA bus at full speed.

Network Storage

Network storage or *hosted storage* is accessed over a LAN in your own home or office, a wide area network (WAN) with computers in different countries, or anything in between. This section discusses four options for network storage: file servers, NAS, shared volumes, and ad hoc networks.

NOTE   Technically all Internet-accessed storage is network storage, but we'll discuss Internet storage later in this chapter.

File Servers

Networked computers called *servers* are dedicated full-time to assisting (serving) other computers. There are many kinds of server, including e-mail servers that store and forward e-mail, authentication servers that manage user identities, Web servers that respond to requests for Web pages, and file servers that grant users access to the server's local storage.

A *file server* has fast, high-capacity HDDs or SSDs for storing files that multiple users need to access. When users connect to the file server, they can view and edit files that they have permission to use.

NOTE   It isn't on the exam, but it is worth knowing that many file servers use *Redundant Array of Inexpensive Disks (RAID)* technology, which combines more than one physical drive to improve performance or protect against data loss.

Network-Attached Storage

Network-attached storage (NAS) typically describes a simple stand-alone device that contains one or more hard drive slots, a pared-down file server, and a network connection. It doesn't have a keyboard, mouse, monitor, or full-blown operating system (users can interact with its simple operating system via a Web browser); it just shares access to the installed hard drives.

NAS appliances designed for home use (see Figure 4-10) are sometimes marketed as *home media servers* since a common use is to share music and video collections within a household.

Shared Network Volumes

You don't *need* a file server or NAS appliance to share files on a LAN. You can share a local folder on your own PC with network users and set permissions that control who can view and edit that folder's content.

The main drawback to this kind of *peer-to-peer file sharing* is that the files are available only when your computer is on the network to act as a file server. If your computer is offline for some reason, nobody will be able to access the shared folder (this also applies when you share connected printers). See Chapter 10 for more information about setting up and using a local area network.

Figure 4-10
A network-attached storage appliance

NOTE As a noun, a *network share* is a shared folder or printer.

Ad Hoc Networks

An *ad hoc network* connects devices directly without any "infrastructure" hardware such as a switch, router, or server. Some examples of ad hoc networks include the following:

- **Direct link** Two computers can be physically connected directly to one another via cables. When this is done via the Ethernet ports (RJ-45), you must use a specially wired cable called a *crossover cable*.

- **Ad hoc wireless network** In some cases you can use the wireless LAN adapters in two or more computers to create an impromptu network. Because of the security risks involved in this kind of network, modern versions of Windows have made doing so more difficult, though.

- **Bluetooth** A Bluetooth device such as a keyboard, mouse, headset, or printer might connect directly to a computer, tablet, or smartphone. Chapter 10 explains Bluetooth in more detail.

Online Storage

Online storage is, as you might guess, accessed via the Internet. Online storage is not that different from network storage because the Internet is itself a network. Most users will see it as distinct, though, because the software used to access it creates a different experience. The following sections look at three types of online storage: cloud, FTP, and Web-based.

Cloud Storage

As you learned in Chapter 1, *cloud computing* is the use of (ideally secure) applications or data storage that you access over the Internet. Many commercial businesses with employees all over the globe use cloud computing to provide their employees with standardized applications and file storage no matter where they are.

You can access thousands of cloud-based services and applications for free or as a paid subscription. When you use Microsoft Office Online (www.office.com) to access files stored in OneDrive (Microsoft's online storage service), for example, you are cloud-computing. Other free cloud storage services include iCloud (Apple), Dropbox, and Google Drive.

EXAM TIP Because someone else does the work of hosting these online services, you can think of them as *hosted storage*.

File Transfer Protocol (FTP)

File Transfer Protocol (FTP), which predates the Web, is one of the oldest types of online file sharing still in use today. It is still popular because it's a simple way to move files from one place to another.

FTP is a protocol (a set of standards or rules for accomplishing something) that FTP applications use to transfer files. FileZilla (shown in Figure 4-11) is a popular free FTP application (www.filezilla-project.org). FTP is sometimes used as a verb, as in "I'll FTP those over to you this afternoon." An FTP server supports file upload and download via the protocol.

Like most protocols its age, FTP is not secure. It can require a login, but it sends the credentials (and any files you transfer) in the clear (without encryption) where anyone watching can see them. Developers have created multiple secure (encrypted) versions, including Secure FTP (SFTP) and FTP over SSL (FTPS), which you should use if possible. Despite the similar letters, SFTP and FTPS aren't synonyms.

 EXAM TIP The CompTIA IT Fundamentals objectives expect you to compare FTP, FTPS, and SFTP as sharing and storage methods. While these acronyms are stable, people interpret them differently. CompTIA's list of IT Fundamentals acronyms uses *File Transfer Protocol over SSL* and *Secure File Transfer Protocol*, but you can find tons of variations in different resources, such as *File Transfer Protocol Secure* and *SSH File Transfer Protocol*.

FTPS secures the connection with either TLS or SSL, which you'll read more about in the next section. SFTP piggybacks on the Secure Shell (SSH) protocol.

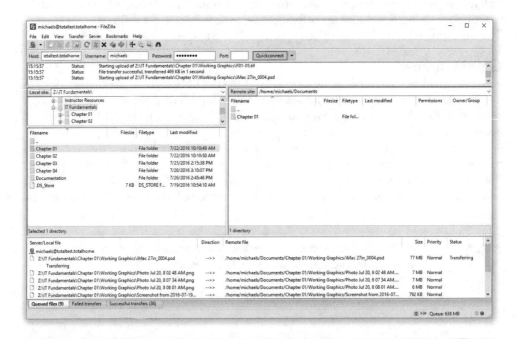

Figure 4-11 FileZilla transferring files via FTP

Figure 4-12   A secure address in Google Chrome (top), Internet Explorer, and Microsoft Edge (bottom)

Web-Based File Downloads and Storage

Many Web sites have files you can download by clicking a hyperlink. Sometimes these are software or documents made by the site owner, but other file-sharing sites allow registered or even anonymous users to upload files. Beware these file-sharing sites. Outside of reputable app stores and developer Web sites, there are few guarantees you aren't downloading a copy that is seeded with *malware*—programs that can damage your computer or steal from you.

For downloading and everything else you do online, it's important to understand that regular (insecure) Web sites use the Hypertext Transfer Protocol (HTTP). Secure Web sites, in contrast, use HTTP over SSL (HTTPS), a variant that establishes an encrypted link between the Web server and the user's browser originally using a security protocol called Secure Sockets Layer (SSL). HTTPS-based Web sites today use the more robust Transport Layer Security (TLS), but developers kept the original name of the protocol. You don't need to know how HTTPS and SSL work, but you should know how they indicate that they are keeping you safe.

- HTTPS (not HTTP) shows as the prefix for the address (shown in Figure 4-12) in the browser's address bar.

- A lock symbol appears in the address bar.

Chapter Review

In this chapter, you learned the basics of how magnetic, optical, and solid-state storage works in a variety of modern devices. The magnetic storage you'll see most are the spacious hard disk drives that have dominated computing for years, though they are being slowly edged out by faster, lighter, and more-efficient solid-state drives as prices fall and capacities rise. Optical media and drives are still common, but they too have been shoved aside by two other solid-state memory formats, memory cards and USB flash drives.

You learned how to classify storage locations as local, network, or online; how systems connect to these types of storage; and the benefits and drawbacks of each location type. Local storage is directly connected from within your system or with an external expansion port such as USB, eSATA, or Thunderbolt, while network storage relies on wired (RJ-45) or wireless network connections to reach drives on other networked computers or in special file servers and NAS systems. Online, we have access to files through cloud storage, FTP servers, and direct downloads from Web sites. Applications and data storage in the cloud play an important role in having access to the same data and software from multiple devices.

Questions

1. Which kind of device stores data in patterns of magnetic polarity?

   A. DVD

   B. CD

   C. USB flash drive

   D. HDD

2. Which unit of measurement describes approximately 1 trillion bytes of storage?

   A. Terabyte

   B. Gigabyte

   C. Megabyte

   D. Kilobyte

3. Which of these is *not* an optical disc?

   A. DVD

   B. SSD

   C. BD-R

   D. CD-RW

4. How can a single DVD hold more than 4.7 GB of data? (Choose all that apply.)

   A. Multiple actuator arms

   B. Multiple sides

   C. Multiple layers

   D. High-density recording

5. Which type of optical disc is rewriteable multiple times?

   A. DVD-ROM

   B. BD

   C. CD-RW

   D. BD-R

6. What kind of drive reads CompactFlash storage?

   A. USB flash drive

   B. Card reader

   C. HDD

   D. SSD

7. Which of these is *not* a benefit of SSD over HDD?

   A. Quieter

   B. Uses less power

   C. Faster

   D. Less expensive

8. Which of these is an external storage connection?

   A. ePATA

   B. eSATA

   C. PATA

   D. SATA

9. Which of these is an ad hoc network?

   A. PATA

   B. NAS

   C. RAID

   D. Direct link with crossover cable

10. Which of these is a secure protocol for transferring files?

   A. SFTP

   B. FTP

   C. HTTP

   D. USB

Answers

1. **D.** A hard disk drive (HDD) uses magnetic polarity to store data. DVD and CD are both optical, and a USB flash drive is solid-state.

2. **A.** A terabyte is approximately 1 trillion bytes. A gigabyte is approximately 1 billion bytes; a megabyte is approximately 1 million bytes; and a kilobyte is approximately 1 thousand bytes.

3. **B.** SSD stands for solid-state drive. All the others listed are optical discs.

4. **B, C.** A DVD can have multiple sides and multiple layers. Optical drives do not have actuator arms. DVDs cannot have higher-density recordings than the standard for DVDs.

5. **C.** Rewriteable discs end in *RW* or *RE*. Discs that are not writeable end in *ROM*. Discs that are writeable only once end in *R*.

6. **B.** A card reader reads from a variety of flash memory cards, including CompactFlash. All other drive types listed contain their own storage and do not accept cards.

7. **D**. SSD has all the advantages listed except it is more expensive than HDD.

8. **B**. eSATA is external serial ATA. SATA and PATA are internal. There is no such thing as ePATA.

9. **D**. One kind of ad hoc network is a direct connection between two PCs using a crossover cable. PATA is a technology for an internal local hard drive connection. NAS is network-attached storage. RAID combines multiple hard disks into a single logical pool of storage.

10. **A**. SFTP is a secure form of File Transfer Protocol (FTP). HTTP is the protocol for Web pages. USB is a type of external port on a PC.

PART II

Setting Up and Using Computers

Setting Up and Configuring a PC

In this chapter, you will learn how to
- Prepare the work area
- Unpack and set up a new desktop computer
- Complete post-setup tasks

Suppose a neighbor or relative calls you, breathless and excited. "I just bought a new computer! Can you come help me set it up?" Of course you can help. After all, you're CompTIA IT Fundamentals certified, right? Or you soon will be. Besides, it'll be fun.

In this chapter, we provide a lot of practical advice on setting up and configuring new computers. You'll learn how to choose a good location for a desktop computer, how to navigate the computer's setup process, and what to do after the initial setup to make sure the computer is connected, secure, and ready for users.

Preparing the Work Area

Preparing the work area for a desktop computer takes into consideration several factors. First, you should look at environmental conditions, such as average temperature and level of dust. Second, you should pick an optimal location. Third, you should evaluate comfort issues. Fourth, you should examine possible interference issues. Finally, you should ensure reliable power. Let's take a look.

Evaluating Room Conditions

Environmental conditions can make a huge impact on the computing experience. You need to analyze the room conditions for temperature, humidity, and airborne particles.

The *ideal* room for a computer is probably cooler than you would find comfortable. Performance and stability will suffer if the system gets too hot, but as long as the temperature is between 50 and 75 degrees Fahrenheit or so, it should be fine.

 CAUTION You want cool but not cold. Condensation can form when cold air heats up around the hot chips and cause short-circuiting.

Humidity is the amount of water vapor in the air. The ideal humidity level is about 50 percent. High humidity reduces electrostatic discharge (static electricity), an enemy of computer chips. However, extremely high humidity, like 75 percent or more, creates dampness, also an enemy of computer chips.

The computer's room should be as clean as possible and free of dust or other airborne particles that could potentially get inside the PC and interfere with its cooling. By airborne particles in a small office/home office (SOHO) environment, we mean pet hair and dander. If you plan to operate the computer in a dusty or hairy environment, you'll need to regularly clean out the inside of the PC. See "Cleaning a Computer" in Chapter 13.

 EXAM TIP Make sure you can identify the impact of environmental factors such as airflow, humidity, temperature, and dust/dander when selecting a location for a computer.

Choosing Where to Set Up the PC

Once you choose a room, where will you put the computer? Is there a desk or table you have your eye on? Make sure there is a grounded (three-prong) power outlet nearby. Don't use an extension cord unless it's absolutely necessary, and if you do, make sure it's a grounded one (or better yet, a surge protector power strip, discussed later in this chapter).

 NOTE A grounded plug has two prongs for electric current, and a third ground prong to avoid fire and electric shock. Prong layouts and voltage (see "Ensuring Reliable AC Power") are common international power differences, so make sure you get the right plug!

When positioning a desktop PC case, make sure there is adequate airflow all around it, especially vents and fans. Don't back up a desktop PC tightly to a wall, because the fan on the back won't have enough space around it. Some computer desks have lower cabinets with doors to hide the case, but we don't recommend these because of poor airflow.

While we're on the subject of case placement, make sure that the PC case is not in a location where it is likely to get kicked, bumped, or knocked off a table. Strike a balance between open-air and out of harm's way.

Making a Work Area More Comfortable

Have you ever noticed that when you sit at some desks, you are comfortable all day, but at others your back and arms start to hurt after an hour or so? The difference between a work area that stresses your body and one that doesn't is *ergonomics,* the study of how humans and equipment interact.

 NOTE A product marketed as *ergonomic* is (the marketer claims, at least) designed to place less stress on the body during use than a product not marked as such.

Figure 5-1
An ergonomically
designed
keyboard

Good ergonomic design and positioning of equipment can enable people to use the equipment extensively with no adverse effects on the body. Bad ergonomics can cause eyestrain, neck and shoulder problems, backaches, and tendon problems such as carpal tunnel syndrome.

Here are some tips for good ergonomics at a computer workstation:

- If possible, use an ergonomic keyboard and mouse. For example, some keyboards curve the keys, with half slanting to the left and half to the right, as shown in Figure 5-1. This helps users keep their wrists straight as they type. An ergonomic keyboard may also have a built-in wrist rest.

- The keyboard should either be flat or be tilted toward the user at up to a 25-degree angle, depending on user preference.

- The display should be 16 to 24 inches from the user's eyes. When looking straight ahead, the user's gaze should fall at the top of or just above the display (Figure 5-2).

- The distance between the floor and the keyboard should be between 23 and 28 inches, or whatever height is necessary for the user's forearms to be perpendicular to the floor while typing.

Figure 5-2
Ergonomically
correct monitor
placement

- If using a traditional chair (with a rigid seat parallel to the floor), the distance between the floor and seat should be 16 to 19 inches, or whatever height is necessary so that the user's thighs are parallel and calves are perpendicular to the floor when sitting upright with feet flat on the floor.

 EXAM TIP The IT Fundamentals objectives expect you to understand ergonomic concepts such as proper keyboard and mouse placement, sitting positions, and proper monitor level placement.

Avoiding ESD and EMI Problems

Electrostatic discharge (ESD) happens when objects with different electrical charges come close enough for the excess charge to jump quickly to equalize the charge between them. A low-charge object experiences this as a high-voltage electrical shock (Figure 5-3). You've experienced it when touching a door knob in the winter time. Ouch!

 NOTE Voltage is a measurement (in volts) of the strength of the electrical current. Amperage (or amps) is a measurement of the rate at which the current flows.

Sensitive computer components can easily be damaged if ESD sends thousands of volts surging into a device designed for somewhere between 3 and 12 volts. The component (or entire device) might not work right after that, or it might be weakened so that it fails sometime in the future. The tricky thing about ESD is that you can transfer enough voltage to damage the device without feeling a thing. You probably won't know you've ruined an expensive motherboard until your computer fails to start.

Touching the outside of a computer won't cause ESD damage, but touching components inside might. Anytime you open a PC's case, touch the frame to equalize the

Figure 5-3
ESD in action

Figure 5-4
Inside the case,
touching the
power supply to
ground the tech

electrical potential between you and the case (Figure 5-4). Do it periodically as you work inside the computer case to dissipate any difference in potential that might build up.

For even better protection, wear an antistatic wrist strap, as shown in Figure 5-5. This is a band you wear around your wrist with a cable that clips to the PC's frame, so electrostatic charge stays the same between the tech and the computer.

Other choices can also minimize ESD problems, such as wearing natural fibers and rubber-soled shoes. When possible, work on smooth floor (no carpet). Don't walk around in polyester socks on nylon carpet before working inside a computer unless you *want* to ruin hundreds of dollars of equipment.

Electromagnetic interference (EMI) occurs when a cable runs too close to something that generates a strong electromagnetic field. EMI is not permanently damaging, but it can garble the data flowing through the cable, and having to retransmit reduces performance.

Figure 5-5
An antistatic
wrist strap
is helpful if
you regularly
work inside
computers.

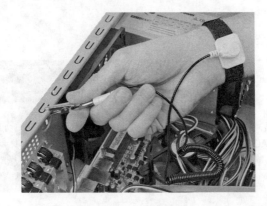

The most common source of EMI is fluorescent lighting; don't run cables near fluorescent light fixtures. If it can't be helped, use EMI-resistant cables.

 EXAM TIP The IT Fundamentals objectives expect you to know ESD and EMI concepts. Make sure you understand the difference between them and how to minimize or avoid each.

Ensuring Reliable AC Power

Electrical devices rely on the wall outlet to carry a consistent, well-defined voltage. In the United States, standard alternating current (AC) power is between 110 and 120 volts, often written as ~115 VAC (volts of alternating current). Most of the world uses 220-240 VAC, so power supplies with *dual-voltage options* work with either standard.

Before you plug a PC into a wall outlet in another country, you should use a power voltage adapter, replace the PC's power supply with a compatible model, or confirm the power supply's voltage selection switch is in the correct position. As shown in Figure 5-6, this switch is next to the power supply's three-prong power port (where you connect the primary power cable from the wall outlet).

Conditions anywhere between the electric company and your home or office can cause power instability that can damage a computer. A *power outage* is just what it sounds like—power from the electric company isn't reaching your location. Many things can cause this *blackout* such as storms knocking down power lines.

A *surge* and a *spike* are basically the same thing: a sudden, dramatic increase in the voltage. Computer components are designed to operate at precise low voltages, and they are easily damaged by higher voltages. A lightning strike at or near your home can send a spike of high-voltage electricity through your AC power outlets and into connected devices.

External devices help compensate for these problems. A typical multi-outlet *surge suppressor* (Figure 5-7) can absorb excess power during a surge or spike to prevent it from reaching the plugged-in devices. Surge suppression capacity is measured in *joules*. The higher the joule rating, the greater the protection provided by the surge suppressor. Many (but not all) grounded power strips are surge suppressors; read the package carefully.

Figure 5-6
Make sure the switch on the power supply, if present, is set to your country's AC voltage.

Figure 5-7
A surge
suppressor

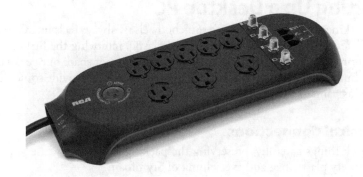

A *power sag* is insufficient voltage. Power sags don't usually damage hardware, but they can cause it to temporarily malfunction, resulting in memory storage errors that can cause the operating system to unexpectedly freeze up or restart. When that happens, you may lose unsaved data in open applications.

A *power conditioner* enhances the features of a surge suppressor by storing extra voltage in a capacitor and then releasing it onto the power line to smooth out power sags.

EXAM TIP Collectively, CompTIA IT Fundamentals calls these outages, surges, spikes and sags *power limitations*. Make sure you know these conditions and which devices can correct them.

An *uninterruptible power supply (UPS)* combines a surge suppressor, a power conditioner, and a battery backup. A UPS (shown in Figure 5-8) can protect against surges and spikes and provide power briefly to deal with sags and power outages. This helps avoid problems (such as storage errors) that occur when a computer can't shut down correctly. A typical UPS connects to the PC (usually via universal serial bus [USB]) so the operating system (OS) can shut itself down automatically when the UPS reports a power outage.

Figure 5-8
An uninterruptible
power supply

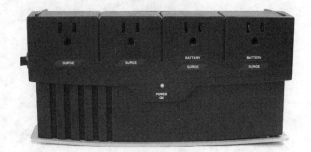

Setting Up a Desktop PC

Unpacking a new PC, even if it's somebody else's, always feels like Christmas morning to us. Carefully unwrapping the protective plastic, removing the little tape tabs and Styrofoam protectors…there's nothing like it. You may not share our geeky enjoyment of this task, but there's nothing to fear. The following sections provide some tips for making the setup as painless as possible.

Physical Connections

Unpack things carefully, preserving the packing materials in case you have to return it. Save every plastic bag and every hunk of Styrofoam.

Plug the cables in snugly, referring to the instructions that came with the PC or using your own knowledge from Chapter 3. The basic connectors are as follows:

- **Keyboard and mouse**   Any USB port. Figure 5-9 shows a USB connector ready to be plugged into one of several USB ports on the back of a desktop PC.

- **Monitor**   Digital Visual Interface (DVI) or High-Definition Multimedia Interface (HDMI) port if available; Video Graphics Array (VGA) is your backup plan. On a Mac, use Thunderbolt or Mini DisplayPort.

- **Internet**   Connect an *Ethernet cable* to an RJ-45 port on the router or broadband modem and another on your system, or plan to set up a wireless connection to a wireless modem or router later.

- **Speakers**   3.5-mm speaker jack. Make sure you use the one for speakers and not the similar-looking input port for a microphone. Most manufacturers use green for the speaker port and pink for the microphone.

Figure 5-9
Connect USB
external devices
to any USB port
on the PC.

EXAM TIP Make sure you know which ports to connect which components to on a desktop PC. Practice this by unplugging all the cords on the back of a desktop PC (turned off) and then reconnecting them.

Cable Management

With all the connections you've just made, you may have a tangle of cables on the back of the PC, running every which way. There's nothing wrong with that, as long as the cables don't become a trip-and-fall hazard or a dust-bunny hideout.

If ugly haphazard cables aren't acceptable (for example, a computer out in the open on a receptionist's desk) or you're worried about stray cables as hazards, the solution is cable management. That sounds fancy, but it really just means adding channels for cables to run through in an orderly way or binding groups of cables with cable ties.

Cable management is a much bigger deal in businesses where many computers share a fairly small space and cable proliferation can get out of hand. Figure 5-10 shows a particularly messy bunch of cables in need of some organizing. Figure 5-11 shows a well-ordered mass of cables on a network panel sorted out with cable ties.

Figure 5-10
Disorganized
cables

PART II

Figure 5-11
Well-organized
cables

Operating System Setup

The first time you press the power button to start a new computer, a setup program runs for the already-installed operating system. The specifics will vary by OS and version, but it generally configures the following:

- **Localization** What time zone are you in, and does the time change for daylight saving time in your area? What country are you in? (Country affects the default currency symbol and some other details.)

- **Screen resolution** This is selected for you automatically and silently; the setup program detects your display adapter and monitor, determines the maximum resolution, and sets the OS to that resolution.

- **Audio settings** Like screen resolution, your audio hardware settings are also autodetected and set up in the OS.

- **Internet connectivity** The setup program looks for an Internet connection and asks whether you want to use the connection it finds. If it doesn't find one, the setup program may prompt you to configure an Internet connection or to skip that step for now.

- **User account** Most operating systems support multiple user accounts on a computer. The setup program will insist that you create at least one user account to start. This default user account will have full administrative permissions. You can create more accounts later.

This step isn't brain surgery; just follow the prompts and skip anything optional that you don't understand.

Completing Post-Setup Tasks

You need to take several other steps to prepare a PC for use, such as installing security software, making sure the network connections are working, configuring peripherals, and installing additional software. You might also want to set up other user accounts. The following sections explain each of these tasks.

 EXAM TIP You should be able to list the post-installation tasks involved in setting up a new PC, covered in the following sections.

Verify and Configure the Internet Connection

If the OS found an Internet connection during its initial setup, great. If that connection is wireless, make sure it's secure. Connecting to a wireless access point that doesn't require authentication can put your computer at risk for snooping by anyone who happens to be nearby on that network.

If you own the wireless access point, enable its security. If you are using someone else's unsecured Wi-Fi, at a minimum you should turn off File and Printer Sharing in your operating system so others cannot browse your files. See Chapter 10 for more on both of these.

Install Security Software

Before you start using the PC, make certain it has adequate security software installed. Windows comes with a program called Windows Defender, which provides basic anti-virus and anti-malware protection, and it's enabled by default. However, depending on your situation, you may want to install a more full-featured security program, such as one that your employer or school provides. Chapter 12 explains security software and how it works in more detail.

Run Software and Security Updates

Between the time the OS was installed on your new computer and now, some updates have probably been released. It's important to have the latest OS updates because many of the updates fix security holes. So before you go any further, you should make sure your OS is up to date. By default, Windows is set to download and install updates automatically.

PART II

In Windows, use the Windows Update feature to download and install updates. Here's how to run it in the last several Windows versions:

- **Windows 7/8/8.1**   Open the Control Panel, click System and Security, and under the Windows Update heading, click Check for updates.
- **Windows 10**   Click Start | Settings, click Update & security, and under Windows Update, click Check for updates, as shown in Figure 5-12.

On a Mac, you get OS updates via the App Store. Open the App Store and then click Updates. If any OS updates are available, they will appear in the list of available updates. Apple will push some important OS updates to you more aggressively so that a message pops up on the screen inviting you to install the update.

Configure Peripherals

You might have additional hardware that you want to set up on the new PC. Many folks add an additional input device (such as a touchpad) or output device (such as a printer). In many cases you can plug a new device into a USB port and the OS will automatically recognize and install a driver for the device.

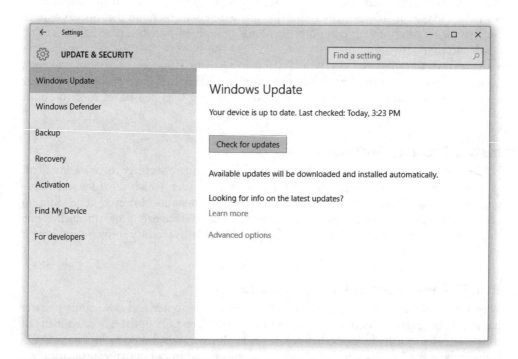

Figure 5-12   Checking for Windows updates

If a peripheral comes with its own setup disc, that disc may contain helpful applications. A scanner might include an optical character recognition (OCR) application that converts images of scanned text to text you can edit in a word processing program. Pop the disc in the PC's optical drive and let it run its setup program. If you don't have a disc, download the latest version of the device's setup program from the device manufacturer's Web site.

CAUTION   The included software is occasionally essential, especially for less common devices or ones with special features that only work with the manufacturer's software. Read the instructions before you connect the device to the PC for the first time; you may need to run the setup program first and connect the device only when the setup program prompts you.

After you've installed a peripheral, you can configure it in the OS settings. For a standard input device like a keyboard or mouse, you can use the Options dialog box from the Control Panel for that particular device type (for example, Mouse Properties in Figure 5-13). For devices with proprietary software, run the software to configure the device. If the device has a memory-resident component, there may be an icon for the device in the notification area in Windows. If you see one, right-click the icon and choose Properties or Options (or similar) to configure the device's settings.

Figure 5-13
Configuring a
device via its
Properties box

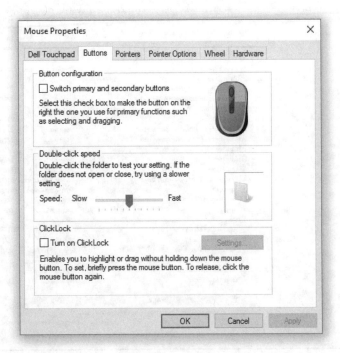

Uninstall Unneeded Software

Many new computers come with what technicians not so affectionately refer to as *bloatware*—applications most people don't need (or want) preinstalled because their developers paid the PC manufacturer. This can include trial versions of useful software, marginally useful software, and stuff that is downright annoying. Part of the post-setup cleanup is removing some of this bloatware.

To remove an application in Windows, open the Control Panel and run the Programs and Features applet. Select the application you want to remove and then click the Uninstall button (or Uninstall/Change in some cases), as shown in Figure 5-14. Then just follow the prompts to uninstall it.

 EXAM TIP It's mostly for advanced users, but Programs and Features can also add and remove optional *OS features*. Just click Turn Windows features on or off and check or uncheck the specific features. Don't mess with these unless you understand a feature's risks and benefits or are following instructions from a tech who does.

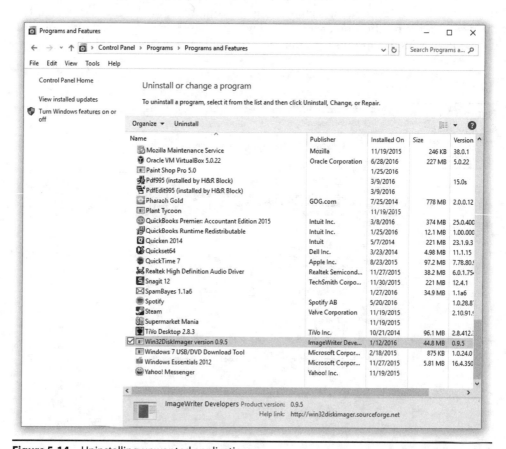

Figure 5-14 Uninstalling unwanted applications

To remove an application in macOS, open Finder and choose Applications in the navigation pane on the left. Then right-click an application to remove and choose Move to Trash. You might need to type your password to confirm.

Install Additional Software

Now it's time to install software you actually want on the new computer, such as applications you bought for a previous computer. To install an application from disc, insert the disc and follow the prompts that appear. If nothing happens, open Windows Explorer, File Explorer, or Finder (or equivalent file management program) and double-click the icon for the optical drive. If a file listing appears, double-click the Setup file in that listing.

 NOTE The Setup file may appear as Setup.exe. The .exe part is the file's extension. Extensions identify file types; .exe is short for "executable" (in other words, a program). You'll learn more about file types and extensions in Chapter 7.

In some cases, the file that starts the setup program isn't named Setup. It might be Install, RunMe, or some other intuitive name.

Increasingly, you can just download software. You download a setup file and then run that file to install the application. If you still have a setup file on an older computer, you can transfer it to the new computer via USB flash drive, a writeable optical disc, or a network connection. It's best to use this as a fallback, though, since the programs will likely be out of date and may be vulnerable to widely available exploits until you update them.

Create More User Accounts

The user account that you set up when you do the initial computer setup has Administrator privileges. That means the account can install and remove software, change system settings, and do anything else that needs to be done. "Great!" you may be thinking. "I never have to worry about not having high enough permission levels to do whatever I want to the computer."

Using an Administrator account all the time increases the security risk. If malware infects your computer and tries to make changes to system files, for example, it can do serious damage with the power of an Administrator account. For this reason, Microsoft recommends you create a Standard account for daily use. A Standard account can change settings that affect only that one account. Microsoft recommends that you sign into your Administrator account only when you need to make system changes, such as installing new software or updating device drivers. You can also create Child accounts (Mac calls these Managed with Parental Controls), which are like Standard accounts except you can restrict what Web sites they can visit, what times of day they can use the PC, and so on.

In Windows 8.1 and 10, user accounts are tied to an e-mail address registered with Microsoft. These accounts are also known as *Microsoft accounts* because Microsoft manages the account permissions and passwords online. A Microsoft account has advantages such as access to your OneDrive and Windows settings from any PC you sign into.

An alternative is a Local account, which is not registered with Microsoft and exists only on the local PC. Microsoft tries to discourage this type of account by making it more difficult to set up.

To create a new account in Windows 10, click Start | Settings | Accounts. Click Family & other users. To add a family member (such as a Child account), click Add a family member. To add other users, click Add someone else to this PC. Then just follow the prompts, which differ for Microsoft accounts and Local accounts. The prompts are also affected by whether an e-mail address has already been registered with Microsoft on some other computer.

Chapter Review

In this chapter, you learned about the process of setting up a new computer. Before you begin, it's important to pick out a work space that is good for the computer (good airflow, cool temperature, low dust, appropriate humidity, reliable power, and so on) and has good ergonomics for the user. During setup, maintenance, and operation, make sure you take steps to protect the system from ESD and EMI.

The setup process itself begins with carefully unpacking the components in case you need to return the system, physically cabling and connecting the components, and using any desired cable management devices to keep all of the cords and cables in order. Once all of these are connected, you're ready to insert the operating system's installation media and follow the onscreen prompts.

There are a few things left to go over once the OS is up and running. First, you need to verify that the system has a functioning, secure Internet connection. Once you have a secure Internet connection, you can install current security software as needed and update your OS and applications to fix known security issues.

Now that the system is protected, you can install additional peripherals, remove any preinstalled software you don't need, install the applications you plan to use, and create user accounts for anyone else who'll be using the system. The next time someone asks you for help with their new PC purchase, you will be prepared to walk them through the process with confidence.

Questions

1. In which environment would a desktop computer be safest and operate the best?
   A. Inside a small, tightly sealed cabinet
   B. In a clean room with a powerful air conditioner running
   C. On the balcony at a tropical beachfront condo
   D. On a TV tray in a living room

2. How far should a user's face be from a monitor screen for most comfortable viewing?
   A. 10 to 12 inches
   B. 12 to 16 inches
   C. 16 to 24 inches
   D. 24 to 32 inches

3. Which of these is the flow of static electricity?

   A. EMI

   B. ESD

   C. AC

   D. DC

4. What device can help correct power sags?

   A. Power supply

   B. Power strip

   C. Surge suppressor

   D. UPS

5. What kind of cable is most often used to connect a PC to a broadband modem or router?

   A. VGA

   B. DVI

   C. Ethernet

   D. RJ-11

6. What should you install before you download and install additional software on a new PC?

   A. Security software

   B. Nothing

   C. Updates to other applications

   D. Drivers for hardware devices

7. What component protects against occasional electrical spikes?

   A. Surge suppressor

   B. Motherboard

   C. Hard disk drive

   D. Printer

8. Where in Windows can you access the configuration settings for hardware devices like mice and printers?

   A. File Explorer

   B. EMI

   C. Start menu

   D. Control Panel

9. Where in the Control Panel can you remove unwanted applications?

   A. Programs

   B. Ergonomics

   C. Setup

   D. Start menu

10. Which of these is a type of Windows user account?

   A. Kid

   B. Standard

   C. Supervisor

   D. Normal

Answers

1. **B**. A computer would operate very well in a clean room (no dust) with a powerful air conditioner (cold). A tightly sealed cabinet would not allow enough airflow. A balcony in a tropical location would be too warm and humid. A TV tray would be unstable and easy to knock over.

2. **C**. The optimal distance is 16 to 24 inches.

3. **B**. ESD is short for electrostatic discharge, the flow of static electricity. EMI is electromagnetic interference, a magnetic field that can cause problems to nearby data. AC is alternating current, the power from a wall outlet. DC is direct current, the power used by computer components.

4. **D**. A UPS combines a power conditioner, battery backup, and surge suppressor. None of the other options listed does anything for sags, although surge suppressors can help with power surges and spikes.

5. **C**. An Ethernet cable is used to connect to a broadband modem or router. VGA and DVI are used for monitors. RJ-11 is used for dial-up modems.

6. **A**. You should make sure security software is installed before downloading anything else.

7. **A**. A surge suppressor can protect against power surges and spikes.

8. **D**. Use the Control Panel to configure hardware devices. File Explorer is the file management interface. EMI is electromagnetic interference, which is not a Windows feature. The Start menu does not contain settings for hardware devices.

9. **A**. Uninstall applications from the Programs section of the Control Panel. None of the other options listed is a section in the Control Panel.

10. **B**. Standard is one of the Windows user account types. The others listed are not.

Understanding Operating Systems

In this chapter, you will learn how to

- Explain the functions of an operating system
- Discuss operating system characteristics
- Describe operating system interfaces
- Compare operating system features

Operating systems enable users of computing devices to interact with those devices in many ways. The various operating systems have features in common and stark differences. This chapter looks at the primary desktop operating systems you'll run into in the wild. While the CompTIA IT Fundamentals exam focuses a lot on Microsoft Windows, you'll get questions on three other desktop operating systems: Apple macOS, Linux, and Google Chrome OS. We'll start with an analysis of functions common to all operating systems and discuss characteristics of operating systems. Next, we'll survey the interfaces of the four most common desktop operating systems. The chapter finishes with a side-by-side comparison of features.

NOTE Chapter 9 dives into the three major operating systems for mobile devices—iOS, Android, and Windows Mobile.

The Functions of an Operating System

As you'll recall from earlier chapters, the *operating system (OS)* is a layer of software that enables the hardware and application software to work together. The OS also enables you to tell the computer what to do and enables the computer to show you the results. A typical OS performs five functions, summarized in Figure 6-1.

- *An OS provides an interface between user and machine.* This interface can be a graphical user interface (GUI) or a command line. A GUI enables you to click onscreen elements to interact with the OS. You type commands at the command-line interface (CLI) to tell the OS to do things.

Displays structure/directories
for data management

Coordinates hardware
components

Provides environment
for software to function

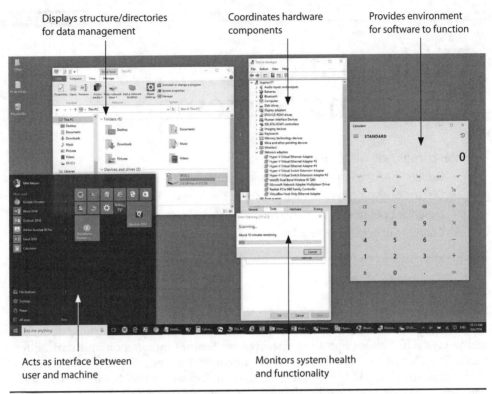

Acts as interface between
user and machine

Monitors system health
and functionality

Figure 6-1 The five functions of an OS, illustrated in Windows 10

- *An OS enables coordination of hardware components.* Each hardware device speaks a different language, but the operating system can talk to and manage them all through translation files called *device drivers.*

- *An OS provides an environment for software to function.* In GUI operating systems such as Windows and macOS, applications run within a consistent, graphical desktop environment.

- *An OS monitors system health and functionality.* Each OS comes with utility programs that help keep the system in good condition by checking storage drives for errors or monitoring system activity for malware.

- *An OS displays structure/directories for data management.* You can view file and folder listings and issue commands to act on those files and folders (move, copy, rename, delete, and so on).

Operating System Characteristics

Operating systems differ in three primary characteristics: licensing, software compatibility, and complexity. These different categories define strengths and limitations both among OS versions and among editions within those versions.

Licensing

Operating system developers want you to use their OS. They really do! They make their OS available to acquire in three basic ways: open source, free, or commercial.

As you learned in Chapter 1, Linux is an *open source* operating system, meaning that anyone can download and modify it. Open source operating systems can benefit from improvements contributed by thousands of programmers. Some people choose open source operating systems out of an anti-establishment spirit; others choose them as a practical matter because they are free.

 NOTE *Public domain* software is a step beyond open source. Not only is it free to use and modify, but the owner has renounced ownership of it.

A *free OS* doesn't have to be open source. Some of them may be free to download and use but unavailable to modify. The OS remains owned by an individual or company that limits who can modify and distribute it. Google owns and manages Chrome OS, for example, and makes it free to use. Not just anyone can modify it.

Commercial operating systems are privately owned by companies that charge money for them. Examples include Microsoft Windows and Apple macOS. You need to pay for the right (or *license*) to use computers that run commercial operating systems.

Software Compatibility

Programmers write applications to work with a specific OS. In other words, applications work only on the OS for which they were written. One reason to choose a certain OS over another is software compatibility. Microsoft Office doesn't run on a Linux system, for example, and Linux software won't run in Windows. If you are choosing a computer to do a specific task, make sure any programs you *need* are available for your OS. Figure 6-2 shows a Mac failing to run an application not written for it.

Software compatibility can also be an issue with different versions of the same OS. For example, an application written for Windows 10 might not work under Windows 7. Check each application's advertised system requirements when assessing whether a particular application will work with your computer.

Figure 6-2
An OS will report an error if you try to run software not designed for it.

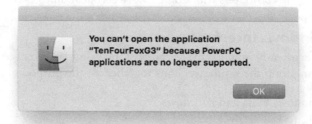

NOTE Many application developers make versions of their programs for multiple operating systems. Microsoft develops similar (but not identical) versions of Microsoft Office, for example, for both macOS and Windows. A retail DVD containing an application might contain application versions for multiple operating systems, but only the one for your OS will install or function.

Complexity

In Chapter 2 you learned that modern central processing unit (CPU) manufacturers produce both 32-bit and 64-bit versions of their processors. The bit support of a CPU refers in large part to the complexity of programming it can handle, including the programming or code that makes up the OS.

Operating systems also come in 32-bit and 64-bit editions. The 64-bit edition of an operating system has advantages over the 32-bit edition, such as the ability to use more random access memory (RAM). (The 32-bit editions of Windows are limited to 4 GB of RAM, for example.) A computer with a 64-bit CPU can run either a 32-bit or a 64-bit OS, but a computer with a 32-bit CPU can run only a 32-bit OS.

NOTE As we'll discuss in Chapter 7, applications also come in 32-bit and 64-bit versions. Most 32-bit applications will work on 64-bit operating systems, but not *vice versa*. Certain applications that work very closely with the operating system, however, such as anti-malware programs, must match the OS.

Comparing OS Interfaces

Each of the operating systems examined in this chapter has a graphical interface based on a desktop metaphor, where a colored background is the surface on which you open windows and click icons. The following sections show you the interfaces of the four operating systems you'll find in the wild: Windows, macOS, Linux, and Chrome OS.

EXAM TIP Every desktop OS has a command-line interface as well as a graphical user interface. The CompTIA IT Fundamentals exam pretty much ignores the CLI—with a few exceptions noted in this book—focusing instead on the GUI. Save serious study of the CLI if you decide to go further in computers with CompTIA A+ certification.

The Windows Interface

Microsoft currently supports five versions of the Windows interface for desktop computers, but we can group the similar versions together for the purposes of discussion:

- Windows Vista and Windows 7
- Windows 8 and Windows 8.1
- Windows 10

The CompTIA IT Fundamentals exam doesn't distinguish among the versions of Windows or even among the different editions within each version. Instead, you'll see questions that you can answer the same way regardless of version or edition. This section goes into a little more detail because you should be familiar with the most popular desktop OS on the planet.

Windows Vista/7

Figure 6-3 shows the standard interface for Windows 7, a traditional multifunction computer. Windows uses a graphical user interface primarily, so you engage with the mouse or other pointing device and click elements. The background is called the *Desktop*. The open applications are Internet Explorer, Window's default Web browser, and a Windows Explorer window showing the Windows 7 default Libraries.

Other visible items are as follows:

- The open applications demonstrate *transparency*, where the edges of the applications show blurred background images. This feature is called *Aero* or *Aero Glass*.

- Click the *Start button* to get access to applications, tools, files, and folders.

- The *pinned programs* enable you to launch a program with a single left-click.

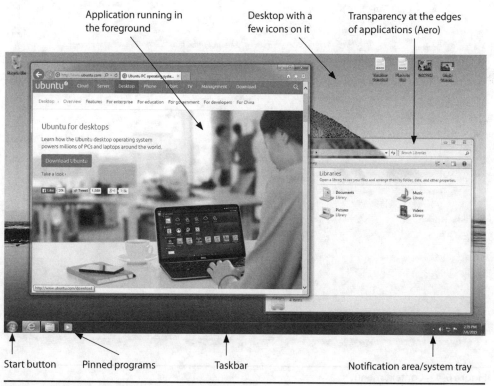

Figure 6-3 Windows 7 with applications open

- The *taskbar* shows running programs.
- The *notification area* shows programs running in the background. Many techs also call it the *system tray*.

Interacting with the classic Windows interface primarily involves using a mouse or touchpad to move the cursor and either left-clicking or right-clicking the icons. Left-clicking selects an item; double-left-clicking opens an item. Right-clicking opens a *context menu* from which you can select various options (see Figure 6-4).

NOTE The context menu offers options specific to the icon you right-click. Right-clicking a file, for example, gives you a context menu that differs greatly from when you right-click an application.

Figure 6-4   Context menu

Gadgets
in the
Sidebar

Windows
Vista
Sidebar

Figure 6-5   Windows Vista

Windows 7's predecessor, Windows Vista, has a similar look and feel. The most visible difference is the Vista feature called the Sidebar. Enabled by default, the *Sidebar* houses one or more *Gadgets,* such as the Clock, Calendar, and speed gauges you can see in Figure 6-5. Windows 7 supports Gadgets but doesn't have a Sidebar.

Windows 8/8.1

Microsoft took a bold chance with Windows 8 (and later 8.1) by making some radical changes. The familiar Desktop is still there, but there is no Start menu. Instead, clicking the Start button opens a Start screen. The *Start screen* covers the entire screen and contains rectangular *tiles* that are shortcuts to *apps,* which are the programs you can run. Note that the screen shows *pinned apps*—the default programs and programs selected by the user—and not all the applications installed on the computer.

The Windows 8 interface, code-named *Metro UI,* works great for touch-enabled devices. The PC becomes in essence a giant tablet. Touch an app to load, drag your finger across the screen to see other apps, and have fun. Figure 6-6 shows the default Windows 8 Start screen.

NOTE   Microsoft dropped the "Metro UI" moniker just before releasing Windows 8 because of legal concerns, replacing it with "Modern UI." A lot of techs and IT industry pros continue to refer to the unique Windows 8/8.1 tiled interface as "Metro."

Windows 8 also features a more classic Desktop, but it's one with the noticeable absence of a visible Start button (see Figure 6-7). You access this screen by pressing the WINDOWS LOGO KEY on a standard keyboard.

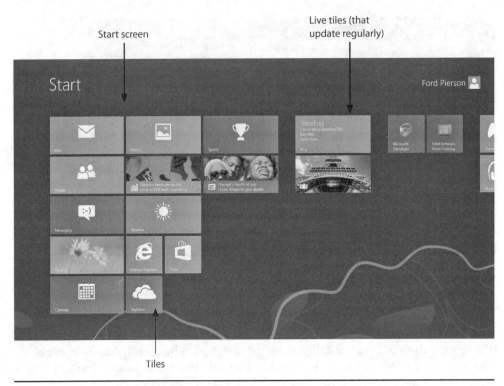

Figure 6-6 The Windows 8 Start screen

Figure 6-7 Windows 8 Desktop

Figure 6-8   Windows 8 Start screen scrolled to the right

Using a keyboard and mouse with Windows 8 bothers a lot of users making the jump from Windows 7. Scrolling with the mouse wheel, for example, scrolls right to left rather than up and down (see Figure 6-8).

With a series of updates culminating in Windows 8.1, Microsoft brought back features such as the Start button, easy access to a Close button for apps, and the ability to boot directly to the Desktop. Figure 6-9 shows the standard interface for Windows 8.1. Note that it's similar to Windows 7.

Windows 8.1 makes it easy to pin apps to the Start screen. Selecting the arrow at the bottom left brings up the Apps pane where you can sort and select apps and utilities (see Figure 6-10). Right-click an icon to pin it to the Start screen.

Windows 8/8.1 offer lots of hidden interface components that activate when you place the cursor in certain places on the screen. Dropping the cursor to the bottom-left corner, for example, activates the Start button (see Figure 6-11) when in the Start screen.

Placing the cursor in the upper- or lower-right corner of the screen reveals the *Charms bar,* a location for tools called *charms*. See the right side of Figure 6-12. Charms include a robust Search tool that enables a search of the computer or even the Internet in one location. There's a Share charm for sharing photos, e-mail messages, and more.

The final version of Windows 8.1 uses the Desktop rather than the Start screen as the default interface. The Start button is visible in the bottom left (see Figure 6-13). You can still access the charms using the cursor and the upper- and lower-right corners of the screen.

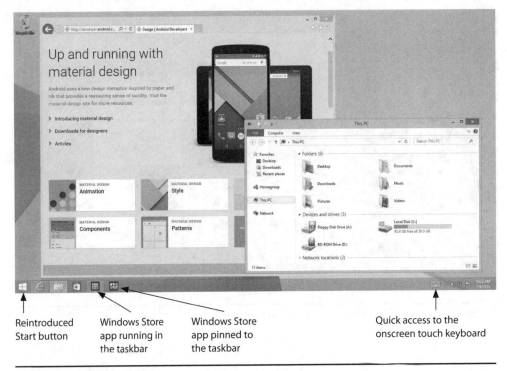

Reintroduced
Start button

Windows Store
app running in
the taskbar

Windows Store
app pinned to
the taskbar

Quick access to the
onscreen touch keyboard

Figure 6-9 Windows 8.1

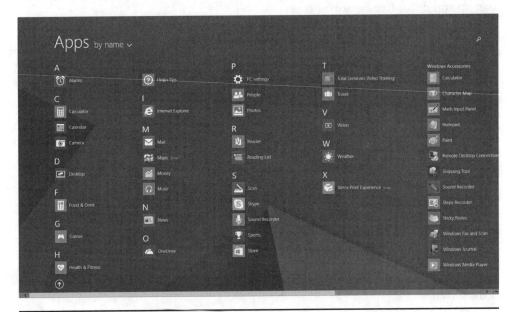

Figure 6-10 Apps sorted by name

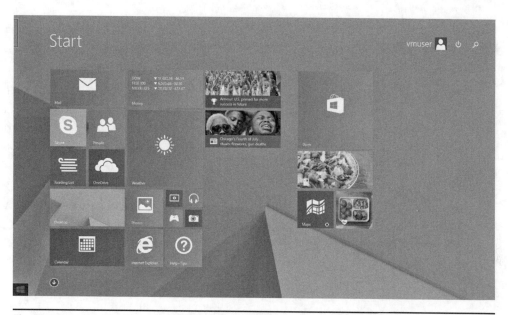

Figure 6-11 Start button magically appears

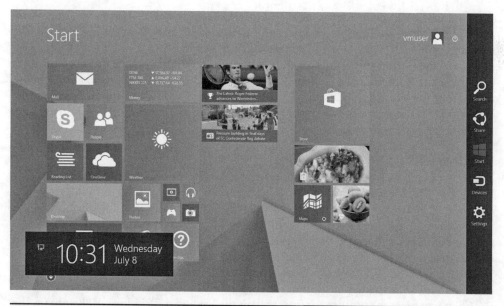

Figure 6-12 Charms accessed by cursor in upper- or lower-right corner

Figure 6-13 Windows 8.1 Desktop

Windows 8.1 also supports a new type of application, called *Modern apps* or *Metro apps*. This type of application resembles the type used on mobile operating systems like iOS and Android. They run full-screen and are optimized for touchscreen use. You download them from the Windows Store, rather than installing them from optical discs or downloads from individual Web sites. They install automatically when you choose them from the Store app. Chapter 7 explains how to acquire and install applications. Windows 8.1 also includes a Settings app, which is an alternative to the Control Panel for changing system settings.

Windows 10

Windows 8 and 8.1 were widely criticized for being too different from the familiar Windows environment of Windows 7 and earlier. Consequently, Windows 10 is a compromise between the look and feel of both Windows 7 and Windows 8.1.

Windows 10 has some features of Windows 8/8.1, such as the ability to download and run Modern apps and the Settings app for changing system settings. It has a Start menu (rather than a Start screen), like Windows 7 does, but the Start menu includes customizable tiles like the Windows 8.1 Start screen has. Figure 6-14 shows the Windows 10 interface with an active application in the foreground.

When you press the WINDOWS LOGO KEY on the keyboard, Windows 10 brings up the Start menu with useful tools and your most used apps on the left and pinned apps on the right (see Figure 6-15). Just like with Windows 8.1, you can click the link helpfully

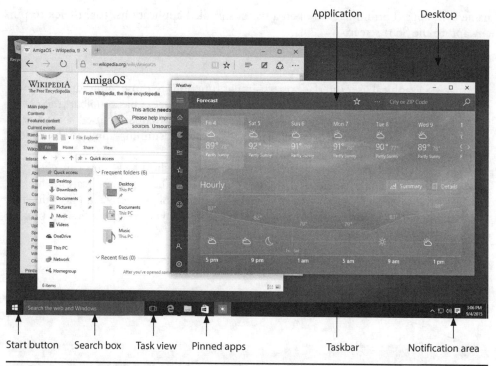

Figure 6-14 Windows 10 with a few applications open

Figure 6-15 Start menu in Windows 10

named All apps (bottom left) to open a list of installed applications. Right-click to pin any app to the Start screen.

The macOS Interface

The macOS graphical user interface offers similar functions to those found on Windows. The background of the main screen is called the *Desktop*. macOS has a toolbar (the *Dock*) at the bottom of the screen where you can pin and access frequently used shortcuts as with the taskbar, Start screen, or Start menu in Windows. Running applications appear in the Dock with a small black dot under them.

If the application you want to run doesn't appear on the Dock, you can click the Launchpad to see a complete list of available applications. The active application's menus appear in the upper-left corner of the screen. Regardless of the active application, the Apple menu (open in Figure 6-16) is always available for you to access System preferences, shut down, log out, and so on.

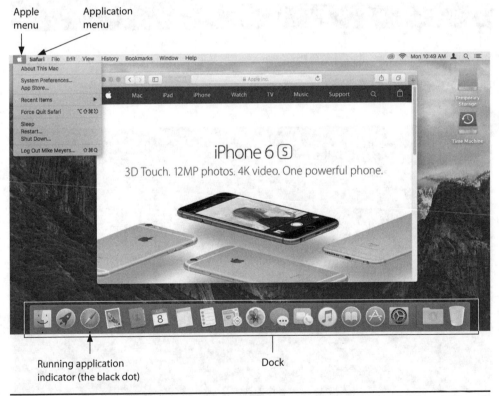

Figure 6-16 macOS Desktop with Apple's Safari Web browser running and the Apple menu open

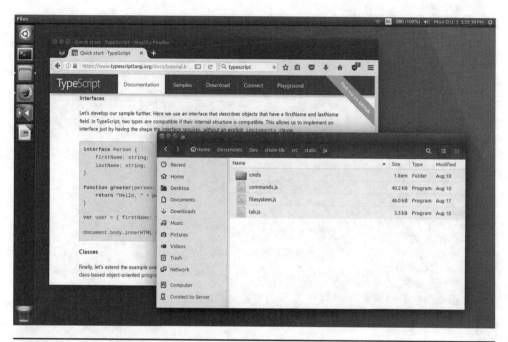

Figure 6-17   The Unity interface, provided with Ubuntu Linux

The Linux Interface

At its heart, Linux is a command-line operating system. However, many distributions (*distros*) come with a *desktop environment (DE)* that provides a GUI for Linux users. One of the most popular distros for casual users, Ubuntu, comes with a DE called Unity (shown in Figure 6-17). Several other popular distros also come with this same GUI interface.

The *Launcher* is the bar along the left side of the screen. It is similar both to the Dock in macOS and to the taskbar in Windows. When an item is open, as the Files utility is in Figure 6-17, the background to its icon on the Launcher appears dark red, rather than the usual gray.

The topmost Launcher button is the *Dash button,* which is roughly equivalent to Windows' Start button. It opens a Dash panel that includes a Search box and shortcuts. Filter icons called *lenses* appear across the bottom of the pane and let you browse by type of item. For example, in Figure 6-18 we're browsing applications. Notice that the Installed section has icons for installed applications; the More suggestions section suggests applications you may want to download.

The Chrome OS Interface

On the surface, computers running Google Chrome OS appear to function similarly to computers running other desktop operating systems. Chrome OS features a desktop background. Along the bottom of the screen you'll find the *shelf* with access to frequently used applications, such as the Chrome Web browser and Gmail for e-mail. Figure 6-19 shows the default interface for Chrome OS with a browser window open and features labeled.

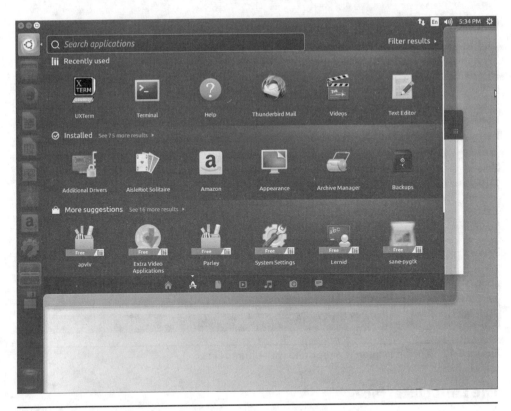

Figure 6-18 The Dash pane

The *Launcher* that you can see in the lower left of the desktop enables you to access all the programs available to the computer. Figure 6-20 shows apps in Launcher. Almost all of the apps are Web-based apps tied to your Google account. In fact, the only way to add an app is through the Google Web store.

The *status tray* (lower right) shows the status of essential computer elements, such as remaining battery life, wireless network connections (including Bluetooth), and current audio volume; it also gives you access to Settings where you can adjust various system features. Figure 6-21 shows the status tray expanded.

Although Chrome OS resembles the other desktop operating systems, it differs substantially under the hood. Google designed Chrome OS with the assumption that users would always be connected to the Internet. This means that Chrome OS relies heavily on Internet-based applications and features. Chrome OS computers usually have tiny local storage, for example, relying instead on the online *Google Drive* associated with the user's account for storing files and folders. You can access Google Drive directly or use the Files app (Figure 6-22).

Desktop background   Chrome Web browser

Launcher   Shelf   Status tray

Figure 6-19   Chrome OS

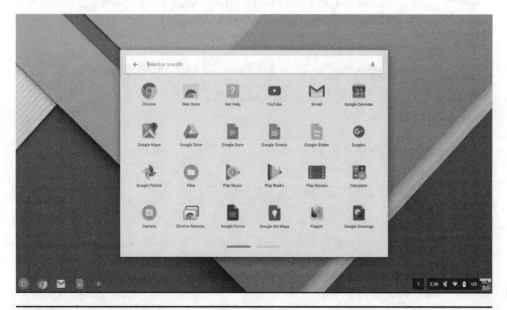

Figure 6-20   Launcher apps

Figure 6-21
Status tray
expanded

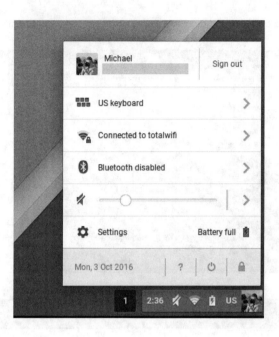

NOTE Chrome OS gets a bad rep in some circles because of its always-connected nature. The assumption often made is that you can't do any work on a Chrome OS computer when you're not connected to the Internet. That's not true. You can do a lot of things offline; when you go online, Chrome OS will sync your files and folders in Google Drive.

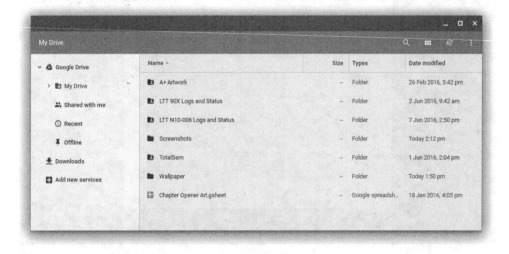

Figure 6-22 Access to the Google Drive contents with the Files app

Feature	Windows	macOS	Linux	Chrome OS
Manage Files	File Explorer	Finder	Files	Files or Google Drive
Browse Programs to Run	Start menu/screen	Launchpad	Dash	Launcher
Change System Settings	Control Panel or Settings	System Preferences	System Settings	Settings

Table 6-1   Feature Equivalents in Windows, macOS, Linux, and Chrome OS

Cross-Referencing Features

Windows, macOS, Linux, and Chrome OS have many of the same tools and features, but they go by different names. Table 6-1 provides a key to finding what you want in one OS if you know what it's called in another.

The next section looks at some of the common features in these operating systems in more detail. It focuses more heavily on Windows because Windows is by far the most popular, but other operating systems are also mentioned where they differ significantly.

Common Features of Operating Systems

Operating systems, both under the hood and in their user interfaces, have many of the same capabilities. That's expected, because users have the same basic needs (such as running programs, managing files, and connecting to the Internet) no matter which OS they use. Every OS also gives users the capability to navigate with hotkeys, create screen captures, and configure accessibility options.

 EXAM TIP   Most of the topics in Objective 5.2 pertain to file management, which is covered in Chapter 8.

Executing Programs

All operating systems execute programs (that is, run applications, or apps). That's the point of a computer: to run programs that do something useful. We cover applications in more detail in Chapter 7.

In a GUI environment, you run a program in one of these ways:

- Double-click an icon or button for the program (or single-click in some cases).
- Open a menu and select the program from the menu, such as the Windows Start menu shown in Figure 6-23.
- Open a file management interface and double-click a data file that is associated with a certain application.
- Press a key combination (a keyboard shortcut) assigned to that program.
- In a touchscreen environment, tap an icon for the program.

Figure 6-23 In Windows, the most common way to execute a program is from the Start menu.

Many of the program buttons or icons you see in a GUI environment are not the actual program files but shortcuts to them. A *shortcut* is a pointer that refers to a file. The actual file that runs the program Notepad in Windows, for example, is stored in C:\Windows\System32, but you can access it from a Notepad shortcut on the Start menu/Start screen. Some shortcut icons have an arrow in their lower-left corner to differentiate them from the actual file (Figure 6-24) and have the word *shortcut* in the name, but that's not always the case. Shortcuts are useful because you can have a shortcut in a convenient location while the original file remains protected. You can also have multiple shortcuts that all point to the same program, giving you multiple ways to start the program.

Figure 6-24
A shortcut icon
may have an
arrow on it.

Notepad

In a command-line environment, you run a program by typing the program's name, a space, and any options needed, and then pressing ENTER.

Managing Files

Computing devices that save data files need some type of file management capability. In Windows, this feature is called File Explorer in Windows 8 and later, or Windows Explorer in earlier versions. In macOS, this feature is called Finder; in Linux it's called Files. With Chrome OS, you can access Google Drive directly or use the Files app for file management. Figure 6-25 compares these, and Chapter 8 explains how to manage files in each OS.

 NOTE   On a simple computing device like a digital music player, you might have to connect the device to a PC to manage files.

Connecting to Hardware

As you learned at the beginning of this chapter, an important OS function is communicating with hardware. Each hardware device has its own language, however, so the OS needs device drivers to translate between them.

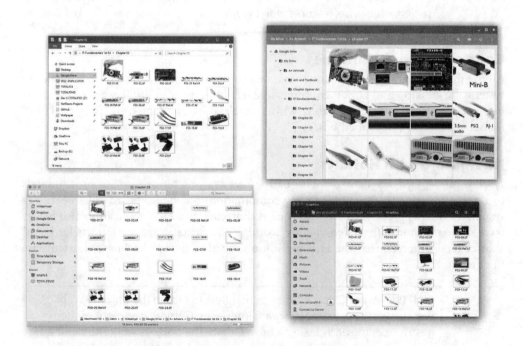

Figure 6-25   File management utilities are similar across operating systems.

Figure 6-26
Windows has automatically connected to new hardware, and it is ready to use.

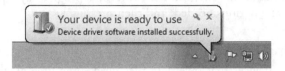

Most modern hardware and operating systems support *Plug and Play,* which enables hardware to report its specifications to the OS and enables the OS to assign resources to the device and install a driver for it if one is available. Operating systems come with a collection of device drivers for common devices. That's why when you connect some new hardware to a computer, it seems to work like magic. A message might appear in Windows in the notification area, at the bottom-right corner of the screen, letting you know the device has automatically been set up, as in Figure 6-26.

If the OS cannot locate a usable device driver for the device, it prompts you to download one or to insert a disc containing the driver. Most devices come with an optical disc containing the needed drivers.

 NOTE Chrome OS doesn't do well with many new devices, because you can't install third-party drivers. If the drivers are built into the OS, you're golden; otherwise, features won't work.

Connecting to the Internet

All the major operating systems for computers support Internet connections. Operating systems for desktop and laptop computers generally support multiple ways of connecting, such as with an Ethernet cable, with a wireless Wi-Fi adapter, or using a dial-up modem (an older, slower method).

Navigating with Hotkeys

Hotkeys, also called *keyboard shortcuts* or *shortcut keys,* enable you to issue commands to the operating system by pressing key combinations on the keyboard. The operating system itself has a predefined set of keyboard shortcuts, and each application also has its own keyboard shortcuts. When you are working in a specific application, its keyboard shortcuts take precedence; when no application is active, the OS keyboard shortcuts are in effect.

 EXAM TIP Many Chrome OS apps manifest as tabs in the Chrome Web browser, not as separate program interfaces. Getting in and out of them means opening and closing a browser tab. The hotkeys work the same way.

Action	Windows	macOS	Linux (Unity)	Chrome OS
Shut down the active app	ALT-F4 from active window	COMMAND-W	CTRL-Q	CTRL-W
Cut the selected item	CTRL-X	COMMAND-X	CTRL-X	CTRL-X
Copy the selected item	CTRL-C	COMMAND-C	CTRL-C	CTRL-C
Paste the selected item	CTRL-V	COMMAND-V	CTRL-V	CTRL-V
Switch between open applications	ALT-TAB	COMMAND-TAB or SHIFT-COMMAND-TILDE (~)	ALT-TAB	SWITCHER
Open Help	F1	COMMAND-?	n/a	CTRL-?

Table 6-2 Some Keyboard Shortcuts (Hotkeys)

To find out the shortcut keys for an OS, look in the Help system in the OS, or look for a list online. Table 6-2 lists some of the most common ones for Windows, macOS, Ubuntu Linux's Unity interface, and Chrome OS.

NOTE F1 and F4 are in the row of the F1–F12 *function keys* across the top of the keyboard. The OS assigns certain commands to them as shortcuts; consult the Help files for a specific OS to find out what each does. Some applications assign their own shortcuts, both alone and in combination with other keys such as SHIFT, CTRL, and ALT. To add another confusing wrinkle, most laptops and some desktop keyboards have an additional kind of function (FN) key. It's often printed in a distinct color. You can issue extra commands on some keys (indicated by icons of the same color) by holding the FN key when you press them.

Creating Screen Captures

A *screen capture* (or *screenshot*) is a digital image of the computer screen. Many of the figures you see in this book are screen captures, and knowing how to create them enables you to teach others how to use an OS or program to accomplish some task. Screenshots also play an important role in showing support staff a problem you're having so they can help you.

Most operating systems include a built-in screen capture feature, involving pressing a certain key or combination of keys. You can also buy third-party applications that capture screenshots with more options. Screen captures are saved with default names (different in each OS) in default locations (which also vary with the OS). Table 6-3 lists the most common procedures.

	OS	Keyboard Shortcut	Default Save Location
Table 6-3 Screen Capture Keyboard Shortcuts	Windows	WINDOWS-PRINT SCREEN	Pictures\Screenshots
	macOS	COMMAND-SHIFT-3 (full-screen) COMMAND-SHIFT-4 (select an area)	Desktop
	Linux (Unity)	PRINT SCREEN	Desktop
	Chrome OS	CTRL-SWITCHER	Downloads

Configuring Accessibility Options

Most operating systems include optional configuration settings that make the OS easier for people with certain types of disabilities to use. These are collectively referred to as *accessibility options*. Accessibility options fall into these categories:

- **Movement**   Features that help people who have limited mobility or dexterity. A user who can use a keyboard but not a mouse, for example, may engage a feature that enables him or her to move the mouse pointer with the keyboard arrow keys. Someone who can use a mouse but not a keyboard, as a further example, might use an onscreen keyboard utility that enables him or her to type by clicking a mouse button. In addition, keyboard and mouse settings can be enabled that will help people with specific movement limitations. You can slow down the reaction rate and repeat rate of keys, for example, and you can enable a click-lock that locks the mouse button down for dragging.

- **Visual**   Features that help people who have limited vision. High-contrast color schemes can help with visibility, as can extra-large mouse pointers and low-resolution display modes. Magnifier utilities can magnify an area of the screen by moving the mouse pointer over it. Screen-reading programs read the contents of windows and dialog boxes aloud.

- **Audio**   Features that help people who have limited hearing. For example, the OS can be configured to flash or blink when a sound is played.

- **Voice**   Programs that can recognize voice commands and data input. This can be useful both to people with movement difficulties and to people with limited vision.

In Windows, you can set up multiple accessibility options in one place (see Figure 6-27) by opening the Control Panel and choosing Ease of Access | Ease of Access Center. In macOS, open the Apple menu in the upper-left corner, and choose System Preferences | Accessibility. Linux (in Unity, at least) has accessibility options under Settings called Universal Access. Finally, you'll find an Accessibilities section in the Settings in Chrome OS.

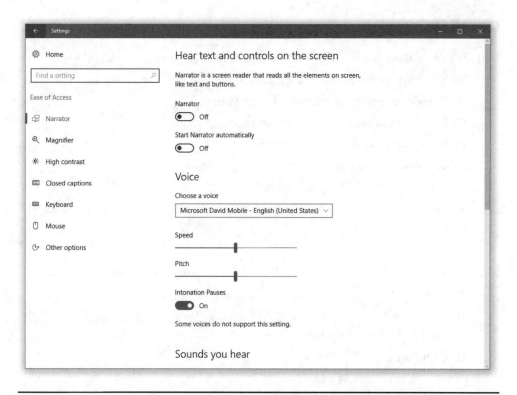

Figure 6-27 The Ease of Access Center helps you set up accessibility options in Windows.

Chapter Review

In this chapter, you learned the five functions of an operating system: providing a machine/ human interface, coordinating hardware activities, providing a software environment, monitoring system health, and providing for data management.

You learned about operating system characteristics. Companies release operating systems under one of three licensing options: open source, free, or commercial. Programmers write applications for specific operating systems; you need to get the software that matches the OS you use. Most companies also make both 32-bit and 64-bit editions of their operating systems.

You toured the basic interfaces of Windows, macOS, Unity (the GUI component of Ubuntu Linux), and Chrome OS, including the major features of each desktop environment. You also learned the differences between Windows Vista/7, 8/8.1, and 10, and what all operating systems have in common. You learned about navigation with hotkeys, screen captures, and accessibility options for people with disabilities.

Questions

1. Which of these is *not* one of the five functions of an operating system?

   A. Monitors system health and functionality

   B. Provides an environment for software to function

   C. Coordinates the activities of hardware components

   D. Sends and receives e-mail messages

2. Which of these is an open source operating system?

   A. Windows

   B. Linux

   C. iOS

   D. macOS

3. If you have a PC with a 32-bit CPU, which operating systems will run on it?

   A. 32-bit only

   B. Both 32-bit and 64-bit

   C. Neither 32-bit nor 64-bit

   D. 64-bit only

4. CTRL-V is an example of what?

   A. Hotkeys

   B. System keys

   C. Function keys

   D. Launch keys

5. Which key combination switches between open applications in Windows and Linux (Unity)?

   A. FI

   B. ALT-F4

   C. ALT-TAB

   D. WINDOWS-PRINT SCREEN

6. Which of these is an accessibility option for people who have limited mobility?

   A. Speech recognition

   B. High-contrast color scheme

   C. Magnifier

   D. Windows flashing or blinking when a sound is played

7. What is the defining feature of a commercial OS?

    A. Open source

    B. Free

    C. Not free

    D. Public domain

8. The Dock on a Mac is equivalent to what feature of a Windows 8.1 desktop?

    A. Start button

    B. Notification area

    C. Launcher

    D. Taskbar

9. What feature in Windows 10 is equivalent to Finder in macOS?

    A. File Explorer

    B. Control Panel

    C. Start screen

    D. Start menu

10. A _____ is a pointer that refers to a file.

    A. Launcher

    B. Taskbar

    C. Shortcut

    D. GUI

Answers

1. **D**. An operating system does not send and receive e-mail messages; that is the function of a mail application. All the other items listed are functions of an operating system.

2. **B**. Linux is open source. Windows, iOS, and macOS are all commercial operating systems.

3. **A**. 32-bit hardware will run only 32-bit operating systems.

4. **A**. CTRL-V is an example of a hotkey, also called a keyboard shortcut. Function keys are the keys across the top of the keyboard that begin with F, as in F1 and F2. There is no such thing as system keys or launch keys.

5. **C**. ALT-TAB switches between open applications. F1 opens Help in Windows. ALT-F4 closes the active application in Windows. WINDOWS-PRINT SCREEN takes a screen capture in Windows.

6. **A.** Speech recognition can help someone who has trouble typing or using a mouse. The magnifier and high-contrast color schemes would help someone with vision limitations. Windows flashing or blinking when a sound is played would be useful for someone with limited or no hearing.

7. **C.** A commercial OS is not free. Open source and public-domain operating systems are free.

8. **D.** The Dock in macOS is like the taskbar in Windows 8.1. The Start button opens the Start screen. The Launcher is the Dock equivalent in Linux (Unity). The notification area is the rightmost section of the taskbar, where icons appear for background programs.

9. **A.** File Explorer in Windows is like Finder in macOS. Control Panel changes system settings. The Start menu helps you run programs in Windows 10. The Start screen is like the Start menu except it's in Windows 8.1.

10. **C.** A shortcut is a pointer that refers to a file. Launcher is the taskbar/Dock equivalent in Linux (Unity). The taskbar is the bar along the bottom of the screen in Windows. A GUI is a graphical user interface.

Working with Applications

In this chapter, you will learn how to
- Run applications
- Install and uninstall applications
- Identify common applications and their uses
- Describe application licensing and distribution

This chapter tells the story of applications, starting with a primer on how to run them in several different operating systems. Second, we'll look at the process used in each operating system (OS) to install applications. The next section looks at the types of applications available today and reviews some common file types. The chapter finishes with licensing issues. We've got a lot of ground to cover, so let's get started!

Running an Application

As you learned in Chapter 6, the operating system handles the computer's basic operation and housekeeping. In contrast, an *application* enables you to do something with the computer. You can produce something of value, such as calculate a budget, touch up a photo, or play music. For convenience and flexibility, each OS has multiple ways of running an application. The procedure for running an application depends on the OS you use.

 NOTE The term *app* is often used as shorthand for application, especially the small applications that run on mobile devices. Some people use the terms *application* and *program* synonymously, but that's not really accurate. Whereas *program* refers to any software, *application* means a program that isn't involved in running or maintaining the computer itself.

Running an Application in Windows

The process of running an application in Windows varies somewhat depending on the Windows version, so let's look each version individually.

153

TIP You can also customize your desktop and taskbar with shortcuts to applications you access regularly.

In Windows 10, click the Start button to open the menu (see Figure 7-1). If there's a shortcut for the desired application in the "Most used" list along the left side or pinned to the Start menu as a tile on the right side, click that shortcut and you're done.

If you don't see the application you want, you have a couple of options. You can scroll down to see a complete alphabetized list of available applications and then click the desired application's shortcut from there. Alternatively, you can begin typing the name of the desired app and then select it from the search results, as in Figure 7-2.

When you click the Start button in Windows 8.1, you get the Start screen rather than the Start menu. You can click a shortcut tile on the Start screen to start an application, or you can click the down arrow at the bottom of the Start screen to display the Apps list. It's the same alphabetical list as before, but (as Figure 7-3 shows) it occupies the entire screen. Like in Windows 10, you can also start typing the name of the application you want to run and then choose it from the search results.

 EXAM TIP The missing Start button in Windows 8 doesn't feature in the CompTIA IT Fundamentals exam. Assume every version of Windows has a Start button.

Figure 7-1 Open the Start menu to access shortcuts to the installed applications.

Figure 7-2
Begin typing an app's name and then select it from the search results.

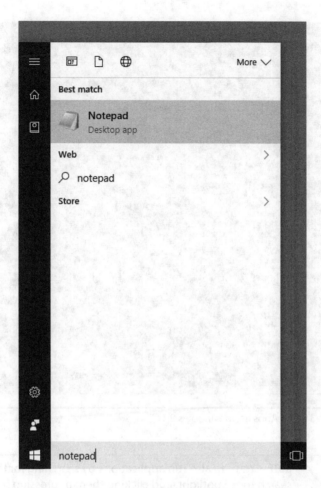

In Windows Vista/7, the process is similar to Windows 10. Click the Start button to open the Start menu. If you don't see the app you want, click All Programs to open an alphabetical list of programs, or click in the Search box near the bottom of the Start menu and type the first few letters of the desired app's name.

Running an Application in macOS

In macOS, the Dock at the bottom of the screen contains shortcuts to frequently used applications, similar to the taskbar and Start menu/screen in Windows. Click an application to run it (Figure 7-4).

If the app you want doesn't appear on the Dock, click the Launchpad button on the Dock to open the Launchpad window, which contains icons for all the installed applications. Click the desired icon from there to start the application.

Figure 7-3   The Apps list in Windows 8.1

NOTE   You can also run applications by searching for them with the macOS search tool, Spotlight, and clicking them or pressing ENTER.

Running an Application in Linux

In any version of Linux, you can use the Terminal (the command prompt) to run command-line applications. The command-line environment is used more for utilities and file management than for applications that directly serve the average user, though, so you will more often run applications within Linux's graphical user interface (GUI). As in Chapter 6, we'll look at the default GUI in Ubuntu Linux, Unity.

Figure 7-4
Click icons in
the Dock to run
the associated
program.

Figure 7-5
Click an icon on the Launcher bar to run an associated program.

If a shortcut for the desired application appears on the Launcher bar along the left side of the screen, click it to start the application (Figure 7-5). If not, you can do the following:

- Click the Dash button (the topmost icon on the Launcher) and then click the Applications button at the bottom of the Dash pane (Figure 7-6).

- Click the Dash button, begin typing the application name, and then click its name in the search results.

Figure 7-6
In Dash, click the Applications button to find more programs.

Figure 7-7
The shelf has
commonly
accessed apps.

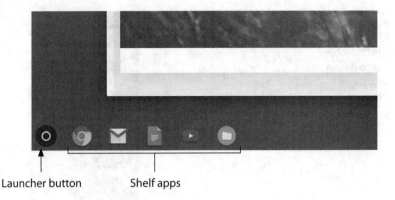

Launcher button   Shelf apps

Running an Application in Chrome OS

To run an application in Chrome OS, right-click one of the apps on the shelf (Figure 7-7) or click the Launcher button (bottom left) to display all the available apps. Click the one you want to open (Figure 7-8).

Switching Between Applications

Each of the desktop operating systems covered in the CompTIA IT Fundamentals exam can run multiple applications at once, but only one *active application* has focus at a time; any text you type or keyboard shortcuts you press will apply to this active application.

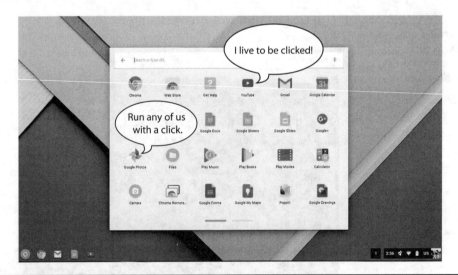

Figure 7-8 Open the Launcher bar and then click All programs to see everything you can currently do on the Chrome OS device.

Other applications can continue to operate in the background, and their displays might update, but you must switch to the app before you can interact with it.

There are many different ways to switch to an application:

- Click the desired application's button in the taskbar (Windows), Dock (macOS), Launcher (Unity Linux), or shelf (Chrome OS).

- If any portion of the application window is visible, click it.

- In Windows, press ALT-ESC. Each time you do so, a different application becomes active.

- Hold down the ALT key (Windows, Linux, Chrome OS) or COMMAND key (macOS) and tap the TAB key. Each time you press and release TAB, a different application becomes active. Release the ALT or COMMAND key when the desired application is active.

- Chrome OS has a couple of quirks that make it different from the other desktop environments. First, many applications run as tabs in the Chrome Web browser. Press CTRL-TAB or ALT-TAB to go to the next or previous tab. Second, dedicated Chrome machines, like a Chromebook portable, have a SWITCHER key that brings up active programs. Click the program you want to bring into focus.

Saving Your Work

Many programs enable you to create data files and save them for later use. Microsoft Word enables you to create and save documents that you can later reopen, edit, save, and print. Saving works the same way across all operating systems and, for the most part, is standard across most applications too.

In any application, look for a Save or Save As command. If the data file has not previously been saved, these commands are identical—they both open the Save As dialog box, from which you can specify a filename, location, and type. Figure 7-9 shows an example. If the file has been previously saved, the Save command re-saves it with the same settings, without opening a dialog box.

Exiting an Application

To close an application, use its Exit command or Quit command. Look for that command on the File menu (in most Windows and Linux applications) or on the menu named after the application (in macOS applications).

Depending on the OS and application, you might be able to exit by closing the application's window. In Windows, Linux (Unity), and Chrome OS, closing an application's window exits the application. In macOS, however, closing the application's window does not exit the application in many cases. (It depends on the application.) The application might still be open in the background. If the application has an icon on the Dock, a black dot under the icon indicates it is still open.

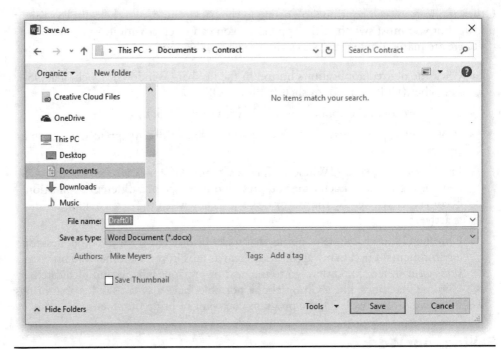

Figure 7-9   A Save As dialog box enables you to save your work.

Installing, Updating, and Removing Applications

Next, let's take a look at the procedures for installing, updating, and removing applica-tions. It's different in each OS (and among some versions/editions of the same OS, of course), but they are all similar.

Installing Applications

You'll probably want to install some additional applications to add capabilities to the computing device. You can buy applications in retail stores, buy and download applica-tions online, or get applications from an app store associated with your OS.

When you get them from an app store, they'll typically install automatically. If not, you'll run a setup program (often called an *installer*) that prepares your system to run the application. The following sections explain the various installation methods.

NOTE   Installer files can have any name the developers want to give them. Installers you download may be named after the application and may also include its version number. These installers are often named Setup, especially if the application comes on removable media such as an optical disc.

Installing a Desktop Application in Windows

Windows desktop applications typically have an installer. To install an application from removable media, insert the media and wait a moment to see whether the system either prompts you to run the installer or runs it automatically. If it does neither, browse the file system for the disc, locate the installer (its extension is usually .exe or .msi), and double-click it to get the ball rolling.

 EXAM TIP This section and the next list common installer file extensions you'll encounter on Windows and macOS. If you aren't already familiar with file formats and extensions, circle back to confirm you understand these sections after you have learned about formats and extensions later in the chapter.

An installer you download may technically be a compressed archive file (with formats such as ZIP, 7z, RAR, and so on), in which case you'll have to double-click it once to unpack the files to a folder on your system. The setup utility might run automatically after that; if not, navigate to the folder the installer unpacked to and double-click it.

 NOTE A *compressed archive file* is a single file that, much like a folder, can contain and compress many files. You'll read more about compression and archive file formats later in the chapter, but for now it's enough to know that compression "packs" data more efficiently so that it uses less space until you "unpack" it later.

Compressed archive files make it easy to bundle up related files (such as an application) and transfer them efficiently. Your OS can pack and unpack the most common compressed archive formats, but you may need a separate application to work with less common formats.

In either case, you may see a User Account Control (UAC) security prompt when you double-click the installer. You'll learn more about this in Chapter 11, but the UAC prompt is your system's way of confirming you (and not some malware) initiated the request. In this case, click Yes to continue—but don't get in the habit of clicking through unexpected UAC prompts unless you understand what caused them and know they are safe.

From here, follow the prompts to install the application. During the setup process, you may be asked to specify a location for the files, as in Figure 7-10 (the default location is usually best), and you might have the choice of installing optional features or doing a custom installation.

 CAUTION It's often fine to pick the default or express installation, but it's safer to pick the Custom option to make sure the installer doesn't add extra software you don't want; you'll learn more about these risks in Chapter 12. If you don't understand specific custom options, stick with the default.

Figure 7-10
Work through
the prompts to
install a desktop
application.

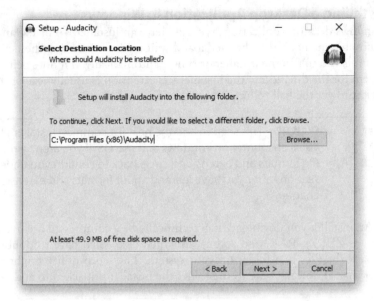

Figure 7-10 Work through the prompts to install a desktop application.

Installing a Desktop Application in macOS

To install an application from a disc, first insert the disc in the computer. A setup utility might run automatically. If it doesn't, browse the disc using Finder. Locate a file named Setup (or similar) and double-click it to start the setup process.

To install downloaded software on a Mac, double-click the file you downloaded. If an error message appears that the application can't be opened because it wasn't downloaded from the Mac App Store, right-click the downloaded file and click Open. Mac installation files come in several different formats: ZIP, PKG, or DMG. If it's a .zip file, double-clicking it unpacks the .zip file into its own folder, and within that folder you will find a .pkg or .dmg file. Double-click it. A .pkg file will install the application for you automatically from that point; a .dmg file may require you to manually drag the app into the Applications folder (using Finder). See Figure 7-11. You can delete the downloaded file when you're done.

Installing an App from an Online Store

All four desktop operating systems have a dedicated online app store so you can download and install programs. The store app enables you to browse applications, make a selection, and click Install. Figure 7-12 shows an app being selected in the Windows Store, for example. It's a free app, so you would click Free to begin the download. The rest of the setup process is completely automated—no choices to make.

Figure 7-11
Manually
installing an app
in macOS

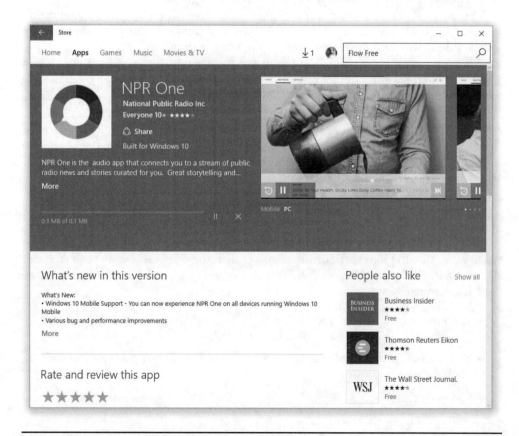

Figure 7-12   Installing a free application from the Windows Store

Using Web-Based Applications

You use Web-based applications directly through a browser or other tool when you connect to the Internet. You do not need to install Web-based applications. Companies provide these applications as a *service* to users, which is why Web-based applications are described as *software as a service (SaaS)*. Some SaaS is "free" to the user (this often means the developer makes money by showing you ads or collecting data about you), but most paid SaaS requires a monthly or yearly subscription.

NOTE Some desktop applications (including Microsoft Office 365) are licensed as SaaS, but downloaded as desktop applications. You pay your first month's "rent" on the application and then you can download its installer. You can use the application anytime, not just when online. Subscription-based software you can use offline may require you to go online once in a while to confirm your subscription is current.

Updating Applications

Like operating systems, applications can be updated to fix problems and add features. An update designed to fix problems is sometimes called a *patch*.

The process for downloading application updates varies depending on the application and the OS. Under Windows, Microsoft Office application updates are automatically installed along with Windows updates by default, for example.

Other applications run a small utility in the background that periodically checks a Web site for updates and informs you of (or even installs) updates. You can often modify the scheduling and frequency of these update checks.

TIP Multiple applications running their own background utility to watch for updates can collectively use enough memory to make system performance suffer. If your system is running slowly, investigate whether you can disable some applications' automatic update features.

Still other applications have a manual "Check for updates" command, such as the one in the Help menu in Figure 7-13.

All of these options compare the installed version number to the latest available number to make sure the new version truly is newer than the one you already have. You can also manually find an application's version number and check its Web site to see whether there is a newer version.

- If there is a Help menu, open it and look for an About command. Figure 7-14 shows the result of such a command in FileZilla.

- In Microsoft Office applications, click the File tab and click Account and then click the About button.

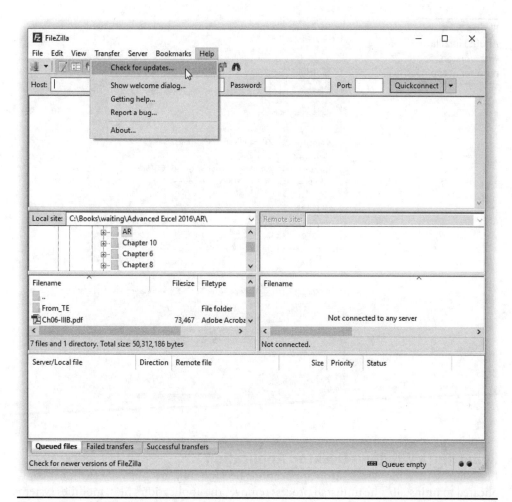

Figure 7-13   FileZilla's update command

Armed with the application's version number, you can also research any compatibility issues. For example, if you are running an older version of Windows and an update is available for your favorite application, it's a good idea to check online for any known compatibility issues between the new version and your OS version.

Removing Applications

In some operating systems and with some application types, uninstalling is kind of a big deal; you have to go through a step-by-step process. In other cases, it's just a few clicks. The following sections summarize the processes you should know.

Figure 7-14
About FileZilla
with version
number at top

Removing a Windows Desktop Application

Let's start with Windows desktop applications because they are generally the most complicated to uninstall. The uninstall process removes the application's files, modifies system files, and deletes the application's shortcuts.

To remove a Windows desktop application, open the Control Panel and click Programs | Uninstall a Program. A list of installed applications appears. Click the one you want to remove, click Uninstall (or Uninstall/Change), and then follow the prompts. The uninstall process is similar to the setup process and usually involves multiple steps. Figure 7-15 shows an example.

NOTE The instructions here assume Control Panel is in the default Category view, which organizes utilities by category. If the drop-down menu in the upper-right corner doesn't say View By: Category, open the drop-down and choose Category.

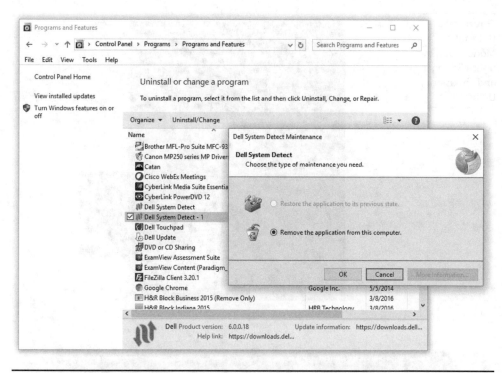

Figure 7-15 Click Uninstall or Uninstall/Change and then follow the prompts.

Removing a Modern Windows App

To uninstall a Modern app (one you download from the Windows Store), first locate it on the Start screen or Start menu. You might have to bring up the full Apps list. Then right-click it and choose Uninstall, as in Figure 7-16.

Removing a macOS Application

On a computer running macOS, drag the application from the Applications folder to the Trash located on the Dock. Then choose Finder | Empty Trash and it's gone.

Removing an App in Ubuntu Linux

In Ubuntu's Unity GUI, click the Ubuntu Software Center icon on the Launcher bar. Then on the toolbar at the top of the window, click Installed to see the installed applications. Expand the category for the app you want to remove so you can find it and then click it and click Remove. Figure 7-17 shows an example.

Removing an App in Chrome OS

To remove an app in Chrome OS, open Launcher and select All Apps. Right-click the app you want to uninstall and select Uninstall. Click Remove and the app goes away. If you have a single button touchpad, hold the ALT key down and single click to access the uninstallation option.

Figure 7-16
Uninstall a
Modern app by
right-clicking it
and choosing
Uninstall.

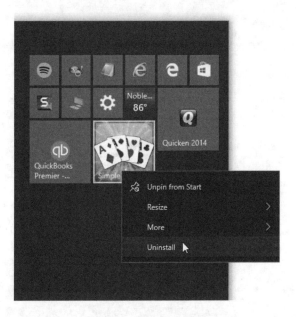

Figure 7-17   Uninstall applications in Ubuntu Linux via the Ubuntu Software Center.

PART II

Common Applications and Their Uses

This section is a whirlwind tour of the various application types and platforms you may encounter. The objectives list for the CompTIA IT Fundamentals exam has more than two dozen application types and three dozen file extensions, but you're not expected to know how to use everything. That would go well beyond the scope of the certification. You should read this section to get a sense of all the types of applications used in modern computing.

 EXAM TIP   You will get questions on the CompTIA IT Fundamentals exam that ask about which file extensions go with which type of software. A good study tool for memorizing the extensions here is to make a handwritten, two-column chart that matches extension to file type. Writing it out helps the memorization process.

Platforms

As you learned in Chapter 1, a *platform* is the hardware on which an OS (and its applications) runs. The platforms listed in Objective 1.2 of the CompTIA IT Fundamentals exam are mobile, desktop, and Web-based, so let's look at each.

Desktop in this context does not mean a desktop PC necessarily but software that runs on a desktop OS such as Windows or macOS. *Mobile* means software that is designed to run on a mobile OS such as Android or iOS. Web-based means software that is accessed through a Web browser. *Web-based* software (such as Office Online at www.office.com) is usually available only when you connect to the Internet and use the app's Web site.

Types

In the context of the CompTIA IT Fundamentals objectives, an application's type refers to its overall purpose. What is it designed to help you do? Does it help you with business documents? Does it help you collaborate? The following sections provide a look at the types listed in the exam objectives. It's not a comprehensive list of every type of software that exists, but it's a good start for understanding what's available.

 EXAM TIP   Objective 1.2 lists five types: Productivity, Collaboration, Utility, Specialized, and Open Source vs. Commercial. Wait, what? That last one doesn't really fit, does it? It's about software licenses, not purpose, so we'll save it for the section "Software Licensing," later in this chapter.

Productivity Software

This rather large class of software includes programs designed to help you do productive tasks associated with making a living, such as writing documents, managing personal information, giving presentations, storing data, and sending e-mail. Table 7-1 lists the types of productivity application the objectives specifically mention and explains each.

Application Type	Purpose	Examples
Word processing	Create business and personal documents such as letters, reports, memos, and manuscripts	Microsoft Word (Windows, macOS) Pages (macOS) LibreOffice Writer (Linux) Google Docs (Chrome OS)
Spreadsheet software	Create worksheets that perform calculations on financial and statistical data	Microsoft Excel (Windows, macOS) Numbers (macOS) LibreOffice Calc (Linux) Google Sheets (Chrome OS)
E-mail software	Send and receive e-mail, manage an address book of contacts	Microsoft Outlook (Windows, macOS) Mail (Windows) Evolution (Linux) Gmail (Chrome OS)
Basic database software	Store and manage structured data, such as lists of contacts, products, or transactions	Microsoft Access (Windows) FileMaker (macOS, Windows) LibreOffice Base (Linux)
PDF viewers/creators	View and create formatted pages for printing or distribution on any platform	Adobe Acrobat (reads and creates) Adobe Reader (only reads)
Presentation software	Create graphical slides to support presentations	Microsoft PowerPoint (Windows, macOS) Keynote (macOS) LibreOffice Impress (Linux) Google Slides (Chrome OS)
Desktop publishing software	Combine text and graphics into page layouts such as magazine pages and brochures	Microsoft Publisher (Windows) Quark Xpress (macOS, Windows)
Personal information manager	Manage contacts, calendars, tasks, notes, and reminders; may also send, receive, and manage e-mail	Microsoft Outlook (Windows) Evolution (Linux)
Remote desktop software	Access the desktop of one computer from another	Windows Remote Desktop

Table 7-1   Productivity Software Types

Collaboration Software

Collaboration software helps people communicate and work with one another, and it helps computers share information. Although this collaboration can be personal in nature, it's more often for business. Table 7-2 lists the collaboration software types you should know for the exam.

Application Type	Purpose	Examples
Online workspace	Provide an online environment for running cloud-based services and applications	Office Online (applications) Microsoft SharePoint (complete environment including file libraries and messaging) Google Docs
Document storage/sharing	Provide private or sharable file storage via cloud-based services	Microsoft OneDrive Google Drive
Screen sharing software	Enable a remote user to see and take control of another user's screen while the original user and others watch	Windows Remote Assistance Can also be built into video conferencing software
Video conferencing software	Place and receive video calls among two or more locations; may also include screen, file, and application sharing	Citrix GoToMeeting
Instant messaging software	Enable two or more people to communicate in real-time using text; may also include video conferencing capability	Yahoo! Messenger AOL Instant Messenger
E-mail software	Sends and receives e-mail messages	Microsoft Outlook

Table 7-2   Collaboration Software Types

Utility Software

Utility software is arguably not in the Applications category because it doesn't do anything directly for the human using the computer. Instead, utilities help keep the computer running smoothly and help manage and distribute files. You should know the utility software types listed in Table 7-3.

Specialized Software

In this category are applications designed to appeal to a specific segment of the population. This can include software for people in professions such as computer-aided design (CAD), medicine, science, and finance, as well as games and entertainment applications designed for people of a certain type or age. Table 7-4 reviews the types mentioned in the exam objectives.

Common File Types

Each application has a default format for its data files, also called its *file type*. On Windows systems, a file's type is specified by its extension, which is a code (usually three characters but not always) that follows the filename, separated by a period, like this: myfile.txt. In other Operating systems, the file type is determined by the OS looking inside the file for that information, so a file's extension, if it has one, is not a reliable way to determine a file's actual type. Still, it's a good starting point.

PART II

Application Type	Purpose	Examples
Anti-malware	Scan a system for malicious software (malware) including viruses, worms, and exploits. See Chapter 12 for more about this kind of software.	Norton Internet Security Symantec Endpoint Protection McAfee VirusScan Malwarebytes Windows Defender
Software firewalls	Prevent hackers from gaining access to a computer remotely via network or Internet.	Windows Firewall Norton Firewall
Diagnostic/ maintenance software	Check hard disks for errors and optimize their performance. Chapter 13 covers several kinds of diagnostic software.	Check Disk / Error Checking Optimize Drives (Windows)
Compression software	Combine and compress multiple files into a single archive file that can be more easily distributed. See "Compression Formats," later in this chapter.	WinZip Compression features built into some operating systems

Table 7-3 Utility Software Types

Application Type	Purpose	Examples
Computer-aided design (CAD)	Create blueprints and 3D renderings of buildings and products.	AutoCAD
Graphic design	Create and edit drawings and other artwork; edit photos.	Adobe Photoshop Adobe Illustrator
Medical	One type provides reference information for medical professionals; another type manages a medical practice, including patient data, scheduling, and medical records.	MedClarity Kareo Accountable
Scientific	One type provides reference information and tools for scientific professionals; another type manages the process of doing scientific research.	LabVIEW Mathematica MATLAB Origin
Financial	Track and manage financial information; many different types exist, from personal finance applications to software that runs large accounting departments.	Quicken TurboTax Peachtree Accounting QuickBooks
Gaming	Entertain (and potentially educate) the user; may run on separate PCs independently or on a network. May be desktop, mobile, or Web-based.	The Sims World of Warcraft Candy Crush
Entertainment (nongames)	Entertain a specific audience, such as playing music or movies or providing digital copies of magazines to read.	Texture Spotify iTunes Windows Media Player

Table 7-4 Specialized Software Types

Extension	File Type
.app	A Mac application bundle. In macOS it looks like an application executable, but the *bundle* is actually a folder containing the application's files. Windows users just see the bundle as a folder.
.bat	A batch file (or *script*) is a list of commands to be executed in sequential order.
.exe or .com	A Windows application. An .exe file may have multiple helper files that work with it; a .com file is normally a stand-alone application.
.msi	An installer package file format used in Windows.
.scexe	A proprietary file extension used by HP for firmware updates.

Table 7-5 Executable File Extensions on the CompTIA IT Fundamentals Exam

PART II

Executables

Files that run programs are known as *executables*. An executable can be part of the OS itself, an application, or an installation package. Table 7-5 lists some common executable formats you should be familiar with for the exam.

EXAM TIP   That last entry in Table 7-5, .scexe, is not one you are likely to encounter. It's anyone's guess why it appears in the exam objectives. The others in Table 7-5, though, are important to know in real life, not just for study.

Compression Formats

Groups of files can be compressed and combined into a single *compressed archive* file, which makes the group of files easier to distribute and transport (Figure 7-18). For example, suppose you have to send ten picture files to someone. You could attach all ten files separately to an e-mail, but it would be better to create a single compressed archive that holds them.

To create a compressed zip archive file out of a group of files in File Explorer, select the files and then right-click the selection, point to Send To, and click Compressed (zipped) folder. Type a name for the compressed archive file (the default is the name of the first file in the selection) and press Enter. Now you can take this .zip file and e-mail, move, copy, or do anything else with it that you can do with a regular file. It will open in File Explorer as if it were a folder if you double-click it. File Explorer will give you the option to extract all of the files, but you can also just select and move or copy specific files out of the .zip file.

You may encounter many other compressed archive formats, but in Windows, .zip (the default) dominates. Some of these formats may require you to use a third-party utility to create and manage their archive files. Table 7-6 lists the compressed archive formats you should know.

Audio and Video Formats

Collectively, files containing audio (such as voice recordings, music, or audio books) and video (movies, music videos, presentations, TV shows, and so on) are often referred to as *media clips*. You'll need to download some media clips before you can play them, but your device can play *streaming media* as the clips transfer from sites and services such as SoundCloud, YouTube, Spotify, and Netflix. There are many different formats for audio and video recordings, each with its own set of benefits and drawbacks.

Figure 7-18
Creating a
compressed
archive file

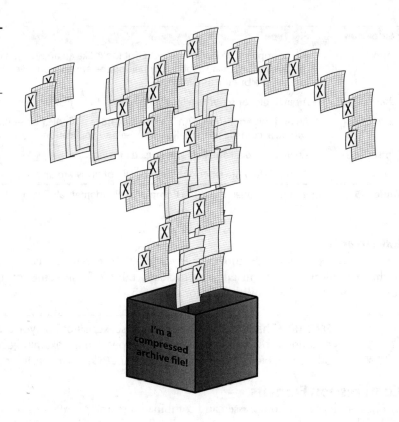

I'm a compressed archive file!

Format	Purpose
7ZIP or 7z	7ZIP is the default format for the file compression utility 7-Zip archiver. 7z is an updated version of the file format, offering better compression and security
DMG	The format of a macOS disc image; similar to ISO but for Mac.
GZIP or GZ	The default format for the gzip utility. The G stands for GNU. GNU is a Linux variant.
ISO	The format of a file that represents an optical disc image; use a DVD burning application to burn an ISO file to removable media such as a blank CD, DVD, or USB flash drive.
JAR	A compression format for Java classes and data. You may encounter this when you work with Java applications.
RAR	The default format of the WinRAR file archive program
TAR	The Linux and UNIX standard archive format. It's an acronym that stands for *tape archive*.
ZIP	A popular compression format for Windows computers. Originally developed for a command-line application called PKZIP, it is now most closely associated with WinZip.

Table 7-6 Compression Formats

No media player supports all formats, so it's important to find one that supports the formats of the clips you want to play. The playback software must have a *codec* installed for each format it supports. Codec is short for "compressor-decompressor," and it refers to the encoding of the clips. Playback software uses the codec to decode clips on the fly. Windows Media Player in some versions and editions of Windows, for example, lacks the codec needed to play most DVD movies; you must purchase a codec as an add-on to the application.

 CAUTION *Compression* can refer to condensed files like the compressed archive files discussed here. It can also refer to the encoding of a media file.

Some clips are *compressed,* meaning they use a special type of encoding that makes the file take up less disk space. You'll find two types of this kind of compression with media files: lossless and lossy.

Lossless compression creates a file that retains the quality of the original file. Media producers use this kind of compression when file size doesn't really matter but quality does.

Lossy compression deletes some of data from the file to make the final file size smaller. That funny cat video on YouTube uses a lossy compression, but it looks good enough on a computer monitor. You would only see the fact that it's missing data if you made the image huge.

Almost all video files are *containers* for data encoded in any of several different formats. Codecs are for the inner content, not the container file type. To play back the clip, the player must have a codec for the formats used inside the file.

Most video files are container files for both visual and audio data, each decoded by a different codec during playback. The playback software needs to know how to talk to the container file and have the correct codecs for the internal data.

Here's where you can run into trouble. A container file gets a file extension, such as .mov. There's no rule that says that data inside a .mov container has to use one type of encoding. You can have two .mov container files with wildly different internal encoding. Even if playback software can talk to .mov files, it needs the codecs for all the internal data as well. With a missing codec, you might hear sound but get no video when playing a media clip.

An audio or video container file may have special features or properties. Some formats support *digital rights management (DRM),* for example, a kind of copy protection that prevents copyrighted clips from being freely shared. (The music and film industries call this a feature, but most of us call it a nuisance!)

 EXAM TIP The list of acronyms for the CompTIA IT Fundamentals exam includes MP3, MP4, and MPEG. All of these share a common source: Moving Pictures Experts Group (MPEG). MPEG is a standards organization that has defined several popular audio and video formats.

Table 7-7 lists the audio and video formats you should know.

Type	Format	Purpose
Audio	AAC	Advanced Audio Coding (AAC) was designed to replace MP3. It has better sound quality than MP3 at similar compression levels and file sizes.
Audio	FLAC	Free Lossless Audio Codec (FLAC) is similar to MP3, but the lossless compression yields a little higher quality.
Audio	M4A	This format is used for music downloads from iTunes that have no copy protection on them. M4A is a container file, and the content inside the container is usually coded as AAC.
Audio	MP3	This is a common general format for music files. It's popular because it uses a high level of lossy compression (so files are small), it lacks copy protection (so files can be freely shared), and almost all music player applications support it. The extension is short for Moving Picture Experts Group Layer 3 Audio.
Audio	WAV	The raw data inside is usually uncompressed CD-quality sound. The files are large, so this format is not usually used for long clips. This is the default container format for the Sound Recorder application in Windows.
Audio	MID/MIDI	This format is not in the exam objectives, but it is in the exam acronyms list. A Musical Instrument Digital Interface (MIDI) file is a text file that takes advantage of the sound-processing hardware to enable the computing device to produce sound. Programmers use these small files to tell the sound card which notes to play; how long, how loud, and on which instruments to play them; and so forth. Think of a MIDI file as a piece of electronic sheet music, with the instruments built into your sound card.
Video	AVI	Audio Video Interleave (AVI) is a Microsoft-created container format for audio and video. It's a common format for short, homemade videos you might find online.
Video	FLV	Flash Video (FLV) is a container file format designed to distribute video online using Adobe Flash Player as the playback application, usually within a Web page.
Video	MP4	This format uses MPEG-4 raw video data and usually AAC or MP3 audio data. The extension is short for Moving Picture Experts Group Layer 4.
Video	MPG/MPEG	The MPG format is a container that can hold either MPEG-1 or MPEG-2 raw video data, plus accompanying audio data. It is an older format but still in use. The extension is an acronym for Moving Picture Experts Group.
Video	WMV	Windows Media Video (WMV) is used in some Microsoft programs that deal with user-created videos, such as Windows Movie Maker.

Table 7-7   Audio and Video Formats

Image Formats

Files that store still images, like photos, are called *image formats*. There are two kinds of image files: raster and vector. A *raster format* is used for photos and digital paintings. It contains color information for each individual dot (pixel) in the entire image. Another name for this kind of image is bitmap (because it is literally a map of bits). Raster image files tend to be rather large, even when compression is applied. (As with audio and video, compression can be lossless or lossy.) The main drawback to the raster format is that the image loses quality when it is resized (particularly when resized larger than the original). Raster images are created and edited in programs like Microsoft Paint and Adobe Photoshop.

A *vector format* is used for line drawings. It uses math formulas to describe each line and curve in the image, like the geometry formulas you might have plotted in high school. Vector drawings are not photorealistic, but they take up a lot less space, and they don't lose quality when resized. Vector format is great for technical drawings and flow charts. You create vector drawings when you use the drawing tools in Microsoft Office applications, for example, or when you use an application like Microsoft Visio or Adobe Illustrator.

 EXAM TIP No vector formats appear in the CompTIA IT Fundamentals objectives, but graphic artists and illustrators often work in vector formats that are easy to re-scale as needed and export in a raster format.

All of the image formats that the CompTIA IT Fundamentals exam objectives mention are raster formats. They each have their own unique mix of file size, compression, and quality, and each has its fans in certain industries. For example, the GIF format has a somewhat unusual extra capability: it can store several versions (frames) of the graphic inside a single file and cycle among them automatically, so it's popular on Web page advertisements that cycle through several ads. Table 7-8 describes the image formats you need to know.

Format	Purpose
BMP	Short for bitmap, the BMP format is one of the oldest raster formats used in personal computing. In the early days of Windows, BMP was the only format that Microsoft's application Paint supported. BMP is widely supported in many graphics applications for backward compatibility but no longer widely used because there are other formats that are more appealing in terms of file size and quality.
GIF	Graphics File Interchange (GIF) is an uncompressed format. It supports only 256 colors, so it's not a great choice for photos, but it is popular for Web page ads because it can store and cycle through several graphics in a single file.
JPG/JPEG	Joint Photographic Experts Group (JPG or JPEG) is a lossy image compression format that sacrifices some image quality but has a very small file size. It's commonly used on the Web and in onscreen graphics, where you can't detect the reduced image quality.
PNG	Portable Network Graphic (PNG) is the successor to GIF. It uses lossless compression and supports 16.7 million colors, a big improvement from GIF's 256 colors. It is one of the most popular formats used on Web pages and in game graphics.
TIF/TIFF	Tagged Image File Format (TFF or TIFF) uses lossless compression and is considered a high-quality format but with a rather large file size. Some digital cameras capture images in this format, and photos in publications that will be printed on paper often use this format because of the high quality.

Table 7-8 Image Formats

Format	Purpose
TXT	A plain-text file, with no formatting. This is the default format for the Notepad app in Windows, as well as most other text editors.
RTF	Rich Text Format (RTF) is a widely accepted generic word processing format. Nearly all word processing applications can read and write this format. It includes all the basic text formatting options, including fonts, attributes, paragraph indentation, margins, bullets and numbering, and headers/footers.
DOC/DOCX	The DOCX format is the current format for Microsoft Word documents and is also used by many other word processing applications for compatibility with Word. The DOC format is an earlier version, used in Word 2003 and earlier and still supported.
XLS/XLSX	Microsoft Excel, the spreadsheet application, uses XLSX as its default format. The XLS format is an earlier version, used in Excel 2003 and earlier and still supported.
PPT/PPTX	Microsoft PowerPoint, the presentation application, uses PPTX as its default format. The PPT format is an earlier version, used in PowerPoint 2003 and earlier and still supported.
PDF	Portable Document Format (PDF) is the default format for Adobe Acrobat and Adobe Reader. This format is designed to make document formatting consistent when distributing documents across platforms. No matter what computer or device you open up a PDF file on, the file looks the same, without any variation in fonts or spacing. You can save to PDF in most Microsoft Office applications; you can also set up a PDF print driver that outputs print jobs to PDF files, useful in applications that do not save to PDF.

Table 7-9   Document Formats

Documents

Our final category of file type to consider is *documents*. It includes not only various types of text-heavy files but also spreadsheets, presentations, and page layouts—all types of data files that you would create in business-oriented applications. Table 7-9 summarizes the document file types you should know.

Software Licensing

Companies distribute software in several ways. When you purchase a computer, it comes with the operating system and some other basic *bundled* (pre-installed) applications such as a text editor, a media player, and a Web browser.

Some software is sold in neat little boxes that include an optical disc or USB flash drive containing the application installer. Most folks use the Internet these days to get software; this includes both programs you download and Web apps (software as a service) that you access with a browser.

All software is subject to licensing and copyright regulations, so you usually have to agree to an *end-user license agreement (EULA)* before using a program or service. The terms vary depending on the type of software, but they're most common when you install, update, or open a downloaded program, and when you register, log in to, or access a Web app. Agreeing to the EULA creates a contract between the software company and the user (you). This contract specifies terms such as how many computers you can install it on and limits the vendor's liability should something disastrous occur as a result of installing the software.

A lot of (often overlapping) terms apply to how software developers sell, distribute, and license their products. Let's look at some of the most common here.

- Software that you can download at no cost—like Adobe Reader or Google Chrome—is called *freeware*. Some freeware includes advertising.

- A related term, *freemium,* applies when the developers offer the basic version for free, but you have to make an in-application purchase or subscribe to get some features.

- Many paid programs and Web apps have a *trial* version. You may see installable trials called *shareware,* though this term has become rare. The trial version is usually limited in either time or functionality. If you pay, you unlock the missing features or get permanent access.

- *Commercial* software must be purchased. You pay for it, and then you get access to it. In some contexts, it indicates that software can be used for commercial purposes.

- *Closed source* software applies when the software developers keep the source code and other information about how the software works private.

- *Open source* software means the software's source code is freely available for anyone to copy, modify, and create new versions of the application. Examples of open source software are Linux and OpenOffice.

EXAM TIP The CompTIA IT Fundamentals objectives include comparing "open source vs. commercial" software as if they are clearly different, but the reality is messy. For the exam, know the following:

- Developers charge money for commercial software, keep the source code private, and prohibit you from selling or giving away copies of their software.
- You are free to use, modify, and redistribute open source software.

Beyond the exam, know there are *many* software licenses that vary in what they permit and require you to do. They may, for example, require commercial users to pay for a commercial-use license, prohibit commercial uses entirely, require you to publish any modifications you make, and more. In short, always consult the license.

- *Public domain* software isn't owned by anyone. When the original developer releases any claim on it, anyone can do as they wish with it. Public domain software is usually (but not always) open source.

- *Proprietary* software is the opposite of public domain. A proprietary application clearly belongs to a company or individual who retains the rights to it, even if they are currently giving it away for free or making its source code available. In practice, proprietary software is usually closed source.

Single and Multi-use Licenses

If you buy software for personal use, you will probably get a *single-user license* that permits you to install the application on a single device or perhaps on a small fixed number of devices.

Schools and organizations can save money by purchasing a *multiple-user license* (also called a *volume license* or *site license*); they can distribute the same software to several users in their network. The organization pays the appropriate licensing and maintenance fees and ensures its users stay within legal bounds.

Multiple-user licensing comes in two main varieties. A *per-seat license* grants permission to install the application on a certain number of computers and has no specifications about how many people can use those computers. A *per-user license* grants permission to a certain number of users, who can use the software on multiple computers.

Product Keys and Activation

When installing an application, you might be prompted for a *product key,* which is a unique string of letters and numbers that identifies your copy of the application. Product keys are common as theft deterrents for high-priced software to prevent people from sharing their copy of the application with others. If you buy the application via download, you will receive an e-mail message containing the product key. Print it, and also keep a digital copy of it. If you buy the application in a retail box, the product key may be on a sticker or card inside or on a sticker on the disc sleeve, USB flash drive, box, or manual.

A product key, by itself, is not an effective theft deterrent, because people can just as easily provide their product key to others along with the setup files. Therefore, after the application setup has completed, you might be prompted to *activate* the software online. Activation locks that particular copy of the application (as indicated by the product key) to a particular computer so it can't be installed on any other computers. Some products that require activation give you a little leeway there, allowing installation on two or three computers before cutting you off.

How does activation work? The actual process is more complex than you probably want to know about, but essentially the setup program examines the computer's hardware components and generates a *hash* (a code created by performing some closely guarded math calculations). It then combines the hash with the product ID to create a unique value and assigns that value to that product key in a database. As a result, that same product key can be reused to install that same software on the same computer again because the hash code will match, but it can't be used on different hardware.

 EXAM TIP Be prepared to apply the software-management best practices in this chapter to specific scenarios. These practices include installation and uninstallation, patching and updates, version identification and compatibility, and licensing.

Chapter Review

This chapter looked at how to run applications in Windows, macOS, Linux, and Chrome OS. In Windows, the entry point for applications is the Start menu/screen, in macOS it is the Dock or the Launchpad application, and in Linux it is the Dash button or the Terminal window. In Chrome OS, you can click application links in the shelf or open Launcher.

It also explains how to install and remove applications. In Windows, the process is different depending on whether it is a desktop application or a Modern app. You can remove desktop applications via the Control Panel and can remove Modern apps from the Start menu/screen. On a Mac, you drag the application from the Applications folder to the Trash. In Ubuntu Linux, you use the Ubuntu Software Center. A right-click and Uninstall in the Launcher gets you there in Chrome OS.

We reviewed common applications and their uses, and you learned about many different file extensions and what kind of applications they are associated with. Along the way, you learned about formats for compressed archives, multimedia clips, and productivity applications.

Finally, we examined software licensing, including shareware, freeware, public domain, open source, and commercial licenses.

Questions

1. Where in Windows 8.1 can you browse installed applications?

   A. Apps list

   B. Dash pane

   C. Dock

   D. Windows Store

2. Where can you see what applications are installed in Ubuntu Linux?

   A. Apps list

   B. Dash pane

   C. Dock

   D. Windows Store

3. How do you install a Modern app in Windows 8.1 or 10?

   A. From the Control Panel

   B. From a downloaded executable file

   C. From the Store app

   D. From the Start menu/screen

4. What is the purpose of an application patch?

   A. Adding new features

   B. Removing the application

   C. Upgrading to a new version

   D. Correcting a problem

5. What can you find out about an application by choosing Help | About?

   A. Most recent data file used

   B. Supported extensions

   C. Application version number

   D. Windows version

6. How can you remove a Windows desktop application?

   A. From the Control Panel

   B. From the Store app

   C. From the Start menu/Start screen

   D. From the Dock

7. Which of these is a graphic format?

   A. PNG

   B. PPTX

   C. AVI

   D. TAR

8. Which of these is a productivity application?

   A. Microsoft Excel

   B. Candy Crush

   C. Windows Firewall

   D. Spotify

9. Which of these is a collaboration application?

   A. TurboTax

   B. Microsoft Word

    C. SharePoint

    D. Symantec Endpoint Protection

10. Which of these is a compression format?

    A. WAV

    B. TXT

    C. XLS

    D. RAR

Answers

1. A. In Windows 8.1, open the Start screen and then click the down arrow to view the Apps list, which shows all installed applications. The Dash pane is in Linux. The Dock is in macOS. The Windows Store is for acquiring new apps, not viewing existing ones.

2. B. The Dash pane shows installed applications in Linux. The Apps list is in Windows 8.1 and Windows 10. The Dock is in macOS. The Windows Store is not in Linux.

3. C. Modern apps come from the Store app. The Control Panel is not a place to install software (although you can remove software from there). A downloaded executable would be for a desktop app, not a Modern app. The Start menu/screen shows already installed apps.

4. D. A patch corrects a problem. New features and new versions are not provided in a patch. A patch does not remove the application.

5. C. Help | About will tell you the application's version number in many applications. It does not report the most recent data file, supported extensions, or Windows version.

6. A. Remove a desktop application from the Programs section of the Control Panel. The Store app installs applications; it doesn't remove them. The Start menu/Start screen could be used to remove a Modern app, not a desktop app. The Dock is used in macOS.

7. A. PNG is a graphic format, PPTX is a PowerPoint data file, AVI is a video file, and TAR is a compressed archive file.

8. A. Excel is a productivity application, used for spreadsheet creation. Candy Crush is a game. Windows Firewall is a utility. Spotify is a music player.

9. C. SharePoint is a collaboration application. TurboTax is a personal finance program. Microsoft Word is a productivity application (a word processor). Symantec Endpoint Protection is a utility.

10. D. RAR is a compression format, WAV is an audio format, TXT is a text file format, and XLS is a spreadsheet format.

Managing Files

In this chapter, you will learn how to
- Manage file storage
- Manipulate files and folders
- Protect files

The operating system (OS) enables you to store, organize, and retrieve data files—working with files is one of its primary functions. Your primary hard drive contains a ton of files, files that make up the OS, the apps, and the data. You can replace the OS and apps pretty easily, but the data needs protection. This chapter looks at organizing, manipulating, and backing up data.

NOTE Unless specifically noted otherwise, *hard drive* in this and other chapters includes both magnetic hard disk drives and flash-based solid-state drives.

Managing File Storage

Operating systems organize hard drives into volumes. A hard drive can have any number of volumes, though most users in Windows at least have a C:\ drive as their primary volume.

Understanding Folders and Paths

Each volume can store files, commonly organized into *folders* (also called *directories*). For example, windows computers have a Windows folder for the OS files, a Users folder to hold user profile information and data, and a Program Files folder to hold installed applications. Any folder can have many layers of subfolders nested inside it.

A *path* or *file path* describes the location of a particular file on a volume. It starts with the drive letter and then lists each folder and subfolder and ends with the file name. Each folder name is preceded by a backslash (\) in a path. Here's an example:

```
C:\Users\Mike\Documents\Projects\Invoice.xlsx
```

In Windows, the address bar in File Explorer shows file paths with arrows rather than slashes, like this:

```
C: > Users > Mike > Documents > Projects > Invoice.xlsx
```

In a graphical file management interface like File Explorer in Windows or Finder in macOS, folders are represented by icons that look like paper folders. When you display the contents of a folder, subfolders also appear as folder icons.

 EXAM TIP Make sure you understand the hierarchical way folders are nested on a volume and how to navigate between levels to find files.

At the top of the file hierarchy is the *root directory* of the volume—that is, the top level, not inside any other folder. Under the root directory are folders, along with any files stored in the root directory. (A few system files may be stored there, depending on the OS.) In a path, the root directory appears as a backslash all by itself (no folder name), as in C:\.

 CAUTION Avoid storing data files in the root directory of your system volume (your main hard drive). If you get into the habit of manipulating files in that location (for example, renaming them or deleting them), it becomes all too easy to accidentally delete an important system file.

Because folder structures can be complex, involving multiple layers of nesting, it is sometimes easier to look at a folder structure as a tree. In Windows' File Explorer, you can see a graphical view of the tree structure in the Navigation pane (the left pane). Figure 8-1 shows this tree structure.

Figure 8-1
A graphical tree helps visualize the folder structure in some file management utilities.

File Management Tools

In Windows 8 and later, File Explorer handles the file management chores. Earlier versions of Windows came with a similar tool called Windows Explorer. Look for the following features of File Explorer in Figure 8-2:

- **Address bar** This shows the current location's path.
- **Navigation pane** This shows the folder tree and shortcuts to common locations.
- **Files pane** This lists icons for files and folders in the current location.

 TIP Drag the divider between panes to adjust their relative sizes.

- **Ribbon** This multitabbed toolbar provides commands you can issue.
- **Back and Forward buttons** Click the Back button to return to the previously displayed location. This activates the Forward button, which you can click to get to the next location.

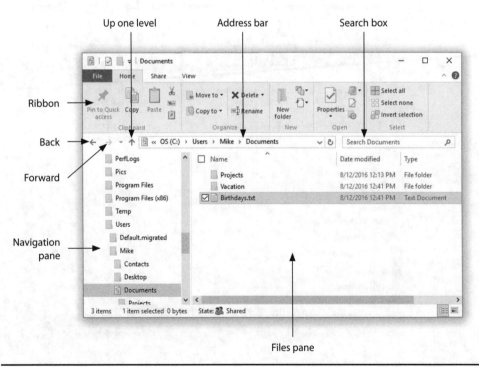

Figure 8-2 File Explorer in Windows 10

- **Up One Level**   Click here to move up one level in the folder hierarchy (that is, one step closer to the root directory).

- **Search box**   Click here and type a keyword to search for a file or folder.

In macOS, the Finder utility manages files. It has many of the same features as File Explorer. A toolbar across the top provides buttons for changing the view, adjusting settings, sharing files, and changing file properties. A Navigation pane at the left provides shortcuts to some locations, and a Search box enables you to search for a specific file or folder. Back and Forward arrow buttons are present as well.

Finder doesn't have an expandable folder tree (like the one in Figure 8-1) in its navigation pane, but you can see an expandable tree (shown in Figure 8-3) if you choose the List view (from the View buttons at the top of the window).

The Files utility in the Linux Unity GUI has a navigation pane without an expandable folder tree. It also indicates the current location in the path bar (though you can't click into it to manually edit the path without jumping through a few hoops). Figure 8-4 shows the Files utility's interface.

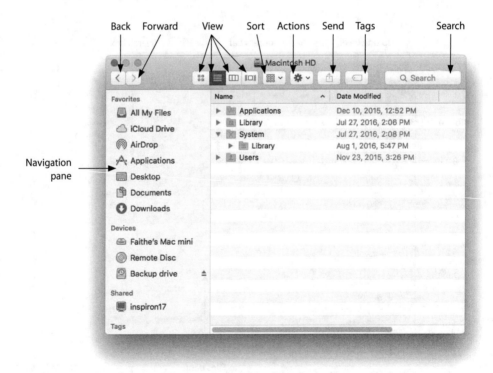

Figure 8-3   The Finder utility in macOS provides a graphical user interface (GUI) file management interface.

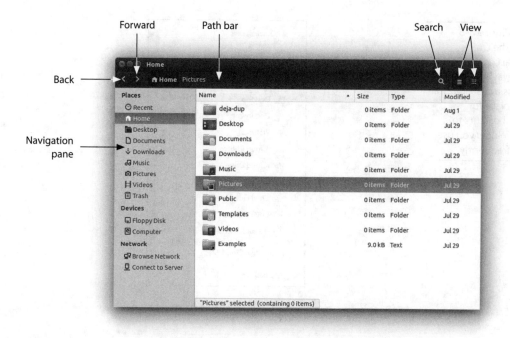

Figure 8-4   The Files utility in Unity provides a simple file management interface.

Any of these file management utilities can perform the actions you'll learn about in the "Manipulating Files" section later in this chapter, but the steps may differ slightly. The rest of this chapter focuses on the more common Windows interface.

EXAM TIP   As you prepare for the CompTIA IT Fundamentals exam, you might want to explore the macOS and Linux file management utilities on your own. See if you can perform the actions in this chapter on each OS.

Navigating a File Structure

You can navigate between locations in a file management utility in many ways. The easiest way is to click the location's shortcut in the Navigation pane. In Figure 8-2, for example, you can jump from the Mike\Documents folder to the Temp folder by clicking Temp in the Navigation pane.

EXAM TIP   Navigating a file structure (as Objective 5.2 calls it) means moving between file storage locations—from folder to folder and from volume to volume. If someone provides you with a path, you should be able to open that location in a file management utility.

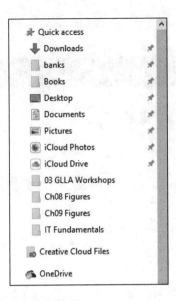

Figure 8-5
The Quick
access list in the
Navigation pane
is a customizable
place for
shortcuts to
folders you use
frequently.

At the top of the Navigation pane in File Explorer is a Quick access section, shown in Figure 8-5. Shortcuts appear here for recently used locations, as well as some common locations such as Documents, Pictures, and Desktop. You can also drag your favorite folders and files from the Files pane into the Navigation pane's Quick access section to pin them there. You can modify the look and feel of File Explorer to suit your needs. Figure 8-5 shows File Explorer with the banks and Books folder shortcuts added. Locations without a pushpin icon, by the way, appear temporarily because they have been used recently and may scroll off over time.

If the Navigation pane doesn't contain a shortcut to the desired location, you can browse for the location by starting at the top level of the volume and drilling down. In Windows 10, click This PC (called Computer in earlier Windows versions) in the Navigation pane to see a list of the local volumes in the Devices and Drives section of the Files pane. Double-click the desired volume, then double-click the desired folder, and keep double-clicking until you arrive at your destination.

You can also navigate to a folder by clicking its name in the path in the Address bar. Clicking the arrow between two folder names in the Address bar opens a menu of subfolders in the folder left of the arrow (see Figure 8-6); click a folder on that menu to jump to it.

EXAM TIP Objective 5.2 includes explaining the difference between shortcuts and files. Shortcuts, explained in Chapter 6, are pointers that refer to a file. They can appear not only on the desktop and Start menu but also in the file list for any folder.

Figure 8-6
Subfolder menu
in the Address
bar

File and Folder Properties

Each file and folder has a number of properties that describe it, such as its size, its type, and its creation date. A file's properties are sometimes referred to as its *metadata,* which literally means "data about the data." Let's look at attributes, file size, keywords, and program association.

Basic File Attributes

Attributes (sometimes called *flags*) are yes/no values for a file. There are four basic file attributes: read-only, system, hidden, and archive.

- **Read-only**   *Read-only* marks a file as unchangeable. You can read the file, but if you modify the file, you need to save it under a different name. Read-only protects the original file from change.

- **System**   A file marked *system* is hidden by default and protected from accidental deletion.

- **Hidden**   A *hidden* file acts like its name would suggest, hiding from the default view in File Explorer.

- **Archive**   A file with the *archive* attribute active indicates the file has changed since the last system backup. When a backup utility backs up a file, it turns this attribute off. When the file changes, the OS turns the attribute on, so the backup program will know that it needs to be backed up again next time it runs.

Advanced File Attributes

Most hard drives in Windows systems use a file system called *NTFS* file system. NTFS offers additional advanced attributes, such as indexing, compression, and encryption.

Indexed   Windows (and some applications) can search file contents for something the user wants to find, but this can take a long time (especially on slow or large drives). Allowing a file's content to be indexed makes those searches go faster.

Compressed   NTFS enables file compression so files take up less space on the volume. This compression is invisible to the user; the only thing you might notice is that the file takes slightly longer to open and to save. Compression can be enabled for individual files, though it is more often enabled for entire folders thus affecting all files they contain.

Encrypted   In some Windows editions, NTFS enables file encryption. This encryption is invisible to the file's owner. When another user on the same local computer tries to access the file or folder, however, its access is protected by the encryption.

NOTE   If encryption isn't available on your PC, you probably don't have a Windows edition that supports it. Encryption is available only on professional editions such as Windows 7 Professional, Enterprise, or Ultimate; Windows 8.1 Pro; or Windows 10 Pro.

Folder Attributes
Many file attributes can also be applied to folders. An attribute applied to a folder applies to all files within that folder, so assigning attributes at the folder level is a great time-saver.

File Size and Other Noneditable Properties
Some file properties simply describe the file. You can change them only by modifying the file. These include the file's size, when it was created, when it was last modified or accessed, and so on.

Keywords
Certain kinds of data files can have Details assigned to them. Details can include tags (keywords), a subject, the authors' names, categories, and comments.

Viewing and Modifying Properties
To view (and optionally modify) properties via a file's Properties dialog box, right-click the file's name in File Explorer and choose Properties.

On the General tab, shown in Figure 8-7, you can see many of the noneditable properties, such as size and creation date/time. You can also mark or clear the Read-only and Hidden attribute check boxes.

To access other attributes, click the Advanced button to open the Advanced Attributes dialog box (shown in Figure 8-8). Here you can toggle the attributes that control whether the file is archived, indexed, compressed, and encrypted.

To access other properties such as the title, subject, and tags, click the Details tab, shown in Figure 8-9. Click next to an item in the Description area to edit it. You can't edit the properties in the Origin section.

File and Folder Size
As you saw in Figure 8-7, a file's size describes how much space it occupies on the volume. A folder technically has no size of its own; it is just a container. In practice, though, a folder's size is shown as the sum of the size of every file it holds. To see a folder's size, open its Properties box and look on the General tab. You'll also see a summary of what the folder contains. In Figure 8-10, for example, the folder contains 1536 files and 560 subfolders.

Figure 8-7
View a file's
properties from
its Properties
dialog box.

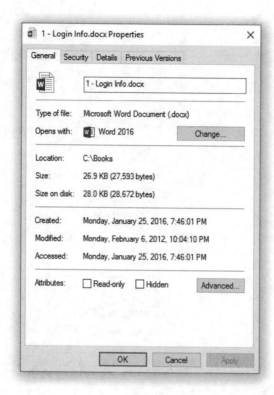

Figure 8-8
Use the
Advanced
Attributes dialog
box to turn other
attributes on/off.

PART II

Figure 8-9
Set other
properties on the
Details tab.

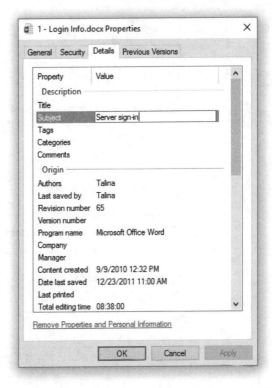

Figure 8-10
Viewing a folder's
information

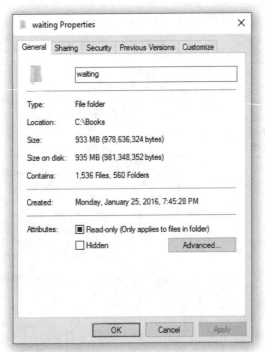

Manipulating Files and Folders

You will likely need to take some actions on the data files you create in various applications. For example, you might need to edit, rename, copy, move, or even delete a file. The following sections summarize how to perform the most common file manipulations in Windows.

Opening, Editing, and Saving Files

There are several ways to open a data file. Here are some of the easiest:

- **Open an application** that can work with data files of that type and then use the Open command in the application to select and open the desired file.

- **Double-click the data file** in File Explorer to open the file (in the default application).

- **Double-click a shortcut** to the data file. For example, you might have created a shortcut on the Windows desktop to a file that you use frequently.

TIP   To create a shortcut on the desktop for a data file, right-drag the data file out of File Explorer and onto the desktop. (In other words, drag it using the right mouse button, rather than the left one.) When you release the mouse button, a menu appears. Select Create shortcuts here.

How does Windows know which application to open the data file in when you double-click a data file? It all depends on the file extension. As you learned in Chapter 7, a file's extension lets the OS know what kind of file it is. A .txt file is a text file, for example, and a .bmp file is a graphic file. Each data file extension has a default application assigned to it. This is called its *association*. When you double-click a data file, Windows opens it with the default application listed in its internal table of file associations.

If the application supports editing the file, you can make and save changes to it in the application. Microsoft Word can edit the text—for example, change the formatting, or insert new content, such as a graphic. If you don't know how to make a certain kind of edit, use the application's help system to find out. Pressing the F1 key will open the help system in most applications.

To save a file, use the Save command in the application. See the section "Saving Your Work" in Chapter 7 for details.

EXAM TIP   Be sure you know how and where to open, edit, and save files within an operating system or application.

Moving and Copying Files and Folders

Moving and copying are similar activities, so we cover them as a pair. When you move a file, you remove it from one location and put it in another location. When you copy a file, you *don't* remove it from the first location; you just place a copy of it somewhere else.

To move or copy files (and folders) between locations, you have three methods to choose from: drag-and-drop, the Clipboard (cut/copy/paste), and the Move and Copy commands in File Explorer.

Selecting Multiple Files and Folders

You will eventually want to move or copy multiple files and folders at a time. To select multiple files and folders, use these techniques:

- To select multiple *contiguous* items (located next to each other), click the first one, hold down SHIFT, and click the last one. All the items between the two files are selected. Alternatively, drag with the mouse to draw a selection box around the files you want to include.

- To select multiple *noncontiguous* items (not located next to each other), click the first one, hold down CTRL, and click each additional item that you want.

Drag-and-Drop

As the name implies, drag-and-drop means selecting the files and/or folders and then using the mouse to move them or copy them somewhere else.

You can open two separate File Explorer windows, navigate to a different location in each, and then drag between them. As you drag, a thumbnail of the file appears on the mouse pointer, along with a label that tells whether it will move (as in Figure 8-11) or copy them.

 TIP To open a second File Explorer window when one is already open, right-click the File Explorer window's button on the taskbar and choose File Explorer. You can also just drag-and-drop files onto one of the location shortcuts in the Navigation pane without opening another File Explorer.

Figure 8-11   Drag-and-drop to move or copy.

How do you specify that you want a move versus a copy? It's a bit tricky. When you drag-and-drop between locations on the *same* volume, Windows moves the files by default. If you want to copy instead, hold down the CTRL key as you drag. When you drag-and-drop between locations in *different* volumes, Windows copies by default; if you want to move instead, hold down the SHIFT key. If you aren't sure whether the locations are on the same volume or not, you can still hold down CTRL to copy or SHIFT to move. You can also just right-drag, in which case a menu pops up when you release the mouse button asking what you want to do.

TIP   Holding down ALT as you drag creates a shortcut.

Cut-and-Paste

The Cut, Copy, and Paste commands use the Clipboard, which is a temporary holding area in memory. When you select a file (or a group of files or folders) and issue the Cut command, the selected items are removed from their current location and placed on the Clipboard. If you issue the Copy command, in contrast, a copy is placed on the Clipboard, and the original stays in place.

EXAM TIP   Make sure you understand the relationship between the Clipboard and the Cut, Copy, and Paste commands.

The Clipboard can hold the contents of only one Cut or Copy operation at a time. (A Cut or Copy operation can be performed on a multifile/multifolder selection, though, so it's not like you have to move or copy files individually.) When you choose Cut or Copy again, whatever was previously on the Clipboard is replaced with the new content.

NOTE   If you use the Clipboard feature in Microsoft Office applications, an enhanced Clipboard is available that can hold up to 24 selections at once.

File Explorer supports two methods of accessing Clipboard commands.

- **Shortcut keys**   CTRL-C for copy, CTRL-X to cut, CTRL-V to paste.
- **Shortcut menu**   Right-click the selection and click Cut, Copy, or Paste. Figure 8-12 shows the shortcut menu for a group of selected files. The Paste command doesn't appear in Figure 8-12 because there is currently nothing to paste. (Nothing has yet been cut or copied.)

Move to and Copy to Commands

Here's one more method for moving and copying. In File Explorer, the Home tab of the ribbon contains Move to and Copy to buttons. Select the desired items and then click one of these buttons; a menu of recently accessed locations will appear. Select a location

Figure 8-12
Right-click for the
shortcut menu
and then choose
Cut, Copy, or
Paste.

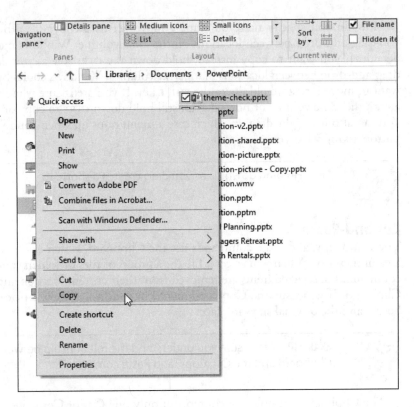

from the menu to complete the operation. If you don't see the location you want, click Choose Location from the bottom of the menu.

Renaming Files and Folders

To rename a file or folder in File Explorer (you can't rename more than one at a time), use one of these methods:

- Right-click the item, click Rename, type the new name, and press ENTER.
- Select the item, press F2, type the new name, and press ENTER.
- Click the item and then click it again to move the insertion point into the name. Edit the name and press ENTER.
- Select the item, click Rename on the Home tab of the ribbon, type a new name, and press ENTER.

CAUTION File extensions are not displayed for known file types by default in File Explorer. You can toggle their display on/off from the View tab, with the File name extensions check box. When file extensions are displayed, you can change a file's extension when you rename it. Be careful: Windows relies on the file extension to know what kind of file it is and which app should open it.

Deleting and Undeleting Files and Folders

Deleting unneeded files and folders keeps your file system orderly and frees up disk space. However, deleting a file or folder doesn't automatically remove it from your hard drive. By default, the Delete command sends the files or folders to a special folder called Recycle Bin. You can restore deleted items from the Recycle Bin to correct any deletion mistakes.

 TIP The Recycle Bin works only for local hard drives; it doesn't retain deleted files from network shares, USB flash drives, or optical discs.

To delete files or folders (and send them to the Recycle Bin, if available for the volume you are working with), select them and then do one of the following:

- Press the DELETE key.
- Right-click the selection and choose Delete.
- On the Home tab on the ribbon, click Delete, or click the down arrow on the Delete button and click Recycle Bin.

To delete files or folders permanently (without sending them to the Recycle Bin), do one of the following:

- Press SHIFT-DELETE.
- On the Home tab, click the down arrow on the Delete button and click Permanently delete.

To undelete, open the Recycle Bin by double-clicking its icon on the desktop. All the deleted content appears there. Figure 8-13 shows some deleted content in the Recycle Bin. Select an item; then on the Manage tab, click Restore the Selected Items. You can also right-click an item and choose Restore.

To permanently delete an item, delete it from the Recycle Bin. (Select it and press the DELETE key.) To empty the entire Recycle Bin at once, click Manage | Empty Recycle Bin.

 TIP To empty the Recycle Bin without opening the Recycle Bin window, right-click the Recycle Bin icon on the desktop and choose Empty Recycle Bin.

Searching, Sorting, and Displaying Files

As you accumulate files on your computer, it's easy to forget where you stored a certain file or what you named it. There are several ways of displaying file listings that can make it easier to find what you need, such as searching, sorting, and changing the display view.

Searching for Specific Files

For a quick search, use the Search box in the upper-right corner of the File Explorer window. Just type what you know about the file, either the name or the content, and press ENTER. Results appear in the Files pane.

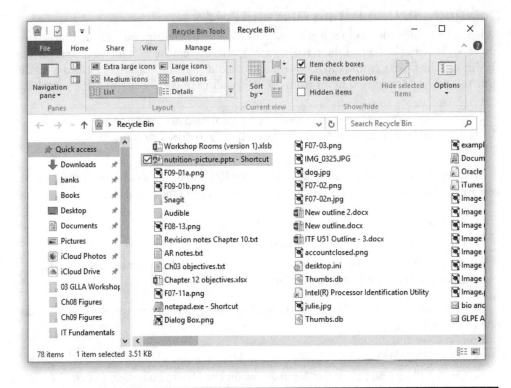

Figure 8-13 You can restore deleted files from the Recycle Bin.

For a more advanced search, click the magnifying glass icon in the Search pane to open the Search tab in the ribbon, as shown in Figure 8-14. Then use the options that appear to refine the search criteria as desired. You can limit the search to a certain file type, for example, or to size or date modified.

Changing the View

On the View tab in File Explorer you can select a view from the Layout group, shown in Figure 8-15. Different views work for different situations.

- The Small icons and List views show files in a compact way that helps when working with many files at once.
- The Details view (see Figure 8-15) shows multiple columns of data about the files, such as Size, Type, and Date Modified, making it ideal for browsing files by size, date, name, and so on.
- The Extra large icons, Large icons, and Medium icons views show a preview of the file if possible, which is great for finding images and documents by look instead of name (see Figure 8-16).

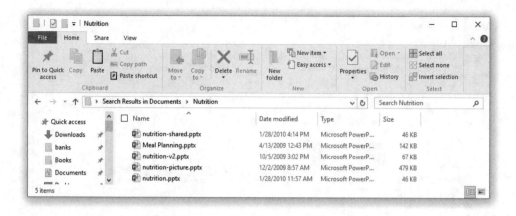

Figure 8-14 Use the Search tab on the ribbon in File Explorer to specify search criteria.

Also on the View tab are additional controls that affect the way you see the file listing, including these:

- **Navigation pane** Clicking this button opens a menu containing three options:
  - **Expand to open folder** Expands the folder tree to show the path to the folder displayed in the Files pane
  - **Show all folders** Shows additional shortcuts in the Navigation pane for locations such as the Control Panel, Recycle Bin, and folders on the desktop
  - **Show libraries** Shows shortcuts to the Libraries folders in the Navigation pane

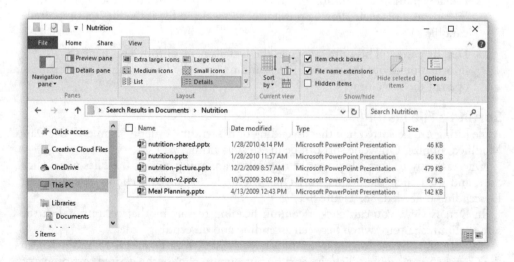

Figure 8-15 Details view

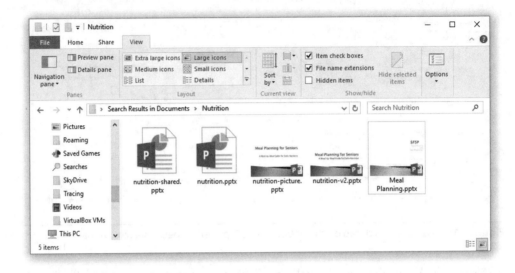

Figure 8-16 Large icons view

 NOTE Libraries, introduced in Windows 7, is a virtual location that combines the contents from multiple locations in a single window, as if all the files and folders were in one location. This way, you can use many folders on more than one volume to organize your pictures, videos, or music but still have a single place to browse all of your pictures at once.

- **Preview pane** This button toggles the Preview pane on/off to the right of the Files pane. This pane shows a preview of the selected file if the file is a supported data file.

- **Details pane** This button toggles the Details pane on/off. This pane shows information about the selected file. You can't have the Preview and Details panes open at the same time.

Sorting a File Listing

A file listing can be sorted in either ascending or descending order by Name, Type, Date Modified, or Size. Only one sort can be in effect at a time.

One easy way to sort a listing is to right-click an empty area of the Files pane, click Sort, and then click the desired sort type. Right-click again and choose Ascending or Descending if needed. See Figure 8-17.

In Details view, you can click a column heading to sort by that column. Click the same column again to switch between ascending and descending order.

You can also change sorting from the View tab (shown in Figures 8-15 and 8-16), in the Current View group. Click the Sort by button and choose the desired sort property. There are more properties available to sort by on this menu than on the right-click menu.

Figure 8-17
You can sort
using the right-
click menu.

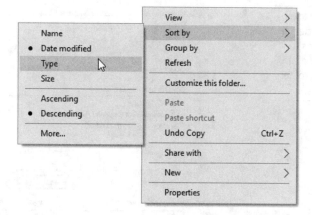

Protecting Files

In this final section of the chapter, we'll look at some ways you can protect your files from snooping by other people who use your computer and how you can back up your files as an insurance policy against hard drive failures.

File and Folder Permissions

Your files are your own private business…until someone else who uses your computer starts snooping around. Protect your privacy by setting restrictions on who may view or edit certain folders on the local hard drives. These are called *local permissions*. The word *local* differentiates these permissions from *sharing*, which occurs across networks.

On a computer that multiple people share, you can set up a separate user account for each person. You can then restrict access to certain folders to only certain users (or only you). You can set permissions for individual files, but it is better to set permissions at the folder level. That way everything in the folder has the specified permissions, and you can set permissions for other files just by moving them into that folder.

To set a folder's permissions, right-click the folder in File Explorer, choose Properties, and then click the Security tab. On the Security tab, you can view permissions for specific users or groups of users. Some groups are built-in so that when you assign permissions to that group, everyone in that group also has those permissions. The Administrators group, for example, includes all user accounts with Administrator permissions. (The default is Standard permissions.)

To make a change, click the Edit button on the Security tab, opening the Permissions dialog box (see Figure 8-18). From here you can add users to the Group or user names list, and you can set Allow or Deny permissions for each file management activity for each group or user. Figure 8-18 shows that user Mike can view the selected folder but can't modify it.

CAUTION   Avoid using the Deny permission option. Yes, it works, but it's all too easy to create tough-to-troubleshoot problems if you start mixing Allow and Deny permissions for different groups. If a user is a member of multiple groups and one group is allowed and one group is denied, the effective permissions can become a confusing mess. A lack of Allow stops access, so just stick to allowing or not allowing.

Figure 8-18
Modify folder
permissions to
control who can
access the folder
locally.

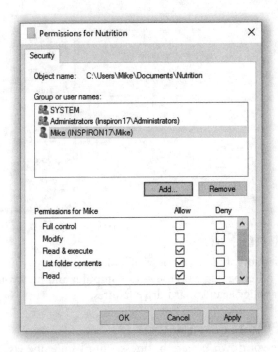

Backing Up and Restoring Data

On most computers, the stored data is more valuable than the computer itself. Let's say your hard drive dies and you suddenly lose access to everything it contains. Or, perhaps a child in your household decides to delete everything in your Documents folder to clear out space for the new game he wants to install. How bad would that be? Catastrophic? Panic-inducing just to think about? That's why backups are so important.

Backups can be performed automatically via a backup utility, or manually by copying files to an external drive using the Copy command in File Explorer. Both methods have their advantages.

Backup Software vs. Manually Copying Files

Most businesses have an automated backup system that backs up files from individual computers daily, usually in the middle of the night when network traffic is low. As a result, the average employee doesn't have to think about backups. Backups just happen.

Home and individual users, however, don't have access to an IT department and need to think about their own backup needs. A consumer-level backup utility is one option. Using a backup utility, since it is automated, takes less time, and you don't have to remember to do it. A backup utility also compresses the files as it backs them up, so the backups take up less drive space than the originals. However, the backups it creates aren't ready-to-use versions of the files; they're compressed into archive files. If you ever need to access the backed-up files, you must use the same backup utility to extract them.

Copying files manually to a volume results in ready-to-use backup copies, which is convenient if you need quick access to a backed-up file. You need to exercise discipline if you plan to go the manual route.

There are three main classes of backup applications. The first kind makes an image of the entire hard drive and then restores the disk image to new hardware in the event of a drive failure. This is sometimes called *imaging software*. Some popular imaging applications include StorageCraft ShadowProtect and Acronis True Image.

A second kind backs up individual files and folders that you specify. Microsoft Windows 7 comes with a Backup utility that does this kind of backup. Windows 8 and later offer a third style of backup called File History that uses an additional storage drive to back up personal documents. Apple includes Time Machine with macOS to take snapshots of user documents.

Online Storage as Backup Media

If you use a cloud storage service like OneDrive or online storage provided by your employer, you might want to back up your important files to the cloud. This can be a simple, cost-effective way to keep your files safe because it doesn't involve any special utilities. In Windows, each user has a OneDrive folder in his or her user folders; a shortcut to it appears in the Navigation pane in File Explorer. When you place files in that folder, they are saved locally on your hard drive, but they are also uploaded to the OneDrive cloud, and any changes you make to the local copies are mirrored automatically in the online versions. Other cloud-based file storage systems can be configured to work similarly.

Backup Scheduling and Frequency

Whether you use a backup program or make backup copies manually, you should have a schedule in place to make sure you have recent backups available at all times. A backup utility will have a scheduling component that you can set up to perform a backup at specified intervals. If you're making your own backup copies, you'll need to create a reminder for yourself, perhaps in a calendar program.

Most data security experts recommend performing a weekly or monthly backup of the full set of your important data files as a starting point and then saving incremental daily changes.

Backup Storage Media

For maximum safety (in terms of your data surviving catastrophic what-ifs), you should back up to a different physical location than where your computer resides. If your home or office burns to the ground or gets swept away by a hurricane or earthquake, at least one copy of your data should ideally be far from danger.

There are several methods:

- You can back up to an off-site cloud-based location via the Internet.
- If your company has multiple locations, you could use the company's network to send your backup files to a network drive located in a different city or in a different building, city, or even continent.
- You could also make backups to an external locally attached storage device (such as an external hard drive, USB thumb drive, or optical disc) and then physically carry (or ship) it somewhere else (take it home, for example, or leave it in a safe-deposit box).

If your data is not so important that you need to go to all that trouble, a lower level of protection would be to duplicate the data outside of your computer. Send it via LAN to network attached storage (NAS), for example, or back up to an external drive. *Network attached storage* connects to your network independently of any particular computer, such as a file server or a *NAS appliance* (a specialized network-enabled external drive that multiple users can share).

 EXAM TIP Objective 5.4 lists three storage media to be aware of for backups: locally attached storage, off-site/cloud-based storage, and network attached storage. Make sure you understand the convenience and safety trade-offs for each of these storage locations.

Backup Verification and Testing

If you go to the trouble of setting up a backup schedule (and perhaps purchasing backup software), make sure it works. Don't wait until disaster strikes and you need to restore your files before you test the process!

The first time you use a new backup method, verify the backups. Test them by going through the restoration process, and make sure the files are completely and accurately restored to their original locations. After you have verified that the process works, spot-check it regularly. The more critical the data, the more often you should check.

Chapter Review

In this chapter, you learned about folders and paths and how to navigate them using an OS file management utility. You worked mostly with File Explorer in Windows but learned that the equivalent utilities are Finder in macOS and Files in (Ubuntu) Linux.

You learned how to view and change file and folder properties using the Properties box in File Explorer and about the four basic attributes: read-only, system, hidden, and archive. You saw that file properties include size, dates created and modified, and keywords.

You learned how to manipulate files and folders in Microsoft Windows including how to open, edit, save, move, copy, rename, and delete. You also learned how to search, sort, and display file listings, as well as how to protect your important files with local permissions and backups.

Questions

1. Which of these is a correctly written file path?

   A. C:>Books/Mike\birthdays.txt

   B. C:/Books/Mike/birthdays.txt

   C. C:\Books\Mike\birthdays.txt

   D. C:\\Books\Mike\birthdays.txt

2. What is a root directory?

    A. The top-level storage location on a volume

    B. The folder containing the system files

    C. The folder containing the boot files

    D. The folder containing the signed-in user's personal files

3. What is the file management tool in macOS?

    A. File Explorer

    B. Dock

    C. Launcher

    D. Finder

4. Which of these is an on/off flag for a file?

    A. Size

    B. Archive

    C. Date modified

    D. Date created

5. Which file property makes a search faster for content within files?

    A. Archive

    B. Indexed

    C. Compressed

    D. Encrypted

6. What action opens a data file for editing in the application associated with its extension?

    A. Double-click

    B. Right-click

    C. CTRL-click

    D. SHIFT-click

7. How do you select multiple noncontiguous files in a file listing?

    A. CTRL-click

    B. SHIFT-click

    C. Double-click

    D. Right-click

8. CTRL-V is a keyboard shortcut in Windows for what activity?

   A. Copy

   B. Paste

   C. Cut

   D. Delete

9. In File Explorer, from which tab can you select a different view?

   A. View

   B. Share

   C. Details

   D. Home

10. Which utility in macOS backs up user files automatically?

   A. Backup

   B. File Explorer

   C. File History

   D. Time Machine

Answers

1. C. A correctly written path begins with the drive letter, a colon, and one backslash, and separates locations with backslashes. The other options don't follow this pattern.

2. A. The root directory is the top-level location on a volume. The other options don't describe the top-level location.

3. D. Finder is the macOS file management utility. File Explorer is the Windows file management utility. Dock and Launcher are components of macOS and Linux, respectively, but not involving file management.

4. B. Archive is an on/off flag (attribute). The others all have specific values.

5. B. Indexed allows a file's content to be indexed, speeding up searches. Archive indicates whether a file has changed since it has been backed up. Compressed and Encrypted are NTFS-specific properties that control how the file is stored.

6. A. Double-click a data file to open it. Right-click it to see a shortcut menu. CTRL-click and SHIFT-click select multiple files in a file listing.

7. A. CTRL-click each item to select them. SHIFT-click selects multiple contiguous files. Double-click opens a file. Right-click displays a shortcut menu.

8. B. CTRL-V is for Paste. CTRL-C is for copy. CTRL-X is for cut. DELETE is for deletion.

9. A. Change the view on the View tab. The Share and Home tabs do not contain view commands. Details is not a tab; it is a pane that you access from the View tab.

10. D. macOS uses Time Machine to back up user files automatically.

Setting Up and Configuring a Mobile Device

In this chapter, you will learn how to

- Describe features that mark mobile devices
- Set up and manage mobile device security
- Establish wireless connectivity and pairing
- Configure e-mail
- Configure synchronization
- Install and remove apps

Writers and teachers on computing devices tend to focus on the desktop computers running Windows or macOS. Some might tip the hat to laptops or Chromebooks, but those devices run standard desktop operating systems.

The vast majority of consumers around the world, on the other hand, use a radically different computing device—a mobile device like a smartphone.

The CompTIA IT Fundamentals exam likewise focuses on Windows PCs, but you need to understand a lot about mobile devices to function in today's mobile world. This chapter goes a little beyond the exam objectives, but offers very relevant information for any computer user.

The chapter starts with an overview of mobile devices. It then hits five major aspects of the mobile computing experience:

- How to set up a mobile device
- How to establish wireless connections
- How to configure e-mail
- How to sync with other devices
- How to install and remove apps

We have a lot of ground to cover, so let's get started.

Mobile Devices: A Quick Overview

Mobile devices have three features that distinguish them from desktop computing devices: size, interface, and OS.

Size matters. Mobile devices come in four basic formats, all designed to hold in your hand or wear like jewelry:

- Smartphone
- Tablet
- Phablet
- Wearable

A *smartphone* combines a mobile phone and a small handheld computer, and a *tablet* is a slate-style touchscreen device, which may or may not have cell phone capability. Tablets that have phones in them are referred to as *phablets*. There are also several kinds of specialty mobile devices, such as mobile media players, fitness trackers, and e-readers, but they are less popular because smartphones and tablets can do the same things they do and more. A *mobile media player* is a device that plays music or videos but does little else.

EXAM TIP Objective 2.1 of the CompTIA IT Fundamentals exam mentions mobile media players. A decade or so ago, you would find mobile music players like iPods in almost every pocket, but they are a dying breed in everyday life today because smartphones and tablets play video and audio so well.

Mobile devices have *touchscreen* interfaces (which you know from earlier chapters), but you can also use a pen-like input device. A simple *stylus* affects most touchscreens like a finger would, but a few devices with advanced digitizers support a pressure-sensitive stylus tailored for digital writing, drawing, and painting on the device.

The major operating systems for mobile devices are Android, iOS, and Windows. Android enjoys the most market share with about 84 percent, probably because it is free (so Android devices tend to be more affordable). Apple's iOS comes in second at around 15 percent. Mobile Windows devices use special versions of Windows that differ from the Windows you know as a desktop and laptop operating system. Windows Phone has a paltry 0.7 percent of the market, and the BlackBerry OS, once a powerhouse player in mobile devices, now has only 0.2 percent. This chapter focuses on Android and iOS, though it touches on potential exam questions about the others.

NOTE These statistics refer to the first quarter of 2016 and come from www .gartner.com/newsroom/id/3323017. The exact figures change constantly, but the general trend holds steady: Android and iOS are the main mobile operating systems, and everything else trails far behind.

Setting Up the Device

When you unpack a new mobile device, connect it to alternating current (AC) power and press its power button to turn it on and start the setup routine. Some devices require you to hold the power button down for a few seconds until something appears on the screen or until you feel the device vibrate briefly. Check the documentation to find the power button if needed.

The device will go through a setup process the first time you turn it on, which may include entering information about yourself and your location, calibrating the touchscreen, and granting permission for the device to use certain online services and apps. Just follow the prompts.

Understanding the Interface

Both Android and iOS use the same basic desktop metaphor for navigation. The Home screen features a collection of icons. Each icon represents a different feature or app. You can customize this Home screen by reordering the icons and creating groups to organize them. Figures 9-1 and 9-2 show the Android and iPhone interfaces, respectively.

Figure 9-1
Android
smartphone
Home screen

Figure 9-2
iPhone Home
screen

NOTE The iOS experience is fairly consistent because it runs only on Apple hardware, but Android runs on so many different brands of hardware that there are different procedures. For example, some Android phones have a hardware Home button, and others don't. Most companies customize the version of Android that they put on their devices. (Like Linux, Android is open source.) If you have an Android device that doesn't work as described, it's probably because of some brand-specific differences; check your device's documentation or online support site.

To return to the Home screen, press the Home button, which may be a hardware button on the device or an onscreen icon (Figure 9-3). Returning to the Home screen does not exit open apps.

To switch among open apps in Android, tap the Recent Apps icon at the bottom of the screen or press and hold (also called a *long press*) the Home button, depending on the device. Small images (*thumbnails*) of the open apps appear. Tap the one you want.

Figure 9-3
Home and
Recent Apps
icons

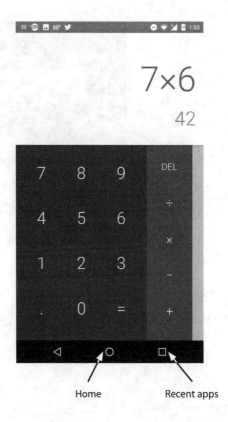

Home   Recent apps

In iOS, double-press the Home button (Figure 9-4). Images of the open apps appear, as shown in Figure 9-5. You can page through them by swiping left or right and then tap the one you want. To close an open app, swipe upward on it when in this view.

Figure 9-4
Home button on
an iPhone

Home button

Figure 9-5
Swipe through
the open apps
and tap the one
you want in iOS.

Using Gestures

Gestures—various actions using one or more finger—enable you to interact with a touch-screen. These input options are called *gesture-based interaction*. Here are some examples:

- **Tap**   Briefly touch the surface with a fingertip.
- **Double-tap**   Rapidly touch the surface twice with a fingertip.
- **Swipe**   Touch the screen and then drag your finger across it in a certain direction. For example, you could swipe left or right. In some apps, swiping left (that is, moving your finger from right to left) goes back to the previous screen or page.
- **Pinch**   Touch the surface with two fingers spread apart and then pinch them closer together to zoom out. To zoom in, start with your fingers together and spread them apart. Some people collectively call these pinch in/closed and pinch out/open gestures *pinch-to-zoom*.

- **Rotate** You can touch the surface with two fingers as you would to zoom out but then rotate them on the screen. This is often used to rotate images in photo-viewing or editing programs or to rotate the map orientation in a navigation app.

 EXAM TIP Objective 1.4 of the CompTIA IT Fundamentals exam calls these touchscreen actions *gesture-based interaction*.

Understanding Kinetics

Many mobile devices include *kinetics*—electronic sensors that track the device's position and movement in 3D space. You don't have to do anything to these sensors. They just exist, doing their jobs and reporting their data to any apps that ask for it. For exam prep, understand the concept of kinetics and the types of sensors included under that umbrella.

The sensors inside a typical smartphone or tablet include the following:

- **Accelerometer** Determines how fast the device is moving through space, like a speedometer does for an automobile.
- **Magnetometer** Works like a compass to detect the device's orientation relative to the earth's magnetic north.
- **Gyroscope** Measures the rotational velocity and position along three axes (in 3D space). This is also called the Attitude sensor or the Rotation sensor. This is the sensor that, among other things, senses the orientation of the device and rotates the screen.

 EXAM TIP For the Kinetics topic in Objective 1.4, make sure you understand the sensors inside a mobile device that detect its position and movement: the accelerometer, magnetometer, and gyroscope.

Controlling Screen Orientation

By default, smartphone and tablet screens change their orientation automatically depending on the orientation of the device. So, for example, if you turn your iPhone clockwise, the interface rotates and changes to wide-screen mode. You can optionally lock the screen in either portrait (tall) or landscape (wide) orientation if you prefer.

In iOS, you can lock or unlock the screen orientation by doing the following:

1. If you want to lock the screen to a particular orientation, start in that orientation.

2. From the Home screen, swipe upward from the bottom.

3. Tap the Orientation Lock icon (Figure 9-6).

Figure 9-6
Orientation Lock

Here's how to do the same thing in Android:

1. If you want to lock the screen into a particular orientation, start in that orientation.

2. Swipe down from the right side of the top panel.

3. Tap the Auto Rotate button.

Alternatively, in Android you can go to Settings | Accessibility and select Auto-rotate screen.

Security Features

All modern tablets and smartphones include security capabilities that keep unauthorized users out of your device. The following sections explain some of the security features you can employ.

 EXAM TIP Chapters 11 and 12 cover more security features on both mobile and desktop computing devices, such as disabling unused features like Bluetooth so they cannot be used by attackers.

Setting and Changing a Lock Passcode

If you set a device's *screen lock*, it will always wake up to the *lock screen*. You can just swipe to unlock the simplest screen locks, but more secure locks prompt you for a password or short *passcode*, as in Figure 9-7.

Depending on the OS type and version, different passcode options may be available. For example, you might be able to choose between a four-digit number, a six-digit number, or an alphanumeric code (letters and numbers). A six-digit alphanumeric combination offers the highest security. Figure 9-8 shows these options on an iPhone. On some newer devices you can authenticate your identity with a fingerprint reader.

On an Android phone, tap the Settings icon and tap Lock Screen to access the passcode options. In iOS, tap the Settings icon (which looks like a gray cog) and then tap Touch ID & Passcode. From there you can set and change your passcode.

TIP   You might also want to change the lock timeout (how long the device can idle before the screen turns off and locks). A shorter time makes for better security, but a longer time is more convenient.

Figure 9-7
Prompting for a
passcode

Figure 9-8
Choose the level
of passcode
security you want
to use.

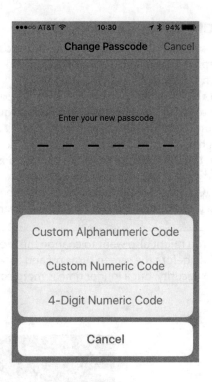

Configuring Account IDs and Passwords

Some activities require extra authentication beyond unlocking the phone. When you make purchases in an app store using a stored credit card number, for example, the store typically prompts you for a password. For an Android phone, this is your Google Account. For an iPhone, this is your Apple ID.

Managing Lost Device Security

So, you've lost your smartphone or tablet, and you are panicking—not so much for the loss of the device itself, although that's an inconvenience, but for the violation of your privacy. Maybe you had all your account passwords stored there for various Web sites, or your deepest darkest secrets were kept in your phone's diary.

If it's an Android device signed into a Google account, you can use the Android Device Manager on any device with a Web browser to show your device's location (Figure 9-9). For this to work, the device needs to have a Wi-Fi or mobile data connection and an active SIM card. In other words, whoever holds the device can just turn it off or pop the SIM card out to keep you from locating it. The Android Device Manager also allows you to remotely ring, lock, or erase the device.

If you successfully locate it, the device itself will show a notification (Figure 9-10). This is good (for you) if *someone else* has managed to access your Google account and is

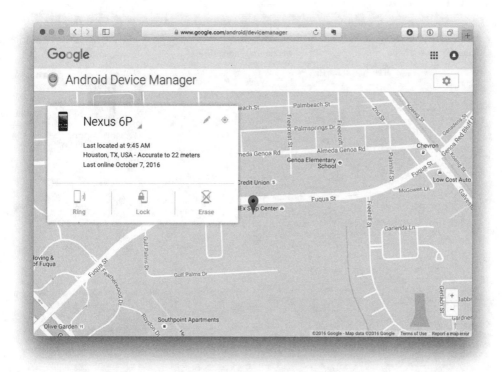

Figure 9-9   Android Device Manager finding a lost smartphone

using it to locate you, but if *someone else* has the device in-hand, they may notice that you're locating the device. If you're coming to wipe private information, be prepared to act swiftly.

On an iOS device, sign into iCloud using a Web browser and select Find iPhone. Then click All Devices and select the desired device (Figure 9-11).

Figure 9-10
Android phone
receiving a
notification
that it has been
located

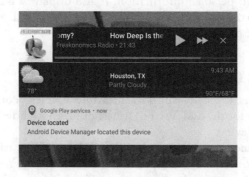

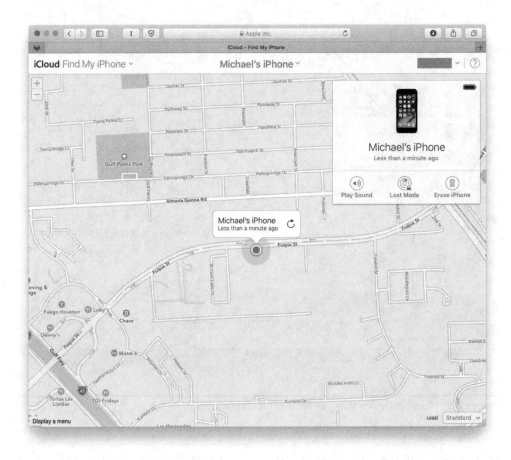

Figure 9-11   iCloud finding a lost iPhone

The next step depends on whether you think the phone was lost or stolen. If you think it's lost and the person who has it might want to return it to you, click Lost Mode. Lost Mode locks the device with a passcode (if you didn't already have one set) so that others can't access your personal information. It also displays a custom message on the screen, such as how to contact you. If you think it was stolen and you want to delete all the data on it, click Erase iPhone.

Wireless Connectivity

Mobile devices typically support multiple wireless connectivity types, including 4G/LTE, Bluetooth, and Wi-Fi. You should know how to configure each of these on a mobile device.

Cellular, sometimes referred to as *3G, 4G,* or *LTE,* is wireless service from a cellular phone network, accessed via cell phone towers in your area. You get this kind of connectivity when you pay a monthly fee for phone service with a provider such as AT&T or Sprint.

This type of service can include voice calls, text messages, and Internet data. The amount of data you use (in gigabytes) is metered, and if you exceed the amount specified by your plan, you are charged extra.

Bluetooth is a short-range wireless connection used for wireless peripherals like headsets and wireless speakers. Bluetooth can also be used for data transfer between two Bluetooth-enabled computing devices, such as a smartphone and laptop. There are different classes of Bluetooth devices, with different maximum ranges. Most devices are Class 2, with a range of 10 meters (33 feet).

Wi-Fi is a friendlier name for the IEEE 802.11 standard of wireless networking. This is the type of connection that most people associate with Internet connectivity, as the Internet wireless access points in most businesses and public accommodations use Wi-Fi. Most mobile devices support Wi-Fi, but it might not be on by default.

EXAM TIP The list of IT Fundamentals acronyms says *Wi-Fi* is short for "wireless fidelity." Wi-Fi *is* a play on *hi-fi* (short for "high fidelity"), a term used for stereo equipment and recordings. Wi-Fi isn't technically short for anything. It's just a marketing name, like *Kodak*.

Near Field Communication (NFC) is a specialized, low-power, short-range wireless communication method. It is built into some Android devices. If your device has one, you can use the Android Beam app to share certain kinds of files with other nearby Android phones. It works great with photos, but it doesn't share most other types of files. More recent iPhones have NFC hardware, but they can't share files this way because it's only included to support Apple Pay (a way to pay at credit card terminals with your phone); some Windows Phone devices, however, can join in on the fun.

Verifying Wireless Capabilities

To find out what wireless capabilities your device has, look in its Settings app. There will be configuration options there for each kind of wireless connectivity that the device supports. For example, in Figure 9-12, you can see that this smartphone supports Wi-Fi, Bluetooth, and cellular.

Figure 9-12
Check a device's Settings app to see what kinds of wireless it supports.

	•••••○ Ting 🛜	1:30 PM	🔋 🔋 ∗ 95% ▪
		Settings	
✈	Airplane Mode		⚪
🛜	Wi-Fi		totalwifi >
∗	Bluetooth		On >
🗼	Cellular		>
⭕	Personal Hotspot		Off >
📞	Carrier		Ting >

Pairing via Bluetooth Devices

Pairing establishes a connection between two Bluetooth-enabled computing devices. Pairing can occur between two computing devices (such as tablets) or between a computing device and a peripheral (such as a smartphone and a wireless headset). Pairing with a wireless device enables a safer way to use a phone while driving, called *hands-free calling*; in some states it's the only *legal* way to use a phone while driving.

 EXAM TIP *Hands-free* is a term listed in Objective 1.5. Make sure you can explain how Bluetooth pairing enables hands-free calling and how hands-free calling improves driver safety.

To pair devices, you must first enable Bluetooth on both devices. Many devices have Bluetooth disabled by default to extend battery life, though some peripherals may have no way to disable it. You'll find a Bluetooth setting in the Settings app. In iOS, you can also swipe up from the Home screen and tap the Bluetooth icon to toggle Bluetooth on or off.

Some Bluetooth devices are automatically discoverable by other devices whenever Bluetooth is enabled. On other devices (like laptops), you must issue a separate command to put them in Pairing (or Discovery) mode. Consult the documentation for each device to find out how to do this. (Look for Bluetooth in the Settings app on Android and iOS devices.) Figure 9-13 shows a Windows 10 laptop pairing with an iPhone.

Some devices require a security confirmation when pairing. This happens most frequently when both devices have a display screen. One device will provide an authorization code onscreen, and that same code must be confirmed on the other device. Figure 9-14 shows an authorization code in Windows 10 for the pairing initiated in Figure 9-13.

Transferring Data with Bluetooth

If you are accustomed to sharing files wirelessly between computers on a Wi-Fi network, you might expect to be able to do the same when the two computers are connected via Bluetooth—just open File Explorer and drag and drop the files between locations, right? Unfortunately, Bluetooth file transfer doesn't work that way. Bluetooth file transfer is not true network sharing of a location; it's only the sending and receiving of individual files.

Furthermore, Android, Windows Phone, and BlackBerry all support Bluetooth file transfers, but Apple iOS devices do not (at least at the time of this writing). Among the operating systems that do support it, you must use the Share feature to share the file with another nearby Bluetooth device. In Android, for example, you would open the Gallery app, select a photo, tap Share, and then select Bluetooth (as shown in Figure 9-15). You will be prompted to set up the Bluetooth pairing between the devices if needed.

 TIP Bluetooth isn't a great way to share lots of files. A better way is to connect your smartphone or tablet directly to a personal computer (PC) via universal serial bus (USB) cable or use an Internet file-sharing service like OneDrive or Dropbox.

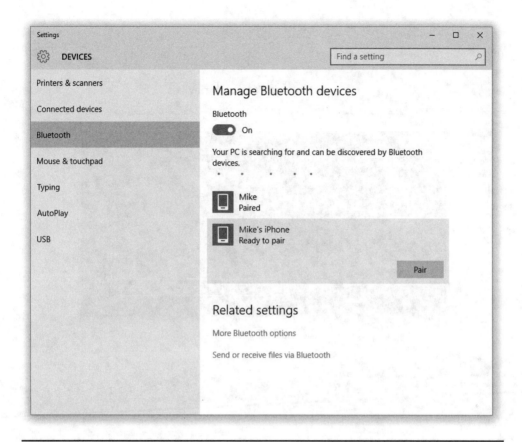

Figure 9-13   Use the Bluetooth app on your device to pair with another device.

Connecting to a Wi-Fi Network

Wi-Fi is a type of wireless Ethernet networking, the kind of network used to share files and printers between personal computers in homes and businesses all over the world. A Wi-Fi connection connects your device to a router, which in turn provides access to other networks (such as the Internet).

Enabling Wi-Fi on a Mobile Device

Most mobile devices support Wi-Fi, but many have the Wi-Fi transmitter/receiver turned off by default to increase battery life.

To turn on Wi-Fi, do one of the following:

- From the iOS Home screen, tap Settings and then tap Wi-Fi. If the Wi-Fi slider is not set to On, tap or drag it to turn it on.

- On an Android device's Home screen, tap Apps and then tap Settings. Ensure that the Wi-Fi setting is On. If it's not, tap or drag it to turn it on.

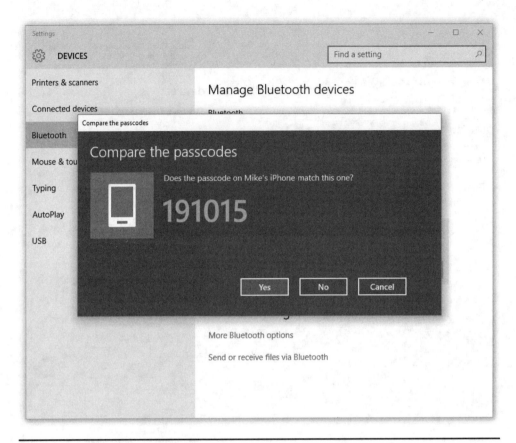

Figure 9-14 Some Bluetooth pairings require an authorization code.

Selecting a Wi-Fi Access Point

Next, choose a *wireless access point (WAP)* to which to connect. Depending on where you are, there may be more than one WAP to choose from. Each one has a name, which is set by the WAP's owner, called the service set ID (SSID). The SSID might be generic, like Linksys for a Linksys-brand access point, or it might be set to the name of the business or family who owns it.

 EXAM TIP The list of IT Fundamentals acronyms defines WAP as the Wireless Application Protocol, a standard for using data on cellular networks. Be prepared to see the acronym used this way, but know that when someone says WAP in most IT and networking contexts, they are referring to a wireless access point as discussed here.

Figure 9-15
Sharing a photo
via Bluetooth
on an Android
smartphone

Each available wireless network within range appears on a list (see Figure 9-16) below the Wi-Fi slider. Next to the SSID will be an icon showing how strong the wireless signal is and whether the connection is secure.

NOTE Chapter 11 covers connecting to a wireless network using a desktop or laptop computer.

Some access points are open; you don't need a password to connect. Most are protected with some type of security and require a password (see Figure 9-17). The device remembers the password for future connections. You can tell whether an access point is protected or not by looking for a Lock icon next to it on the list of available connections. In Chapter 11 you will learn how to configure a wireless access point to use security and to set the password.

After you establish the connection, verify Internet access by opening a Web browser and trying to visit a few Web sites. If you can't, either your device isn't connected correctly to the access point or the access point doesn't have Internet access.

Figure 9-16
Choose from
the available
connections.

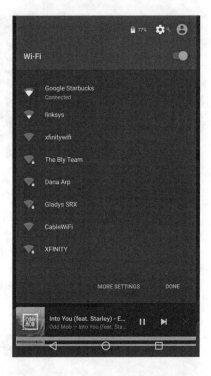

Figure 9-17
Enter the
password for a
secure access
point.

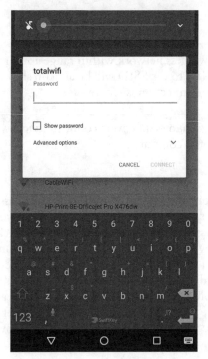

NOTE   Most wireless access points are also routers, so the terms *wireless access point* and *wireless router* are roughly synonymous in practical use.

Sharing a Phone's Cellular Connection with Other Devices

A smartphone with cellular data service and Wi-Fi capability can turn itself into an impromptu wireless access point, allowing other nearby Wi-Fi enabled devices to share it. Depending on the OS, this is called either *tethering* or *personal hotspot*. In iOS, this feature is called Personal Hotspot, and it's accessed from the Settings app. In Android, open the Settings app, find the Wireless Networks section, tap More and then tap Tethering & portable hotspot.

Disabling All Wireless Connections with Airplane Mode

When you fly on an airplane, you are supposed to turn off all electronic devices for take-off and landing because some wireless signals can interfere with the plane's navigation system. If you put the device into airplane mode, however, you don't have to power it down, because Airplane Mode disables all wireless capabilities.

Both Android and iOS have an Airplane Mode setting you can access from the Settings app. In iOS, you can also swipe up from the Home screen and tap the Airplane Mode icon to turn it on or off.

Configuring Mobile E-mail

You can send and receive e-mail on a mobile device via its Mail app. Setting up an e-mail account on a mobile device enables you to send and receive e-mail on the go, even when Wi-Fi is not available. Mail can be sent and received through the cellular data service that the device itself uses. You must configure each e-mail account separately if you have more than one.

EXAM TIP   Objective 1.5 of the CompTIA IT Fundamentals exam includes three *protocols* (standards) for sending and receiving e-mail: Post Office Protocol 3 (POP3), Internet Mail Access Protocol (IMAP), and Simple Mail Transfer Protocol (SMTP). The technical differences aren't important to understand, but remember that POP3 and IMAP receive e-mail and SMTP sends e-mail.

You should also be aware that when you set up an e-mail account on your mobile device, the setup process will ask which type of account you have. In some cases it might also ask for the address of the POP, IMAP, and/or SMTP server. You can get these addresses from your e-mail provider. Most have three parts separated by periods, as in pop.secureserver.net.

Setting up e-mail does not start with the Mail app, as you might expect, but with the Settings app. The steps vary somewhat between Android and iOS.

In Android, here are the steps:

1. From the Home screen, tap Settings.

2. Scroll down to the Personal section, tap Accounts & sync, and then tap Add Account.

3. Tap the type of account you want to set up. You can choose Microsoft Exchange, IMAP, or POP. If you don't know what kind of account it is and you can't easily ask someone, tap E-mail for general settings.

4. The steps diverge at this point depending on the type of account you chose. Follow the prompts, filling in the information requested to complete the process.

In iOS, here are the steps:

1. From the Home screen, tap Settings.

2. Scroll down and tap Mail, Contacts, Calendars; then under the Accounts heading, tap Add Account. A list of popular mail services appears.

3. If your service appears on the list, tap it and fill out the form that appears to connect your phone with the service. It asks for different information depending on which service. If you don't see your service on the list, tap Other and then tap Add Mail Account. Then fill out the forms that appear to follow the setup process to its completion.

After setting up your mail accounts, use the Mail app to send and receive mail. The way the Mail app works varies depending on the operating system, but they all have the same basic features.

You can return to the Settings app later to fine-tune the way the Mail program handles mail. For example, you can choose whether it organizes messages by thread, whether it asks before deleting messages, and which e-mail account it uses by default for sending new messages.

Configuring Synchronization

Synchronization means updating data between two locations so that both locations contain the same files and versions. You might have photos you've taken using your mobile device's camera, for example, and synchronizing your mobile device with your laptop PC might copy those photos to the laptop. There are several ways to keep data synchronized, depending both on the mobile OS and on the type of data being synced.

Synchronizing with a Cloud Service

You can employ a cloud service to synchronize data between devices automatically. The advantage of this method is that it's "set it and forget it." You configure automatic synchronization, and then it just happens going forward.

For Android, you can synchronize with your Google account to keep your contacts, system settings, apps, calendar, and e-mail data coordinated. For Apple, you use iCloud, an Apple-provided cloud service.

In Android, open the Settings app and tap Privacy. Check the boxes for Back up my settings and Automatic restore. Choose your Google account for the Backup account.

In iOS, open the Settings app, select iCloud, and enter your Apple ID and password. This signs you into iCloud on that device and enables synchronization across all your Apple devices that use iCloud. (That's mainly Apple devices, but there are also iCloud apps you can install in other operating systems, like Windows.)

Synchronizing Photos

In Android, Google's Instant Upload service handles photo synchronization. When that feature is enabled, any photo or video you take is uploaded to Google+ in a private album called From the Phone. You can enable or disable Instant Upload via the Settings app.

In iOS, there is a separate cloud app for photos called iCloud Photo Stream. To configure it, open the Settings app, choose iCloud, choose Photos (or Photos & Camera), and then turn My Photo Stream on or off. When it is on, new photos you take are uploaded to iCloud when your device is connected to the Internet using Wi-Fi.

Synchronizing with a Computer

When you connect your mobile device to a computer via a USB cable, you can synchronize all data and settings between the two devices. This includes music and video, which is essential if you use your mobile device as a mobile player.

For iOS devices, the iTunes app provides computer syncing capabilities. Download and install iTunes if needed (from Apple.com) and then connect your iOS device to the computer using a USB cable. Right-click the device's icon in the navigation bar in iTunes and choose Sync. See Figure 9-18.

For Android, you'll need to work with a third-party app to synchronize music and videos. One of the most popular is called doubleTwist. You might even have it installed already; some phone services like T-Mobile make it available on the Android phones they sell.

If you are syncing with a Windows 10 PC, you can also use the Phone Companion app that comes preinstalled with Windows. (That goes for both Android and iOS devices.)

Installing and Removing Apps

Installing an app is probably one of the more important skills to have when using any mobile device. Apps allow you to extend your device's capabilities, adding everything from scientific calculators to mindless games.

Finding and Installing an App

The same app may be available for both Android and iOS, but they are not interchangeable. You get Android apps from the Google Play Store or other third-party app stores.

Figure 9-18 In iTunes, right-click the device and choose Sync.

You get iOS apps from the Apple Store (Figure 9-19). Each of those stores is an app on your device. To download a new app, you open the store app and make your selection.

 TIP When installing an app, you should connect your device to Wi-Fi if possible so you don't use your cellular plan's data (unless, of course, you are on an unlimited data plan). An app download can use tens or hundreds of megabytes.

Some apps cost money (usually less than $10), but many are free. Free apps are more likely to have advertisements in them or have limited features to entice you to pay for a premium version. When you shop for apps, pay attention to the costs.

If you pay money for an app, the store will automatically charge whatever credit card you have on file for your Google or Apple account. The first time you open the store app, you may be prompted to sign in with your Google or Apple account and to set up a payment method.

In Android, to open the Play Store, tap the Apps icon at the bottom of the Home screen and then swipe left and right to locate the Play Store app and tap it. Once you get

Figure 9-19
The Apple Store

into the store, tap Search (magnifying glass) and type the name of the app you're looking for or a keyword.

In iOS, tap the App Store icon on the Home screen to open the Apple Store. In the store, tap Search at the bottom of the screen and type a name or keyword.

Once you find an app that looks interesting, follow the prompts to get it. The app will download and install on your device, and you'll find its icon on the Home screen.

Removing an App

So that app you downloaded didn't turn out to be so great? Dump it! It's easy to remove (uninstall) an app in a mobile OS.

In Android, open the Settings app, and then tap Apps, Applications, or Application Manager (depending on version). Select the Downloaded (or Downloads) tab to see only the apps you have downloaded. Find and tap the app you want to delete, and tap the Uninstall button.

On iOS, it's even easier. On the Home screen, press and hold the app you want to get rid of. When the icons start shaking, tap the X in the upper-left corner of the app's icon. A confirmation appears, as in Figure 9-20. Tap Delete. Then press the Home button again to stop the other icons from shaking and return to normal use.

Figure 9-20
In iOS, hold your finger on an app icon and then tap the *X* in its corner to uninstall it.

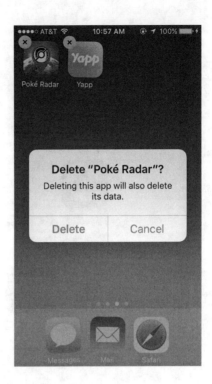

Resetting a Mobile Device

You might need to reset a mobile device to troubleshoot or make the device fresh for a new owner. *Reset* means two very different things, called soft and hard.

A *soft reset* is basically just a reboot. Sometimes when a device locks up or starts acting all squirrelly, a soft reset will do the trick. A *hard reset* wipes out everything on the device and takes it back to its original factory settings. Avoid *hard resets* if at all possible because you'll lose time setting the device up again and any data, files, and preferences you don't have backed up elsewhere. The only time you should prefer a hard reset is when you give or sell your phone to someone else.

Performing a Soft Reset

To perform a soft reset in Android, press and hold the Power button until a message appears offering to turn the device off. Select Power off or select Restart. See Figure 9-21. If the device is locked up, though, that method won't work. With a locked-up device, you need to do a *force restart*. One way is to take the battery out for a few seconds if it's removable. If it's not, try holding down the Power button and the Volume button at the same time until the screen goes black. Then hold down the Power button until the device restarts.

On an iOS device, if it will respond at all, press and hold the Sleep/Wake button until the red slider appears. Then drag the slider to turn the device completely off. After the

Figure 9-21
Powering off an
Android phone

device turns off, press and hold Sleep/Wake until you see the Apple logo. If the device is locked up, press and hold both the Sleep/Wake and Home buttons until you see the Apple logo (ten seconds or longer).

Performing a Hard Reset

Now you'll learn to reset the device the hard, ugly way—the way you have to do when you are out of other options.

On an Android device, you will want to access the Factory data reset screen. The tricky part is that different phone brands and models access this screen differently. Look up the exact steps for your model online. On one phone, for example, with it powered off, hold down Volume Down and Power together. When you see the brand logo, release the Power button only and then immediately press it again; then release both buttons when the Factory reset data screen appears. If that sounds as awkward as a game of Twister, it is. It's difficult on purpose so you don't do it accidentally.

On an iOS device, you need a computer with iTunes installed. Connect the device to the computer and open iTunes. Then press and hold Sleep/Wake and Home at the same time, but *don't* release the buttons when you see the Apple logo. Keep holding them until you see the Recovery Mode screen. A message appears in iTunes that there's a problem with the phone that requires it to be updated or restored. Click Update and wait for iTunes to fix the device.

Getting Your Data Back After a Hard Reset

If you're lucky enough to have backed up or synced the phone's settings before the disaster occurred, you can restore them as follows.

On an Android device, after a hard reset, you are prompted to walk through a setup process. As part of it, you're prompted to sign in to Google. When you do so with the same Gmail account you used for syncing, your data is automatically restored to the device.

On an iOS device, when the device comes back up after a hard reset, the Setup Assistant runs. Go to Set up your device, tap Restore from a Backup, and sign in to iCloud. Tap Choose backup and then select the backup you want to use and follow the prompts.

Chapter Review

In this chapter, you learned how to set up and navigate a smartphone or tablet interface. While Android is the most popular mobile OS, iOS is a strong second-place contender. You learned about gestures for interacting with a touchscreen, such as tap, swipe, pinch, and rotate, and you learned how kinetic sensors such as gyroscopes, magnetometers, and accelerometers help a mobile device orient itself spatially.

You learned the importance of basic security measures like assigning a lock passcode on a device; to access this and most other settings, use the Settings icon on the main screen. You learned what to do if your device is lost or stolen and how to reset a malfunctioning device.

We reviewed wireless technologies in mobile devices, including Bluetooth, Wi-Fi, and NFC, and you learned how to pair a Bluetooth device to a phone or tablet and how to establish and configure a Wi-Fi connection and set up e-mail. You also learned how to configure synchronization with a cloud service and how to install and remove apps.

Questions

1. What is the gesture where you touch the surface with two fingers spread apart and then drag them closer together?

   A. Rotate

   B. Tap

   C. Pinch

   D. Spread

2. Which of these terms is *not* associated with kinetics?

   A. Magnetometer

   B. Gyroscope

   C. Barometer

   D. Accelerometer

3. How is screen orientation determined, if it is not locked?

  A. The user sets it once, and it never changes.

  B. Orientation hardware button.

  C. Orientation command.

  D. Physical orientation of the device.

4. Which of these passcodes is more secure?

  A. Six-digit alphanumeric.

  B. Six-digit number.

  C. Four-digit number.

  D. All are equally secure.

5. 3G, 4G, and LTE are all kinds of what kind of wireless communication?

  A. Wi-Fi

  B. Bluetooth

  C. Cellular

  D. NFC

6. What kind of wireless connectivity is Bluetooth best suited for?

  A. Sending and receiving phone calls

  B. Connecting to a wireless headset

  C. Connecting to the Internet

  D. Connecting to a computer in a nearby building

7. Connecting a Bluetooth peripheral to a smartphone is known as:

  A. Pairing

  B. Wi-Fi

  C. 4G

  D. NFC

8. The name of a Wi-Fi access point is its:

  A. POP

  B. IMAP

  C. NFC

  D. SSID

9. Which of these is *not* a protocol for sending or receiving e-mail?

  A. IMAP

  B. SMTP

  C. POP3

  D. NFC

10. What app does an iPhone use to synchronize music and videos from a computer?

    A. iMusic

    B. iTunes

    C. Google Play

    D. doubleTwist

Answers

1. **C.** Dragging fingers closer together is called *pinching*.

2. **C.** A barometer is not a kinetics term; all the others are.

3. **D.** When screen orientation is not locked, the physical orientation of the device determines the screen orientation.

4. **A.** An alphanumeric passcode is most difficult to guess and therefore most secure.

5. **C.** 3G, 4G, and LTE are types of cellular communication.

6. **B.** Bluetooth works well for pairing a wireless headset. It would not work for any of the other activities listed.

7. **A.** Connecting a Bluetooth peripheral to a device is called *pairing*.

8. **D.** An access point's name is its service set ID (SSID).

9. **D.** Near Field Communications (NFC) is not an e-mail protocol; the others are.

10. **B.** The iTunes app is used to synchronize music and videos with an iOS device.

PART III

Networking, Security, and Maintenance

CHAPTER 10

Configuring Network and Internet Connectivity

In this chapter, you will learn how to

- Understand basic network terminology
- Choose, set up, and configure a SOHO router
- Choose between wired, wireless, and cellular connectivity
- Use a LAN to share files and printers

Few computers are islands unto themselves. To experience the full power of computers, you must connect them to other computers. Imagine you receive a new computer, but it's not on a network, so you can't send e-mail, download music, or interact across the Internet with your friends. How boring would that be?

When you link computers to share files and communicate, you create a *network*. Networks range in size from two computers connected together to the largest and most complex network of all—the Internet.

In this chapter, you will learn the basics of home networking. You'll learn how to choose and configure a router, share files and printers on a network, connect to the Internet, and share data online.

Understanding Network Basics

Networks come in many sizes and vary widely in the number of computers attached to them. Some people connect two computers in their house so that they can share files and play games together—the smallest network you can have. Some company networks connect thousands of employees in dozens of countries to get work done.

LANs and WANs

Network folks put most networks into one of two categories: LANs and WANs.

A *local area network (LAN)* covers a small area, where all the computers connect via cables, wireless signals, or a combination of the two, through connecting boxes (Figure 10-1). LANs usually cover a single building or group of nearby buildings. Typical LANs include home

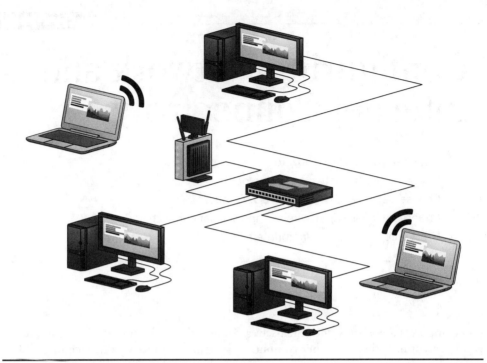

Figure 10-1 A local area network

and small office networks. A *wireless local area network (WLAN)* is a LAN that connects components wirelessly.

A *wide area network (WAN)* covers a large area and can have a substantial number of computers (Figure 10-2). Usually, a WAN is composed of two or more LANs connected together. All the LANs in all of the schools in your district, for example, might link together to form a WAN. The largest WAN in existence, the *Internet,* is a worldwide network that connects millions of computers and networks.

Clients and Servers

People use two kinds of computers on a network: clients and servers. In a nutshell, *servers* share things such as files, folders, and printers, and *clients* access those shared things (Figure 10-3). One of the most common client computers is a *workstation,* which is a PC or macOS box that handles general computing chores. Almost any personal computer can serve as either a client or a server. Microsoft and other developers also make server-specific operating systems, such as Windows Server.

Computers running Windows, macOS, and the many varieties of Linux make up the vast majority of clients. You'll also find other client devices, though, such as game consoles, smartphones, tablets, and digital video recorders (DVRs). Servers manage network resources (such as printers, e-mail, and other stuff that makes a network valuable), provide

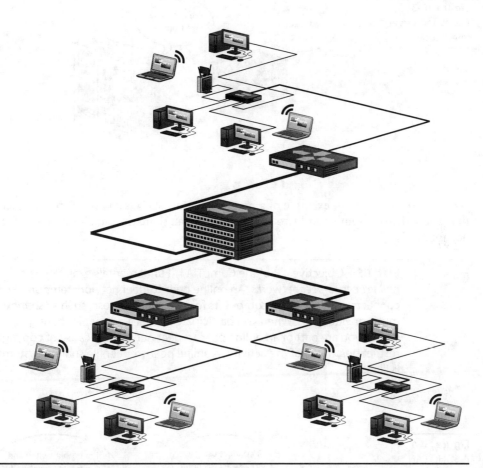

Figure 10-2 A wide area network

central storage of files, and provide services for the users (such as having the printer server tell the printer to print or having the e-mail server send your e-mail).

Networks are traditionally classified into *client/server* or *peer-to-peer,* depending on the role played by each computer in the network. In a client/server network, one or more computers act as servers while the remaining computers act as clients. An example of a client/server network is a corporate network at a large company, where IT professionals maintain multiple servers that provide the individual computers that the employees use (the client computers) with a variety of services.

On some home or small office networks, however, there may not be a separate server. Instead, every computer on the network acts as both a client and a server. Each computer mostly does its own client thing, functioning as a normal computer, and also shares resources with the other computers on the network. Such networks are called

Figure 10-3
Client and server
interaction

peer-to-peer networks. An example of a peer-to-peer network is a network in a residence that allows five computers and two smartphones to all share the same printer and Internet connection.

EXAM TIP   Objective 4.3 of the CompTIA IT Fundamentals exam refers to *online peer-to-peer networks*. An online peer-to-peer network temporarily connects multiple client computers for a specific purpose, such as sharing music or video files. When you participate in peer-to-peer file sharing online, you are part of an online peer-to-peer network. Because of copyright restrictions, much of the activity in online peer-to-peer file sharing systems is illegal.

Figure 10-4
A SOHO LAN
with both wired
and wireless
clients

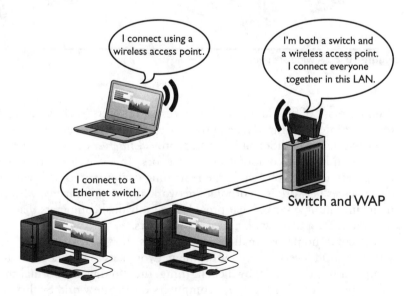

The CompTIA IT Fundamentals exam focuses on LANs for the most part, more specifically on *small office/home office (SOHO)* networks. A *SOHO network* is a small network operated in a home or a small business.

Switches and Routers

In a LAN, each computer connects to a central gathering point, either using a cable or wirelessly via radio frequency (RF) signals. Wired LAN computers connect to a *switch*; wireless LAN computers connect to a *wireless access point (WAP)*. Many SOHO networks use a box that combines both connection options (see Figure 10-4). The switch or WAP keeps track of the computing devices on the network and makes sure network traffic gets to the proper computer.

A *router* connects two networks. Connecting a SOHO LAN to the Internet therefore requires a router. The router acts as a gateway between the LAN and the *Internet service provider (ISP)* that provides that essential Internet connection. Most SOHO networks use some kind of *broadband* connection, such as a cable modem, to make the high-speed connection between the router and the ISP. Figure 10-5 shows a simplified LAN connection to an ISP and then on to the Internet.

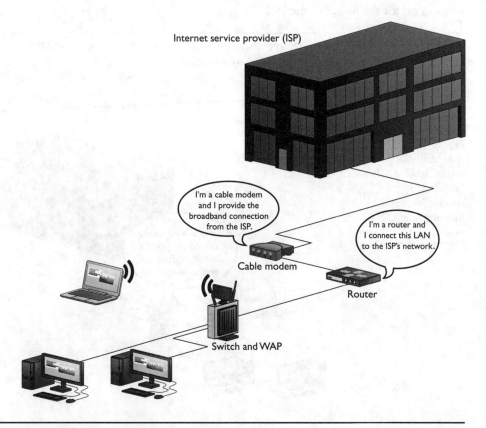

Figure 10-5   Adding a connection to an ISP

A typical SOHO LAN that connects to the Internet, therefore, has five types of devices. Here's the list:

- Workstation or other computing device that people use to connect and do work
- Switch that enables the wired connections among devices so that a LAN happens
- WAP that enables the wireless connections among devices so that a LAN happens
- Router that provides the connection between the LAN and another network, specifically the Internet service provider
- Broadband box (cable or other) that provides the physical connection between the router and the ISP

At this point, the consumer labeling of devices can cause a little confusion. Most SOHO users have a *single* magic box that does it all: switch, WAP, router, and broadband connection rolled into one (Figure 10-6). Worse, most people call this magic box a *SOHO router* or *broadband router*. As a CompTIA IT Fundamentals student, you need to understand the functions that make the magic box work at each level. Switches and WAPs create LANs. Routers connect networks. Broadband devices provide the physical connection for the router to the ISP.

 EXAM TIP Connecting computers to a switch or WAP creates a LAN. Connecting two LANs requires a router.

Figure 10-6
A switch, WAP, router, and broadband connection rolled into one magic box

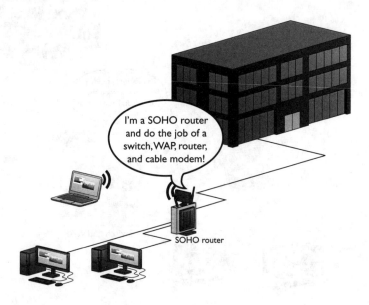

I'm a SOHO router and do the job of a switch, WAP, router, and cable modem!

SOHO router

Local Ad Hoc Networks and Direct Links

You can join a few computers in a direct connection without going through a connecting device such as a WAP. This is called an *ad hoc network*. An ad hoc network is typically wireless (Wi-Fi). Although you could set up this type of network in Windows 7 and earlier, security risks led Microsoft to remove the option of setting up an ad hoc network in Windows 8 and later. It is technically still possible to do in Windows 8 and later, but it involves typing long strings of commands at a command prompt and is best left to computer professionals and technical enthusiasts.

A *direct link* connection (PC to PC) is a one-to-one connection between two computers via their Ethernet ports. It is technically a kind of ad hoc network (in that there is no central gathering point like a switch), although it's not usually called that. To create a direct link, you need a specially wired *crossover cable*.

Setting Up and Configuring a SOHO Router

Most SOHO routers work pretty well right out of the box, but you should check basic configuration options to ensure proper security. Security is important on a router to keep would-be hackers from spying on your computer usage and stealing your Internet bandwidth. Follow along with the upcoming sections to learn how to make your SOHO router work just the way you want it to work.

 NOTE Many Internet service providers lease equipment to customers that is both a modem and a wireless router. The modem portion provides the Internet connection, and the router portion creates a small LAN and allows all the computers on the LAN to share the Internet connection. If you have one of these combo boxes, you might not have to go through most of the activities outlined in the upcoming sections. Just follow the advice of your ISP and you will likely be good to go.

Choosing an Appropriate Router

There are two main considerations when choosing a SOHO router. The first is whether or not it should support wireless connections. This isn't a difficult question—the answer is almost always *yes, it should*. Even if you don't have any wireless devices right now, you might have some in the future, or a guest in your home or office might have one. A typical wireless SOHO router also supports wired (cable) connections, usually at least four ports, so it's not an either-or proposition.

Second, you should determine which wireless standard the SOHO router supports. New wireless routers you buy today will almost all support the 802.11ac standard, which is the newest one. If you pick up a second-hand wireless router or buy one on clearance, it might support an older standard, like 802.11n or 802.11g. Those are okay, but you won't achieve the same data speeds with the older models.

Setting Up a SOHO Router

Follow the instructions that come with the SOHO router to set it up physically. This usually involves plugging it into a wall outlet and placing it in a location reasonably near where the wireless devices will be. Some lights will flash on it, and after a minute or two it will be ready for use.

 TIP In most cases a SOHO router will work right out of the box with its default settings. You should still go through a configuration process to enhance its security.

Making a Wired Connection

To configure a SOHO router, you will need to connect a computer to it with an Ethernet cable. This is called a *wired connection*. For a wired connection you must use a computer that has an Ethernet port (an RJ-45 port). There are USB-to-Ethernet adapters that may work in a pinch, but it's better and easier to use the Ethernet port.

Connect one end to the computer's Ethernet port and the other end to an Ethernet port on the back of the SOHO router. There should be several generic-looking Ethernet ports there and one special one (perhaps a different color or with a label like "Internet"). Use any of the generic-looking ports. See Figure 10-7.

Checking for Basic Internet Connectivity

If you plan to use the SOHO router for Internet access, connect the Internet to the SOHO router. Do this by running an Ethernet cable from the broadband box (which is often called a *modem*) to the special port on the SOHO router. This may be labeled "Internet" or "Modem" or have some such wording. This port may be a different color than the others or be offset from the others. Make sure you connect to this special port and not one of the generic ones. This step isn't necessary if the broadband modem is also a SOHO router.

To verify your connection, try accessing any Web site with a Web browser. If you get Internet access, great! It'll make it possible for you to check for firmware updates, which you'll do later in this chapter. If not, don't sweat it for now. If you still don't have Internet connectivity after you complete the configuration process, check with your ISP to see what extra steps you might need to take.

Figure 10-7
Connect a computer to any of the four Ethernet ports.

EXAM TIP   For Objective 4.1 of the CompTIA IT Fundamentals exam, make sure you know how to verify a wired connection and to verify Internet connectivity—and make sure you can explain the difference between the two. To verify a wired connection, look for blinking lights on the NIC and on the switch that indicate a connection, and try browsing shared folders on another computer connected to the same SOHO router. To verify Internet connectivity, open a Web browser and try to display a Web page.

Accessing the SOHO Router Configuration Utility

Read the documentation that came with the SOHO router to find out how to access its configuration interface with your browser. The process probably involves the following:

1. Connect a computer to the SOHO router with an Ethernet cable. Follow this step even with a computer that will connect to the SOHO router wirelessly in the future.

2. Look up the SOHO router's default IP address in the documentation. The *IP address* functions as the unique name for that device. It will probably start out with 192 and be something like this: 192.168.1.1 (see Figure 10-8). If you don't have the documentation, find the documentation online to get this information.

3. Open a Web browser, click into the address bar, type **http://** followed by the SOHO router's IP address, and press ENTER. The SOHO router interface should open as a Web page.

The configuration interface will vary by SOHO router make and model. Figure 10-8, for example, shows the interface for a combination AT&T broadband modem and wireless router, while Figure 10-9 shows the interface for an older Belkin wireless SOHO router.

Logging In and Changing the Password

Before you can change any settings, you will need to log in to the SOHO router. If it's a new SOHO router, look up the default user ID and password in the documentation if you are prompted for that information. If it's not new but you don't think anyone has changed the password yet, look up the router's documentation online to find out the default information. If it's already been changed, you'll need to know the current password to continue.

TIP   If you can't find the SOHO router's password anywhere and it's been changed, you'll need to do a hard reset of the router to reset the password to the default. Look at the router documentation online to find out how to do this, as the process varies.

The login screen in Figure 10-10 has a hint that the router's default password is blank. In other words, just click Submit without typing anything.

PART III

Figure 10-8 Configuration interface for a combination broadband modem/wireless router

A blank password does not provide good security, especially when the login screen provides a helpful hint. So, first change the password. The process depends on the interface. Check the router's documentation or look for a Help command in the configuration interface. This setting is called Administrator Password on the router in Figure 10-11; it's found in Utilities | System Settings. The Login Timeout setting determines how long your configuration session can be idle before you have to log in again.

Updating the SOHO Router Firmware

Before you get too far into SOHO router configuration, you should check for updates to the router's firmware. Firmware, as you may recall from earlier chapters, is programming stored on a chip inside the device to perform the device's basic functions. The configuration utility itself is stored in firmware, for example, as is the software that the SOHO router uses to start up and do its job.

Figure 10-9 Configuration interface for a wireless router

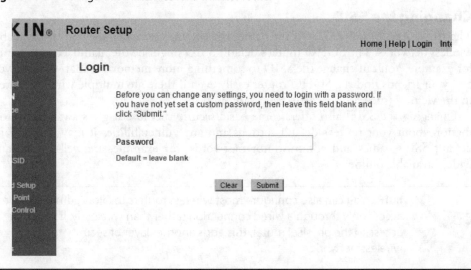

Figure 10-10 Login screen with a hint about the default password

IN® **Router Setup**

Home | Help | Logout   Internet S

Utilities > System Settings

Administrator Password:
The Router ships with NO password entered. If you wish to add a password for more security, you can set a password here. More Info

- Type in current Password >

- Type in new Password >   ••••••

- Confirm new Password >   •••••• |

- Login Timeout >   10   (1-99 minutes)

Figure 10-11   Change the password to prevent unauthorized access to the configuration utility.

NOTE   You might have to postpone the firmware update if the SOHO router isn't connected to the Internet yet, but familiarize yourself with the button's location and come back to it when you can.

Look in the configuration program for a Firmware Update button or hyperlink. If an Internet connection is available, click Check Firmware and then follow the prompts to install an update if one is found. See Figure 10-12.

EXAM TIP   Because the procedure for updating firmware varies among SOHO routers, you don't need to know the specific steps; however, you should understand why router firmware should be updated and how to find the button or hyperlink to accomplish an update in the router's setup utility.

Changing the SSID

The *service set identifier (SSID)* is the name wireless users see when they browse available wireless networks. The SOHO router's default SSID might be the manufacturer's name, for example. You can change the SSID to something more memorable that will help you and your friends find the SOHO router easily even if there are multiple wireless routers in the vicinity (such as in an apartment building).

Changing the SSID also offers some basic security because it gives away less information about your router's default settings and any vulnerabilities it may have. Many default SSID names and administrator passwords, for example, are well-known and widely available online.

NOTE   You can also configure most wireless routers to allow administrative access only through a wired connection rather than wirelessly. If you limit access to the physical router, this adds another layer of security to the wireless network.

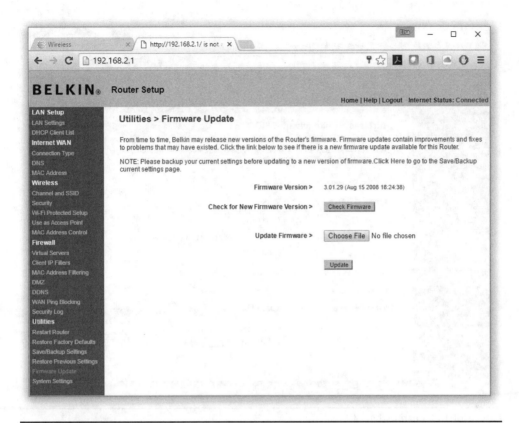

Figure 10-12   Update the firmware if an update is available.

To change the SSID, look for that setting in the configuration utility (in Figure 10-13 it is located under Wireless | Channel and SSID).

Setting Up Wireless Security

Wireless security refers to a system of authentication for the wireless clients that connect to the SOHO router. If a router's security is set to Open, that means it has no security. Anyone with a computer with Wi-Fi can connect to the SOHO router and use the resources on the network. Unless you *want* to provide free Internet access to the public, having an Open wireless SOHO router is a bad idea, especially if you share files on your network. It's an open invitation to hacking.

In the Security section of your SOHO router's configuration utility, you can select a security mode. You will see several options, such as WEP, WPA, and WPA2.

WEP

Wired Equivalent Privacy (WEP) encryption was meant to secure data transmitted wirelessly. WEP encryption uses 40-bit encryption (that is, a 40-digit coding system of ones and zeroes) to scramble data. Many vendors also support 104-bit encryption.

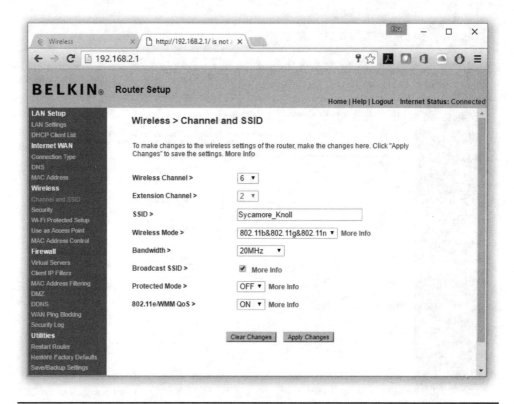

Figure 10-13 Change the SSID.

WEP has some serious security flaws. Shortly after it was released, hackers demonstrated that WEP could be cracked in a matter of minutes using software readily available off the Internet. WEP is better than nothing, but it will not deter any serious hacker. The industry quickly came out with a replacement called WPA.

WPA and WPA2

Wireless Protected Access (WPA) encryption addressed the weaknesses of WEP, and it functions as a sort of security protocol upgrade for WEP-enabled devices. WPA offers security enhancements such as an encryption key integrity-checking feature and user authentication through the industry-standard *Extensible Authentication Protocol (EAP)*. The use of EAP is a huge security improvement over WEP. User names and passwords are encrypted and therefore much more secure. WPA uses an encryption standard called *Temporal Key Integrity Protocol (TKIP)*.

Wireless Protected Access 2 (WPA2), the most secure authentication method for a SOHO wireless network, offers additional benefits over WPA, making WPA2 the strongest available encryption today. WPA2 uses an improved encryption standard called *Advanced Encryption Standard (AES)*. You don't need to know the technical details of the differences between TKIP and AES.

There might be some options available with WPA2, depending on your router. For example, one of the choices might be *WPA2 – Default Key*. The default key is a pre-assigned password for the router that is difficult to guess, usually a long random string of numbers, letters, and symbols. This is the default option on most modem/router combinations because it's extra-safe—no easy-to-guess passwords. The drawback is that every time a new user needs to access the router, you have to look up its password, because there's no way anyone can remember it.

An alternative, WPA2-PSK (PSK stands for "pre-shared key"), uses a password (or key) you specify and share with people who need access. The drawback is that most people don't make this password strong enough. Use a combination of letters, numbers, and symbols that is easy to remember but difficult to guess. See the section "Authenticating Users" in Chapter 11 for more information about selecting strong passwords.

Setting Up Security

In the router's configuration utility, open the Security section and choose a security mode. You might also be prompted to choose an authentication type or encryption technique. In most cases, the best choice is WPA2-PSK with AES as the encryption technique, as in Figure 10-14.

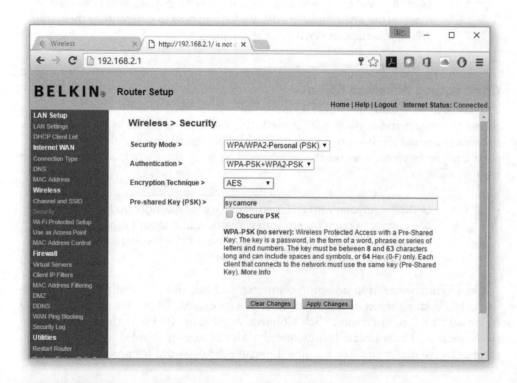

Figure 10-14   Choose a security mode and encryption technique.

WPS

The easiest way to set up a client to access a secured router is with *Wi-Fi Protected Setup (WPS)*. There are a few different WPS methods; the method you use depends on the device's capabilities. With push-button configuration (PBC), you push a button on the router to place it in a special mode where it accepts new connections for a brief time. During those few minutes anyone can connect wireless devices to the router without knowing its password. The device and the router come to an understanding, and the device is approved for future use of the router. Not all routers support WPS, but many of the SOHO routers sold today do.

A second WPS method requires a device to enter a personal identification number (PIN) to join the network. The SOHO router might have a PIN sticker, or it may generate a different PIN each time. The third WPS method uses *near-field communication (NFC)*, which is a *very* short-range wireless networking technology that allows devices to connect when they are within a few inches of each other. Chapter 9 discussed NFC.

You can enable or disable WPS. Find the WPS setting in the router's security properties and choose Enabled or Disabled.

When you finish configuring the router, close the browser window to exit the configuration utility.

EXAM TIP Make sure you know how encryption options rank from least to most secure (in order, WEP, WPA, WPA2) and how to differentiate them from WPS. In practice, use WPA2 if at all possible.

Connecting Wireless Clients

The last step in setting up a SOHO router offers the most benefit: enabling wireless clients to connect and become part of the LAN. You learned earlier in the chapter how to connect a wired client—run an Ethernet cable between the back of the router's switch ports and the Ethernet port on the computer. The setup for a wireless client, however, requires a few steps.

CAUTION Anyone with an Ethernet cable can walk right up to a SOHO router and connect a computer to your network; router security applies only to wireless connections. Therefore, you should lock up your router if it's in an environment you don't trust or can't control.

On a Windows desktop or laptop computer, you can view the available wireless networks by clicking the network icon in the notification area. Then click the desired SSID to connect to that router and click Connect. See Figure 10-15. If the router is open (insecure), you'll be connected automatically. If it has security enabled, the first time you connect to the router you'll be prompted to enter the password (or pre-shared key).

Figure 10-15
Select the desired wireless network to which to connect.

Wired, Wireless, and Cellular: Making the Right Choice

You just learned how to set up a SOHO router, which can act as an on-ramp to the Internet if you connect a broadband modem to it (or if the broadband modem is built into it). You also learned that you can access that router via a wired connection or wirelessly. These two methods aren't equal. There are benefits and drawbacks to each.

Let's also throw a third option into the mix for Internet connectivity: *cellular*. You can connect to the Internet via smartphones or tablets that have cellular service, as an alternative to using a broadband Internet connection in your home or office. You can also buy a cellular modem that connects to a desktop or laptop computer to allow you to access the Internet via the same cellular data network that smartphones use.

Let's examine each of these methods, focusing on costs and benefits, so you can make the right choice in a given situation. This section tackles these seven things to consider:

- Mobility
- Availability
- Bandwidth

- Latency
- Reliability
- Number of concurrent connections
- Security

 EXAM TIP For Objective 4.2 of the CompTIA IT Fundamentals exam, make sure you can identify the strengths and weaknesses of cellular, wireless, and wired data connections in all of the categories listed here. You need to know which technology provides high mobility, for example, versus another technology that provides low mobility. These distinctions will make more sense as we hit each category.

Mobility

Mobility describes how far you can travel and still access network resources. Ranked in order from highest to lowest mobility are cellular, wireless, and wired.

When you're on the go, cellular Internet gets the top score. Different cell phone networks have different technologies available in certain locations, such as 3G, 4G, or LTE, that can affect the speed at which you surf, but basic data service is available just about anywhere. You can be within several miles of the nearest cell tower and still get good service.

Wireless LAN connections are in the middle, mobility-wise; they start to fade out at 100 to 250 feet from the WAP, depending on the WAP's technology (with newer WAPs having better range in general).

When considering mobility, however, don't overlook the availability of public wireless access points (or *hot spots*) like at restaurants, coffee shops, and hotels. If a business offers free Wi-Fi, you and your mobile device can connect to it, just like you do your wireless router at home.

In contrast, wired LAN connections to the Internet are only as mobile as the length of your cable. That's definitely not very mobile.

Availability

Availability refers to the probability that a system will be functional. In other words, when you want to use a service, can you depend on it? Wired network connections win this battle because they don't commonly have interference problems. Cellular networks do a little better than Wi-Fi, but both can suffer from interference.

Throughput/Bandwidth

Throughput refers to the data transfer rate. How quickly does your e-mail download, and how long do you have to wait for a Web page to load? *Bandwidth* relates to throughput in terms of getting data from point A to point B but refers more to the size of the connection. In practical networking terms, both result in the same order of technologies.

The clear winner is wired LANs. Wired connections on modern SOHO networks run at somewhere between 1 and 10 gigabits per second (Gbps), depending on the hardware used. That is *much* faster than any other Internet connection technology discussed here runs, so a wired LAN connection is rarely going to be the cause of speed limitations when you surf the Web.

> **NOTE** Many people equate bandwidth with speed, but it's more properly analogous to volume. Think about drinking through a wide straw versus a narrow one. The liquid might be moving at the same rate, but more of it arrives in your mouth per second with the wider straw; it has greater bandwidth.

In second place is a wireless LAN. Depending on the technology of the router and the network interface on the device, a wireless LAN can transfer data at between 11 and 433 megabits per second (Mbps). Many broadband Internet providers like cable and DSL offer connection speeds of 25 to 110 Mbps, so as long as you have reasonably current networking hardware, the wireless connection should not be a barrier to taking full advantage of your SOHO Internet connection speed.

Last in the race for throughput is cellular. Even the best cellular services today, boasting the latest technology, top out at between 5 and 40 Mbps. (At the time of this writing, U.S. cellular carriers rarely surpass 10 Mbps, so they run a lot slower than many Asian carriers using the same technology. Go figure.)

Connection Delay (Latency)

Latency refers to the *connection delay* between a request and the response to that request. You always want that delay minimized, so low latency is preferred over high latency. In networking terms, a wired connection will always respond the quickest. Electrical pulses on a copper wire move very fast indeed.

Wi-Fi networks come in second, because the distances between the client and the WAP are short. Cellular connections need to travel to the cell tower and back, creating a slightly bigger delay.

Reliability

Reliability refers to the quality of the data received and the error-checking and correcting capabilities of the technology. Does the data match what was sent or have errors been introduced? How frequently does data need to be sent again because the receiving computer detected errors?

Wired connections offer the highest reliability because so little typically can cause problems on a copper wire. Wi-Fi and cellular seem to offer similar strengths and weaknesses in reliability. The shorter distances and lower chance of interference from things like storms put Wi-Fi marginally in second place.

PART III

Number of Concurrent Connections

The phrase *number of concurrent connections* can have a couple of different meanings. In classic networking terms, connections refer to unique conversations between a client and a server, called a *session*. This gets complicated quickly because modern servers handle all sorts of connections and a single client computer can have multiple sessions with a single server at the same time. Here's an example of this beyond the CompTIA IT Fundamentals definition. Open a complicated Web site, like www.yahoo.com. Then open a command prompt, type **netstat**, and press ENTER. See all those TCP lines that say "ESTABLISHED"? Those are connections.

This classic definition of concurrent connections seems to fall well outside the scope of the exam. So let's look at a more English-based definition of concurrent connections in terms of access to the Internet. Which type of Internet connection enables more simultaneous users to access the Internet?

Wired networks scale up easily, so they support the most users. Cellular towers can support hundreds of users. A wireless access point supports a small number of wireless clients at which point it taps out.

 EXAM TIP We think CompTIA is using the phrase *concurrent connections* to mean simultaneous access by users. When ranking connections from high to low, pick wired, cellular, and Wi-Fi, in that order.

Level of Security

When we talk about security in the context of the Internet (and we'll do so a lot more in Chapter 12), we mean the risks involved in, for example, sending bank account or credit card information online. Which type of service is most or least likely to be snooped or hacked?

Wired LAN wins the most secure ranking here. Because it's all about the cables, there's little opportunity for someone to hack into it without physically plugging a cable into your switch.

Cellular data travels miles to reach the cell tower, so there's a lot of ground between you and the tower and more places for hackers to intercept data. Cellular networks all use proprietary technologies for connectivity, however, so it's less likely a hacker has access to the software needed to hack into any given cell phone network than the oh-so-standardized Wi-Fi network type. More specifically, Apple and Google look closely at every app that goes on their phones before making that app available for download. And it's hard to install an app on a smartphone in secret.

Properly set up and configured Wi-Fi networks, with a good password on the WAP and encryption enabled, offer a high level of security. Bad guys can capture the radio signals, however, and creative people work hard to break encryption standards. What drops Wi-Fi to third place in the security game is that you can set up a network with woefully poor security. An open-access Wi-Fi point network, like at a coffee shop, is fertile hacking ground, because anyone can join that network. Short version: don't do your banking at a public Wi-Fi hotspot.

Using a LAN to Share Files and Printers

So you've got a LAN up and running in your home or small business and everyone is happily using your shared Internet connection. Now what? You might want to look at ways to share data (such as your music collection) between the individual computing devices within your local network. Let's get to work on that!

To share files and printers you need to turn on File and Printer Sharing and then organize networked computers in some fashion so they can see networked shares. Then you have to share folders and printers actively.

Enabling File and Printer Sharing

The first time you connect to a network using a Windows device, a box pops up asking about the network location. Depending on what you choose, Windows loosens network security settings for more trusted home or work networks and tightens them for less trusted public networks. Choosing Home or Work as the network location enables File and Printer Sharing; choosing Public disables it.

File and Printer Sharing enables the device to share folders and any directly connected printers with other devices on the network. Without it, none of the other sharing settings described in the upcoming sections are possible.

Here are the steps to check or adjust File and Printer Sharing settings:

1. Open the Control Panel (in Windows 8.1 or Windows 10, just right-click the Start button and select Control Panel).

2. Open the Network and Sharing Center applet.

3. Click *Change advanced sharing settings*.

4. In the *Network discovery* section, make sure *Turn on network discovery* is selected. This setting enables other computers to see your shared assets when they browse the network.

5. In the *File and printer sharing* section, make sure *Turn on file and printer sharing* is selected. See Figure 10-16.

6. If you made any changes, click *Save changes*.

Network Organization

Microsoft organizes networked Windows computers in three ways: workgroups, domains, and homegroups. Each network organization offers distinct advantages and disadvantages.

Workgroups

All PCs belong to a single *workgroup* by default, called WORKGROUP. Being in the same workgroup enables users to share access to files, folders, and printers. You can see your current workgroup name by opening the System applet in Control Panel (Figure 10-17).

The WORKGROUP name carries no special magic, and you can change it at will. The key thing to keep in mind is that computers need to share a workgroup to share files, folders, or printers.

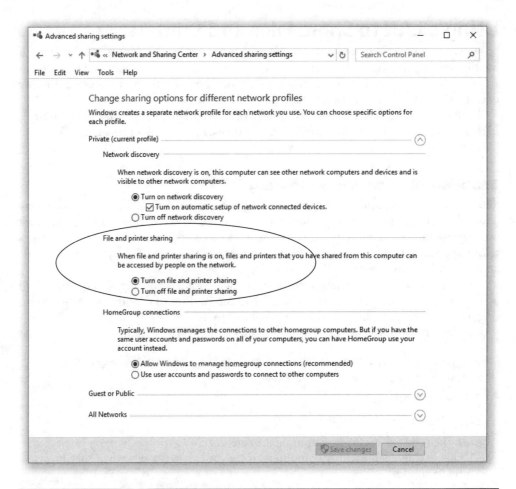

Figure 10-16 Enable File and Printer Sharing if needed.

  NOTE Savvy readers might note that this discussion of workgroups does not use the term *LAN*. Workgroups and LANs function together but function differently. You can have ten computers plugged into the same LAN, for example, and have five set to a workgroup named BARCELONA and five set to a workgroup named MADRID. The BARCELONA computers can see and share with other BARCELONA workgroup members. They can't see or share with any of the MADRID workgroup computers.

The BARCELONA computers need to share a LAN *and* a workgroup name to see and share successfully. The LAN provides physical connectivity. The workgroup provides the sharing capability.

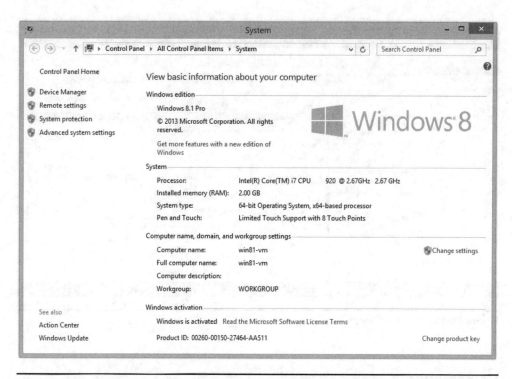

Figure 10-17 System information for a Windows 8 device in the default workgroup.

Workgroups lack central control; this works fine for small networks but falters when securing those with many users. The lack of central control means you have to log on to each individual system to use its resources. Either you need a password for a local account on each system or the system's administrator needs to set one up for you. All of these accounts quickly become an administrative chore as the workgroup grows.

Domains

Larger networks use *domains,* in which a server running Windows Server (Figure 10-18) controls access to network resources. A *domain* requires one or more computers to act as domain controllers, which are central hosts that store the user names, passwords, and permissions of every user who has access to the domain. Users can log in from any computer connected to the domain—what's called *single sign-on*—and have access to everything they have permission to access. Domains rock, but fall well outside the scope of the CompTIA IT Fundamentals exam. You'll see the domain options when you click around in the System applet. Ignore domains until you're ready to start studying for CompTIA A+.

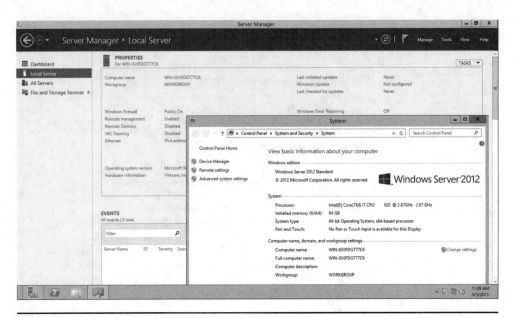

Figure 10-18 Windows Server

Homegroups

Workgroups provide almost no security and require lots of signing on to access resources; domains provide single sign-on and security at a cost. To split the difference, Microsoft introduced HomeGroup in Windows 7.

NOTE Homegroups are not available in Windows Vista, macOS, or any Linux distro.

Most people just want to share types of data, such as music, so homegroups just share Windows libraries. A homegroup connects computers (which can join only one homegroup at a time) via a common password—no extra user names required.

NOTE *Libraries* group files of specific types together, regardless of where they reside on mass storage. You can access all your music files from the Music library, for example. Sharing that library makes your music accessible to all computers attached to the homegroup.

Figure 10-19
Create a
Homegroup
dialog

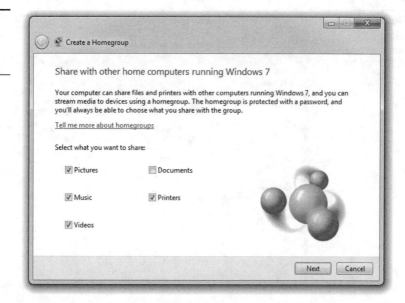

You create homegroups from the HomeGroup applet. If you're in one already, you'll have options to edit relevant settings. If you're in a workgroup and not a homegroup, you can click the *Create a homegroup* button to bring up the Create a Homegroup dialog (Figure 10-19), from which you select library types. When you click Next, you'll see the generated homegroup password (Figure 10-20).

Figure 10-20
The homegroup's
password

Figure 10-21
Using
homegroups

If you go to another computer on the network and open the HomeGroup applet, it will prompt you to join the existing homegroup. Just click the *Join now* button, enter the password, and pick libraries to share. You can browse your new homegroup through Windows Explorer or File Explorer (Figure 10-21). To add additional folders or librar-ies, right-click either, select *Share with* (Figure 10-22), and choose a Homegroup option.

Figure 10-22
The Share with
menu

Sharing

Windows systems can share files, folders, entire drives, printers, faxes, Internet connections, and much more—but the CompTIA IT Fundamentals exam limits its interest to folders and printers. You've already seen how to share with homegroups, but there are other ways to share folders and printers.

Sharing a Folder

The manual way to share a folder is to right-click it, select Properties, go to the Sharing tab, and select Advanced Sharing. From here, select the *Share this folder* check box and name the network share (Figure 10-23). By default, new Windows shares have only Read permission; click the Permissions button to set your share to Full Control (Figure 10-24).

A simpler (less powerful) method is to right-click a file or folder and select Share (or Share with) | Specific people to open the File Sharing dialog and select user accounts from a drop-down list. These will be local accounts unless your system is in a workgroup or domain, in which case you can select or search for remote accounts. When you select one, you can choose Read or Read/Write permissions (Figure 10-25).

Figure 10-23
Advanced
Sharing dialog

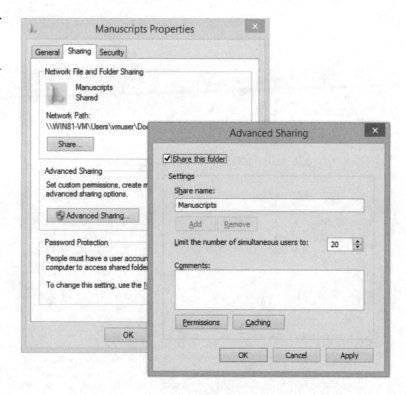

Figure 10-24
Setting the share
to Full Control

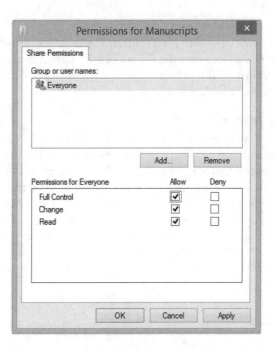

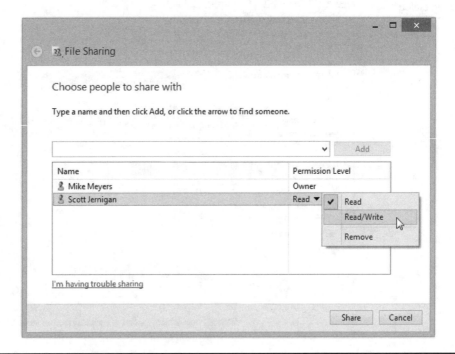

Figure 10-25   File Sharing dialog permissions options

Accessing Shared Network Volumes

To browse shared content on other computers, open File Explorer and click Network in the Navigation pane. From here, double-click the icon in the Computer section for the computer you want to browse.

If the user's shared folders are password-protected, you'll be prompted to enter a user name and password for that computer. See Figure 10-26. If you don't have access to a user account on that computer, you won't be able to access the shared folders.

If you can access the system, you'll see icons for the shared folders. They are much like any other folder icons in File Explorer except they have a green network connector symbol underneath them, as shown in Figure 10-27.

Installing and Sharing a Printer

There are two ways to share a printer on a network. One is to use a network-enabled printer (one with a built-in wired or wireless network adapter). Another way is to connect the printer directly to an individual computer, set it up as a local printer like you did in Chapter 3, and then make it available as a shared resource on the LAN. Let's look at sharing networked and local printers on both wired and wireless networks.

Network-Enabled Printers

You can connect a network-enabled printer directly to your switch. If the printer has a wireless network adapter in it, you can connect the printer to the WAP. (Most likely, your SOHO router includes both devices.) Follow the instructions in the printer's documentation to learn exactly how. You will need to enter the network's password (the pre-shared key) from the printer, most likely using the printer's LED display (and hardware buttons unless it is a touchscreen). This can be a bit tedious, but hang in there and follow the instructions; you shouldn't have to do this often.

Figure 10-26
You might be prompted for credentials when attempting to access shared assets.

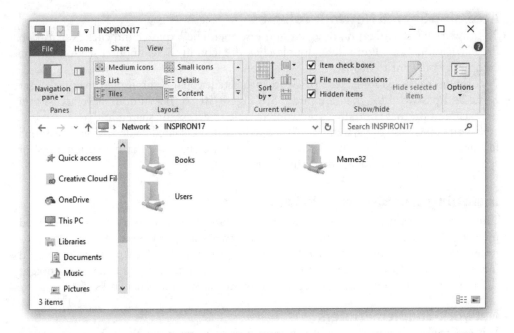

Figure 10-27   Shared folders in File Explorer

Any computer attached to the network should then have access to the printer. As you'll recall from Chapter 3, each workstation requires drivers installed for the specific printer. That includes printers directly connected to the network. Choose the *Add a printer* option in the Devices and Printers Control Panel applet to add a printer.

Sharing a Local Printer with Other Computers on the LAN

To share a printer attached to a workstation, open the Control Panel and open the Devices and Printers applet. Right-click the icon for the printer you want to share and select *Printer properties*. Click the Sharing tab and select the *Share this printer* check box. In the *Share name* box, type the name that will appear to other users on the LAN and click OK. See Figure 10-28.

EXAM TIP   For Objective 4.3 of the CompTIA IT Fundamentals exam, make sure you can explain the difference between network and local printing.

Figure 10-28
Share a printer with other computers on your LAN.

Chapter Review

In this chapter, you learned a little about networks. A LAN covers a small area, where all the computers connect via cables, wireless signals, or a combination of the two, through switches or WAPs. A WAN is a larger collection of connected LANs. Clients are the user PCs, and servers are the workhorses of a network. Client/server networks have both clients and servers, whereas peer-to-peer networks have only clients, each one of which takes on a bit of server responsibility to make it work.

To join a network, computers need a wired or wireless connection to a switch or router. Routers provide a path outside of the LAN, enabling SOHO networks to share an Internet connection. A SOHO router works with no configuration, but you should configure its security settings. This includes changing the SSID and router password and securing the network by enabling encryption.

When choosing among wired, wireless, and cellular, you learned that cellular excels at mobility. A wired connection gets great marks for availability, bandwidth, latency, reliability, number of concurrent connections, and security. Wireless falls in between in these areas.

PART III

To share files and printers on a LAN, first make sure File and Printer Sharing is enabled. Create or join a HomeGroup if desired. Computers that can't use HomeGroup can still connect to other computers on the LAN via workgroup. To share a folder, right-click it and choose *Share with*. Share a printer via the Sharing tab of the Printer Properties dialog box.

Questions

1. Which of these terms best describe a SOHO network? (Choose two.)

   A. Peer-to-peer

   B. Client/server

   C. WAN

   D. LAN

2. What differentiates a router from a switch?

   A. Routers are for WANs, and switches are for LANs.

   B. A router provides a path out of the LAN, such as to the Internet.

   C. A switch provides a path out of the LAN, such as to the Internet.

   D. Routers are for client/server networks, and switches are for peer-to-peer networks.

3. When shopping for a SOHO router, look for the latest available standard, which is:

   A. 802.11b

   B. 802.11ac

   C. 802.11n

   D. 802.11g

4. What kind of ports are on the back of a SOHO router for making wired connections?

   A. VGA

   B. DVI

   C. RJ-45

   D. RJ-11

5. How do you access a router configuration utility?

   A. Buttons on the top of the router

   B. Buttons on the back of the router

   C. IP address in a Web browser

   D. Domain name in a Web browser

6. What is the router's SSID?

   A. Network name

   B. IP address

   C. Serial number

   D. Model number

7. Which wireless encryption standard is the most secure?

   A. WEP

   B. WPA

   C. WPA2

   D. WPS

8. In which way is a cellular Internet connection superior to wired and wireless?

   A. Bandwidth

   B. Mobility

   C. Number of concurrent connections

   D. Security

9. What is an advantage of using a HomeGroup?

   A. Higher security level

   B. Easier folder and printer sharing

   C. Makes router use less power

   D. Faster file transfer

10. Where in the Control Panel would you go to connect to a network printer on a client PC?

    A. Devices and Printers

    B. System and Security

    C. Network and Internet

    D. Ease of Access

Answers

1. **A, D.** A SOHO network is a peer-to-peer LAN. A WAN is a wide area network, where clients are not located near each other. A client/server network is a larger network that uses a server.

2. **B.** A router, not a switch, provides a path out of the LAN. Both routers and switches can be used with either WANs or LANs and with both client/server and peer-to-peer networks.

3. **B**. 802.11ac is the latest wireless standard. The others, from oldest to newest, are 802.11b, 802.11g, and 802.11n.

4. **C**. The RJ-45 ports on the back of a SOHO router are for wired Ethernet connections. An RJ-11 connector is for a telephone landline. VGA and DVI are video connectors.

5. **C**. Access a router's configuration utility by typing its IP address into a Web browser. You cannot access the router configuration with buttons on the router. The router does not have a domain name.

6. **A**. The SSID is the router's network name. Its IP address is the address by which you access it for configuration. The serial number and model number have no role in router naming or configuration.

7. **C**. WPA2 is the most secure wireless encryption standard. WEP and WPA are not as good. WPS is not an encryption standard; it is a way of configuring a network connection by pressing a button on the router.

8. **B**. Wired connections excel at bandwidth, concurrent connections, and security. Cellular is better for mobility.

9. **B**. A homegroup simplifies folder and printer sharing. It does not change the security level, the router power, or the file transfer speed.

10. **A**. Printer settings are accessed from Devices and Printers in the Control Panel.

CHAPTER 11

Local Computer Security Threats and Best Practices

In this chapter, you will learn how to

- Explain the threats to local PC security
- Describe physical access control and device hardening
- Select appropriate user account types

These days, you can't afford to be blissfully unaware when it comes to computer security. Threats to your security, privacy, and computer lurk around every corner. Through your devices, a malicious person (an *attacker*) can gain valuable information about you and your habits. An attacker can steal your files or run programs that log your keystrokes to pilfer account names and passwords, credit card information, and more. An attacker could even run software that takes over your computer to send spam or steal from others. The threats are real and immediate.

 NOTE In computing and technology circles, *hacker* is often a term of reverence for talented experts driven to expand, extend, improve, overcome, and repurpose existing hardware, software, and systems. Since these talents can be used for good or bad (or even just for fun) and because some of the threats you'll see in this chapter are astonishingly low-tech, I've used the more generic term *attacker*.

This chapter and the next both deal with security. Because the topic is so big and important, we've broken down security information into two broad categories. In this chapter we'll look at local security threats. These can include viruses and other malware spread from other computers on your LAN to yours, physical security issues, and attempts to guess your passwords. We'll consider ways to make your computer less vulnerable to local problems. Then in Chapter 12, we'll talk about threats that come from *outside* your local environment (primarily from the Internet).

Understanding Local Security Threats

A local security threat originates from your local environment. For example, a disgruntled employee might try to access private salary data or delete the customer database, or someone might steal the receptionist's laptop when he steps away for a moment. Many people are vigilant for viruses and other malware originating online (covered in Chapter 12) but overlook equally real threats from inside the building.

Unauthorized Access

Unauthorized access occurs when a person accesses resources (such as data, applications, and hardware) without permission. A user can alter or delete data; access sensitive information, such as financial data, personnel files, or e-mail messages; or use a computer for purposes the owner did not intend.

Not all unauthorized access is malicious—often this problem arises when users who are randomly poking around in a computer discover that they can access resources in a fashion the primary user did not intend. Unauthorized access becomes malicious when outsiders knowingly and intentionally take advantage of weaknesses in your security to gain information, use resources, or destroy data.

Password Cracking

The most common way of gaining unauthorized access is to obtain a password that you aren't authorized to have.

Professional computer criminals often employ a technique called *password cracking* to obtain passwords. Cracking is more than just random guessing—it's a disciplined technique for obtaining a password through rapid-fire trial and error, often by employing password-cracking software. Password crackers who know something about the owner of the password can further target their guessing by including names and words that would be meaningful, like a spouse or dog name or an anniversary date. Strong passwords should be used to make it more difficult for password cracking programs to acquire your password. Later in this chapter you'll learn what constitutes a *strong password*.

 NOTE Some people use the term *cracking* to broadly describe *malicious* hacking.

Even more common than software-based password cracking, however, is seeking out or stumbling upon, a written password that has been poorly guarded. For example, a user might have a really difficult-to-guess password, but then he might write it on a slip of paper that he keeps in his desk drawer. That's great for keeping out everyone who doesn't have access to his desk drawer, but it does nothing to keep out those who do. Use common sense and don't write your password down and leave it laying around for prying eyes to see!

Dumpster Diving

Dumpster diving is the generic term for anytime an attacker goes through your refuse, looking for information. The amount of sensitive information that makes it into any organization's trash bin boggles the mind! Years ago, I worked with an IT security guru who gave me and a few other IT people a tour of our office's trash. In one 20-minute tour of the personal wastebaskets of one office area, we had enough information to access the network easily, as well as to embarrass more than a few people. When it comes to getting information, the trash is the place to look! To prevent this threat, shred sensitive information using a paper shredder.

Shoulder Surfing

Another type of theft to worry about when computing in public is theft of your passwords. *Shoulder surfing* is when people spy on you from behind, watching what you type. Even though most passwords appear on the screen as dots rather than characters you typed, the thief could be watching your fingers and memorizing keys you press. The danger from shoulder surfing increases the more frequently you work in a specific place. Each day, an observant person with bad intent can get another keystroke or two. Check before you type! Computer screen privacy filters are often used to prevent shoulder surfing by making a screen harder to read at an angle or from a distance.

Unauthorized Wi-Fi Usage

As you learned in Chapter 10, failing to secure a wireless router means unauthorized users can join the network. If a PC on the network has File and Printer Sharing enabled, the intruder could read and even modify or destroy that user's files. Even if all of your individual systems are locked down, they could use your network to commit fraud, attack other networks, or engage in piracy and other illegal activities that could get traced back to you. The best defense against unauthorized Wi-Fi use is to implement wireless encryption methods such as WPA2.

Data Destruction

Along with unauthorized access may come unauthorized modifying or deleting of files or changing of system settings. For example, suppose a family member signs into your PC with your password and deletes some of your files to make room to install a new game. There goes your final paper or your tax return files for the last five years! Data destruction can also be intentional and purposeful, such as an unhappy (or recently fired) employee destroying valuable company records and databases.

Theft

Thieves steal whatever you don't have locked down, either physically or electronically. If you turn your back on your laptop or tablet at the local coffee shop, for example, someone might take it. Even worse than the physical loss of your hardware, however, is the loss of the data that it contained and the loss of your privacy. If you stored passwords and credit card numbers on the stolen device, they are now in the hands of a thief.

Figure 11-1
A standard
laptop lock that
protects against
casual theft

Amazon and other retailers sell laptop lock cables that work just like a bike chain. Most laptops have a small security port where you insert the lock after wrapping the cable around something immovable, like a table leg or post (Figure 11-1).

Another, less obvious form of theft is the stealing of software and software licenses. Let's say you bought a copy of Microsoft Office and its license allowed you to install it on two computers (that is, to use the product key to activate it on two computers). If someone gets ahold of your product key, they can use (or sell) an activation of the software.

Malware

Networks are without a doubt the fastest and most efficient vehicles for transferring computer malware among systems. Malware is malicious software written to do something unwelcome to your computer. Malware takes many forms; we'll cover malware in detail in Chapter 12.

News reports focus attention on the many malware attacks from the Internet, but a huge amount of malware comes from users who bring in programs on USB drives and writable optical discs.

Physical Security

Once you've assessed the threats to your computers and local networks, you need to take steps to protect those valuable resources. This section explores physical security, including access control and device hardening.

Access Control

The first order of security is keeping people who shouldn't have access away from the actual hardware. This isn't rocket science. Lock the door. Don't leave a PC unattended when logged in. In fact, don't ever leave a system logged in, even with a Guest or Standard user account. I pity the fool who walks away from a server still logged in as an Administrator. Don't tempt fate.

For that matter, when you see a computer logged in and unattended, do the user and your company a huge favor. Just walk up and press the WINDOWS LOGO KEY-L combination on the keyboard to lock the system so it requires anyone who wants access to reenter the active user's password. It works in all versions of Windows.

Device Hardening

One important component of local device security is the practice of *device hardening,* which means to make the device as difficult as possible for unauthorized people to access by changing hardware and software settings. Let's look at the following ways you can harden a device, whether it's a desktop or laptop, a tablet, or a smartphone:

- Disable unused wireless features.
- Set up lockout times.
- Enable security features.
- Use encryption.

Disable Unused Wireless

Disable any wireless features that you are not using, such as Wi-Fi, Bluetooth, and near-field communication (NFC). You can easily reenable them when you want to use them, and keeping them turned off during downtimes ensures that nobody can gain access to your device through them without your permission. On a mobile device you can do this via the Settings app. On a laptop, there may be hardware buttons on the computer that toggle wireless receivers on/off, or there may be an Airplane mode that does the same via software. You can also disable wireless adapters in Device Manager, which you can access via Control Panel | Hardware and Sound | Device Manager. In Figure 11-2, for example, you can tell that the Bluetooth adapter is disabled by the down-pointing arrow symbol on the device icon.

Configure Lockout

You can configure a lock-out time so that a lock screen appears after a certain period of idleness; a password or PIN must be entered to get back in. This prevents someone from snooping around your device if you leave it unattended. Set the lock-out time to the shortest option that doesn't drive you up the wall. Even a minute alone with an unlocked system is enough time for a cool-headed attacker to insert a USB drive, install malware, and walk away like nothing happened. On a mobile device, set the Lock Screen setting. In Windows, enable a screensaver in the Control Panel and set it to display the logon screen when waking from it. Then set the delay before the screensaver starts. See Figure 11-3.

Enable Security Features

Different operating systems have different security features that you can optionally enable to increase security. Windows has Windows Defender for malware, for example, and Windows Firewall for network attacks; some smartphones have fingerprint recognition and enhanced passcodes. You'll learn more about Windows Defender and Firewall in Chapter 12.

PART III

Figure 11-2
You can disable wireless adapters that you don't regularly use.

Figure 11-3
You can require a password when the PC wakes up from the screensaver.

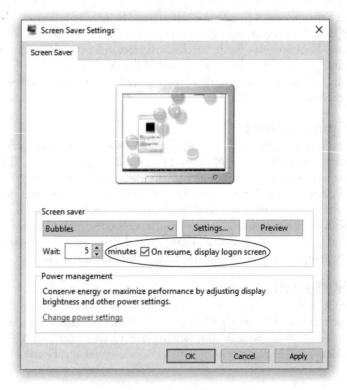

Encryption

Encrypt files. If your device uses a file system and OS version that support encrypting files on the hard drive, do so for all files containing sensitive data. That way even if your hard drive is stolen, nobody can view the files without signing in with your credentials. You learned about encrypted files in Chapter 9. You can also encrypt your entire hard drive with a feature such as BitLocker (in Windows), which makes a hard drive unreadable if removed from the original PC in which it is installed.

 EXAM TIP Make sure you can explain why device hardening is important and list several ways to accomplish it.

Users and Passwords

User accounts play a huge role in the security of any computing device. A secure system controls user accounts types and implements authentication practices such as good password rules. Windows also has UAC to help you secure systems. Let's take a look.

Using Appropriate Account Types

Every desktop/laptop OS enables you to create user accounts and grant different permissions to different kinds of accounts. In Windows, an Administrator account has full permission to do anything, whereas a Standard account can only make changes affecting that one account. Standard accounts can't easily affect other accounts. A Guest account can run only a few applications, such as a Web browser, and can't change any settings.

When you install Windows, the first account you create is automatically an Administrator account. You must maintain at least one Administrator account on the computer. For better local security, however, create a Standard account for everyday use. Even if that *Jack* guy steals your password and signs in to your Standard user account, he won't be able to harm the system as a whole (although he will be able to delete or change your personal files). Jack won't be able to remove applications or install malware.

Create a new account, set its account type to Standard, and make that your main account. Sign in using an Administrator account only when you need to do something that the Standard account can't do, such as install new applications or make system changes. Figure 11-4 shows the screen in the Control Panel where you would change the account type. To get there, open the Control Panel and choose User Accounts | Change Account Type, select the account and choose Change Account Type.

If a guest in your home or business wants to use your PC, have that person sign in using the Guest account. This account has limited permissions, and the user won't be able to do too much damage.

 EXAM TIP Make sure you understand the difference between (and appropriate uses for) Administrator, Standard, and Guest accounts. The CompTIA IT Fundamentals exam doesn't include Windows 10 as of this writing, but note that Microsoft removed the Guest account from Windows 10.

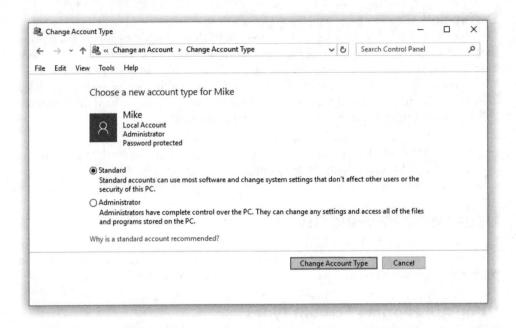

Figure 11-4   You can change the account you use for everyday activities to a Standard account.

Authenticating Users

Authentication is verifying a user's identity to permit or block certain actions on a system. Most authentication relies on two things you know: user names and passwords. Because both are *knowledge factors*, we call this scheme *single-factor authentication*. More secure *multi-factor authentication* schemes add a *possession factor* (such as a key or card that you have), or an *inherence factor* (things you *are*, such as fingerprints, retinal scans, facial recognition). Let's explore how to create and manage passwords for networks, online services, and operating systems.

In the following sections, you'll learn how to create and manage passwords. The same basic guidelines apply for both OS passwords and passwords you use on various Web sites and online services.

Password Complexity

Always use a *strong password,* one too complicated for bad guys to crack easily. That means no words you'd find in the dictionary or encyclopedia—anything that a password cracking program might try.

According to the CompTIA IT Fundamentals exam, a strong password:

- Is at least eight characters long
- Has both uppercase and lowercase letters
- Has numbers and symbols

Examine the following passwords. Can you guess which one is the strongest?

- abc768xyz5
- p1eRsqUred
- Fa$$1on8
- 1haveadreamthatallpeople

According to the exam objectives, the third password wins in security terms. What makes it unique? Of the four, it alone has uppercase and lowercase letters, numbers, and nonalphanumeric characters. And it meets the minimum eight-character threshold.

 EXAM TIP   Remember that a strong password has at least eight characters and a mix of letters, numbers, and special characters.

Some operating systems enable you to set lock-outs for passwords, and many secure Web pages use time-outs as well. In Windows 7 and later you can set lock-outs via the Local Security Policy app (found in the Control Panel under Administrative Tools). In the app, navigate to Security Settings | Account Policies | Account Lockout Policy. To set the number of wrong guesses allowed, set the Account lockout threshold. For the lockout duration, set the Account lockout duration.

Password Confidentiality

Even a strong password is no good if you don't keep it confidential. Don't write down passwords (if you can possibly help it), and if you do write them down, guard that paper as carefully as you would guard other important confidential information. That means don't tape it to the underside of your mouse pad or desk drawer! Don't send passwords via e-mail, text, or instant messaging. If you store your passwords in a document on your computer, create it in a program that allows you to password-protect data files, like Microsoft Word or Microsoft Excel. Don't use the same password for multiple services or Web sites.

If you forget a password and need to have it reset by an administrator, make sure you change it immediately after logging in. If you're an administrator, force the issue by requiring the user to change his or her password when logging in. This creates a temporary *one-time password*, keeping the user safe from any future potential mischief by an administrator.

Along those same lines, when you sign up for an online service or a secure Web site, you might be assigned a default password. It's a good idea to change this at your first login to that site.

Password Expiration and Reuse

On some business networks, the network administrators set up password expiration to force each user to change his or her password at certain intervals. This helps with overall security because the older a password is, the more likely someone unauthorized has gotten ahold of it. Similarly, these password change policies may prohibit users from reusing the same passwords they have used in the past, so, for example, you can't toggle back and forth between two different passwords each time a change is required.

Password Management

Most companies have a password management policy, which establishes rules for several aspects of password usage, including complexity, expiration, and confidentiality. You can create your own password management policies for yourself and your home or small business by thoughtfully creating rules in each of those areas.

For example, you might have a policy like this:

- **Complexity**   Passwords must be at least eight characters and must include at least one uppercase letter, one number, and one symbol.
- **Expiration**   Passwords must be changed every six months.
- **Reuse**   Users may not reuse the last three passwords used.
- **Confidentiality**   Users may not store passwords in unsecured files on any device; any password file must itself be password-protected. If passwords are stored on paper, the paper must be locked in a secure cabinet or drawer.

Single Sign-on Passwords

On some computer systems, password use is simplified by a single sign-on. That means you sign in once, and then that same authentication is used for multiple purposes. When you sign in to Windows using a Microsoft account, for example, you are also automatically signed into the OneDrive online file storage system. Similarly, many Web sites allow you to sign in using your Facebook credentials so that you don't have to create separate accounts.

Single sign-on systems can be convenient and can relieve you of the responsibility of remembering multiple passwords. They can also pose a security risk, however, because if the single password is compromised, all its other uses are compromised.

User Account Control

Windows uses *User Account Control (UAC)* to prevent malware or rogue Web sites from making system changes without your knowledge and consent. When UAC is enabled (and it is enabled by default) and you attempt to make a system change that would affect other user accounts (such as installing new software), UAC opens a prompt that asks if you really want to do it. You must click Yes to continue. See Figure 11-5.

In addition, if you use a Standard Windows account, UAC will prompt for the PIN or password of an Administrator account before it will allow the change to be made. That way you don't actually have to sign out of the Standard account and into the Administrator account in order to provide permission. See Figure 11-6.

You can adjust the UAC setting from the Control Panel. Choose System and Security, and under the Security and Maintenance heading, click Change User Account Control settings. Drag the slider up or down to control the UAC level. Keep in mind that the highest level may become annoying because of its frequent prompting, whereas the lowest level may not offer adequate protection. See Figure 11-7.

Figure 11-5
User Account
Control when
signed in as an
Administrator

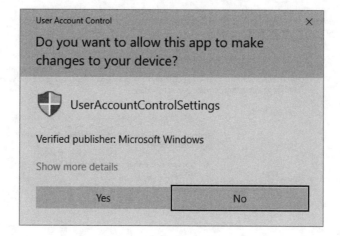

Figure 11-6
User Account
Control when
signed in as a
Standard user

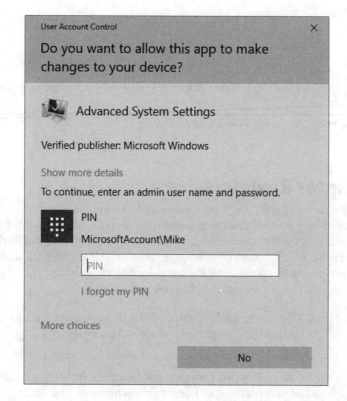

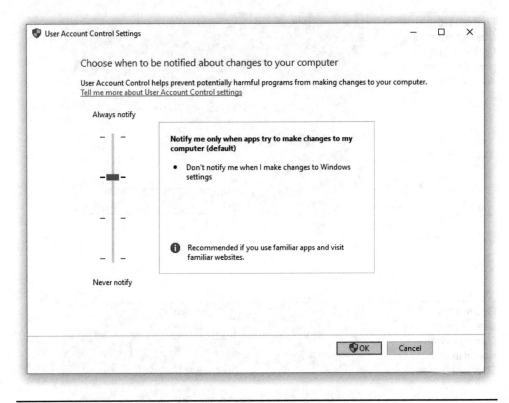

Figure 11-7   Adjust the level of UAC protection.

Chapter Review

Local security threats are often overlooked but are very real. A computer can be compromised by password cracking, dumpster diving, or shoulder surfing, for example. The network can be threatened by unauthorized users on the network, such as someone joining the Wi-Fi network without permission. Unauthorized access can result in data destruction, theft, spying, and the introduction of malware.

To combat local threats, you must control access:

- Harden devices to make them as difficult as possible for unauthorized people to access by changing hardware and software settings.

- Use Standard user accounts rather than Administrator accounts for everyday use.

- Employ safe password management practices, including establishing rules for password complexity, confidentiality, expiration, and reuse.

- Use the appropriate level of User Access Control that balances convenience with security.

Questions

1. What is a person doing when searching trash for useful information?

   A. Dumpster diving

   B. Garbage mining

   C. Cracking

   D. Trash talking

2. Edward loiters at the local café, taking notes on what people type on their computers, especially at the login screens. What kind of theft does he practice?

   A. Cracking

   B. Dumpster diving

   C. Infiltration

   D. Shoulder surfing

3. Disabling the Bluetooth adapter on a laptop when it is not in use is an example of:

   A. Dumpster diving

   B. Cracking

   C. Device hardening

   D. Hardware theft prevention

4. Which of the following can prevent people from snooping on a device that you leave unattended for several minutes?

   A. Configuring a lock-out time

   B. Shoulder surfing

   C. Using a strong password

   D. Disabling Wi-Fi

5. Which type of Windows account would be appropriate for a visitor to your home?

   A. Standard

   B. Guest

   C. Administrator

   D. Limited

6. Which type of Windows account does Microsoft recommend for daily use?

   A. Standard

   B. Guest

   C. Administrator

   D. Limited

7. What is password confidentiality?

    A. Selecting a password that uses a detail from your life you are confident no one else knows

    B. A binding legal agreement that support people won't share or disclose your password, so that it is safe to tell it to them

    C. Keeping your password secret by not using default passwords, not writing it down, not using it in many places, and not sending it through insecure communications

    D. None of the above

8. Which of these is the stronger password?

    A. 1234567890

    B. MikeMeyers

    C. explication

    D. M!keM3y3rZ

9. Which of these is *not* a factor in password management?

    A. Confidentiality

    B. Expiration

    C. Guest

    D. Complexity

10. What Windows feature prevents unauthorized system changes?

    A. UAC

    B. DVI

    C. NFC

    D. WPS

Answers

1. **A**. Digging through the trash looking for useful information is called dumpster diving.

2. **D**. Edward uses shoulder surfing to gain access to people's accounts.

3. **C**. Device hardening involves blocking all unnecessary points of access, such as an unused wireless connection.

4. **A**. A lock-out time will lock the device after a certain idle time period, preventing snoops from looking at it.

5. **B**. The Guest account is designed for temporary, untrusted users such as visitors. The Standard account type is appropriate for everyday use; the Administrator account type is used only when system changes need to be made. There is no such thing as a Limited account.

6. A. The Standard account type is appropriate for everyday use; the Administrator account type is used only when system changes need to be made. The Guest account is designed for temporary, untrusted users such as visitors. There is no such thing as a Limited account.

7. C. Password confidentiality involves following many recommendations to avoid disclosing your password in ways that make it easier to steal.

8. D. The strongest password uses numbers, letters (upper and lowercase), and symbols and is not a proper name or a word from the dictionary.

9. C. Guest is a type of user account. The others are all factors involved in password management.

10. A. User Account Control (UAC) requires confirmation before system changes are made. DVI is a type of video interface adapter. NFC is a type of wireless communication. WPS is a way of connecting a Wi-Fi device to a router securely.

CHAPTER 12

Online Security Threats and Best Practices

In this chapter, you will learn how to
- Define and compare types of malicious software
- Protect against malware and social engineering
- Describe browser privacy and security issues

In Chapter 11, you learned about how to protect a local computer from unauthorized access and other attacks, but connecting a computer to a network opens it up to an entirely new set of dangers. Viruses and other malicious software can sneak into your system and destroy your data from anywhere in the world. You need to know how to stop these infiltrators and recover from any successful intrusions.

This chapter looks at issues involving Internet-borne attacks and how to defend against them. Not only will studying these topics help you on the CompTIA IT Fundamentals exam, but it will help you keep your computer secure and private.

Malicious Software

The Internet enables you to access resources from just about anywhere on the globe, all from the comfort of your favorite chair. This connection, however, runs both ways, and people can potentially access your computer from the comfort of their evil lairs. The Internet is awash with malicious software—*malware*—that is, even at this moment, trying to infect your systems.

 EXAM TIP   While a lot of malicious software comes from the Internet or some type of storage device, it can also come from a local area network. Be careful when you connect to open (or free) wireless networks, such as those at coffee shops and bookstores.

Malware consists of computer programs designed to break into computers or cause havoc on computers. Malware uses your computer to do work you don't want it to do—work that usually harms you, benefits someone else, or both. What kind of work? Well, because malware can also use every other resource connected to the device, the only limit we've seen so far is imagination. It could quietly spy on you, hijack your accounts to post bogus reviews, hold your family photos ransom, or force your system to join a cyber-attack against a government server.

This first section looks at common types of malware, such as adware, spyware, and spam. We examine social engineering—attacks that directly manipulate people—and then wrap up with viruses, Trojan horses, and worms.

Adware

Adware is software that displays unsolicited advertisements on your computer. It may come to you in the form of a program that seems helpful, such as a toolbar for your browser, but instead of (or in addition to) whatever it purports to do, it causes ads to display. These ads are usually in the form of pop-ups, although the ads can also show up in other ways too.

Adware has three main symptoms that clue you in to its presence: home page redirection, search engine redirection, and constant pop-ups.

- **Home page redirection** The adware changes your home page (the one that loads every time you open your browser). The adware company is hoping you won't know how to change it, and they'll profit from the extra ad views. In some really nasty adware installations, it locks the home page redirection in place, so you can't change back to your preferred page, or your preference is ignored.

- **Search engine redirection** Each browser has a default search engine. When you enter keywords in the Address bar, the default search engine processes them. Adware might change your browser's default to one tailored to serve search results that the company will profit from every time you click.

- **Constant pop-ups** A *pop-up* is an uninvited browser window that "pops up" when you visit certain Web sites. Web site designers sometimes code pop-ups into their pages (usually to generate ad revenue), although it's considered bad Web manners to do so. In addition, some adware pops up advertisement windows that may or may not have anything to do with the current Web site.

 EXAM TIP Home page redirection, search engine redirection, and constant pop-ups are all symptoms of adware installed, as outlined in Objective 3.3 of the CompTIA IT Fundamentals exam.

Closing a pop-up window can actually be rather tricky. Some pop-up browser windows don't look like browser windows, but more like dialog boxes, as in Figure 12-1. Some pop-up browser windows are deliberately designed to mimic OS alerts and dialogs to trick you into clicking them.

To avoid clicking in the pop-up window and possibly triggering more ads to appear, use alternate means of closing a pop-up window. For instance, you can right-click the browser's icon in the taskbar and select Close. You can also press ALT-TAB to bring the browser window in question to the forefront and then press ALT-F4 to close it.

Figure 12-1 A pesky pop-up

The larger question, of course, is how to prevent pop-ups in the future. Most Web browsers have features to prevent pop-up ads in the first place. In addition, you can use browser add-ons or extensions (such as Adblock) to block a variety of ads, including pop-ups. Note that some of these blocking programs can interfere with legitimate Web site content.

If you see constant pop-ups, you won't be able to control the problem with simple pop-up blockers. The underlying problem is adware infection; these are not normal pop-ups from Web pages.

NOTE Browser toolbars from reputable companies (such as Yahoo! and Google) are adware too. They don't display constant pop-ups, but they do change your default home page and search engine to sites that generate revenue for their parent companies. The express or default install options for some free software include one of these "helpful" toolbars (or change your default search engine and home page). Choose the custom install option and pay careful attention to the choices.

When you see any adware symptoms, the first place to look is for some sneaky adware installed as a Windows program, such as a browser toolbar or unknown utility. Open the Control Panel, go to Programs and Features, and scan through the list of programs to find something with *toolbar* in the name, or some utility program that you don't recognize. It's probably an adware program that you have inadvertently installed or that installed itself when you downloaded some software. Try removing it as you would uninstall any application.

 CAUTION When removing adware from Windows, the uninstaller might make it difficult for you, so pay attention to the prompts. We've seen all manner of trickiness, including "Are you sure?" messages where the Yes and No buttons are reversed in position from normal.

In other cases, the uninstaller redirects you to a Web site where it tries to force you to enter feedback about why you are uninstalling. Use ALT-F4 to close those Web sites. Don't click anything.

Some adware acts more like a virus than an application and can't be uninstalled via the Control Panel. In such cases, an anti-malware application may be able to help, or you can try manual removal instructions you find online. See "Anti-malware Programs," later in the chapter.

Spyware

Spyware monitors your computer usage habits and reports the information to the program's owner. The data collected might be used for minimally intrusive purposes, such as to gather anonymous data about which Web sites or browsers are most popular, but some types of spyware go considerably beyond the level of simple data collection.

Sensible people don't download and install something that they know is going to compromise their computer. Malware developers know this, so they bundle their software with some other program or utility that purports to give you some benefit.

Would you like free access to movies, music, or games that you would normally have to pay for? Could you use a handy *e-wallet* utility that remembers your many screen names, passwords, and credit-card numbers to make online purchases easier and faster? How about browser enhancements, performance boosters, custom cursor effects, search utilities, buddy lists, file savers, or media players? Programs for *any* purpose could simply be window dressing for the *real* purpose of the software. So you see, for the most part, malware doesn't need to force its way into your PC. Instead, it saunters calmly through the front door.

 CAUTION There are plenty of sketchy software-download sites that repackage legitimate software made by others with malware. Even if you recognize the name of the program and its developer, make sure you download the software itself from a reputable site.

Some spyware makers use more aggressive means to get you to install their software. Instead of offering you some sort of attractive utility, they instead use fear tactics and deception to try to trick you into installing their software. One popular method is to use pop-up browser windows crudely disguised as Windows' own system warnings. When clicked, these may trigger a flood of other browser windows or may even start a file download. An even worse type of spyware installs a *keylogger* utility, which records every keystroke you make, including when you type user names and passwords.

The lesson here is simple: *don't install these programs!* Careful reading of the software's license agreement before you install a program is a good idea, but realistically, it does little to protect your PC.

Use anti-malware software to remove spyware. See the section "Protecting Against Malware," later in the chapter, to see the steps.

Spam

E-mail that comes into your inbox from a source that's not a friend, family member, or colleague, and that you didn't ask for, can create huge problems for your computer and you. This unsolicited e-mail, called *spam,* accounts for a huge percentage of traffic on the Internet. Spam comes in many flavors, from real businesses trying to sell real products to scammers who just want to take your money (Figure 12-2). Hoaxes, pornography, and get-rich-quick schemes pour into the inboxes of most e-mail users. They waste your time and can easily offend.

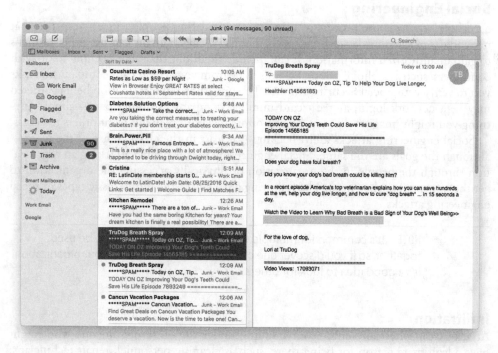

Figure 12-2   A spam message

Even e-mail that comes from a friend can contain spam. If a friend's e-mail address is hijacked or his computer is infected with malware, it might send out spam from his e-mail account without permission. When you get it, you think he is the source, so you are less careful than you ought to be. If a message seems to come from a friend but doesn't sound like that friend, call or text them and ask if they really sent it.

CAUTION   The Unsubscribe link in some spam doesn't actually unsubscribe you from anything; instead, it just confirms that your e-mail address is valid, and you get more spam. On the other hand, commercial messages from mainstream retail sites usually have a reliable unsubscribe link in them. It's sometimes a tough call to know how to proceed. If you have any doubts about the origin of an e-mail, it's best to delete it.

You can use several options to cope with the flood of spam. The first option is defense. Never post your e-mail address on the Internet. One study tested this theory and found that *more than 97 percent* of the spam received during the study went to e-mail addresses that had been posted on public Web sites.

Filters and filtering software can block spam at your mail server, at your service, or at your computer. You can set most e-mail programs to block e-mail from specific people—good to use if someone is harassing you. You can block by subject or keywords.

Social Engineering

Social engineering is the process of using or manipulating people to gain access to that network from the outside—which covers the many ways humans can use other humans to gain unauthorized information. It can include situations that have nothing to do with computers, such as a phone call that claims to be from your credit card company and asks you to verify your Social Security number. The unauthorized information being gathered may be a network login, a credit card number, company customer data—almost anything you might imagine that one person or organization may not want others to access.

Social engineering attacks aren't hacking—at least in the classic sense of the word—although the goals are the same. Social engineering means people attacking an organization through the people in the organization or physically accessing the organization to get the information they need. The following are a few of the more classic types of social engineering attacks.

NOTE   It's common for multiple social engineering attacks to be used together, so if you discover one of them being used against your organization, it's a good idea to look for others.

Infiltration

Attackers can physically enter your building under the guise of someone who might have a legitimate reason for being there, such as cleaning personnel, repair technicians, or messengers. They then snoop around desks, looking for whatever they can find.

They might talk with people inside the organization, gathering names, office numbers, and department names—little things in and of themselves, but powerful tools when combined later with other social engineering attacks. This is called *infiltration*.

Dressing the part of a legitimate user—with fake badge and everything—enables malicious people to gain access to locations and thus potentially to your data. Following someone through a door as if you belong, what's called *tailgating,* is a common way to infiltrate.

Telephone Scams

Telephone scams are probably the most common social engineering attack. In this case, the attacker makes a phone call to gain information. The attacker attempts to come across as someone inside a trusted organization and uses this to get the desired information.

Probably the most famous of these scams is the "I forgot my user name and password" scam. In this gambit, the attacker first learns the account name of a legitimate person in an organization, usually using the infiltration method. The attacker then calls someone in the organization, usually the help desk, in an attempt to gather information, in this case a password.

Hacker: "Hi, this is John Anderson in accounting. I forgot my password. Can you reset it, please?"
Help Desk: "Sure, what's your user name?"
Hacker: "j_w_Anderson."
Help Desk: "OK, I reset it to e34rd3."

Telephone scams aren't limited to attempts to get network access. There are documented telephone scams aimed at getting cash, blackmail material, or other valuables.

E-mail Phishing

Phishing is the act of trying to get people to give their user names, passwords, or other security information by pretending to be someone else electronically. A classic example is when a bad guy sends you an e-mail that's supposedly from Twitter or Instagram saying that your account is on hold for some violation and you need to click the Login link provided in the e-mail to straighten out the problem. Banking scams are also very popular, as shown in Figure 12-3.

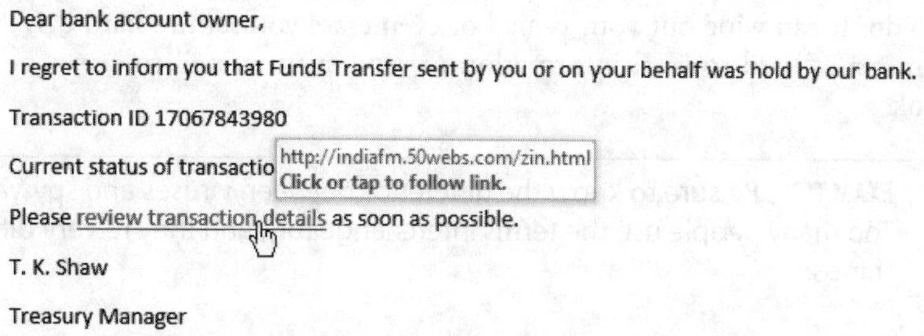

Dear bank account owner,

I regret to inform you that Funds Transfer sent by you or on your behalf was hold by our bank.

Transaction ID 17067843980

Current status of transactio http://indiafm.50webs.com/zin.html
Click or tap to follow link.

Please review transaction details as soon as possible.

T. K. Shaw

Treasury Manager

Figure 12-3 A phishing message

A phishing e-mail might contain a hyperlink that appears to point to a legitimate destination but actually points to a server run by the phisher. In Figure 12-3, for example, notice how the underlined text in the e-mail says one thing, and when you hover the mouse pointer over the link, the pop-up showing the actual address says quite another thing. Here are some other clues in this message that it is not legitimate:

- It does not identify the recipient by name in the body of the message.
- The banking institution is not named. There is no business name after the signature line.
- The first sentence contains a grammatical error ("was hold by our bank").

Security Messages: Fake and Real

Another way social engineering scammers try to trick users is by popping up fake security alerts. When you view a Web site, for example, a pop-up might appear saying that your computer has been infected by malware, prompting you to click a link to download a malware removal utility. It's fake, though—you don't have malware yet. If you click that link, one of two things will happen: (1) you will actually *get* malware of some sort or (2) someone will try to sell you software that will "fix" a problem that doesn't exist.

It can be difficult to distinguish such messages from legitimate security software alerts. If in doubt, shut down all browser windows by right-clicking their icons on the taskbar and choosing Close. If the alert persists, it was not generated by a pop-up. Next, verify the warning is from a security application you actually have installed. Look in the Control Panel in the Programs section to see if the program names match.

It's important to act on *legitimate* security software alerts instead of ignoring them, so close the alert window, open the full version of the security software, and run a full system scan. If the error reappears, it's probably legitimate. Illegitimate alerts are a good hint your device has malware.

Viruses

Just as a biological virus gets passed from person to person, a computer *virus* is a piece of malicious software that gets passed from computer to computer. A computer virus is designed to attach itself to a program on your computer and execute when the program executes. It could be your e-mail program, your word processor, or even a game. Whenever you use the infected program, the virus goes into action and does whatever it was designed to do. It can wipe out your e-mail or even erase your entire hard drive! Viruses are also sometimes used to steal information or send spam e-mail to everyone in your address book.

 EXAM TIP Be sure to know the difference between viruses and spyware. Too many people use the terms interchangeably, and they're very different things.

Trojan Horses

Trojan horses (sometimes just called *Trojans*) are freestanding programs that do something other than what the person who runs the program thinks they will. Much as the Trojan horse in antiquity, you invite these programs in, unaware of what lurks inside. An example of a Trojan horse is a program that a person thinks is an antivirus program but is actually a virus. Some Trojan horses are quite sophisticated. It might be a game that works perfectly well but causes some type of damage when the user quits the game.

Worms

Similar to a Trojan horse, a *worm* is a complete program that travels from machine to machine, usually through computer networks. Most worms are designed to take advantage of security problems in operating systems and install themselves on vulnerable machines. (Remember in Chapter 11 when we talked about the importance of keeping the OS up to date? This is why.) They can copy themselves over and over again on infected networks, potentially creating so much activity that they overload the network by consuming bandwidth. A fast-spreading worm might even bring chunks of the entire Internet to a halt.

 EXAM TIP Make sure you understand the differences between the various types of malware, including spyware, viruses, Trojan horses, and ransomware.

Ransomware

One particularly nasty type of malware, *ransomware,* locks down your computer and holds it for ransom, displaying some threatening warning that if you don't pay up (usually by sending money via wire transfer), your files will be deleted. Some smoke-and-mirrors ransomware doesn't actually harm your PC beyond locking it down until you pay or remove the ransomware; other versions actually do delete files. What differentiates this from most types of malware is that it's not a sneaky attack. It's blatant, obvious extortion. Figure 12-4 shows an example. This type of malware is usually spread via infected .zip files sent as e-mail attachments.

There are three basic types of ransomware: scareware, lock-screen, and encryption.

- **Scareware** This is ransomware that just scares you. It tries to sell you bogus antivirus or cleanup tools to fix a problem that doesn't exist. You can still use your PC but you might be bombarded with pop-ups, or you might be prevented from running programs. These are the easiest to remove.

- **Lock-screen** This type doesn't allow you to use your PC in any way. It shows a full-size window warning you that you have violated the law and must pay a fine. Figure 12-4 shows this form.

- **Encrypting** This is the worst stuff because it encrypts and locks your personal files until you pay. Even if you manage to remove the malware, your files are useless without the decryption key, which you can't get without paying.

PART III

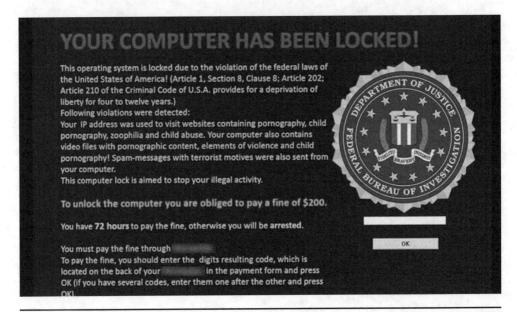

Figure 12-4   A ransomware warning (Courtesy of Motormille2 at Wikimedia Commons, CC BY-SA 4.0)

Protecting Against Malware

You can do several things to protect yourself and your data against online threats. First, keep the OS patched. Second, make sure your computer runs up-to-date anti-malware software, especially if you connect to the Internet via an always-on broadband connection. You should also be protected by a firewall, either as part of your network hardware or by means of a software program. (See the sections on anti-malware programs and firewalls coming up in this chapter.)

Windows Update

Because malware can infect systems through security flaws in operating systems, the next defense against them is to make sure you have the latest security patches installed on your version of Windows. A *security patch* is an addition to the operating system to patch a hole in the operating system code. Keeping your patches up to date, called *patch management,* goes a long way toward keeping your system safe.

Microsoft's Windows Update tool is handy for Windows users, as it provides a simple method to ensure that your version's security is up to date. Windows Update is set to download and install updates automatically by default. (You should not change that setting unless specifically directed to do so by your IT department.) You might occasionally be prompted to give permission to install a certain update, but for the most part, Windows Update works silently and automatically behind the scenes.

You can adjust Windows Update settings through the Control Panel or the Settings applet (in Windows 10). You can configure several settings.

- **Change active hours**   Windows will not automatically restart between the hours you specify here, so an update won't interrupt your work.

- **Restart options**   When a restart is scheduled, this option is available to specify an exact restart time (on a one-time basis).

- **Advanced options**   Here you can choose whether to also receive updates for Microsoft applications with Windows Update.

NOTE   Application updates were covered in Chapter 7.

Anti-malware Programs

An *anti-malware* program, such as a classic *antivirus program,* protects your PC in two ways. It can be both sword and shield, working in an active seek-and-destroy mode and in a passive sentry mode. When ordered to seek and destroy, the program scans the computer's files for viruses (as shown in Figure 12-5) and, if it finds any, presents you with the available options for removing or disabling them. Antivirus programs can also operate

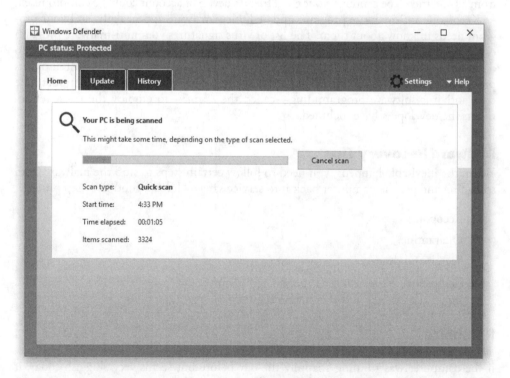

Figure 12-5   Windows Defender scanning Windows 10 for viruses and other malware

as *virus shields* that passively monitor your computer's activity, checking for viruses only when certain events occur, such as a program executing or a file being downloaded.

The antivirus program uses a library of signatures to detect viruses. A *signature* is the code pattern of a known virus. The antivirus program compares an executable file to its library of signatures. Sometimes a perfectly clean program coincidentally holds a virus signature. Usually the antivirus program's creator provides a patch to prevent further false alarms.

 NOTE The term *antivirus* (and *antispyware,* or anti-anything) is becoming obsolete. Viruses are only a small component of the many types of malware. Many people continue to use the term as a synonym for anti-malware.

Malware Prevention Tips

The secret to preventing damage from a malicious software attack is to keep from getting malware in the first place. As discussed earlier, all good anti-malware programs include a malware shield that scans e-mail, downloads, running programs, and so on, automatically.

Know the source of any software before you load it. Although the chance of commercial, shrink-wrapped software having malware is virtually nil (there have been a couple of well-publicized exceptions), that illegal copy of Modern Warfare 3 you downloaded might really make you *pay*. Be very careful with e-mail attachments and hyperlinks. If the e-mail they arrive in is even remotely suspicious, don't open, click, or download them. Even if the e-mail is from a good friend, be cautious: your good friend's device or account could be compromised.

Keep your anti-malware program updated. New malware appear daily, and your program needs to know about them. The list of virus signatures your anti-malware program can recognize is called the *definition file,* and you must keep that definition file up to date so that your antivirus software has the latest signatures. Fortunately, most antivirus programs update themselves automatically. Further, you should periodically update the core antivirus software programming—called the *engine*—to employ the latest refinements the developers have included.

Malware Recovery Tips

When the inevitable happens, you need to follow certain steps to stop the malware from spreading and get the computer back into service safely. Here's a good five-step process:

1. Recognize.
2. Quarantine.
3. Search and destroy.
4. Remediate.
5. Educate.

Recognize

The first step is to recognize that a potential malware outbreak has occurred. For example, if the computer was running snappily the day before but seems very sluggish today, it could be a symptom of a virus or other malware attack.

Quarantine

Malware can spread, so you need to quarantine the infected computer to cut it off from the rest of the network. One easy method for doing this is to disconnect the network cable from the back of the system and disable any wireless adapters. Once you are sure the machine isn't capable of infecting others, you're ready to find the malware and get rid of it.

Search and Destroy

Once you've isolated the infected computer (or computers), you need to find the malware using an anti-malware application, and allow the application to remove it. The process varies among the various anti-malware tools available. Follow the developer's instructions that apply to your OS.

E-mail is still a common source of malware, and opening infected e-mail is a common way to get infected. Viewing an e-mail in a preview window opens the e-mail message and exposes your computer to some malware. Download files only from sites you know to be safe; the less reputable corners of the Internet are the most likely places to pick up computer infections.

Remediate

Malware can do a lot of damage to a system, especially to sensitive files needed to load Windows, so you might need to remediate formerly infected systems after cleaning off the drive or drives. *Remediation* simply means that you fix things the malware harmed. This usually means replacing corrupted or destroyed files with your backups—you did make backups, right? The Backup and Restore applet in the Windows Control Panel will walk you through restoring the backed-up files to your PC. Time Machine in macOS can likewise restore damaged or missing files.

Educate

The best way to keep from having to deal with malware is education. Educate other people in your home or office who may be inadvertently putting their own computer and others at risk, explaining what you have learned in this chapter. Any user who understands the risks of questionable actions on their computers will usually do the right thing and stay away from malware.

 NOTE   If, at any point, you don't think you can fix the problem or are unsure if you completely removed the malware, be sure to *escalate* the issue. Escalation is the process of handing off your task to someone else, such as an IT professional. For example, you might decide that you need to hire an expert to come to your home or take your computer to a repair shop.

Being a Smart Web User

Many of the ways you can protect your system while browsing the Web aren't tied to any particular setting but are instead a combination of being skeptical and understanding what you are seeing. The following sections explain some best practices for browsing.

Understanding the Risks of Public Workstations

In many places, such as hotel lobbies, conference centers, and libraries, you may find public workstations that anyone can use to access the Internet and run basic applications. Use these with great caution. You never know what malware lurks there. An unsupervised terminal could even contain a keylogger program that can steal user names and passwords. The company providing the terminal is probably not out to steal your data, but if the workstation's maintenance and upkeep is left to unqualified staff who don't know how to lock down the security on a workstation, any public user can accidentally or intentionally install malware on it.

Public workstations also pose privacy risks. Some browsers are set to automatically remember the text you enter into form fields, so they could remember your name, address, and even credit card data for the next person to see who sits down at that workstation. Other users can also review the history in the browser to see what Web sites you have used.

When using a browser on a public workstation, your best bet is to use the high-privacy mode for that browser. In Internet Explorer and Microsoft Edge it is called InPrivate Browsing (see Figure 12-6), and you activate it by pressing CTRL-SHIFT-P or pressing

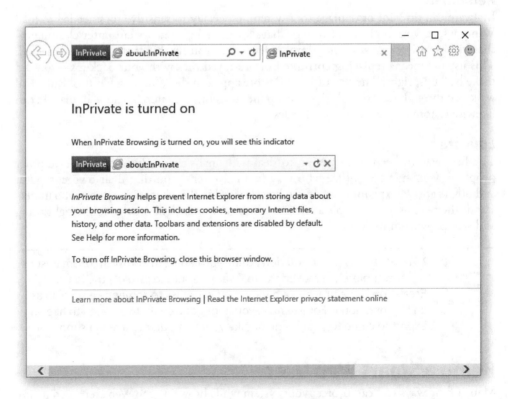

Figure 12-6   InPrivate Browsing protects your privacy as you use a public workstation.

ALT-T to open the Tools menu and then clicking InPrivate Browsing. In this high-privacy mode, nothing about your session is retained in the browser: no form fields, no history, no temporary files. An InPrivate session continues until you close its window. Some other browsers have their own high-privacy modes. For example, in Google Chrome the feature is called Incognito Window.

NOTE You can use high-privacy settings in just about every browser, including the ones on mobile devices. Apple Safari and Mozilla Firefox both enable you to open a private session by selecting File | New Private Window. Safari in iOS has a Private toggle button to go into Private Browsing mode.

Playing Smart with Secure Web Sites

You should enter private information (such as credit card numbers) only on secure, trusted Web sites. A *secure* site is one that encrypts the transmission between you and the Web site so that it cannot be intercepted and snooped along the way. A *trusted* site is one that you trust will not do anything illegal or unethical with the information you provide.

NOTE It is much easier to determine whether a site is secure than whether you should trust it. Anyone can set up a secure site and prove that it is secure, but trust is more subjective. Will that online merchant safeguard your credit card data adequately? Will they sell your contact information to a marketing company? That's where reference organizations like the Better Business Bureau come in.

Recognizing a Secure Web Site

A secure Web site uses encryption protocols (rules) to create secure communications between your computer and the server hosting the Web site. One popular protocol is *Transport Layer Security (TLS);* it is a modern update of the older *Secure Sockets Layer (SSL)* protocol. A Web site address that use SSL or TLS starts with *https://* (which stands for Hypertext Transfer Protocol over SSL) instead of http://. So one way to recognize a secure site right off the bat is to look for https:// in the address bar.

Another clue that a Web site is secure is a lock symbol in or near the address bar. In some browsers the address bar turns green when using a secure URL. Figure 12-7 shows a secure URL in Internet Explorer.

EXAM TIP You should be able to recognize the signs of a secure connection in a browser window, including https:// and the lock symbol.

Figure 12-7 A secure URL

Recognizing Invalid Certificate Warnings

Encrypted transmission by itself doesn't guarantee *who* you are communicating with, so the identity of a secure site is authenticated by a digital certificate. In other words, you know that when you receive data from PayPal.com, it's really from PayPal.com and not from some rogue site intercepting the transmission and pretending to be PayPal. When a company sets up a secure Web site, they buy a certificate from a certificate authority.

When you visit a secure Web site, your browser asks for verification from the certificate authority that the secure site is authentic. If all goes well with that transaction, it's invisible. However, if there's a problem with the certificate, you might see a certificate warning. It might report, for example, that the certificate has expired or the name on the certificate doesn't match the name sent with the request.

In some cases a certificate warning can be safely dismissed, especially if it's for a company you know to be reputable and the warning is about a minor issue like the name not matching exactly. However, if it's for a company you don't know and trust or if anything looks amiss with the Web site, be cautious about providing any personal or financial information on that site. If the error is that the security certificate was not issued by a trusted certificate authority or was issued for a different Web site's address, that could indicate a fraudulent site.

Recognizing Untrusted Source Warnings

In the course of your Web browsing, you might see a message when attempting to open a Web page that the source is untrusted, as in Figure 12-8. Depending on the browser and the exact problem, this warning may be worded in a number of ways.

A source (that is, a Web site) may be untrusted for any of several reason. Its certificate may not have been issued by a trusted certificate authority. It might be a known phishing site that your browser (or a security add-on) has on its "do not trust" list. The Web site might attempt to load software when you visit it, which is suspicious and triggers some browsers to warn you.

Pay attention to these warnings! If there is any doubt about the site's safety (or you don't understand the warning), do not proceed.

Recognizing Suspicious Links

On a Web site or in an e-mail message, there are a number of ways to spot a hyperlink that is likely to get you into trouble.

First, take a look at the address that the hyperlink really points to. Hover the mouse pointer over the hyperlink to see the actual URL, either in a pop-up ScreenTip or in the browser's status bar at the bottom of its window.

Beware of URLs that use an IP address instead of a domain name. Usually when someone uses the IP address, they're trying to make it hard for you to see the domain name for some reason.

When evaluating a URL, find the first single / in the address and read backward from there to see the domain name of the site. For example, in http://answers.yahoo.com /question/index;_ylv=3, the first slash comes after .com. The text immediately before that slash is yahoo.com, which is a well-known site, so this URL is probably safe.

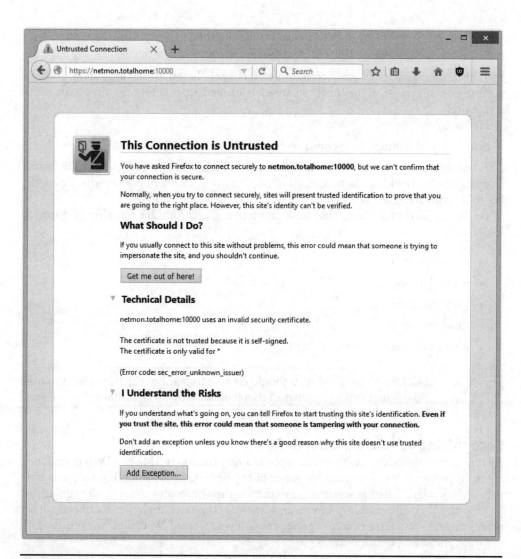

Figure 12-8   A certificate warning may be harmless, or it may indicate a fraudulent site.

On the other hand, if there is some other domain name before the first slash, it is probably a fraudulent site. Here is an example:

http://hackerz.com/chaseonline.chase.com/survey.html

In that one, even though the URL contains a legitimate domain name (chase.com), it's not before the *first* slash. This URL would actually direct you to hackerz.com.

Here's another example:

http://www.chase.com@209.131.36.168/survey.jsp

Yes, this example includes chase.com, but immediately before the slash is an IP address, not the domain name. Remember, whatever is immediately before the first slash is the actual site.

Here's another one:

http://onlinebanking-chase.com/survey.php

This one does have chase.com immediately before the slash, but look closely. The actual domain is onlinebanking-chase.com, which is an entirely different domain that has nothing to do with the real chase.com.

Be careful also of variants that look right at a glance but are actually malformed, like these:

- wwwchase.com
- www-chase.com
- www.chasecom.com
- chase.com.cc
- www.chase.com-sweepstakes.info

 EXAM TIP Given a link, you should be able to point out characteristics in the address that make you suspect that it either is or isn't fraudulent.

Recognizing Suspicious Banner Ads

Banner ads are the advertisements that appear along the top or side of a Web page. They are third-party ads, not provided by owner of the site you are visiting. For the most part they are harmless. They generate ad revenue for the site owner so he or she can afford to keep the Web site running. However, some unscrupulous malware distributors have been known to use banner ads, even at well-known, trusted Web sites, to spread nasty malware, including ransomware.

There are no ironclad ways to tell whether a banner ad is legitimate just by looking at it. If a banner ad promises something that sounds too good to be true, however, or is obviously trying to manipulate you into clicking it by dangling some tantalizing piece of information in front of you, be wary. Watch also for poor-quality, low-resolution graphics in the banner and for ads that seem oddly placed (for example, a banner ad for "adult content" on a site that sells children's toys). Banner ad space is sometimes sold on a clearinghouse basis, where the actual company purchasing the ad space is not the company that chooses and places the ad there. A legitimate site could contract with a legitimate banner ad company, which could in turn subcontract that space to a company that had malicious intent, and nobody would notice until people started getting phished or scammed.

You can protect your computer from banner ads with malicious content by not clicking them. You can also minimize your risk by uninstalling any third-party browser extensions that you don't use, such as Adobe Flash, Oracle Java, and Microsoft Silverlight. It's also important to install updates for your browser as soon as they become available and to use the 64-bit version of your browser if possible.

Limiting Use of Personally Identifiable Information Online

It's amazing how much *personally identifiable information (PII)* a determined sleuth can find out about you online. There are databases that have your phone number, your current and last several addresses, your employers, and even your government records like parking tickets and arrests, available to anyone with a credit card.

You can't stop people from searching public records, so it's difficult to keep your personal information off the Internet entirely. You don't have to volunteer it up to anyone who asks. Here are some tips for limiting the amount of personal information you share online:

- Have a separate e-mail address that you use only for filling in online forms and making online purchases. Don't use your main e-mail address. This will help minimize the amount of spam you receive.

- When asked to enter a phone number in an online form, unless you are making a purchase, use a fake phone number, or use 000-000-0000. The same goes for entering a mailing address. If you're not making a purchase, they don't need to know where you live.

- When a site asks for your birthdate, indicate that you are younger than 13. It is illegal in many places for marketers to market to people younger than 13, so they will exclude you from any marketing they send out. (Of course, don't do this if you are visiting a site that has a minimum age to use the site.)

- Look yourself up on sites that offer personal information about people and see whether there is a way to have your information removed. Most such sites will remove your data if you go through the proper channels to make such a request.

 EXAM TIP You should be able to identify the risks involved in putting personal information on the Internet and some strategies for minimizing your exposure while still participating in online activities.

Updating Browsers and Plug-ins

Most malware that comes through a Web browser does so because of exploits from out-of-date browser software or plug-ins. The classic *plug-ins* added functionality to early Web browsers for various purposes. Some enabled you to access more interactive features of a site that supported those plug-ins. Most modern browsers don't use them (see "Disabling Unneeded Plug-ins, Toolbars, and Extensions" for more details).

It's essential, therefore, that you keep browsers updated, installing the latest versions whenever they become available. Windows Update will update Internet Explorer and Microsoft Edge browsers automatically for you. Other browsers may update themselves automatically when you run them. In Google Chrome, you can check whether your version is up to date by choosing Tools | Settings | About. In Mozilla Firefox, choose Tools | Options | Advanced | Update to get to a screen where you can enable or disable automatic updates.

While we're on the subject of browsers, note that *legacy browsers* (that is, older versions of the browser) suffer from all of the same security risks as an un-updated browser of the current version. For example, if you're using a computer with Windows XP on it, you're probably using Internet Explorer 7, which is woefully underprepared for today's Web security threats. In some cases you can install a newer browser version, but in very old operating systems you cannot go past a certain level. For example, you can't install IE 11 on Windows XP. Because of this, I don't recommend Web browsing on a Windows XP system.

Configuring Browser Security and Privacy Settings

Some of the settings for your browser are purely superficial; you can customize the size and type of fonts used on Web sites with your own styles. But you also have power over privacy and security features such as cookies, the Internet cache, and add-ons that enhance the abilities of your browser. If these settings are configured improperly, you may be opening yourself up to outside attacks. The exact names of the settings and the processes of accessing them vary between browsers; in this chapter we examine them in Internet Explorer.

Adjusting Browser Security Settings

In a browser context, *security* means the ability to prevent your computer from being harmed by malware. When you crank up security settings, you minimize the chance that visiting Web site with malicious code will infect your computer and cause problems. High security settings may prevent some Web sites from performing as intended, though; for example, some shopping sites won't work with security settings at their highest levels.

Internet Explorer has a special security feature that most other browsers lack: it uses multiple security zones. This feature enables you to differentiate between risky sites and safe ones. A *security zone* is a group of settings that are applicable to a certain trust level for Web sites. There are four zones: Internet, Local intranet, Trusted sites, and Restricted sites. Internet is the default. The other three zones enable you to assign Web sites to them. To control which sites are in a zone, click the zone and then click the Sites button. Using zones enables you to have different security settings for sites that you trust, like your banking institution, than from sites you don't trust, like one that illegally streams live sporting events.

To change the security level for a zone, choose Tools | Internet Options in Internet Explorer and click the Security tab. Click the zone icon at the top and then drag the slider bar up or down (see Figure 12-9). You can also click Custom level and fine-tune the security settings for the chosen zone.

Clearing Your Cookies

When you go to a Web site, browsers store copies of the graphics and other items so the page will load more quickly the next time you access it. These are part of the *Internet cache* or *Temporary Internet Files*. One of the types of information that a Web site may

Figure 12-9
Change the
security settings
for a particular
zone.

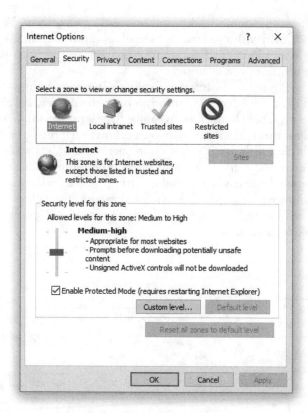

store on your computer is a cookie. A *cookie* is a small text file containing information
about you. The data stored in cookies is used for a variety of purposes:

- To authenticate or identify you as a registered user of a Web site so it will
  remember you on future visits
- To track items in your shopping basket or cart
- To present different content to different users
- To style or theme the site based on user preference
- To track your access to Web sites, including what products you look at, even if
  you don't buy them

Not all cookies (or Temporary Internet Files) are happy and friendly, though. Malicious cookies, installed by some type of malware, can track your Internet activities and
report to its creator. This information is often sold to advertisers so that they can better target you. The best way to defend against these bad cookies is to guard against all
malware. Some browsers and browser add-ins can be set to partially or completely block
cookies.

Cookies come from two different sources. A *first-party cookie* comes from the Web site you are actually visiting. First-party cookies can be helpful. A *third-party cookie* comes from another source, such as an advertisement on the Web page. Third-party cookies have no benefit to you as a user.

On the Privacy tab in Internet Explorer's Internet Options dialog box (Figure 12-10), you can click the Advanced button to open the Advanced Privacy Settings dialog box. From here you can choose how to handle first-party and third-party cookies. Your choices are to allow them, block them, or get a prompt each time one tries to write to your hard drive. You can click the Sites button to open a dialog box where you can indicate certain Web sites to always allow or always block from using cookies.

Microsoft Edge has fewer cookie settings you can change. Choose Tools | Settings | View Advanced Settings and then scroll down to the Cookies section. Open the Cookies drop-down list and then choose Block all cookies, Block only third party cookies, or Don't block cookies.

Figure 12-10
On the Privacy tab you can control the use of cookies and pop-ups.

Clearing the History and Temporary Internet Files

Most browsers track the Web sites you visit over time—your history—and store any relevant information about the site as temporary Internet files. You can remove the history and temporary Internet files to erase your tracks.

In Internet Explorer, choose Tools | Internet Options, and on the General tab, select the *Delete browsing history on exit* check box. That takes care of the future. To wipe up the past, click the Delete button and then mark or clear the check boxes for the types of content you want to delete. For example, you can wipe out cookies and Web site data from here, as well as history, temporary Internet files, and saved passwords. See Figure 12-11. Then click Delete.

In Microsoft Edge, choose Tools | Settings and under the Clear browsing data heading, click Choose what to clear. Select or clear the check boxes for the various types of content and click Clear.

 EXAM TIP Make sure you understand the benefits and drawbacks of clearing the browser cache, history, and cookies.

Figure 12-11
Clear your browsing history and other information about your browsing habits.

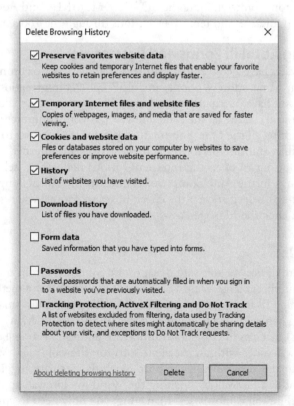

Disabling Unneeded Plug-ins, Toolbars, and Extensions

The problem with classic plug-ins was that they exercised a lot of control over the user's Web browser and could do malicious things.

According to the CompTIA IT Fundamentals exam, you should uninstall unused plug-ins. Get that correct on the test. For Web browser use today, in contrast, don't use any classic plug-in. Instead use extensions (more on these shortly).

Various third-party companies create toolbars for browsers that add certain features. The Yahoo! toolbar, for example, added a Yahoo! search field, access to Yahoo! mail, a stock ticker, and so forth. A lot of people enjoyed the added features (though Yahoo! stopped making the toolbar in favor of a customized Firefox browser).

The problem with toolbars comes from less-reputable companies that add aggressive toolbars during installation of other programs. They can prove to be hard to remove and use up valuable resources. If you accidentally install one of these predatory toolbars, such as Jeeves from Ask.com, uninstall it immediately.

Modern browsers use extensions to add functionality. Extensions are usually tightly written code with discrete functions. Adblock, for example, just blocks ads from appearing on Web pages you visit. It doesn't take over your browser or redirect you somewhere. It just does its job.

You can and should disable unused extensions. Figure 12-12 shows the Extensions list in Google Chrome browser. Note the 3D Viewer for IKEA and Adobe Acrobat are disabled. You can add, disable, and remove extensions through the Tools menu in most browsers.

Disabling AutoFill Forms and Passwords

Most browsers have a convenient feature that allows you to automatically fill in forms that ask for your name, address, phone, and other contact information, as well as passwords for Web sites you have previously signed into. This feature saves a lot of time on a computer that is physically secure all the time. However, if your computer is not under your control and monitoring all the time, you might not want the browser to save that kind of data.

To disable autofill for forms and passwords in Internet Explorer, choose Tools | Internet Options to open the Internet Options dialog box, select the Content tab, and click Settings in the AutoComplete section. In the AutoComplete Settings dialog box (Figure 12-13), select or clear the check boxes to control what is saved. To manage saved passwords, click the Manage Passwords button there.

Firewalls

Firewalls are devices or software that protect computers from unauthorized access to and from the Internet at large. Hardware firewalls use a number of methods to protect networks, such as hiding IP addresses and blocking TCP/IP ports. Most small office/home office networks use a hardware firewall built into the SOHO router. Many routers use access control lists (ACLs) that can filter by port number, IP address, or several other attributes.

Windows comes with an excellent software firewall called Windows Firewall. It can also handle the heavy lifting of port blocking, security logging, and more. You can access Windows Firewall by opening the Windows Firewall applet in the Control Panel. Windows Firewall is mostly self-managing; you only need to configure it if it is blocking an application that you want to use.

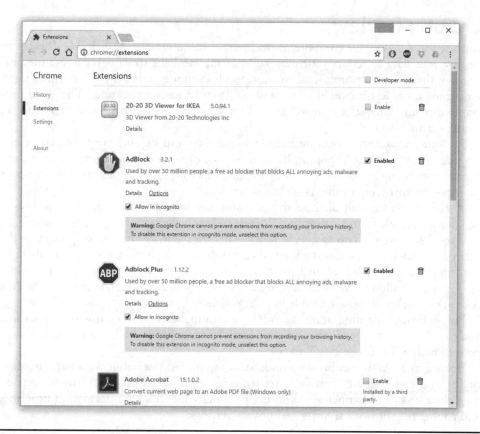

Figure 12-12 Extensions in Chrome

Figure 12-13
Choose
what your
browser saves
automatically
when you enter
passwords and
fill in forms.

Chapter Review

You need to defend your computer from Internet-based attacks. Malicious software can destroy your data or report your personal information back to whoever wrote the program. Viruses, Trojan horses, and worms can all infiltrate your system, often posing as something more legitimate, like (not without irony) a malware scanner. These bad programs also have a habit of growing worse over time, as they destroy more data or infect more systems.

Spyware and adware do not necessarily do harm to your PC, but they can make using it a pain by causing ads to pop up in front of your browser or slowing down your computer. Spam is any unwanted e-mail that appears in your inbox. These are usually scams for money. Don't reply to them—delete them.

There are tools for all of these that scan for any malware currently on your system and defend against future infiltration. If your system becomes infected with malware, be sure you know what to do to get rid of it: recognize the malware attack, quarantine the entire PC, search for and destroy the malware using anti-malware software, remediate by restoring your PC with previously made backups, and educate yourself and anyone else who may have allowed the infection to occur. Also, be sure to escalate the problem to a boss or co-worker if you are unable to fix it yourself.

Proper browser configuration can often prevent malware from getting onto your PC. You can delete history, cookies, and temporary Internet files, which can be used to track your browsing. Don't use classic plug-ins.

Being a smart Web user includes understanding the risks of public workstations, identifying and using secure Web sites, recognizing invalid certificates, untrusted sources, suspicious links and banner ads, limiting personally identifiable information exposure, and configuring browser security and privacy settings.

Questions

1. Which of these types of programs is bothersome but not necessarily dangerous?

   A. Worm

   B. Adware

   C. Virus

   D. Trojan

2. Which of the following are alternative methods of closing a pop-up window? (Choose two.)

   A. Clicking inside the pop-up

   B. Pressing ALT-F4

   C. Right-clicking the program's taskbar icon and selecting Close

   D. Running your antivirus software

3. What is spam?

   A. Unwanted e-mail messages

   B. A type of virus

   C. An antivirus program

   D. A type of firewall

4. Besides using anti-malware software, what two things can you do to protect your Windows machine from intruders? (Choose two.)

   A. Install all available Windows updates.

   B. Use only Internet Explorer.

   C. Back up your data.

   D. Use a firewall.

5. After you have recognized that there is a virus on your PC, what is the next step to removing the virus?

   A. To educate

   B. To search and destroy

   C. To quarantine

   D. To remediate

6. How can you defend against malware delivered by e-mail?

   A. Delete old messages regularly.

   B. Don't open attachments from unknown senders.

   C. Only use the preview window.

   D. Only use Mozilla Thunderbird.

7. Which type of file tracks your activities on the Internet?

   A. Spam

   B. Java

   C. Pop-up

   D. Cookie

8. Which of the following might you want to disable to protect your privacy?

   A. Autofill forms

   B. Hyperlinks

   C. Certificates

   D. InPrivate browsing

PART III

9. Which type of malware tries to get you to pay a fee to decrypt your files?

   A. Trojan

   B. Worm

   C. Spyware

   D. Ransomware

10. What indicates that you've browsed to a secure Web page? (Select two.)

   A. The Web address starts with http://.

   B. The Web address starts with https://.

   C. A small lock appears in the browser.

   D. A small key appears in the browser.

Answers

1. **B.** Adware can cause annoying pop-ups and browser redirection but it doesn't necessarily attack your PC.

2. **B, C.** To close a pop-up window safely, you can either press ALT-F4 or right-click the program's taskbar icon and select Close.

3. **A.** Spam is the name for the unwanted e-mail messages that can clog your inbox.

4. **A, D.** Updating your operating system and using a firewall are two things that will help protect you from hackers.

5. **C.** After you recognize that there is a virus on your machine, you need to quarantine, either by using anti-malware software or by disconnecting the infected machine from the network.

6. **B.** The best defense against e-mail messages with malware is not opening e-mail messages from unknown senders.

7. **D.** Web browsers use cookies to track certain things you do on the Internet.

8. **A.** Autofill forms can make your previously entered form data available to others who use your computer.

9. **D.** Ransomware holds your data for ransom by demanding that you pay a fee.

10. **B, C.** Secure Web pages have addresses that start with https://, and a small lock appears in the browser.

Computer Maintenance and Management

In this chapter, you will learn how to
- Manage power usage
- Clean and maintain hardware
- Dispose of computer equipment responsibly

Keeping a computer working well isn't that difficult these days. Most of the maintenance utilities that IT professionals used to recommend you run manually are now handled automatically in the OS, including running Windows Update and checking the hard drive for storage errors.

So what's left for the average user to do? The main things are to manage the computer's power usage effectively, keep it clean (inside and out), and recycle or dispose of it properly when it's beyond repair or no longer cost-effective to upgrade. In this chapter, we look at those three important topics, all of which are covered in Objective 5.5 of the CompTIA IT Fundamentals exam.

 EXAM TIP This chapter provides good general guidelines, but you should also check, be aware of, and follow the manufacturer's safety guidelines. These guidelines help you use, maintain, repair, and dispose of your devices safely.

Power Management Basics

Broadly, *power management* means controlling how a computer uses power, with a focus on using less power and making sure power is available when needed (for example, by conserving battery life).

Choose Energy-Efficient Devices

In addition to the power management changes you can make in Windows (covered next), you can also achieve some power savings by choosing energy-efficient devices. Look for components that have the Energy Star logo; these are certified to be energy efficient. An energy-efficient device may have special power-conserving features, such as shutting itself off or putting itself in a low-power mode after a period of inactivity.

317

EXAM TIP An *energy-efficient device* uses less energy overall than nonefficient equivalents and may have special energy conservation features. Look for comparative questions on the exam.

What do you do when you're going to be away from the computer for a while? The following sections can help you decide.

Leave the PC Running

Some people like to leave their computers on 24/7, so they never have to wait for the computer to start up when they want to use it. That's okay, but it has some consequences.

First, there's the financial side. If you leave a desktop computer on all the time, you will pay about $200 a year for its electricity (assuming a cost of about 12 cents per kilowatt/ hour). A laptop is much less, around $65 per year. That's not a bank-breaker, but it's not small change, either.

Next, there's the fact that a running computer generates heat, and heat is an enemy of computers. If certain chips (like the CPU) get too hot, they stop working until they cool down enough. Very high temperatures can damage a chip immediately, but damage from less intense heat can also accumulate until the chip fails. That's why there are all those heat sinks and fans inside a computer, as you learned in Chapter 2. Even with all that heat-reducing equipment, though, heat is still an issue.

Finally, if your computer runs on battery power, leaving it on all the time drains the battery. That's fine if you are close to an AC outlet where you can recharge the battery, but you won't always be.

For all those reasons, you should consider either shutting the computer down entirely or putting it in a low-power mode whenever you are going to be away from it for more than a few minutes.

Shut Down the PC

Shutting down completely eliminates all three of the problems described earlier, but it has one big disadvantage: it's inconvenient. A typical Windows PC takes a minute or two to start up, and meanwhile you're sitting there drumming your fingers on the desk impatiently. If you're coming back to the computer relatively quickly (say, within a day or so), you might want to consider an alternative that will enable you to resume your work more quickly.

Low-Power Modes

Windows supports two power-saving modes.

- **Sleep**   Keeps memory powered but shuts down all other components. As a result, the computer uses very little power—just enough to allow the memory to retain its contents. On battery power, a laptop can last about a day in this mode (depending on battery capacity and condition, of course). Resuming from Sleep mode is very fast, just a few seconds in most cases.

- **Hibernate**   Copies memory content to a reserved area of the hard drive and then powers off all components. Since the PC is not using any power, it can remain in Hibernate mode indefinitely. Resuming from Hibernate takes slightly longer than from Sleep, about 15 seconds on the average.

NOTE   In Windows 8 and later, Sleep mode is actually a hybrid sleep. It starts out in Sleep mode, but if the battery reaches a critically low threshold or if a certain amount of time passes (as specified in Power Options), Windows switches to Hibernate automatically.

To enter Sleep mode manually, click the Start button, click Power, and then click Sleep or Hibernate. See Figure 13-1. You can also configure the PC to enter Sleep or Hibernate mode automatically after a certain amount of idle time by setting that up in a power profile, described next.

If Hibernate doesn't appear on the Power menu (as it doesn't in Figure 13-1), you can make it appear by marking the Hibernate check box in the Control Panel, in Hardware and Sound | Power Options | System Settings (shown later in this chapter in Figure 13-5). If the check box isn't selectable, click the *Change settings that are currently unavailable* hyperlink near the top of the dialog box. Be aware, however, that on systems where Hibernate is not enabled by default, it is sometimes because the hardware doesn't work well with the feature. If you experience a problem using Hibernate, you might decide it's better not to use it.

TIP   If your PC won't wake up from Sleep or Hibernate, press and hold the Power button on the computer for 10 seconds and then press it again to restart.

Figure 13-1
Put the PC to sleep before you walk away.

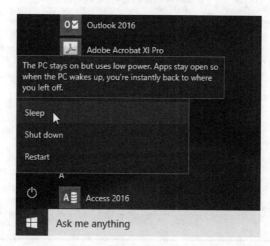

PART III

Power Plans

A *power profile* is a collection of settings that determine how Windows manages power use. All Windows PCs have at least three power plans corresponding to three levels of power-saving aggressiveness.

- **High performance**   Use when power consumption and battery life are less important than the PC always being instantly available.
- **Balanced**   This provides moderate power savings; this is the default.
- **Power savings**   This gives the most power savings; use this when conserving power and/or battery time is important.

You can choose one of these power profiles and use its default settings, or you can modify the settings. You can easily switch between power profiles whenever your needs change.

To access the power profiles, open Control Panel | Hardware and Sound | Power Options. Then, click the option button of the desired power plan. Choose the one that describes your general situation the best, as in Figure 13-2. Then click the Change plan settings hyperlink for the chosen plan.

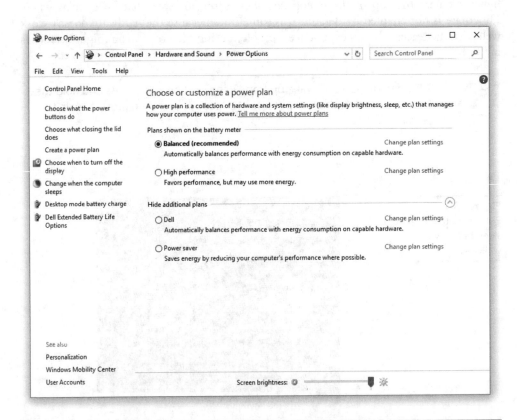

Figure 13-2   Select a power plan.

TIP There may be an additional power plan, such as the Dell plan shown in Figure 13-2.

The Edit Plan Settings section (shown in Figure 13-3) enables you to choose two important aspects of the power plan: when to just turn off the display and when to put the whole computer to sleep. On a laptop you'll see separate settings for On battery and Plugged in and also be able to adjust display brightness for the plan.

For even more control, click Change advanced power settings, opening the Power Options dialog box. From here you can fine-tune many subtle aspects of the power plan, such as when/whether to turn off wireless adapters, USB ports, and PCI Express slots. If you expand the Sleep section in this dialog box, you come to settings (shown in Figure 13-4) for the amount of idle time before Sleep and Hibernate start.

EXAM TIP Make sure you know how to edit a power plan (which the exam objectives call a *Power profile*) and that you can differentiate Sleep and Hibernate.

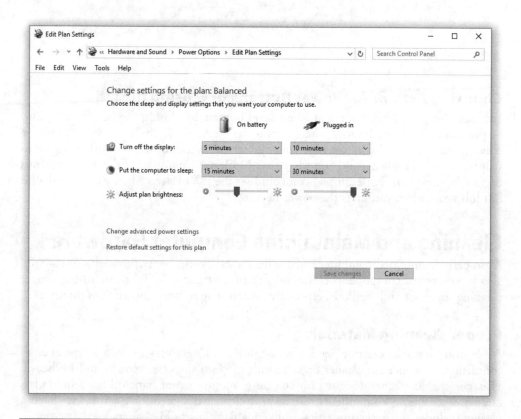

Figure 13-3 Edit the power plan.

Figure 13-4
Fine-tune the
power plan.

Choosing Actions for Power Buttons or Closing the Lid

You can also put the computer in Sleep or Hibernate by closing the lid (for a laptop) or pressing a hardware button. These actions will have some effect on your system by default, but you can also adjust how your system will respond to them. Just navigate to Control Panel | Hardware and Sound | Power Options | Choose what the power buttons do (see Figure 13-5). For example, you could set the PC to sleep when you close the lid but hibernate when you press the power button.

Cleaning and Maintaining Computer Hardware

A properly maintained computer starts with a clean, orderly environment. You should also keep external components clean and free of dust and hair. Take care to use proper cleaning solutions and methods, especially for sensitive components such as monitors.

Proper Cleaning Materials

Aside from dust, the exterior parts of a computer don't get very dirty in a typical environment. Use a vacuum cleaner or soft cloth to clean the case, mouse, and keyboard. Use special glass cleaner designed for computer monitors, not standard household glass cleaner. For exterior components, use a spray cleaner designed for electronics. (Such a cleaner includes antistatic properties, unlike regular household cleaners.)

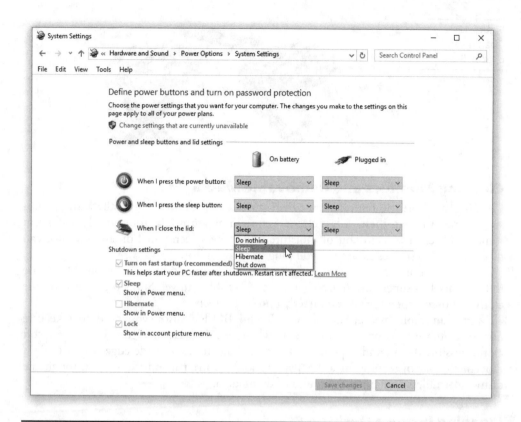

Figure 13-5 Defining power buttons and lid action

TIP Special vacuum cleaners are available for use on computer equipment and other electronics, but they're mainly useful when cleaning the inside parts. See the section "Cleaning Inside," later in this chapter, for details.

In a nontypical environment, the game changes and more aggressive cleaning is required. For a PC in an automotive shop or other high-grime environment, use a *mild soap and water* solution on exterior components. Unplug keyboards from the PC first and allow them to dry out completely before reattaching. If you plug in a keyboard with any moisture inside, it'll short out and become more landfill fodder. You may prefer to use denatured alcohol when cleaning a keyboard.

EXAM TIP Use mild soap and water with a soft cloth to clean any dirty external parts of the computer.

Figure 13-6
Cleaning an
optical disc

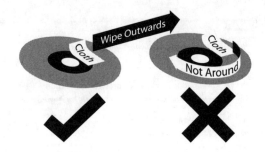

Cleaning Monitors and Removable Media

Cleaning monitors and removable media requires a little caution, especially with the substances used to clean them. Glass cleaners containing ammonia, for example, will harm some LCD screens. A tiny bit of moisture under the screen panel on any monitor can take out the electronics as soon as you plug in the monitor.

To clean a monitor, use a damp cloth or a mild soap and water solution. Make sure the cloth itself is super-soft, like a chamois or microfiber towel. Spray the cleaner on the cloth and then wipe; don't spray directly onto the screen.

With removable media, such as CD-R and BD-RE discs, you need to take care not to scratch, crack, or warp the media when cleaning. As in Figure 13-6, use a soft cloth, possibly damp, and wipe from the inside edge to the outside edge with a straight movement (*not* by wiping in a circular motion). Don't run optical discs through the dishwasher unless you enjoy the sound of dying data.

Cleaning Inside a Desktop PC

Computers aren't solid; they're a collection of parts inside a box. The box or case usually has vents, and over time the inside can accumulate dust and hair. If too much debris builds up, the computer could overheat and break down. It is important to open the case and clean the inside every once in a while.

The first step is getting inside. Some desktop cases have a side panel that you can remove with two screws, as in Figure 13-7. Others have a clamshell design that unlatches when you press buttons, and still others have a single U-shaped cover that exposes three sides at once when removed.

Figure 13-7
Remove these
two screws and
the side will
come off.

Figure 13-8
Touching the
power supply

Avoiding ESD

Electrostatic discharge (ESD) can permanently damage or destroy computer components inside the case. ESD is the transfer of static electricity from you to something you touch. If you've ever been shocked when touching a door knob in the winter time, you know exactly what ESD feels like. Unlike you, though, a computer component can't say "Ouch!" and flinch from the contact. It just dies a little, inside, where it counts.

As soon as you open the case, touch the metal of the power supply (Figure 13-8). This will discharge any static electricity you have without harming anything.

If you plan to be inside the computer case for a while, purchase an *antistatic wrist strap*. Connect one side to your wrist and the other to the power supply or case (Figure 13-9). This keeps everything safe from ESD.

EXAM TIP Connecting to the power supply or metal frame of a case with an antistatic wrist strap is the best way to avoid ESD when working inside a computer.

Figure 13-9
An antistatic
wrist strap
connected to
a PC

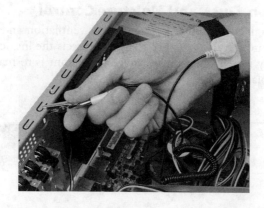

Figure 13-10
Compressed air

Cleaning Inside

Once inside the case, you have two basic options for getting rid of dust and hair inside a PC: you can blow the dust out, or you can vacuum it out.

You use a product called *compressed air* to blow out dust, cat hair, and anything else out of the case. Compressed air comes in small cans like spray paint, usually with a little tube for precise aiming (Figure 13-10). You can purchase compressed air at any electronics or computer retail store. Just make sure to do the blowing outdoors, not inside! Otherwise, you'll make a huge mess.

You can use a special vacuum cleaner designed for electronics to vacuum out the inside of the case (Figure 13-11). Normal vacuum cleaners create a static electricity charge as the dust flows through the plastic nozzle, so you shouldn't use them inside a computer. You can find electronics or *antistatic vacuums* at computer and electronics stores.

CAUTION Don't vacuum up spilled toner from a laser printer toner cartridge with a regular household vacuum. The filter is not usually fine enough to catch the particles. The particles can become airborne and irritate your lungs if you inhale them. Wipe up spilled toner with a damp paper towel.

Ventilation, Dust, and Moisture Control

A well-maintained computer ensures proper ventilation and limits the amount of dust that comes into the case. Further, the case protects the inside from any unwanted moisture. The key issue from a maintenance standpoint is to make sure the case covers are properly in place.

Figure 13-11
Antistatic
vacuum

Figure 13-12
Drive cover
missing on the
front of a PC

Case manufacturers design cases for air to flow across the drives and motherboard. The front of the PC usually has extra covers for drives you might want to add later, and the back usually has slot covers for unused expansion slots. Don't leave unused covers off, as in Figure 13-12 and Figure 13-13, because missing covers can disrupt the flow (causing overheating) and let in even more airborne debris.

Figure 13-13
Slot cover
missing on the
back of a PC

Environmentally Aware Computer Disposal

When a computer (or component) reaches the end of its useful life, don't just throw it in the trash can along with your everyday waste! Many computer components contain materials that are bad for the environment, such as cadmium, mercury, and lead. In addition, the plastics and metals will probably end up in a landfill with your regular trash, when they could possibly be recycled into some other product.

Most computer part makers have adopted the *Restriction of Hazardous Substances (RoHS) Directive* to make their products more environmentally friendly and thus easily disposed of (Figure 13-14). The RoHS guidelines are a European Union (EU) standard that regulates toxic substances, such as lead, mercury, and cadmium. RoHS has helped change the way manufacturers create circuit boards. *Solder* is used to make a connection point (which resembles a little glob of solid silver) between wires. In recent years, most computer part makers have shifted from lead-based solder to tin-based solder. This helps reduce the risk of lead exposure to the people who work in electronics recycling around the world.

Many major cities offer convenient recycling centers for hazardous household materials, and some electronics retailers have electronics-specific recycling programs. Check online to find the nearest recycling center that will take electronics.

 EXAM TIP Make sure you can identify proper disposal methods for CRTs, scanners, batteries, ink, toner, and hard drives.

Here are some basic guidelines for recycling some of the most environmentally unfriendly components:

- **CRT monitors** Not only are they large and boxy, taking up lots of landfill space, but CRTs also contain lead (to shield the viewer from radiation). This is the number-one component to take to a recycling center rather than put out with the trash.

- **Scanners and printers** Recycling programs accept scanners and printers, either working or nonworking. If they are working, some programs can find homes for them; many scanners end up in schools, shelters, food banks, and other organizations. If not, they can recycle the plastics and reclaim lead from the circuit boards.

Figure 13-14
RoHS-
compliance
labeling

- **Batteries** Small alkaline batteries can be thrown in regular trash (except in California, where they must be recycled), but rechargeable batteries such as those in laptops should be taken to a recycling center. Never incinerate a battery; the heat can cause it to explode.

- **Ink/toner** Ink cartridges are not so much hazardous as they are wasteful, being thrown away after just one brief use. Toner cartridges are similarly wasteful, but the toner itself can also be harmful to humans. It's easy to inhale airborne toner (a mixture of iron and plastic), which can damage the lungs. Rather than throwing ink and toner cartridges away, send them to a company that reconditions and refills them. Your local office supply store may be a drop-off point.

- **Hard drives** A hard drive has a small circuit board in it, which may contain some lead. The big risk in discarding a hard drive is to your privacy. If the hard drive is still operational, make sure you delete all the data from it; for extra security, reformat it too. If the data it contained was very sensitive, you might even consider using a service that guarantees to totally destroy any data remaining on a drive before disposing of it.

Chapter Review

Power management features in Windows (and other operating systems) save electricity or battery charge time by placing the computer in a low-power state after a certain time idle. In Windows, you can define the parameters of that low-power state using Power Options. This can include specifying when Sleep and Hibernate modes occur.

Clean the exterior of a PC with a mild (preferably antistatic) cleaner. Don't use regular glass cleaner on a monitor. When cleaning inside a PC, you should use compressed air or an antistatic electronics vacuum cleaner to clean the inside of the case. Touch the power supply or use an antistatic wrist strap to avoid damaging components with ESD. Keep slot covers in place to make sure the computer cools things properly and the dust stays outside.

When disposing of computer equipment, use your local recycling center for large plastic items like CRTs, printers, and scanners, and for items that contain circuit boards with lead in them. Recycle ink and toner cartridges when possible too. Recycle rechargeable batteries such as from laptops; small alkaline batteries can be disposed of with regular trash (except in California, where they must be recycled).

Questions

1. In Sleep mode, the _____ remains powered; everything else shuts off.
   A. Hard drive
   B. Monitor
   C. Memory
   D. CPU

PART III

2. How long can a laptop remain in Hibernate mode without running out of battery power?

   A. 36 hours.

   B. 12 hours.

   C. It depends on the battery condition and capacity.

   D. Indefinitely.

3. How should you clean removable media, such as a DVD?

   A. Use a soft cloth and wipe with a circular movement.

   B. Use a soft cloth and wipe inside to outside with a straight movement.

   C. Use a soft scrub brush and wipe left to right.

   D. Put the disc in the dishwashing machine.

4. Rich has inherited a computer that used to live in his uncle's machine shop. What should he use to clean up parts such as the case, keyboard, and mouse?

   A. A dry, soft cloth

   B. A soft cloth with distilled water

   C. A soft cloth with mild soap and water

   D. A soft cloth with a commercial cleaning solution

5. What standard offers computer part makers guidelines for making environmentally friendly parts?

   A. FTC

   B. RIAA

   C. RoHS

   D. VHS

6. What can you use to prevent ESD from damaging components when cleaning inside a computer?

   A. Antistatic wrist strap.

   B. Antistatic bag.

   C. Antistatic wipe.

   D. ESD presents no danger to components, so nothing special is needed.

7. What should you use to remove dust and animal hair from inside a computer case?

   A. Blow dryer

   B. Compressed air

   C. Household vacuum cleaner

   D. Mild soap and water

8. What problem can missing slot covers on the case cause?

   A. Electromagnetic interference from other electronics nearby

   B. Electrostatic discharge from dust and animal hair

   C. Disruption of airflow inside the computer leading to overheating

   D. Disruption of airflow outside the computer leading to overheating

9. What computer component contains a lot of lead and must be recycled?

   A. CRT

   B. Toner cartridge

   C. Ink cartridge

   D. Hard disk drive

10. In California, how should small alkaline batteries be disposed of?

    A. Regular trash

    B. Recycling center

    C. Incinerated

    D. Any of the above

Answers

1. **C.** Memory remains powered in Sleep mode; everything else turns off.

2. **D.** Hibernate mode uses no power, so it can remain in that state indefinitely, regardless of the battery state or capacity.

3. **B.** To clean removable media discs, use a soft cloth, possibly damp, and wipe from the inside edge to the outside edge with a straight movement.

4. **C.** Mild soap and water are about as fierce a solution as may be needed for cleaning external parts of the computer.

5. **C.** The Restriction of Hazardous Substances (RoHS) Directive has guidelines for making products more environmentally friendly.

6. **A.** Connect to the power supply with an antistatic wrist strap to protect the PC from ESD.

7. **B.** Use compressed air outdoors to blow out dust and hair. An electronics or antistatic vacuum will also work.

8. **C.** Missing slot covers can disrupt airflow inside the case and can lead to overheating. They can also lead to excessive dust and animal hair inside the case. This can cause overheating too.

9. **A.** A CRT monitor contains lead, so it must be disposed of properly, not thrown out with regular trash.

10. **B.** In California, small alkaline batteries must be taken to a recycling center. Elsewhere in the U.S., they can be thrown in the regular trash. Batteries should never be incinerated.

CHAPTER 14

Computer Troubleshooting and Problem-Solving

In this chapter, you will learn how to
- Troubleshoot common computer problems
- Get help with your computer

Most people don't realize how dependent they are on their computers until that moment when the computer won't work as usual. If you've experienced that moment, then you know the anxiety that comes with it. *How will I get my work done? Are my files okay? How much is this going to cost to fix?*

Computer users should know how to troubleshoot basic computer problems. Plus, you need to know how to get help when the problem goes beyond your current knowledge. Just like every rider should know what to do when a chain pops off the sprocket on his or her bike, savvy computer users can fix typical issues such as a frozen computer or a dead PC.

This chapter looks first at problems that happen when external factors intervene, such as a jostled cable or an operating system (OS) that hangs at boot up. The second part of the chapter explores ways to get help when you need it.

Solvable Common Computer Problems

You can solve common problems by recognizing symptoms and implementing solutions. Typical problems you'll run into include no power, physical damage, failed boot, application failure to load, and peripherals that don't function as they should. Let's take a look at each issue.

No Power

It's dead, Jim.
          —*Dr. McCoy*

You press the power button and nothing happens. *Nada*. No lights, no sound, nothing on the screen. Don't panic!

First, make sure the device has power. If the device runs off batteries, make sure the battery has a charge or plug it into AC power if possible. If the device runs on AC, check for a firm power cord connection and confirm the outlet works. If the workstation uses a power strip, surge protector, UPS, or the like, make sure it isn't switched off and confirm the device itself is connected.

Some PCs fail to come out of Sleep or Hibernate mode and get stuck there, so they seem completely dead. To make sure that isn't the case with your dead PC, hold down the power button for five to ten seconds and then release it and press it again. This resets any low-power mode that might be in effect.

An apparently-dead handheld mobile device like a smartphone or tablet can sometimes be rescued with a reset. Try a soft reset first (one that does not destroy data); if that doesn't work, try a hard reset. Check the device documentation or search online for the procedure. See Chapter 9 for more on resetting mobile devices.

 CAUTION Before assuming your dead mobile device needs to be reset, make sure that the problem is not just a drained battery. Plug the device into AC power for at least four hours to make sure.

If the device remains completely lifeless after trying all that, it may be time to consult a professional.

 EXAM TIP Make sure you can explain several reasons why a device might not power up and how to differentiate between them. Check for dead batteries, loose cables and power connections, and possible physical damage, which is covered next.

Physical Damage

Aside from the occasional move, desktops don't have many chances to get seriously damaged. As portable and mobile devices become more popular, though, more and more of us have had to watch a device drop, slide, fly, clink, shatter, crunch, or splash its way to a violent end or watery grave.

Computers like to run in a cool and dry environment, but extreme heat or cold won't usually bother them as long as they are not running. When bringing a computer in from a hot or cold environment, wait for it to come to room temperature before starting it.

 CAUTION Still, don't tempt fate. Many devices use plastics or adhesives that may melt as they warm, and intense heat can also damage batteries. If you *can* avoid exposing a device to extreme temperatures, do.

Water is the number-one enemy of electronics, including computers and smartphones. Unfortunately, water damage is common for smartphones. People drop them into toilets, fountains, and wishing wells all the time. Even if you aren't the least bit clumsy, you (and your device) can get caught out in a rainstorm. If your device is on when it gets wet, it will probably short-circuit, which may or may not ruin a circuit board inside it. If the device is off (completely off, not just sleeping), you stand a slightly better chance of avoiding damage. Some newer smartphones are splash-resistant or even waterproof, but don't rely on that to save you.

EXAM TIP You should understand the causes and consequences of physical damage to both desktop and portable computing devices, how to assess the level of damage, and what the repair options are.

If the battery is removable, act quickly to pop it out; if not, turn off the device. Let the device dry out completely. Take it apart if possible, and let the pieces air-dry. Put it in a bag of rice to help absorb the moisture. Don't try to turn it back on for at least 72 hours. If there's any water remaining when you turn it back on again, you run the risk of further short-circuiting.

A cracked display screen is also common. If you can still see the display panel updating properly—without any strange visual artifacts—under the cracked glass, it probably just needs a glass replacement; the screen itself (that is, the LCD or OLED panel) is likely still intact. Consult a repair shop that specializes in your type of device.

A dropped computer might suffer from the trauma, but circuit boards inside a case are not particularly vulnerable to these physical jolts. If a computer doesn't work after a fall, it might have some loose cables inside. If it's a desktop, open up the case and look for any loose or disconnected cables. Checking all of the connectors in mobile and portable devices is best left to a specialist—it takes special tools and expertise to take one apart without breaking or losing anything.

NOTE Hard drives, because they have moving parts, don't fare as well; falls can damage the mechanical parts or even the surface of the platters (though the latter aren't usually immediately apparent). Thankfully, many modern devices use solid-state memory or drives with no moving parts.

Won't Start Up Normally

If the computer won't start up, think about it like a detective would. What has changed? Did you install any new hardware or software? Has the computer been moved, such that some cables might have come loose? Did the OS restart itself after installing an update?

Occasionally after an OS update, the computer might start up badly (that is, slowly, or with errors). Sometimes you can fix that by simply rebooting. If that doesn't help and you're using Windows, try using the System Restore feature to revert to a previous day's restore point. Using a restore point will not cause you to lose any recent data file edits. Here's how in Windows 10:

1. Right-click the Start button and click System.

2. Click System protection.

3. Click System Restore.

4. Click Next.

5. Select a restore point. If you have a choice (there's just one available restore point in Figure 14-1), pick the one immediately before the problem started.

NOTE When Windows Update installs system updates, it sometimes erases all the restore points to prevent users from creating system file problems by reverting to earlier versions that the update doesn't support. If you don't have many (or any) restore points available, that's probably why.

6. Follow the prompts to complete the restoration of the system files to that point in time.

System Restore is completely reversible; just run it again and follow the prompts to undo the restoration.

If the OS won't start at all, you might see a prompt offering to boot into a recovery or troubleshooting mode. Do that, if it's offered. If it's not, try booting from the operating system's removable installation media, if you have it, and choosing the Repair option to enter the Windows Recovery Environment (RE). You can also get there in Windows 10 through the Settings app (Update & Security | Recovery | Advanced Startup | Restart Now).

Figure 14-1
Choose a restore point.

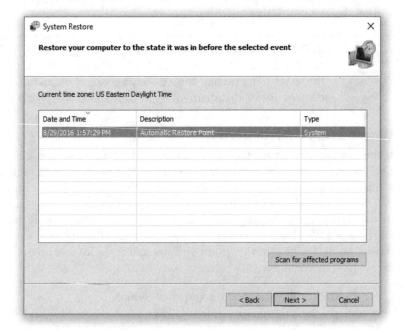

A Certain App Won't Install or Run

Problems with a specific application are often due to hardware incompatibility, especially with the display adapter. The latest games often require specific, high-powered display adapters with the latest driver versions. The application's installation program should check your hardware and let you know if there are any problems. If it doesn't and you experience problems after starting the application, check online for any known incompatibilities between that application and certain hardware. Try updating your video card (display adapter) driver by downloading the latest driver version from the adapter manufacturer's Web site.

Next, look at the application manufacturer's Web site to see whether there is a patch or update available for download. If you can't find patches for or information about problems that match what you're experiencing, it's probably a glitch in your own system, such as a minor incompatibility between the application, the OS, and some piece of hardware. Try uninstalling and reinstalling the application; this fixes the problem more often than you might think.

Still no luck? Check to see what version of Windows the application requires. If it's designed for an older Windows version, see if there's a newer version of the software available. If not, try using Compatibility Mode to see if you can get it to run better by emulating an earlier Windows version. To use the Program Compatibility Troubleshooter, right-click the shortcut for running the application (or its executable file) and choose Troubleshoot compatibility. Click Try recommended settings to let Windows try to guess the right settings. See Figure 14-2. You can also manually troubleshoot compatibility from the Compatibility tab in the program's Properties box, choosing a specific older Windows version to emulate.

Figure 14-2
Try configuring Compatibility Mode for an application that doesn't run well.

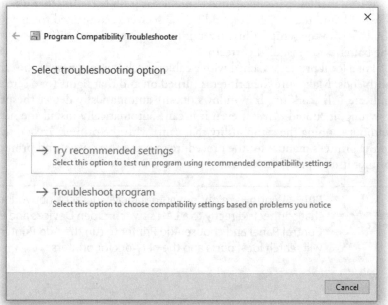

Program Compatibility Troubleshooter

Select troubleshooting option

→ Try recommended settings
Select this option to test run program using recommended compatibility settings

→ Troubleshoot program
Select this option to choose compatibility settings based on problems you notice

Cancel

Peripherals Won't Work

When peripherals don't work, it's usually for one of these reasons:

- The cable/cord is bad or isn't snugly connected on each end.
- If wireless, the device's power switch may be off, its batteries drained, or the transceiver (the wireless transmitter/receiver that plugs into the USB port) isn't snugly connected to the computer's USB port.
- If the device uses AC power and you've confirmed the connection, the power cord or the outlet may be bad.
- The device itself is defective.
- The port on the computer is defective.

Check the items on this list to make sure there is no physical problem. If the peripheral came with software, run the setup program for it. Try a different port. There could be a problem with the peripheral's driver, especially if you didn't follow the installation instructions. You can start over by disconnecting the device from your system and uninstalling the driver. To remove a driver in Windows, right-click the peripheral in Device Manager, select Properties, switch to the Driver tab, and click Uninstall.

NOTE   If a mouse is dirty, the pointer may stutter or jump around onscreen as you try to use it; remove any dirt or hair from around the sensor on the bottom of the mouse if this occurs. On a trackball, remove the ball and clean out any debris from underneath it.

If it's a cordless peripheral, make sure it has fresh batteries, that it's turned on (if it has a switch), and that the corresponding transceiver is connected to an appropriate port on the PC. Run the setup utility, try a different port, and try different batteries. Make sure the batteries are installed correctly.

For a local printer attached with a cable, check the snugness of the cable connection at both ends. Make sure the printer is turned on and that lights (or a screen) on the printer indicate it is working. If Windows doesn't automatically detect the printer, something is wrong; it should *detect* it even if it can't automatically install the needed driver for it without running the setup utility that came with the printer. Try a different cable. Look in the printer's manual for the procedure to print a test page, and print one to ensure the printer itself works.

NOTE   Windows might not automatically detect a network-capable printer that connects directly to a LAN's switch. Open Devices and Printers from the Control Panel and choose Add Printer to run the Add Printer Wizard, which will search local ports and the network for printers.

Getting Help

Thanks to the Internet, you can get help for most computer problems. If someone has solved a similar problem to the one you face, you can find an article about it online. The following sections review the many places to look for help with your computer difficulties.

 EXAM TIP You should able to list several sources of help and the pros and cons of each. Make sure you understand the difference between manufacturer documentation, manufacturer Web sites, technical community groups, Internet search results, and technical support.

Manufacturer Documentation and Web Sites

Any hardware or software you buy comes with documentation. It could be a printed booklet in the box, a document file on the installation media, or a downloadable file from the company's Web site. The original documentation should explain how the item works and may also provide some basic troubleshooting information. Documentation quality and detail varies widely, from nicely formatted 100-page manuals to a few vaguely English sentences on a half-sheet of paper. The manufacturer documentation (including additional documentation on a manufacturer-maintained Web site) is the most authoritative source of information about the device or software.

If you've misplaced the original printed documentation, you can probably find it online, either at the manufacturer Web site or at a third-party site. There are Web sites that specialize in providing PDFs of product manuals, for example. Manufacturers also build documentation into the application in the form of a Help file. Look on the menu bar or ribbon for a Help command. More and more manufacturers save money by including documentation only in electronic form, rather than providing a printed manual.

Manufacturer Web sites can provide excellent information. Depending on the size of the company, the Support section of the Web site may integrate with the main site, or it may be a separate host like http://support.microsoft.com. On a manufacturer's Web site you might find any of the following:

- Downloadable updates and patches
- Downloadable product manuals and setup utilities
- A customer support message board, with help both from company representatives and from other customers
- Press releases regarding new versions
- Existing-customer discounts for upgrading to new versions
- Product registration forms
- Warranty claim information
- Information about known problems and conflicts with certain hardware or software
- Contact information for technical support and customer service

NOTE *Technical support* provides help for operating the product; if the product isn't working as expected, you contact technical support. *Customer service* helps with financial and authentication matters, such as creating a user account, placing or cancelling orders, and getting refunds. *Sales* is normally just for new sales, not billing or cancellations.

Some support Web sites request the exact model number or serial number of your computing device to customize the information presented. The Dell Product Support site shown in Figure 14-3, for example, identifies the exact model number of my laptop and offers to diagnose problems I might behaving.

Technical Support

The best way to get technical support for a product is usually via the Web site. Technical support Web sites can help you diagnose problems, update drivers and firmware, get product enhancements, and more. Your problem may appear in the Frequently Asked Questions (FAQ) section of the Web site. If not, you can send an e-mail message asking for help.

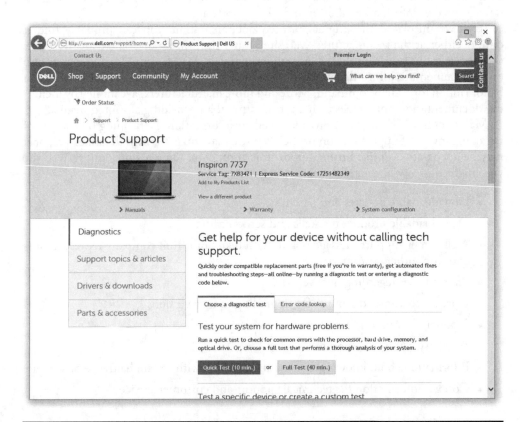

Figure 14-3   Dell's product support Web site for my Inspiron 7737 laptop

NOTE Sometimes the FAQ is just a document with common questions; some companies use a *knowledge base,* which is a little like a cross between the FAQ and a support forum. A knowledge base typically highlights the most common questions but also includes less frequently asked questions.

The *Contact us* link on a tech support Web site usually leads to a form you can use to submit a support request. This is usually your best bet if you don't need an immediate answer. You might have to wait 24 hours for a response (usually via e-mail), but that's 24 hours where you can be doing something else. With phone support, you might get an answer after being tortured for an hour with low-quality elevator music and automatic reassurances about *how much your call matters* and how *we are experiencing unusually high call volume* and *your call will be answered in the order it was received.*

NOTE With luck, you'll be able to use some of the more compassionate support improvements pioneered in recent years, such as the ability to chat with a support person in your browser or to go about your business and receive a callback when a representative is available.

A phone call to the company's technical support line is usually a last resort. Some companies make it really easy to find the tech support phone number on the Web site; others bury it in the fine print, hoping that you won't be able to locate it. They do this because phone support costs a lot to provide, so don't be surprised if finding the phone number is only the first hurdle. Telephone support systems commonly include long automated menus crafted to avoid connecting you to a living, breathing human.

Internet Searches and Community Groups

If the manufacturer's Web site and tech support department let you down, the next step is to see what the Internet at large has to offer. Use one of the popular search engines, such as Google or Bing, to see what's out there for your particular model number or product name. Keep in mind that the results of such searches aren't authoritative, so take what you find with a grain of salt. For example, one person might write about some complicated system file hack he used to solve a similar problem to yours, but don't assume that it is safe to try on your system.

Internet searches can connect you to user posts that mirror or match the trouble you have. Sometimes, an Internet search points you to that perfect solution. Implement it and you're on your way. Other times you might discover that you simply can't solve the current problem directly. You might find out, for example, that it's a known problem that your game won't run on systems with a certain type of video card or that you can circumvent a particular error by making a BIOS/UEFI setting change.

CAUTION Don't download anything from an untrusted site. Don't download a driver for your display adapter that is supposed to be "better than" the one that the manufacturer provides, for example, and be wary of free antivirus, system repair, and disk cleaner tools. A lot of them are malware disguised as helpful programs.

If you're lucky, you'll find a technical community group (such as a support message board or chat room) specifically for the device or software that's causing problems for you. You may also be able to find computer user groups that meet regularly in your town. (Yes, actual people in a room together physically! Such wonders still exist.)

Chapter Review

This chapter provided some advice for situations where a computer, mobile device, peripheral, or application isn't working properly.

If the computer or device seems dead, it's probably disconnected or not getting power. If your device gets wet, don't turn it on until it's bone-dry. Take it apart to let it air out if possible. You can also put it in a bag of rice to dry it out. If a device stops working after you drop it, check to make sure no cables inside have come unplugged; it's easy enough to open up a desktop and look, but mobile and portable devices may need to go to a specialist. For a cracked screen, you'll need to take it to a repair shop.

If the computer starts performing poorly after an update or system change, use System Restore or the Windows Recovery Environment. If a certain app won't run, try uninstalling and reinstalling it. You can also try the Program Compatibility Troubleshooter. If a peripheral isn't working, check the connection, cord, and batteries.

Some places you can get help include manufacturer documentation, manufacturer Web sites, technical support, Internet searches, and community groups, both online and in-person.

Questions

1. Which of these could *not* be the cause of a computer appearing completely dead?

   A. Hibernate mode

   B. Bad power cable

   C. Disconnected power cable

   D. Bad keyboard

2. Which of these is the most hazardous to a desktop computer or mobile device?

   A. Dropping it

   B. Leaving it in a hot car in the summer

   C. Getting it wet

   D. Leaving it in an unheated building in winter

3. What Windows utility returns the computer's system files to previously saved versions?

   A. Control Panel

   B. Compatibility Mode

   C. File Explorer

   D. System Restore

4. Which of these might correct a problem with an application not running correctly?

    A. Delete your data files.

    B. Clean the display screen.

    C. Uninstall and reinstall the application.

    D. Create a shortcut to the application on the desktop.

5. Suppose you have a wireless mouse that doesn't work at all. Which of these is *not* likely to be the cause?

    A. Mouse is dirty.

    B. Power switch on mouse is turned off.

    C. Transceiver is not connected to the computer.

    D. Batteries are dead.

6. You have a printer that connects to your computer via USB cable. The printer can print a test page successfully from its own controls, but the computer doesn't see it. Which of these should you try?

    A. Use a different printer cable.

    B. Replace the ink cartridges.

    C. Turn the printer off and then back on again.

    D. Use a different kind of paper in the printer.

7. Which is the most authoritative source of information about a device?

    A. Friend and relatives

    B. Internet search

    C. Community user groups

    D. Manufacturer's Web site

8. What is an FAQ?

    A. The main page of a manufacturer's support Web site

    B. A Web site page containing frequently asked questions and their answers

    C. An index of all help topics on a Web site

    D. A utility that identifies your product's model number

9. If you need to cancel an online subscription, what department of the company do you need to contact?

    A. Customer service

    B. Technical support

    C. Service

    D. Sales

10. Which of these would likely be found on a manufacturer's support Web site?

   A. Downloadable product manuals

   B. New versions of the device's drivers

   C. Troubleshooting information

   D. All of the above

Answers

1. **D**. A bad keyboard would not prevent the computer from starting up, although you might see an error message.

2. **C**. Water is the most serious hazard to computers.

3. **D**. System Restore allows you to return system files to earlier versions.

4. **C**. Uninstalling and reinstalling an application sometimes corrects problems with the application's performance.

5. **A**. A dirty mouse would not appear completely dead, although it might result in an erratically moving pointer onscreen.

6. **A**. A different printer cable might allow the computer to see the printer. All the other solutions would not be likely to help since the printer has already proven to be working.

7. **D**. The manufacturer Web site is the most authoritative source of information.

8. **B**. FAQ stands for Frequently Asked Questions. It is a Web page commonly found on a manufacturer's support Web site.

9. **A**. Customer service handles financial matters relating to existing accounts.

10. **D**. All of these items are commonly found on a manufacturer's support Web site.

PART IV

Appendixes

Exam Objective Reference

CompTIA IT Fundamentals

The commercial version of the CompTIA IT Fundamentals exam is designed to show that the successful candidate has the knowledge to discuss basic computer components and put together a personal computer (PC). The candidate can install software for productivity, connect the computer to a network, and explain basic security. The candidate can communicate essentials of safety and maintenance. This test is intended for candidates who want to understand modern technology to function well in our increasingly digital world and for those considering becoming a tech.

NOTE The lists under each objective are not exhaustive. Even though they are not included in this document, other examples of technologies, processes, or tasks pertaining to each objective may also be included on the exam.

Domain	Percent of Examination
1.0 Software	21%
2.0 Hardware	18%
3.0 Security	21%
4.0 Networking	16%
5.0 Basic IT Literacy	24%
Total	100%

Topic	Chapter No.	Page No.
1.0 Software		
1.1 Compare and contrast common operating systems and their functions and features		
Types	1	
Mobile	1	22
Apple iOS	1	22
Android	1	22
Windows Phone	1	22
BlackBerry	1	23

Topic	Chapter No.	Page No.
Images	7	176–177
.jpg	7	177
.gif	7	177
.tiff	7	177
.png	7	177
.bmp	7	177
Video	7	173, 175–176
.mpg	7	176
.mp4	7	176
.flv	7	176
.wmv	7	176
.avi	7	176
Executables	7	173
.exe	7	173
.msi	7	173
.app	7	173
.bat	7	173
.scexe	7	173
Compression formats	7	173–174
.rar	7	174
.tar	7	174
.zip	7	174
.dmg	7	174
.iso	7	174
.7zip/7z	7	174
.gzip/gz	7	174
.jar	7	174
1.3 Given a scenario, use software management best practices		
Install/uninstall	5, 6, 7, 14	
OS features	5	120
Applications	7	160–168
Drivers	6, 14	146, 338

PART IV

Topic	Chapter No.	Page No.
Input and output devices	3, 4	
Fax	3	83–84
External storage devices	4	93–98
Flash drive	4	93–94
External hard drive	4	96
CD/DVD/Blu-ray	4	92–93
Network attached storage	4	98
Memory card	4	93–94
Mobile media players	4, 9	93, 210
Smartphone	4, 9	93, 210
Touchscreen display	3	74
2.2 Compare and contrast common computer connector types		
Video	3	69–74
VGA	3	71
DVI	3	70
HDMI	3	70
Display port/Thunderbolt	3	73
USB	3	74
S-video	3	71
Component – RGB	3	71
FireWire	3	65
eSATA	3	65
Thunderbolt	3	64
USB	3	63–64
PS/2	3	65
Parallel	3	65
Serial	3	65
RJ-45	3	61
RJ-11	3	61
Audio	3	77–78
Power	2, 5	52–54, 112
AC/DC	5	112

PART IV

PART IV

About the CD-ROM

The CD-ROM included with this book includes the following:

- A video from the authors introducing the CompTIA IT Fundamentals exam
- A link to download Total Tester practice exam software with 130 practice exam questions
- A link to more than one hour of free video training episodes from Mike Meyers' CompTIA IT Fundamentals Video Training series
- PDF copies of the official CompTIA IT Fundamentals Objectives and Acronyms
- An electronic copy of the book in secured PDF format

System Requirements

The software requires Windows Vista or higher and 30MB of hard disk space for full installation, in addition to a current or prior major release of Chrome, Firefox, Internet Explorer, or Safari. To run, the screen resolution must be set to 1024 × 768 or higher. The PDF files require Adobe Acrobat, Adobe Reader, or Adobe Digital Editions to view.

Playing the Introduction Video

If your computer's optical drive is configured to auto-run, the menu will automatically start upon inserting the CD-ROM. If the auto-run feature does not launch the CD, browse to the disc and double-click the Launche.exe icon.

From the opening screen you can launch the video by clicking the Introduction to IT Fundamentals button. This launches the video file using your system's default video player.

Total Tester Practice Exam Software

Total Tester provides you with a simulation of the CompTIA IT Fundamentals exam. Exams can be taken in Practice Mode, Exam Mode, or Custom Mode. Practice Mode provides an assistance window with hints, references to the book, explanations of the correct and incorrect answers, and the option to check your answers as you take the test. Exam Mode provides a simulation of the actual exam. The number of questions, the types of questions, and the time allowed are intended to be an accurate representation of the exam environment. In Custom Mode, you can select the number of questions and the duration of the exam.

The link on the CD-ROM takes you to a Web download page. On the main page of the CD, click the Software and Videos link, and then select Download Total Tester. Click the download and follow the prompts to install the software. To take a test, launch the program and select IT Fundamentals from the Installed Question Packs list. You can then select Practice Mode, Exam Mode, or Custom Mode. All exams provide an overall grade and a grade broken down by domain.

Mike's Video Training

The CD-ROM comes with a link to more than one hour of Total Seminars training videos, starring Mike Meyers, for the first three chapters of the book. On the main page of the CD, click the Videos link and then select Mike Meyers' Online Video Training. Along with access to the videos from the first three chapters of the book, you'll find an option to purchase Mike's complete video training series.

Objectives and Acronyms

To view the official CompTIA IT Fundamentals exam objectives and list of acronyms, select the Exam Objectives and Acronyms button on the main page of the CD-ROM. On the next page, clicking either the CompTIA IT Fundamentals Objectives button or the CompTIA IT Fundamentals Acronyms button will open the respective PDF. The objectives and acronyms are the actual exam objectives and acronyms from CompTIA as of the date of publication. Please visit the CompTIA Web site for the most up-to-date versions.

Secured Book PDF

The entire contents of the book are provided in secured PDF format on the CD-ROM. This file is viewable on your computer and many portable devices.

- **To view the PDF on a computer**, Adobe Acrobat, Adobe Reader, or Adobe Digital Editions is required. A link to Adobe's Web site, where you can download and install Adobe Reader, has been included on the CD-ROM.

 NOTE For more information on Adobe Reader and to check for the most recent version of the software, visit Adobe's Web site at www.adobe.com and search for the free Adobe Reader or look for Adobe Reader on the product page. Adobe Digital Editions can also be downloaded from the Adobe Web site.

- **To view the book PDF on a portable device**, copy the PDF file to your computer from the CD-ROM and then copy the file to your portable device using a USB or other connection. Adobe offers a mobile version of Adobe Reader, the Adobe Reader mobile app, which currently supports iOS and Android. For customers using Adobe Digital Editions and an iPad, you may have to download and install a separate reader program on your device. The Adobe Web site has a list of recommended applications, and McGraw-Hill Education recommends the Bluefire Reader.

Technical Support

For questions regarding the Total Tester software or operation of the CD-ROM, visit **www.totalsem.com** or e-mail **support@totalsem.com**.

For questions regarding the secured book PDF, visit **http://mhp.softwareassist.com** or e-mail **techsolutions@mhedu.com**.

For questions regarding the book content, please e-mail **hep_customer-service@ mheducation.com**. For customers outside the United States, e-mail **international_cs@ mheducation.com**.

PART IV

%SystemRoot%   The path where the operating system is installed.

4G   Most popularly implemented as Long Term Evolution (LTE), a wireless data standard with theoretical download speeds of 300 Mbps and upload speeds of 75 Mbps.

10BaseT   Ethernet LAN designed to run on twisted pair cabling. 10BaseT runs at 10 Mbps. The maximum length for the cabling between the NIC and the switch (or hub, repeater, etc.) is 100 meters. It uses baseband signaling. No industry-standard naming convention exists, so sometimes it's written 10BASE-T or 10Base-T.

100BaseT   Ethernet cabling system designed to run at 100 Mbps on twisted pair cabling. It uses baseband signaling. No industry-standard naming convention exists, so sometimes it's written 100BASE-T or 100Base-T.

1000BaseT   Gigabit Ethernet on UTP.

10 Gigabit Ethernet (10GbE)   Ethernet standard that supports speeds of up to 10 Gbps. Requires CAT 6 or better twisted pair or fiber optic cabling.

110 block   The most common connection used with structured cabling, connecting horizontal cable runs with patch panels.

16-bit (PC Card)   Type of PC Card that can have up to two distinct functions or devices, such as a modem/network card combination.

2.1 speaker system   Speaker setup consisting of two stereo speakers combined with a subwoofer.

3.5-inch floppy drive   Size of all modern floppy disk drives; the format was introduced in 1986 and is one of the longest surviving pieces of computer hardware.

34-pin ribbon cable   Type of cable used by floppy disk drives.

3-D graphics   Video technology that attempts to create images with the same depth and texture as objects seen in the real world.

40-pin ribbon cable   PATA cable used to attach EIDE devices (such as hard drives) or ATAPI devices (such as optical drives) to a system. (*See* PATA.)

5.1 speaker system   Speaker setup consisting of four satellite speakers plus a center speaker and a subwoofer.

7.1 speaker system   Speaker setup consisting of six satellite speakers (two front, two side, two rear) plus a center speaker and a subwoofer.

64-bit processing   A type of processing that can run a compatible 64-bit operating system, such as Windows 7, 8, 8.1, or 10, and 64-bit applications. 64-bit PCs have a 64-bit-wide address bus, enabling them to use more than 4 GB of RAM.

8.3 naming system   File-naming convention that specified a maximum of eight characters for a filename, followed by a three-character file extension. Has been replaced by LFN (long filename) support.

80-wire ribbon cable   PATA cable used to attach fast EIDE devices (such as ATA/100 hard drives) or ATAPI devices (such as optical drives) to a system. (*See* PATA.)

802.11a   Wireless networking standard that operates in the 5-GHz band with a theoretical maximum throughput of 54 Mbps.

802.11ac   Wireless networking standard that operates in the 5-GHz band and uses multiple in/multiple out (MIMO) and multi-user MIMO (MU-MIMO) to achieve a theoretical maximum throughput of 1 Gbps.

802.11b   Wireless networking standard that operates in the 2.4-GHz band with a theoretical maximum throughput of 11 Mbps.

802.11g   Wireless networking standard that operates in the 2.4-GHz band with a theoretical maximum throughput of 54 Mbps and is backward compatible with 802.11b.

802.11n   Wireless networking standard that can operate in both the 2.4-GHz and 5-GHz bands and uses multiple in/multiple out (MIMO) to achieve a theoretical maximum throughput of 100+ Mbps.

A/V sync   Process of synchronizing audio and video.

AC (alternating current)   Type of electricity in which the flow of electrons alternates direction, back and forth, in a circuit.

AC'97   Sound card standard for lower-end audio devices; created when most folks listened to stereo sound at best.

accelerometer   Feature in smartphones and tablets that rotates the screen when the device is physically rotated.

access control   Security concept using physical security, authentication, users and groups, and security policies.

access control list (ACL)   A clearly defined list of permissions that specifies what actions an authenticated user may perform on a shared resource.

ACPI (Advanced Configuration and Power Interface)   Power management specification that far surpasses its predecessor, APM, by providing support for hot-swappable devices and better control of power modes.

Action Center   A one-page aggregation of event messages, warnings, and maintenance messages in Windows 7.

activation   Process of confirming that an installed copy of a Microsoft product (most commonly Windows or a Microsoft Office application) is legitimate. Usually done at the end of software installation.

active cooling   System designed to remove heat from a processor by using some electrically powered mechanical parts, such as a fan.

active matrix   Type of liquid crystal display (LCD) that replaced the passive matrix technology used in most portable computer displays. Also called TFT (thin film transistor).

active partition   On a hard drive, primary partition that contains an operating system.

active PFC (power factor correction)   Circuitry built into PC power supplies to reduce harmonics.

actively listen   Part of respectful communication involving listening and taking notes without interrupting.

activity light   An LED on a NIC, hub, or switch that blinks rapidly to show data transfers over the network.

ad hoc mode   Decentralized wireless network mode, otherwise known as peer-to-peer mode, where each wireless node is in meshed contact with every other node.

Add or Remove Programs   Applet allowing users to add or remove a program manually to or from a Windows system.

address bus   Set of wires leading from the CPU to the memory controller chip (traditionally the Northbridge) that enables the CPU to address RAM. Also used by the CPU for I/O addressing. On current CPUs with built-in memory controllers, the address bus refers to the internal electronic channel from the microprocessor to RAM, along which the addresses of memory storage locations are transmitted. Like a post office box, each memory location has a distinct number or address; the address bus provides the means by which the microprocessor can access every location in memory.

address space   Total amount of memory addresses that an address bus can contain.

administrative shares   Administrator tool to give local admins access to hard drives and system root folders.

Administrative Tools   Group of Control Panel applets, including Computer Management, Event Viewer, and Reliability and Performance Monitor.

administrator account   User account, created when the OS is first installed, that is allowed complete, unfettered access to the system without restriction.

Administrators group   List of members with complete administrator privileges.

ADSL (asymmetric digital subscriber line) Fully digital, dedicated connection to the telephone system that provides average download speeds of 3–15 Mbps and upload speeds of 384 Kbps to 15 Mbps. *Asymmetric* identifies that upload and download speeds are different, with download usually being significantly faster than upload.

Advanced Encryption Standard (AES) A block cipher created in the late 1990s that uses a 128-bit block size and a 128-, 192-, or 256-bit key size. Practically uncrackable.

Advanced Host Controller Interface (AHCI) An efficient way for motherboards to work with SATA host bus adapters. Using AHCI unlocks some of the advanced features of SATA, such as hot-swapping and native command queuing.

Advanced Startup Options menu Menu that can be reached during the boot process that offers advanced OS startup options, such as to boot to Safe Mode or boot into Last Known Good Configuration.

adware Type of malicious program that downloads ads to a user's computer, generating undesirable network traffic.

Aero The Windows Vista/7 desktop environment. Aero adds some interesting aesthetic effects such as window transparency and Flip 3D.

AGP (Accelerated Graphics Port) An older 32/64-bit expansion slot designed by Intel specifically for video that ran at 66 MHz and yielded a throughput of at least 254 Mbps. Later versions (2×, 4×, 8×) gave substantially higher throughput.

air filter mask A mask designed to keep users from inhaling particulate matter, as when cutting drywall.

airplane mode Mode for mobile devices that disables all wireless and cellular communication for use on airplanes.

algorithm Set of rules for solving a problem in a given number of steps.

ALU (arithmetic logic unit) CPU logic circuits that perform basic arithmetic (add, subtract, multiply, and divide).

AMD (Advanced Micro Devices) CPU and chipset manufacturer that competes with Intel. Produces FX, A-Series, Phenom II, Athlon, Sempron, and Opteron CPUs and APUs. Also produces video card processors under its ATI brand.

AMI (American Megatrends, Inc.) Major producer of BIOS and UEFI software for motherboards, as well as many other computer-related components and software.

amperes (amps or A) Unit of measure for amperage, or electrical current.

amplitude Loudness of a sound card.

analog Device that uses a physical quantity, such as length or voltage, to represent the value of a number. By contrast, digital storage relies on a coding system of numeric units.

AnandTech (anandtech.com) Computer, technology, and Internet news and information site.

Android Smartphone and tablet OS created by Google.

Android application package (APK) Installation software for Android apps.

anti-aliasing In computer imaging, blending effect that smoothes sharp contrasts between two regions—e.g., jagged lines or different colors. Reduces jagged edges of text or objects. In voice signal processing, process of removing or smoothing out spurious frequencies from waveforms produced by converting digital signals back to analog.

antistatic bag Bag made of antistatic plastic into which electronics are placed for temporary or long-term storage. Used to protect components from electrostatic discharge.

antistatic mat Special surface on which to lay electronics. These mats come with a grounding connection designed to equalize electrical potential between a workbench and one or more electronic devices. Used to prevent electrostatic discharge.

antistatic wrist strap Special device worn around the wrist with a grounding connection designed to equalize electrical potential between a technician and an electronic device. Used to prevent electrostatic discharge.

antivirus program Software designed to combat viruses by either seeking out and destroying them or passively guarding against them.

AOL You've got mail!

API (application programming interface) Software definition that describes operating system calls for application software; conventions defining how a service is invoked.

APIPA (Automatic Private IP Addressing) Feature of Windows that automatically assigns an IP address to the system when the client cannot obtain an IP address automatically.

APM (Advanced Power Management) BIOS routines (developed by Intel in 1992 and upgraded over time) that enable the CPU to turn on and off selected peripherals. In 1996, APM was supplanted by Advanced Configuration and Power Interface (ACPI).

app A program for a tablet or smartphone. Also, a program written for the Windows Modern interface.

applet Generic term for a program in the Windows Control Panel.

Applications Name of the tab in Task Manager that lists running applications.

App Store Apple's mobile software storefront, where you can purchase apps for your smartphone, tablet, or other Apple products.

apt-get   Linux command for installing or updating a program using the advanced packaging tool.

archive   To copy programs and data onto a relatively inexpensive storage medium (drive, tape, etc.) for long-term retention.

archive attribute   Attribute of a file that shows whether the file has been backed up since the last change. Each time a file is opened, changed, or saved, the archive bit is turned on. Some types of backups turn off this archive bit to indicate that a good backup of the file exists on tape.

ARM   Energy-efficient processor design frequently used in mobile devices.

ARP (Address Resolution Protocol)   Protocol in the TCP/IP suite used with the command-line utility of the same name (arp) to determine the MAC address that corresponds to a particular IP address.

Ars Technica (arstechnica.com)   Internet technology news site.

ASCII (American Standard Code for Information Interchange)   Industry-standard 8-bit characters used to define text characters, consisting of 96 upper- and lowercase letters, plus 32 nonprinting control characters, each of which is numbered. These numbers were designed to achieve uniformity among computer devices for printing and the exchange of simple text documents.

aspect ratio   Ratio of width to height of an object. Standard television has a 4:3 aspect ratio. High-definition television is 16:9. Desktop computer monitors tend to be either 16:9 or 16:10.

ASR (Automated System Recovery)   Windows XP tool designed to recover a badly corrupted Windows system; similar to the ERD in Windows 2000.

assertive communication   Means of communication that is not pushy or bossy but is also not soft. Useful in dealing with upset customers as it both defuses their anger and gives them confidence that you know what you're doing.

AT (Advanced Technology)   Model name of the second-generation, 80286-based IBM computer. Many aspects of the AT, such as the BIOS, CMOS, and expansion bus, have become de facto standards in the PC industry. The physical organization of the components on the motherboard is called the AT form factor.

ATA (AT Attachment)   Type of hard drive and controller designed to replace the earlier ST506 and ESDI drives without requiring replacement of the AT BIOS—hence, AT attachment. These drives are more popularly known as IDE drives. (*See* IDE.) The ATA/33 standard has drive transfer speeds up to 33 MBps; the ATA/66 up to 66 MBps; the ATA/100 up to 100 MBps; and the ATA/133 up to 133 MBps. (*See* Ultra DMA.)

ATA/ATAPI-6   Also known as ATA-6 or "Big Drive." Replaced the INT13 extensions and allowed for hard drives as large as 144 petabytes (144 million GB).

ATAPI (ATA Packet Interface)   Series of standards that enables mass storage devices other than hard drives to use the IDE/ATA controllers. Popular with optical drives. (*See* EIDE.)

ATAPI-compliant   Devices that utilize the ATAPI standard. (*See* ATAPI.)

Athlon   Name used for a series of CPUs manufactured by AMD.

ATM (Asynchronous Transfer Mode)   A network technology that runs at speeds between 25 and 622 Mbps using fiber-optic cabling or CAT 5 or better UTP.

attrib.exe   Command used to view the specific properties of a file; can also be used to modify or remove file properties, such as read-only, system, or archive.

attributes   Values in a file that determine the hidden, read-only, system, and archive status of the file.

ATX (Advanced Technology Extended)   Popular motherboard form factor that generally replaced the AT form factor.

audio interface   High-end external sound device used by audio engineers and recording artists.

AUP (Acceptable Use Policy)   Defines what actions employees may or may not perform on company equipment, including computers, phones, printers, and even the network itself. This policy defines the handling of passwords, e-mail, and many other issues.

authentication   Any method a computer uses to determine who can access it.

authorization   Any method a computer uses to determine what an authenticated user can do.

autodetection   Process through which new disks are automatically recognized by the BIOS.

Automatic Updates   Feature allowing updates to Windows to be retrieved automatically over the Internet.

AutoPlay   Windows setting, along with autorun.inf, enabling Windows to detect media files automatically and begin using them. (*See* autorun.inf.)

autorun.inf   File included on some media that automatically launches a program or installation routine when the media is inserted/attached to a system.

autosensing   Used by better-quality sound cards to detect a device plugged into a port and to adapt the features of that port.

auto-switching power supply   Type of power supply able to detect the voltage of a particular outlet and adjust accordingly.

Award Software   Major brand of BIOS and UEFI software for motherboards. Merged with Phoenix Technologies.

backlight   One of three main components used in LCDs to illuminate an image.

backside bus   Set of wires that connects the CPU to Level 2 cache. All modern CPUs have a backside bus, which first appeared in the Pentium Pro. Some buses run at the full speed of the CPU, whereas others run at a fraction. Earlier Pentium IIs, for example, had backside buses running at half the speed of the processor. (*See also* frontside bus *and* external data bus.)

Backup and Restore Center   Windows Vista/7's backup utility (Windows 7 drops "Center" from the name). It offers two options: create a backup or restore from a backup.

Backup or Restore Wizard   Older Windows utility that enables users to create system backups and set system restore points.

bandwidth   Piece of the spectrum occupied by some form of signal, such as television, voice, or fax data. Signals require a certain size and location of bandwidth to be transmitted. The higher the bandwidth, the faster the signal transmission, allowing for a more complex signal such as audio or video. Because bandwidth is a limited space, when one user is occupying it, others must wait their turn. Bandwidth is also the capacity of a network to transmit a given amount of data during a given period.

bank   Total number of DIMMs that can be accessed simultaneously by the chipset. The "width" of the external data bus divided by the "width" of the DIMM sticks. Specific DIMM slots must be populated to activate dual-, triple-, or quad-channel memory.

bar code reader   Tool to read Universal Product Code (UPC) bar codes.

basic disk   Hard drive partitioned in the "classic" way with a master boot record (MBR) and partition table. (*See also* dynamic disks.)

baud   One analog cycle on a telephone line. In the early days of telephone data transmission, the baud rate was often analogous to bits per second. Due to advanced modulation of baud cycles as well as data compression, this is no longer true.

bcdedit   A command-line tool that enables you to view the BCD store, which lists the Windows boot options.

BD-R (Blu-ray Disc-Recordable)   Blu-ray Disc format that enables writing data to blank discs.

BD-RE (Blu-ray Disc-REwritable)   Blu-ray Disc equivalent of the rewritable DVD, allows writing and rewriting several times on the same BD. (*See* Blu-ray Disc.)

BD-ROM (Blu-ray Disc-Read Only Media)   Blu-ray Disc equivalent of a DVD-ROM or CD-ROM. (*See* Blu-ray Disc.)

beep codes   Series of audible tones produced by a motherboard during the POST. These tones identify whether the POST has completed successfully or whether some piece of system hardware is not working properly. Consult the manual for your particular motherboard for a specific list of beep codes.

binary numbers   Number system with a base of 2, unlike the number systems most of us use that have bases of 10 (decimal numbers), 12 (measurement in feet and inches), and 60 (time). Binary numbers are preferred for computers for precision and economy. An electronic circuit that can detect the difference between two states (on–off, 0–1) is easier and more inexpensive to build than one that could detect the differences among ten states (0–9).

biometric device   Hardware device used to support authentication; works by scanning and remembering a unique aspect of a user's various body parts (e.g., retina, iris, face, or fingerprint) by using some form of sensing device such as a retinal scanner.

BIOS (basic input/output services) (basic input/output system)   Classically, software routines burned onto the system ROM of a PC. More commonly seen as any software that directly controls a particular piece of hardware. A set of programs encoded in read-only memory (ROM) on computers. These programs handle startup operations and low-level control of hardware such as disk drives, the keyboard, and monitor.

bit   Single binary digit. Also, any device that can be in an on or off state.

bit depth   Number of colors a video card is capable of producing. Common bit depths are 16-bit and 32-bit, representing 65,536 colors and 16.7 million colors (plus an 8-bit alpha channel for transparency levels), respectively.

BitLocker Drive Encryption   Drive encryption software offered in high-end versions of Windows. BitLocker requires a special chip to validate hardware status and to ensure that the computer hasn't been hacked.

Bluetooth   Wireless technology designed to create small wireless networks preconfigured to do specific jobs, but not meant to replace full-function networks or Wi-Fi.

Blu-ray Disc (BD)   Optical disc format that stores 25 or 50 GB of data, designed to be the replacement media for DVD. Competed with HD DVD.

boot   To initiate an automatic routine that clears the memory, loads the operating system, and prepares the computer for use. Term is derived from "pull yourself up by your bootstraps." PCs must do that because RAM doesn't retain program instructions when power is turned off. A cold boot occurs when the PC is physically switched on. A warm boot loads a fresh OS without turning off the computer, lessening the strain on the electronic circuitry. To do a warm boot, press the CTRL-ALT-DELETE keys twice in rapid succession (the three-fingered salute).

Boot Camp   Apple tool used to install and boot to versions of Windows on a macOS computer.

Boot Configuration Data (BCD) file   File that contains information about the various operating systems installed on the system as well as instructions for how to actually load (bootstrap) them.

boot sector   First sector on a PC hard drive or floppy disk, track 0. The boot-up software in ROM tells the computer to load whatever program is found there. If a system disk is read, the program in the boot record directs the computer to the root directory to load the operating system.

boot sequence   List containing information telling the bootstrap loader in which order to check the available storage devices for an OS. Configurable in CMOS setup.

boot.ini   Text file used during the boot process that provides a list of all operating systems currently installed and available for ntldr (NT Loader). Also tells where each OS is located on the system. Used in Windows XP and earlier Microsoft operating systems.

bootable disk   Disk that contains a functional operating system; can also be a floppy disk, USB thumb drive, or optical disc.

bootmgr   Windows Boot Manager for Vista and later versions.

bootrec   A Windows Recovery Environment troubleshooting and repair tool that repairs the master boot record, boot sector, or BCD store. It replaces the fixboot and fixmbr Recovery Console commands used in Windows XP and earlier operating systems.

bootstrap loader   Segment of code in a system's BIOS that scans for an operating system, looks specifically for a valid boot sector, and, when one is found, hands control over to the boot sector; then the bootstrap loader removes itself from memory.

bps (bits per second)   Measurement of how fast data is moved from one place to another. A 56K modem can move ~56,000 bits per second.

bridge   A device that connects two networks and passes traffic between them based only on the node address, so that traffic between nodes on one network does not appear on the other network. For example, an Ethernet bridge only looks at the MAC address. Bridges filter and forward packets based on MAC addresses and operate at Level 2 (Data Link layer) of the OSI seven-layer model.

broadband   Commonly understood as a reference to high-speed, always-on communication links that can move large files much more quickly than a regular phone line.

broadcast   A network transmission addressed for every node on the network.

browser   Program specifically designed to retrieve, interpret, and display Web pages.

BSoD (Blue Screen of Death)   Infamous error screen that appears when Windows encounters an unrecoverable error.

BTX (Balanced Technology eXtended)   Motherboard form factor designed as an improvement over ATX.

buffered/registered DRAM Usually seen in motherboards supporting more than four sticks of RAM, required to address interference issues caused by the additional sticks.

bug Programming error that causes a program or a computer system to perform erratically, produce incorrect results, or crash. The term was coined when a real bug was found in one of the circuits of one of the first ENIAC computers.

burn Process of writing data to a writable optical disc, such as a DVD-R.

burn-in failure Critical failure usually associated with manufacturing defects.

bus Series of wires connecting two or more separate electronic devices, enabling those devices to communicate. Also, a network topology where computers all connect to a main line called a bus cable.

bus mastering Circuitry allowing devices to avoid conflicts on the external data bus.

bus topology Network configuration wherein all computers connect to the network via a central bus cable.

BYOD (bring your own device) An arrangement in some companies' IT departments where employees are permitted to use their own phones or other mobile devices instead of company-issued ones. Also, a feature of some wireless carriers where you can buy an unsubsidized device and use it to get cheaper wireless rates.

byte Unit of 8 bits; fundamental data unit of personal computers. Storing the equivalent of one character, the byte is also the basic unit of measurement for computer storage.

CAB files Short for cabinet files. These files are compressed and most commonly used during OS installation to store many smaller files, such as device drivers.

cache (disk) Special area of RAM that stores the data most frequently accessed from the hard drive. Cache memory can optimize the use of your systems.

cache (L1, L2, L3, etc.) Special section of fast memory, usually built into the CPU, used by the onboard logic to store information most frequently accessed by the CPU.

calibration Process of matching the print output of a printer to the visual output of a monitor. Alternatively, a method used to define the active or touchable area of a touchscreen monitor or phone; primarily found on older, resistive touchscreen devices.

capacitive touchscreen Type of touchscreen that uses electrical current in your body to determine movement of your fingers across the screen.

CAPTCHA (Completely Automated Public Turing Test to tell Computers and Humans Apart) Authentication challenge using images, videos, sounds, or other media to be identified by a user. Computers have a much more difficult time discerning the content of these tests than humans, making the challenge useful in determining if a human or a computer is attempting access.

card reader   Device with which you can read data from one of several types of flash memory.

CardBus   32-bit PC cards that can support up to eight devices on each card. Electrically incompatible with earlier PC cards (3.3 V versus 5 V).

CAT 5   Category 5 wire; a TIA/EIA standard for UTP wiring that can operate at up to 100 Mbps.

CAT 5e   Category 5e wire; TIA/EIA standard for UTP wiring that can operate at up to 1 Gbps.

CAT 6   Category 6 wire; TIA/EIA standard for UTP wiring that can operate at up to 10 Gbps.

CAT 6a   Category 6a wire; augmented CAT 6 UTP wiring that supports 10GbE networks at the full 100-meter distance between a node and a switch.

CAT 7   Supports 10-Gbps networks at 100-meter segments; shielding for individual wire pairs reduces crosstalk and noise problems. CAT 7 is not a TIA/EIA standard.

catastrophic failure   Describes a failure in which a component or whole system will not boot; usually related to a manufacturing defect of a component. Could also be caused by overheating and physical damage to computer components.

CCFL (cold cathode fluorescent lamp)   Light technology used in LCDs and flatbed scanners. CCFLs use relatively little power for the amount of light they provide.

cd (chdir)   Shorthand for "change directory." Enables you to change the focus of the command prompt from one directory to another.

CD (compact disc)   Originally designed as the replacement for vinyl records, has become the primary method of long-term storage of music and data.

CD quality   Audio quality that has a sample rate of 44.4 KHz and a bit rate of 128 bits.

CDDA (CD-Digital Audio)   Special format used for early CD-ROMs and all audio CDs; divides data into variable-length tracks. A good format to use for audio tracks but terrible for data because of lack of error checking.

CDFS (compact disc file system)   File structure, rules, and conventions used when organizing and storing files and data on a CD.

CD-R (CD-recordable)   CD technology that accepts a single "burn" but cannot be erased after that one burn.

CD-ROM (compact disc/read-only memory) Read-only compact storage disc for audio or video data. CD-ROMs are read by using CD-ROM drives and optical drives with backward compatibility, such as DVD and Blu-ray Disc drives.

CD-RW (CD-rewritable) CD technology that accepts multiple reads/writes like a hard drive.

Celeron Lower-cost brand of Intel CPUs.

cellular wireless networks Networks that enable cell phones, smartphones, and other mobile devices to connect to the Internet.

certification License that demonstrates competency in some specialized skill.

Certified Cisco Network Associate (CCNA) One of the certifications demonstrating a knowledge of Cisco networking products.

CFS (Central File System) Method to unify all storage devices within a network or organization to facilitate a single management point and to provide user access to any file or data within the organization.

CFS (Command File System) Along with CFS (Common File System), this term is found in the Acronym List of the CompTIA A+ learning objectives, and nowhere else. After diligent research, your intrepid author has not found a satisfactory reference to this alleged technology and believes that your ability to recognize that CFS can stand for Command File System will be sufficient knowledge to pass any exam questions about this topic on the corresponding test. – Mike Meyers

CFS (Common File System) Along with CFS (Command File System), this term is found in the Acronym List of the CompTIA A+ learning objectives, and nowhere else. After diligent research, your intrepid author has not found a satisfactory reference to this alleged technology and believes that your ability to recognize that CFS can stand for Common File System will be sufficient knowledge to pass any exam questions about this topic on the corresponding test. – Mike Meyers

chain of custody A documented history of who has been in possession of a system.

CHAP (Challenge Handshake Authentication Protocol) Common remote access protocol; the serving system challenges the remote client, usually by means of asking for a password.

charms In Windows 8 and 8.1, tools located in the hidden Charms bar, such as a search function, a sharing tool, a settings tool, and more.

Charms bar The location in Windows 8 and 8.1 of the charms tools. Accessed by moving the cursor to the upper-right corner of the screen.

chassis intrusion detection Feature offered in some chassis that trips a switch when the chassis is opened.

chipset   Electronic chips, specially designed to work together, that handle all of the low-level functions of a PC. In the original PC, the chipset consisted of close to 30 different chips; today, chipsets usually consist of one, two, or three separate chips embedded into a motherboard.

chkdsk (CheckDisk)   Hard drive error detection and, to a certain extent, correction utility in Windows, launched from the command-line interface. Originally a DOS command (chkdsk.exe); also the executable for the graphical Error-checking tool.

chmod   Linux command used to change permissions.

chown   Linux command used to change the owner and the group to which a file or folder is associated.

Chrome OS   A Linux variant operating system designed by Google for thin client systems for Internet usage.

CIFS (Common Internet File System)   The protocol that NetBIOS used to share folders and printers. Still very common, even on UNIX/Linux systems.

clean installation   Installing an operating system on a fresh drive, following a reformat of that drive. Often it's the only way to correct a problem with a system when many of the crucial operating system files have become corrupted.

client   Computer program that uses the services of another computer program. Also, software that extracts information from a server; your auto-dial phone is a client, and the phone company is its server. Also, a machine that accesses shared resources on a server.

client/server   Relationship in which client software obtains services from a server on behalf of a person.

client/server network   Network that has dedicated server machines and client machines.

clock cycle   Single charge to the clock wire of a CPU.

clock-multiplying CPU   CPU that takes the incoming clock signal and multiples it inside the CPU to let the internal circuitry of the CPU run faster.

clock speed   Speed at which a CPU executes instructions, measured in MHz or GHz. In modern CPUs, the internal speed is a multiple of the external speed. (*See also* clock-multiplying CPU.)

clock (CLK) wire   A special wire that, when charged, tells the CPU that another piece of information is waiting to be processed.

closed source   Software that is solely controlled by its creator or distributor.

Cloud computing   A model for enabling and accessing computing storage and other shared (or not shared) resources on-demand. The "cloud" is based on servicing models that include IaaS, PaaS, and SaaS, or hybrid mixtures of these services.

cluster Basic unit of storage on a floppy or hard disk. Multiple sectors are contained in a cluster. When Windows stores a file on a disk, it writes those files into dozens or even hundreds of contiguous clusters. If there aren't enough contiguous open clusters available, the operating system finds the next open cluster and writes there, continuing this process until the entire file is saved. The FAT or MFT tracks how the files are distributed among the clusters on the disk.

CMOS (complementary metal-oxide semiconductor) Originally, the type of nonvolatile RAM that held information about the most basic parts of your PC, such as hard drives, floppies, and amount of DRAM. Today, actual CMOS chips have been replaced by flash-type nonvolatile RAM. The information is the same, however, and is still called CMOS—even though it is now almost always stored on Flash RAM.

CMOS clear A jumper on the motherboard that, when set, will revert CMOS settings to the factory defaults.

CMOS setup program Program enabling you to access and update CMOS data. Also referred to as the System Setup Utility or BIOS setup.

CNR (communications and networking riser) Proprietary slot used on some motherboards to provide a sound interference–free connection for modems, sound cards, and NICs.

coaxial cable Cabling in which an internal conductor is surrounded by another, outer conductor, thus sharing the same axis.

code Set of symbols representing characters (e.g., ASCII code) or instructions in a computer program (a programmer writes source code, which must be translated into executable or machine code for the computer to use).

code names Names that keep track of different variations within CPU models.

codec (compressor/decompressor) Software that compresses or decompresses media streams.

color depth Term to define a scanner's ability to produce color, hue, and shade.

COM port(s) Serial communications ports available on a computer. COM*x* is used to designate a uniquely numbered COM port such as COM1, COM2, etc.

command A request, typed from a terminal or embedded in a file, to perform an operation or to execute a particular program.

command-line interface User interface for an OS devoid of all graphical trappings.

command prompt Text prompt for entering commands.

CompactFlash (CF) One of the older but still popular flash media formats. Its interface uses a simplified PC Card bus, so it also supports I/O devices.

compatibility modes   Feature of Windows to enable software written for previous versions of Windows to operate in newer operating systems.

compliance   Concept that members of an organization must abide by the rules of that organization. For a technician, this often revolves around what software can or cannot be installed on an organization's computer.

component failure   Occurs when a system device fails due to a manufacturing or some other type of defect.

Component Services   Programming tools in Windows for the sharing of data objects between programs.

compression   Process of squeezing data to eliminate redundancies, allowing files to use less space when stored or transmitted.

CompTIA A+ 220-901   The first half of the CompTIA A+ certification for computer technicians. The 901 exam focuses primarily on understanding terminology and technology, how to do fundamental tasks such as upgrading RAM, and basic network and mobile device support.

CompTIA A+ 220-902   The second half of the CompTIA A+ certification for computer technicians. The 902 exam focuses primarily on software, security, and troubleshooting.

CompTIA A+ certification   Industry-wide, vendor-neutral computer certification program that demonstrates competency as a computer technician.

CompTIA Network+ certification   Industry-wide, vendor-neutral certification for network technicians, covering network hardware, installation, and troubleshooting.

computer   A sophisticated machine, also called a computing device, that you can use to create work, play games, and so on. Computers have processing and input/output hardware, an operating system, and application software.

Computer   Default interface in Windows Vista and Windows 7 for Windows Explorer; displays hard drives and devices with removable storage.

Computer Management   Applet in Windows' Administrative Tools that contains several useful snap-ins, such as Device Manager and Disk Management.

computing process   Four parts of a computer's operation: input, processing, output, and storage.

Computing Technology Industry Association (CompTIA)   Nonprofit IT trade association that administers the CompTIA A+ and CompTIA Network+ exams, and many other vendor-neutral IT certification exams.

connectors   Small receptacles used to attach cables to a system. Common types of connectors include USB, PS/2, DB-25, RJ-45, HDMI, DVI, HD15, DisplayPort, and Thunderbolt.

consumables   Materials used up by printers, including paper, ink, ribbons, and toner cartridges.

container file   File containing two or more separate, compressed tracks, typically an audio track and a moving-picture track. Also known as a *wrapper*.

context menu   Small menu brought up by right-clicking on objects in Windows.

Control Panel   Collection of Windows applets, or small programs, that can be used to configure various pieces of hardware and software in a system.

controller card   Card adapter that connects devices, such as a drive, to the main computer bus/motherboard.

convergence   Measure of how sharply a single pixel appears on a CRT; a monitor with poor convergence produces images that are not sharply defined.

copy backup   Type of backup similar to a normal or full backup, in that all selected files on a system are backed up. This type of backup does not change the archive bit of the files being backed up.

copy command   Command in the command-line interface for making a copy of a file and pasting it in another location.

Core   Name used for the family of Intel CPUs that succeeded the Pentium 4, such as the Core i3, Core i5, and Core i7.

counter   Used to track data about a particular object when using the Performance Monitor.

cp   Copy command in Linux.

CPU (central processing unit)   "Brain" of the computer. Microprocessor that handles primary calculations for the computer. CPUs are known by names such as Core i5 and Phenom II.

CRC (cyclic redundancy check)   Very accurate mathematical method used to check for errors in long streams of transmitted data. Before data is sent, the main computer uses the data to calculate a CRC value from the data's contents. If the receiver calculates from the received data a different CRC value, the data was corrupted during transmission and is re-sent. Ethernet packets use the CRC algorithm in the FCS portion of the frame.

credit card reader   Device that can be attached to mobile phones and tablets to take credit card payments.

crimper   A specialized tool for connecting UTP wires to an RJ-45 connector. Also called a *crimping tool*.

CrossFire   Technology that combines the power of multiple AMD graphics cards in a system.

crossover cable   A standard UTP cable with one RJ-45 connector using the T568A standard and the other using the T568B standard. This reverses the signal between sending and receiving wires and thus simulates the connection to a switch.

CRT (cathode ray tube)   Tube of a monitor in which rays of electrons are beamed onto a phosphorescent screen to produce images. Also, a shorthand way to describe a monitor that uses CRT rather than LCD technology.

CSMA/CA (carrier sense multiple access/collision avoidance)   Networking scheme used by wireless devices to transmit data while avoiding data collisions, which wireless nodes have difficulty detecting.

CSMA/CD (carrier sense multiple access/collision detection)   Networking scheme used by Ethernet devices to transmit data and resend data after detection of data collisions.

cylinder   Single concentric track passing through all the platters in a hard disk drive. Imagine a hard disk drive as a series of metal cans, nested one inside another; a single can would represent a cylinder.

DAC (Discretionary Access Control)   Authorization method based on the idea that there is an owner of a resource who may at his or her discretion assign access to that resource. DAC is considered much more flexible than mandatory access control (MAC).

daily backup   Backup of all files that have been changed on that day without changing the archive bits of those files. Also called *daily copy backup*.

daisy-chaining   Method of connecting several devices along a bus and managing the signals for each device.

data classification   System of organizing data according to its sensitivity. Common classifications include public, highly confidential, and top secret.

data roaming   A feature of cellular data systems that enables the signal to jump from cell tower to cell tower and from your provider to another provider without obvious notice.

data storage   Saving a permanent copy of your work so that you can come back to it later.

data structure   Scheme that directs how an OS stores and retrieves data on and off a drive. Used interchangeably with the term file system. (*See also* file system.)

DB connectors   D-shaped connectors used for a variety of connections in the PC and networking world. Can be male (with prongs) or female (with holes) and have a varying number of pins or sockets. Also called D-sub, D-subminiature, or D-shell connectors.

DB-9   A two-row DB connector (male) used to connect the computer's serial port to a serial-communication device such as a modem or a console port on a managed switch.

DB-15 connector   A two- or three-row D-sub connector (female) used for 10Base5 networks, MIDI/joysticks, and analog video.

DB-25 connector   D-sub connector (female), commonly referred to as a parallel port connector.

DC (direct current)   Type of electricity in which the flow of electrons is in a complete circle in one direction.

dd   Linux command for copying entire block volumes.

DDOS (distributed denial of service)   An attack on a computer or network device in which multiple computers send data and requests to the device in an attempt to overwhelm it so that it cannot perform normal operations.

DDR (double data rate)   Shortened reference to memory technology, such as DDR SDRAM. Similarly, DDR2 can refer to DDR2 SDRAM, DDR3 to DDR3 SDRAM, and so on.

DDR RAM (double data rate SDRAM)   Shortened reference to memory technology, such as DDR SDRAM.

DDR SDRAM (double data rate SDRAM)   Type of DRAM that makes two processes for every clock cycle. (*See also* DRAM.)

DDR2 SDRAM   Type of SDRAM that sends 4 bits of data in every clock cycle. (*See also* DDR SDRAM.)

DDR3 SDRAM   Type of SDRAM that transfers data at twice the rate of DDR2 SDRAM.

DDR4 SDRAM   Type of SDRAM that offers higher density and lower voltages than DDR3, and can handle faster data transfer rates. Maximum theoretical capacity of DDR4 DIMMs is up to 512 GB.

DE (desktop environment)   Name for the various user interfaces found in Linux distributions.

debug   To detect, trace, and eliminate errors in computer programs.

decibels   Unit of measurement typically associated with sound. The higher the number of decibels, the louder the sound.

dedicated server   Machine that is not used for any client functions, only server functions.

default gateway   In a TCP/IP network, the nearest router to a particular host. This router's IP address is part of the necessary TCP/IP configuration for communicating with multiple networks using IP.

definition file   List of virus signatures that an antivirus program can recognize.

defragmentation (defrag)   Procedure in which all the files on a hard disk drive are rewritten on disk so that all parts of each file reside in contiguous clusters. The result is an improvement in disk speed during retrieval operations.

degauss   Procedure used to break up the electromagnetic fields that can build up on the cathode ray tube of a monitor; involves running a current through a wire loop. Most monitors feature a manual degaussing tool.

del (erase)   Command in the command-line interface used to delete/erase files.

desktop   User's primary interface to the Windows operating system.

desktop replacement   Portable computer that offers the same performance as a full-fledged desktop computer; these systems are normally very heavy to carry and often cost much more than the desktop systems they replace.

device driver   Program used by the operating system to control communications between the computer and peripherals.

device hardening   Actions to make a computing device as difficult as possible for unauthorized people to access.

Device Manager   Utility that enables techs to examine and configure all the hardware and drivers in a Windows PC.

DFS (distributed file system)   A storage environment where shared files are accessed from storage devices within multiple servers, clients, and peer hosts.

DHCP (Dynamic Host Configuration Protocol)   Protocol that enables client hosts to request and receive TCP/IP settings automatically from an appropriately configured server.

differential backup   Similar to an incremental backup. Backs up the files that have been changed since the last backup. This type of backup does not change the state of the archive bit.

digital camera   Camera that simulates film technology electronically.

digital certificate   Form in which a public key is sent from a Web server to a Web browser so that the browser can decrypt the data sent by the server.

Digital Living Network Alliance (DLNA) devices   Devices that connect to a home network, discover each other, and share media. In theory, DLNA devices should work with minimal setup or fuss, even if sourced from different manufacturers.

digital zoom   Software tool to enhance the optical zoom capabilities of a digital camera.

digitally signed driver   A driver designed specifically to work with Windows that has been tested and certified by Microsoft to work stably with Windows.

digitizer   The touchscreen overlay technology that converts finger and stylus contact into input data for the device to use.

DIMM (dual inline memory module)   32- or 64-bit type of DRAM packaging with the distinction that each side of each tab inserted into the system performs a separate function. DIMMs come in a variety of sizes, with 184-, 240-, and 288-pin being the most common on desktop computers.

DIN (Deutsches Institut für Normung)   Round connector shell with pins or holes that was standardized by the German national standards body. Largely obsolete, DIN and mini-DIN connectors have been used by keyboards, mice, video systems, and other peripherals attached to computers.

dipole antennas   Standard straight-wire antennas that provide the most omnidirectional function.

dir   Command used in the command-line interface to display the entire contents of the current working directory.

directory   Another name for a folder.

directory service   Centralized index that each PC accesses to locate resources in the domain.

DirectX   Set of APIs enabling programs to control multimedia, such as sound, video, and graphics. Used in Windows Vista and Windows 7 to draw the Aero desktop.

Disk Cleanup   Utility built into Windows that can help users clean up their hard drives by removing temporary Internet files, deleting unused program files, and more.

disk cloning   Taking a PC and making a duplicate of the hard drive, including all data, software, and configuration files, and transferring it to another PC. (*See* image deployment.)

disk duplexing   Type of disk mirroring using two separate controllers rather than one; faster than traditional mirroring.

disk initialization   A process that places special information on every hard drive installed in a Windows system.

Disk Management   Snap-in available with the Microsoft Management Console that enables techs to configure the various disks installed in a system; available in the Computer Management Administrative Tool.

disk mirroring   Process by which data is written simultaneously to two or more disk drives. Read and write speed is decreased, but redundancy in case of catastrophe is increased.

disk quota   Application allowing network administrators to limit hard drive space usage.

disk striping   Process by which data is spread among multiple (at least two) drives. Increases speed for both reads and writes of data. Considered RAID level 0 because it does not provide fault tolerance.

disk striping with parity   Method for providing fault tolerance by writing data across multiple drives and then including an additional drive, called a parity drive, that stores information to rebuild the data contained on the other drives. Requires at least three physical disks: two for the data and a third for the parity drive. This provides data redundancy at RAID levels 5, 10, and 0+1 with different options.

disk thrashing   Hard drive that is constantly being accessed due to lack of available system memory. When system memory runs low, a Windows system will utilize hard disk space as "virtual" memory, thus causing an unusual amount of hard drive access.

diskpart   A fully functioning command-line partitioning tool.

display adapter   Handles all the communication between the CPU and the monitor. Also known as a video card.

Display applet   Tool in Windows XP and Windows 7 used to adjust display settings, including resolution, refresh rate, driver information, and color depth. (*For the comparable tool in Windows Vista, see* Personalization applet.)

DisplayPort   Digital video connector used by Apple Mac desktop models and some PCs, notably from Dell. Designed by VESA as a royalty-free connector to replace VGA and DVI.

distended capacitors   Failed capacitors on a motherboard, which tend to bulge out at the top. This was especially a problem during the mid-2000s, when capacitor manufacturers released huge batches of bad capacitors.

distribution (distro)   A specific variant of Linux.

DLP (data loss prevention)   System or set of rules designed to stop leakage of sensitive information. Usually applied to Internet appliances to monitor outgoing network traffic.

DLP (digital light processing)   Display technology that reflects and directs light onto a display surface using micromechanically operated mirrors.

DLT (digital linear tape)   High speed, magnetic tape storage technology used to archive and retrieve data from faster, online media such as hard disks.

DMA (direct memory access) modes   Technique that some PC hardware devices use to transfer data to and from the memory without using the CPU.

DMA controller   Resides between the RAM and the devices and handles DMA requests.

DMZ (demilitarized zone)   A lightly protected or unprotected subnet network positioned between an outer firewall and an organization's highly protected internal network. DMZs are used mainly to host public address servers (such as Web servers).

DNS (domain name service or domain name server)   TCP/IP name resolution system that translates a host name into an IP address.

DNS domain   Specific branch of the DNS name space. First-level DNS domains include .com, .gov, and .edu.

dock   A bar at the bottom of the macOS desktop where application icons can be placed for easy access.

docking station   Device that provides a portable computer extra features such as an optical drive or ExpressCard, in addition to legacy and modern ports. Similar to a port replicator. Also, a charging station for mobile devices.

document findings, actions, and outcomes   Recording each troubleshooting job: what the problem was, how it was fixed, and other helpful information. (Step 6 of 6 in the CompTIA troubleshooting theory.)

Documents folder   Windows folder for storing user-created files.

Dolby Digital   Technology for sound reductions and channeling methods used for digital audio.

domain   Groupings of users, computers, or networks. In Microsoft networking, a domain is a group of computers and users that share a common account database and a common security policy. On the Internet, a domain is a group of computers that share a common element in their hierarchical name. Other types of domains exist—e.g., broadcast domain, etc.

domain-based network   Network that eliminates the need for logging on to multiple servers by using domain controllers to hold the security database for all systems.

DoS (denial of service)   An attack on a computer resource that prevents it from performing its normal operations, usually by overwhelming it with large numbers of requests in an effort to monopolize its resources.

DOS (Disk Operating System)   First popular operating system available for PCs. A text-based, single-tasking operating system that was not completely replaced until the introduction of Windows 95.

dot-matrix printer   Printer that creates each character from an array of dots. Pins striking a ribbon against the paper, one pin for each dot position, form the dots. May be a serial printer (printing one character at a time) or a line printer.

double-sided RAM   RAM stick with RAM chips soldered to both sides of the stick. May only be used with motherboards designed to accept double-sided RAM. Very common.

dpi (dots per inch) Measure of printer resolution that counts the dots the device can produce per linear (horizontal) inch.

DPMS (display power-management signaling) Specification that can reduce monitor power consumption by 75 percent by reducing/eliminating video signals during idle periods.

DRAM (dynamic random access memory or dynamic RAM) Memory used to store data in most personal computers. DRAM stores each bit in a "cell" composed of a transistor and a capacitor. Because the capacitor in a DRAM cell can only hold a charge for a few milliseconds, DRAM must be continually refreshed, or rewritten, to retain its data.

drive letter A letter designating a specific drive or partition.

DriveLock CMOS program enabling you to control the ATA security mode feature set. Also known as *drive lock*.

driver signing Digital signature for drivers used by Windows to protect against potentially bad drivers.

DS3D (DirectSound3D) Introduced with DirectX 3.0, a command set used to create positional audio, or sounds that appear to come from in front, in back, or to the side of a user. Merged with DirectSound into DirectAudio in DirectX 8. (*See also* DirectX.)

DSL (digital subscriber line) High-speed Internet connection technology that uses a regular telephone line for connectivity. DSL comes in several varieties, including asynchronous (ADSL) and synchronous (SDSL), and many speeds. Typical home-user DSL connections are ADSL with faster download speeds than upload speeds.

D-subminiature *See* DB connectors.

DTS (Digital Theatre Systems) Technology for sound reductions and channeling methods, similar to Dolby Digital.

dual boot Refers to a computer with two operating systems installed, enabling users to choose which operating system to load on boot. Can also refer to kicking a device a second time just in case the first time didn't work.

dual-channel architecture Using two sticks of RAM (either RDRAM or DDR) to increase throughput.

dual-channel memory Form of DDR, DDR2, and DDR3 memory access used by many motherboards that requires two identical sticks of DDR, DDR2, or DDR3 RAM.

dual-core CPUs that have two execution units on the same physical chip but share caches and RAM.

dual-scan passive matrix Manufacturing technique for increasing display updates by refreshing two lines at a time.

dual-voltage Type of power supply that works with either 110- or 220-volt outlets.

dumpster diving To go through someone's trash in search of information.

DUN (Dial-up Networking) Software used by Windows to govern the connection between the modem and the ISP.

duplexing Similar to mirroring in that data is written to and read from two physical drives, for fault tolerance. Separate controllers are used for each drive, both for additional fault tolerance and for additional speed. Considered RAID level 1. Also called *disk duplexing* or *drive duplexing*.

DVD (digital versatile disc) Optical disc format that provides for 4–17 GB of video or data storage.

DVD-ROM DVD equivalent of the standard CD-ROM.

DVD-RW/DVD+RW Incompatible rewritable DVD media formats.

DVD-Video DVD format used exclusively to store digital video; capable of storing over two hours of high-quality video on a single DVD.

DVI (Digital Visual Interface) Special video connector designed for digital-to-digital connections; most commonly seen on PC video cards and LCD monitors. Some versions also support analog signals with a special adapter.

dxdiag (DirectX Diagnostics Tool) Diagnostic tool for getting information about and testing a computer's DirectX version.

dye-sublimation printer Printer that uses a roll of heat-sensitive plastic film embedded with dyes, which are vaporized and then solidified onto specially coated paper to create a high-quality image.

dynamic disks Special feature of Windows that enables users to span a single volume across two or more drives. Dynamic disks do not have partitions; they have volumes. Dynamic disks can be striped, mirrored, and striped or mirrored with parity.

ECC (error correction code) Special software, embedded on hard drives, that constantly scans the drives for bad sectors.

ECC RAM/DRAM (error correction code DRAM) RAM that uses special chips to detect and fix memory errors. Commonly used in high-end servers where data integrity is crucial.

effective permissions User's combined permissions granted by multiple groups.

EFI (Extensible Firmware Interface) Firmware created by Intel and HP that replaced traditional 16-bit BIOS and added several new enhancements.

EFS (encrypting file system)   Storage organization and management service, such as NTFS, that has the capability of applying a cipher process to the stored data.

EIA/TIA   *See* TIA/EIA.

EIDE (Enhanced IDE)   Marketing concept of hard drive–maker Western Digital, encompassing four improvements for IDE drives, including drives larger than 528 MB, four devices, increase in drive throughput, and non–hard drive devices. (*See* ATAPI, PIO mode.)

electric potential   The voltage differential between any two objects, one of which is frequently ground or earth, resulting in a degree of attraction for the electrons to move from one of the objects to the other. A large difference between a person and a doorknob, for example, can lead to a shocking experience when the two touch. *See* electrostatic discharge (ESD).

electromagnetic interference (EMI)   Electrical interference from one device to another, resulting in poor performance of the device being interfered with. Examples: Static on your TV while running a blow dryer, or placing two monitors too close together and getting a "shaky" screen.

electromagnetic pulse (EMP)   Short burst or disturbance of electromagnetic energy that can cause damage to electronic devices and equipment.

electrostatic discharge (ESD)   Uncontrolled rush of electrons from one object to another. A real menace to PCs, as it can cause permanent damage to semiconductors.

eliciting answers   Communication strategy designed to help techs understand a user's problems better. Works by listening to a user's description of a problem and then asking cogent questions.

e-mail (electronic mail)   Messages, usually text, sent from one person to another via computer. Can also be sent automatically to a group of addresses (mailing list).

emergency repair disk (ERD)   Saves critical boot files and partition information and is the main tool for fixing boot problems in older versions of Windows. Newer versions of Windows call this a system repair disc (Windows Vista/7) or recovery drive (Windows 8/8.1 and 10).

eMMC (embedded MMC)   A form of embedded flash memory widely seen in mobile devices.

emulator   Software or hardware that converts the commands to and from the host machine into an entirely different platform.

encryption   Making data unreadable by those who do not possess a key or password.

equipment rack   A metal structure used in equipment rooms to secure network hardware devices and patch panels. Most racks are 19 inches wide. Devices designed to fit in such a rack use a height measurement called *units*, or simply *U*.

erase lamp   Component inside laser printers that uses light to make the coating of the photosensitive drum conductive.

e-reader   Mobile electronic device used for reading e-books.

ergonomics   The study of how humans and equipment interact.

Error-checking   Windows graphical tool that scans and fixes hard drive problems. Often referred to by the name of the executable, chkdsk, or Check Disk. The macOS equivalent is the Disk Utility, and Linux offers a command-line tool called fsck.

eSATA (external SATA)   Serial ATA-based connector for external hard drives and optical drives.

escalate   Process used when person assigned to repair a problem is not able to get the job done, such as sending the problem to someone with more expertise.

establish a plan of action and implement the solution   After establishing and testing a theory about a particular problem, techs solve the problem. (Step 4 of 6 in the CompTIA troubleshooting theory.)

establish a theory of probable cause   After identifying a problem, techs question the obvious to determine what might be the source of the problem. (Step 2 of 6 in the CompTIA troubleshooting theory.)

Ethernet   Name coined by Xerox for the first standard of network cabling and protocols. Based on a bus topology.

Ethic of Reciprocity   Golden Rule: Do unto others as you would have them do unto you.

EULA (End User License Agreement)   Agreement that accompanies a piece of software, to which the user must agree before using the software. Outlines the terms of use for the software and also lists any actions on the part of the user that violate the agreement.

event auditing   Feature of Event Viewer's Security section that creates an entry in the Security Log when certain events happen, such as a user logging on.

Event Viewer   Utility made available in Windows as an MMC snap-in that enables users to monitor various system events, including network bandwidth usage and CPU utilization.

expand   Command-line utility included with Windows that is used to access files within CAB files.

expansion bus   Set of wires going to the CPU, governed by the expansion bus crystal, directly connected to expansion slots of varying types (PCI, AGP, PCIe, etc.).

expansion bus crystal   Controls the speed of the expansion bus.

expansion card   Electrical circuit board that can add capabilities to a computer.

expansion slots   Connectors on a motherboard that enable users to add optional components to a system. (*See also* AGP, PCI, *and* PCIe.)

ExpressCard   The high-performance serial version of the PC Card that replaced PC Card slots on laptop PCs over the past decade. ExpressCard comes in two widths: 34 mm and 54 mm, called *ExpressCard/34* and *ExpressCard/54*.

extended partition   Type of nonbootable hard disk partition. May only have one extended partition per disk. Purpose is to divide a large disk into smaller partitions, each with a separate drive letter.

Extensible Authentication Protocol (EAP)   Authentication wrapper that EAP-compliant applications can use to accept one of many types of authentication. While EAP is a general-purpose authentication wrapper, its only substantial use is in wireless networks.

extension   Two, three, four, five, or more letters that follow a filename and identify the type of file. Common file extensions are .zip, .exe, .doc, .java, and .xhtml.

external data bus (EDB)   Primary data highway of all computers. Everything in your computer is tied either directly or indirectly to the external data bus. (*See also* frontside bus *and* backside bus.)

face lock   Technology that enables use of facial features to unlock a mobile device or personal computer.

Fast User Switching   Account option that is useful when multiple users share a system; allows users to switch without logging off.

FAT (file allocation table)   Hidden table that records how files on a hard disk are stored in distinct clusters; the only way DOS knows where to access files. Address of first cluster of a file is stored in the directory file. FAT entry for the first cluster is the address of the second cluster used to store that file. In the entry for the second cluster for that file is the address for the third cluster, and so on until the final cluster, which gets a special end-of-file code. There are two FATs, mirror images of each other, in case one is destroyed or damaged. Also refers to the 16-bit file allocation table when used by Windows 2000 and later NT-based operating systems.

FAT16   File allocation table that uses 16 bits to address and index clusters. Used as the primary hard drive format on DOS and early Windows 95 machines; currently used with smaller-capacity (2 GB or less) flash media devices.

FAT32   File allocation table that uses 32 bits to address and index clusters. Commonly used with USB flash-media drives and versions of Windows prior to XP.

FAT64 (exFAT)   A Microsoft-proprietary file system that breaks the 4-GB file-size barrier, supporting files up to 16 exabytes (EB) and a theoretical partition limit of

64 zettabytes (ZB). Envisioned for use with flash media devices with a capacity exceeding 2 TB.

FCS (Frame Check Sequence)   Portion of an Ethernet frame used for error checking, most commonly with the CRC algorithm.

fdisk   Disk-partitioning utility used in DOS and Windows 9*x* systems.

fiber-optic cable   High-speed cable for transmitting data, made of high-purity glass sealed within an opaque tube. Much faster than conventional copper wire such as coaxial cable.

file   Collection of any form of data that is stored beyond the time of execution of a single job. A file may contain program instructions or data, which may be numerical, textual, or graphical information.

file allocation unit   Another term for cluster. (*See also* cluster.)

file association   Windows term for the proper program to open a particular file; for example, the file association for opening .MP3 files might be Winamp.

File Explorer   A tool in Windows 8/8.1/10 that enables users to browse files and folders.

file format   How information is encoded in a file. Two primary types are binary (pictures) and ASCII (text), but within those are many formats, such as BMP and GIF for pictures. Commonly represented by a suffix at the end of the filename; for example, .txt for a text file or .exe for an executable.

file server   Computer designated to store software, courseware, administrative tools, and other data on a LAN or WAN. It "serves" this information to other computers via the network when users enter their personal access codes.

file system   Scheme that directs how an OS stores and retrieves data on and off a drive; FAT32 and NTFS are both file systems. Used interchangeably with the term "data structure." (*See also* data structure.)

filename   Name assigned to a file when the file is first written on a disk. Every file on a disk within the same folder must have a unique name. Filenames can contain any character (including spaces), except the following: \ / : * ? " < > |

Finder   The file and folder browser in macOS.

fingerprint lock   Type of biometric device that enables a user to unlock a mobile device using a fingerprint.

firewall   Device that restricts traffic between a local network and the Internet.

FireWire (IEEE 1394)   Interconnection standard to send wide-band signals over a serialized, physically thin connector system. Serial bus developed by Apple and Texas Instruments; enables connection of 63 devices at speeds up to 800 Mbps.

firmware   Embedded programs or code stored on a ROM chip. Generally OS-independent, thus allowing devices to operate in a wide variety of circumstances without direct OS support. The system BIOS is firmware.

firmware upgrade   Process by which the BIOS/UEFI of a motherboard can be updated to reflect patched bugs and added features. Performed, usually, through CMOS, though some motherboard manufacturers provide a Windows program for performing a firmware upgrade.

fitness monitor   Devices that encourage physical fitness by counting steps using accelerometers, registering heart rate through sensors, using GPS to track exercise, and offering vibration tools to remind the user to get moving. Fitness trackers fit into one of two type: fobs that clip to the body and more sophisticated fitness watches.

Flash ROM   ROM technology that can be electrically reprogrammed while still in the PC. Overwhelmingly the most common storage medium of BIOS in PCs today, as it can be upgraded without a need to open the computer on most systems.

flatbed scanner   Most popular form of consumer scanner; runs a bright light along the length of the tray to capture an image.

FlexATX   Motherboard form factor. Motherboards built in accordance with the Flex-ATX form factor are very small, much smaller than microATX motherboards.

Flip 3D   In the Aero desktop environment, a three-dimensional replacement for ALT-TAB. Accessed by pressing the WINDOWS KEY-TAB key combination.

floppy disk   Removable storage media that can hold between 720 KB and 1.44 MB of data.

floppy drive   System hardware that uses removable 3.5-inch disks as storage media.

flux reversal   Point at which a read/write head detects a change in magnetic polarity.

FM synthesis   Producing sound by electronic emulation of various instruments to more-or-less produce music and other sound effects.

form factor   Standard for the physical organization of motherboard components and motherboard size. Most common form factors are ATX, microATX, and Mini-ITX.

format   Command in the command-line interface used to format a storage device.

formatting   Magnetically mapping a disk to provide a structure for storing data; can be done to any type of disk, including a floppy disk, hard disk, or other type of removable disk.

FPU (floating point unit)   Formal term for math coprocessor (also called a numeric processor) circuitry inside a CPU. A math coprocessor calculates by using a floating point math (which allows for decimals). Before the Intel 80486, FPUs were separate chips from the CPU.

fragmentation   Occurs when files and directories get jumbled on a fixed disk and are no longer contiguous. Can significantly slow down hard drive access times and can be repaired by using the defrag utility included with each version of Windows. (*See also* defragmentation.)

frame   A data unit transferred across a network. Frames consist of several parts, such as the sending and receiving MAC addresses, the data being sent, and the frame check sequence.

freeware   Software that is distributed for free, with no license fee.

frequency   Measure of a sound's tone, either high or low.

frontside bus   Wires that connect the CPU to the main system RAM. Generally running at speeds of 66–133 MHz. Distinct from the expansion bus and the backside bus, though it shares wires with the former.

front-view projector   Shoots the image out the front and counts on you to put a screen in front at the proper distance.

FRU (field replaceable unit)   Any part of a PC that is considered to be replaceable "in the field," i.e., a customer location. There is no official list of FRUs—it is usually a matter of policy by the repair center.

FTP (File Transfer Protocol)   Rules that enable two computers to talk to one another during a file transfer. Protocol used when you transfer a file from one computer to another across the Internet. FTP uses port numbers 20 and 21.

FTPS (File Transfer Protocol over SSL)   An extension to FTP that uses the Secure Sockets Layer (SSL) or Transport Layer Security (TLS) cryptographic protocol.

full-duplex   Any device that can send and receive data simultaneously.

Full-Speed USB   USB standard that runs at 12 Mbps. Also known as USB 1.1.

fully qualified domain name (FQDN)   A complete, bottom-to-top label of a DNS host going from the specific host to the top-level domain that holds it and all of the intervening domain layers, each layer being separated by a dot. FQDNs are entered into browser bars and other utilities in formats like *mail.totalseminars.com*.

Function (fn) key   Special key on many laptops that enables some keys to perform a third duty.

fuser assembly   Mechanism in laser printers that uses two rollers to fuse toner to paper during the print process.

future-proofing   Configuring a PC so that it will run programs (especially games) released in the coming years.

Gadgets   Small tools, such as clocks or calendars, in Windows Vista and 7 that are placed on the Sidebar.

gain Ratio of increase of radio frequency output provided by an antenna, measured in decibels (dB).

gamepad An input device specifically designed for playing computer games. These usually consist of one or more thumbsticks, a directional pad, multiple face buttons, and two or more triggers.

GDI (graphical device interface) Component of Windows that utilizes the CPU rather than the printer to process a print job as a bitmapped image of each page.

general protection fault (GPF) Error code usually seen when separate active programs conflict on resources or data.

geometry Numbers representing three values: heads, cylinders, and sectors per track; defines where a hard drive stores data.

geotracking Feature in cellular phones that enables the cell phone companies and government agencies to use the ID or MAC address to pinpoint where a phone is at any given time.

gesture-based interaction Various actions using one or more fingers to input on a touchscreen, like on a tablet or smartphone.

giga- Prefix for the quantity 1,073,741,824 (2^{30}) or for 1 billion. One gigabyte would be 1,073,741,824 bytes, except with hard drive labeling, where it means 1 billion bytes. One gigahertz is 1 billion hertz. Commonly used for GB (gigabyte), Gb (gigabit), and GHz (gigahertz).

glasses Wearable computing device that enables a user to perform some computing functions via a pair of glasses.

Global Positioning System (GPS) Technology that enables a mobile device to determine where you are on a map.

globally unique identifier (GUID) partition table (GPT) Partitioning scheme that enables you to create more than four primary partitions without needing to use dynamic disks.

gpresult Windows command for listing group policies applied to a user.

GPU (graphics processing unit) Specialized processor that helps the CPU by taking over all of the 3-D rendering duties.

gpupdate Windows command for making immediate group policy changes in an individual system.

grayscale depth Number that defines how many shades of gray the scanner can save per dot.

grayware Program that intrudes into a user's computer experience without damaging any systems or data.

grep   Linux command to search through text files or command outputs to find specific information or to filter out unneeded information.

group   Collection of user accounts that share the same access capabilities.

Group Policy   Means of easily controlling the settings of multiple network clients with policies such as setting minimum password length or preventing Registry edits.

GSM (Global System for Mobile Communications)   Wireless data standard for mobile devices.

guest account   Very limited built-in account type for Windows; a member of the Guest group.

GUI (graphical user interface)   Interface that enables user to interact with computer graphically, by using a mouse or other pointing device to manipulate icons that represent programs or documents, instead of using only text as in early interfaces. Pronounced "gooey."

gyroscope   Device that can detect the position of the tablet or phone in 3-D space.

HAL (hardware abstraction layer)   Part of the Windows OS that separates system-specific device drivers from the rest of the operating system.

handshaking   Procedure performed by modems, terminals, and computers to verify that communication has been correctly established.

hang   Occurs when a computer or program stops responding to keyboard commands or other input; a computer or program in such a state is said to be "hung."

hang time   Number of seconds a too-often-hung computer is airborne after you have thrown it out a second-story window.

hard drive   Data-recording system using solid disks of magnetic material turning at high speeds to store and retrieve programs and data in a computer. Abbreviated HDD for *hard disk drive*.

hardware   Physical computer equipment such as electrical, electronic, magnetic, and mechanical devices. Anything in the computer world that you can hold in your hand. A hard drive is hardware; Microsoft Word is not.

hardware protocol   Defines many aspects of a network, from the packet type to the cabling and connectors used.

HBA (host bus adapter)   Connects SATA devices to the expansion bus. Also known as the SATA controller.

HD (Hi-Definition)   Multimedia transmission standard that defines high-resolution images and 5.1, 6.1, and 7.1 sound.

HDA (High Definition Audio)   Intel-designed standard to support features such as true surround sound with many discrete speakers. Often referred to by its code name, Azalia.

HDD (hard disk drive)   Data-recording system using solid disks of magnetic material turning at high speeds to store and retrieve programs and data in a computer.

HDMI (High Definition Multimedia Interface)   Single multimedia connection that includes both high-definition video and audio. One of the best connections for outputting to television. Also contains copy protection features.

head actuator   Mechanism for moving the arms inside a hard drive on which the read/write heads are mounted.

headphones   Audio output device that sits on top of or in a user's ears.

heads   Short for read/write heads used by hard drives to store data.

heat dope   *See* thermal compound.

hex (hexadecimal)   Base-16 numbering system using ten digits (0 through 9) and six letters (A through F). In the computer world, shorthand way to write binary numbers by substituting one hex digit for a four-digit binary number (e.g., hex 9 = binary 1001).

hibernation   Power management setting in which all data from RAM is written to the hard drive before the system goes into Sleep mode. Upon waking up, all information is retrieved from the hard drive and returned to RAM.

hidden attribute   File attribute that, when used, does not allow the dir command to show a file.

hierarchical directory tree   Method by which Windows organizes files into a series of folders, called directories, under the root directory. (*See also* root directory.)

high gloss   Laptop screen finish that offers sharper contrast, richer colors, and wider viewing angles than a matte finish, but is also much more reflective.

high-level formatting   Format that sets up a file system on a drive.

high-voltage anode   Component in a CRT monitor that has very high voltages of electricity flowing through it.

Hi-Speed USB   USB standard that runs at 480 Mbps. Also referred to as USB 2.0.

home screen   The default "desktop" of a mobile device.

home server PC   A computer built to store files on a small office/home office (SOHO) network.

HomeGroup   A Windows 7 feature that connects a group of computers using a common password—no special user names required. Each computer can be a member of only one homegroup at a time. Homegroups enable simple sharing of documents and printers between computers.

honesty   Telling the truth—a very important thing for a tech to do.

horizontal cabling   Cabling that connects the equipment room to the work areas.

host   On a TCP/IP network, single device that has an IP address—any device (usually a computer) that can be the source or destination of a data packet. In the mainframe world, computer that is made available for use by multiple people simultaneously. Also, in virtualization, a computer running one or more virtual operating systems.

hostname   Windows command for displaying the name of a computer.

hotspot   Feature that enables a mobile device connected to a mobile data network to be used as a wireless access point (WAP) for other devices. Often these are stand-alone devices, though many cellular phones and data-connected tablets can be set up to act as hotspots.

hot-swappable   Any hardware that may be attached to or removed from a PC without interrupting the PC's normal processing.

HRR (horizontal refresh rate)   Amount of time it takes for a monitor to draw one horizontal line of pixels on a display.

HTML (Hypertext Markup Language)   ASCII-based, script-like language for creating hypertext documents such as those on the World Wide Web.

HTPC   A home theater PC designed to attach to a TV or projector for movie and TV viewing.

HTTP (Hypertext Transfer Protocol)   Extremely fast protocol used for network file transfers in the WWW environment. Uses port 80.

HTTPS (HTTP over Secure Sockets Layer)   Secure form of HTTP used commonly for Internet business transactions or any time when a secure connection is required. Uses port 443. (*See also* HTTP.)

hub   Electronic device that sits at the center of a star topology network, providing a common point for the connection of network devices. Hubs repeat all information out to all ports and have been replaced by switches, although the term "hub" is still commonly used.

hybrid   A network topology that combines features from multiple other topologies, such as the star-bus topology.

hyperthreading   CPU feature that enables a single pipeline to run more than one thread at once.

hypervisor   Software that enables a single computer to run multiple operating systems simultaneously.

IaaS (Infrastructure as a Service)   Cloud-hosted provider of virtualized servers and networks.

I/O (input/output)   General term for reading and writing data to a computer. "Input" includes data entered from a keyboard, identified by a pointing device (such as a mouse), or loaded from a disk. "Output" includes writing information to a disk, viewing it on a monitor, or printing it to a printer.

I/O addressing   Using the address bus to talk to system devices.

I/O advanced programmable interrupt controller (IOAPIC)   Typically located in the Southbridge, acts as the traffic cop for interrupt requests to the CPU.

I/O base address   First value in an I/O address range.

ICH (I/O Controller Hub)   Official name for Southbridge chip found in Intel's chipsets.

icon   Small image or graphic, most commonly found on a system's desktop, that launches a program when selected.

iCloud   Apple cloud-based storage. iCloud enables a user to back up all iPhone or iPad data, and makes that data accessible from anywhere. This includes any media purchased through iTunes and calendars, contacts, reminders, and so forth.

ICS (Internet Connection Sharing)   Windows feature that enables a single network connection to be shared among several machines.

IDE (integrated drive electronics)   PC specification for small- to medium-size hard drives in which the controlling electronics for the drive are part of the drive itself, speeding up transfer rates and leaving only a simple adapter (or "paddle"). IDE only supported two drives per system of no more than 504 MB each, and has been completely supplanted by Enhanced IDE. EIDE supports four drives of over 8 GB each and more than doubles the transfer rate. The more common name for PATA drives. Also known as *intelligent drive electronics*. (*See* PATA.)

identify the problem   To question the user and find out what has been changed recently or is no longer working properly. Step 1 of 6 in the CompTIA troubleshooting theory.

IEC-320   Connects the cable supplying AC power from a wall outlet into the power supply.

IEEE (Institute of Electronic and Electrical Engineers)   Leading standards-setting group in the United States.

IEEE 1284   IEEE standard governing parallel communication.

IEEE 1394   IEEE standard governing FireWire communication. (*See also* FireWire.)

IEEE 1394a   FireWire standard that runs at 400 Mbps.

IEEE 1394b   FireWire standard that runs at 800 Mbps.

IEEE 802.11   Wireless Ethernet standard more commonly known as Wi-Fi.

ifconfig   Linux command for finding out a computer's IP address information.

image deployment   Operating system installation that uses a complete image of a hard drive as an installation media. Helpful when installing an operating system on a large number of identical PCs.

image file   Bit-by-bit image of data to be burned on CD or DVD—from one file to an entire disc—stored as a single file on a hard drive. Particularly handy when copying from CD to CD or DVD to DVD.

IMAP4 (Internet Message Access Protocol version 4)   An alternative to POP3 that retrieves e-mail from an e-mail server, like POP3; IMAP uses TCP port 143.

IMC (integrated memory controller)   Memory controller circuitry built into the CPU that enables faster control over things like the large L3 cache shared among multiple cores.

IMEI (International Mobile Equipment Identity)   A 15-digit number used to uniquely identify a mobile device, typically a smartphone or other device that connects to a cellular network.

impact printer   Uses pins and inked ribbons to print text or images on a piece of paper.

impedance   Amount of resistance to an electrical signal on a wire. Relative measure of the amount of data a cable can handle.

IMSI (International Mobile Subscriber Identity)   A unique number that represents the actual user associated with a particular SIM card. The IMSI is usually available from the carrier, to ensure that stolen phones are not misused. The IMSI number can be used to unlock a phone as well.

incident report   Record of the details of an accident, including what happened and where it happened.

incremental backup   Backs up all files that have their archive bits turned on, meaning that they have been changed since the last backup. Turns the archive bits off after the files have been backed up.

Information Technology (IT)   Field of computers, their operation, and their maintenance.

infrastructure mode   Wireless networking mode that uses one or more WAPs to connect the wireless network nodes to a wired network segment.

inheritance   NTFS feature that passes on the same permissions in any subfolders/files resident in the original folder.

ink cartridge   Small container of ink for inkjet printers.

inkjet printer   Uses liquid ink, sprayed through a series of tiny jets, to print text or images on a piece of paper.

installation disc   Typically a CD-ROM or DVD that holds all the necessary device drivers.

instruction set   All of the machine-language commands that a particular CPU is designed to understand.

integrity   Always doing the right thing.

interface   Means by which a user interacts with a piece of software.

Interrupt 13 (INT13) extensions   Improved type of BIOS that accepts EIDE drives up to 137 GB.

interrupt/interruption   Suspension of a process, such as the execution of a computer program, caused by an event external to the computer and performed in such a way that the process can be resumed. Events of this kind include sensors monitoring laboratory equipment or a user pressing an interrupt key.

inverter   Device used to convert DC current into AC. Commonly used with CCFLs in laptops and flatbed scanners.

iOS   The operating system of Apple mobile devices.

IP (Internet Protocol)   A set of rules used to identify and locate devices on networks; an essential component in the TCP/IP protocol suite, the communications rules that enable the Internet to function.

IP address   Numeric address of a computer connected to the Internet. An IPv4 address is made up of four octets of 8-bit binary numbers translated into their shorthand numeric values. An IPv6 address is 128 bits long. The IP address can be broken down into a network ID and a host ID. Also called *Internet address*.

ipconfig   Command-line utility for Windows servers and workstations that displays the current TCP/IP configuration of the machine. Similar to ifconfig.

IPS (in-plane switching)   Display technology that replaces the older twisted nematic (TN) panels for more accurate colors and a wider viewing angle.

IPsec (Internet Protocol security)   Microsoft's encryption method of choice for networks consisting of multiple networks linked by a private connection, providing transparent encryption between the server and the client.

IPv4 (Internet Protocol version 4)   Internet standard protocol that provides a common layer over dissimilar networks; used to move packets among host computers and through gateways if necessary. Part of the TCP/IP protocol suite. Uses the dotted-decimal format—*x.x.x.x*. Each *x* represents an eight-bit binary number, or 0-255. Here's an example: 192.168.4.1.

IPv6 (Internet Protocol version 6) Protocol in which addresses consist of eight sets of four hexadecimal numbers, each number being a value between 0000 and FFFF, using a colon to separate the numbers. Here's an example: FEDC:BA98:7654:3210:080 0:200C:00CF:1234.

IR (infrared) Wireless short-range device communication technology.

IrDA (Infrared Data Association) protocol Protocol that enables communication through infrared devices, with speeds of up to 4 Mbps.

IRQ (interrupt request) Signal from a hardware device, such as a modem or a mouse, indicating that it needs the CPU's attention. In PCs, IRQs are sent along specific IRQ channels associated with a particular device. IRQ conflicts were a common problem in the past when adding expansion boards, but the plug-and-play specification has removed this headache in most cases.

ISA (Industry Standard Architecture) Design found in the original IBM PC for the slots that allowed additional hardware to be connected to the computer's motherboard. An 8-bit, 8.33-MHz expansion bus was designed by IBM for its AT computer and released to the public domain. An improved 16-bit bus was also released to the public domain. Replaced by PCI in the mid-1990s.

ISDN (integrated services digital network) CCITT (Comité Consultatif Internationale de Télégraphie et Téléphonie) standard that defines a digital method for communications to replace the current analog telephone system. ISDN is superior to POTS telephone lines because it supports a transfer rate of up to 128 Kbps for sending information from computer to computer. It also allows data and voice to share a common phone line. DSL reduced demand for ISDN substantially. (*See also* POTS.)

ISO-9660 CD format to support PC file systems on CD media. Supplanted by the Joliet format and then the UDF format.

ISO file Complete copy (or image) of a storage media device, typically used for optical discs. ISO image files typically have a file extension of .iso.

ISP (Internet service provider) Company that provides access to the Internet, usually for money.

ITX A family of motherboard form factors. Mini-ITX is the largest and the most popular of the ITX form factors but is still quite small.

iwconfig Linux command for viewing and changing wireless settings.

jack (physical connection) Part of a connector into which a plug is inserted. Also referred to as a port.

Joliet   Extension of the ISO 9660 format. Most popular CD format to support PC file systems on CD media. Joliet has been supplanted by UDF.

joule   Unit of energy describing (in this book) how much energy a surge suppressor can handle before it fails.

joystick   Peripheral often used while playing computer games; originally intended as a multipurpose input device.

Jump List   A Windows 7 menu that shows context-sensitive information about whatever is on the taskbar.

jumper   Pair of small pins that can be shorted with a shunt to configure many aspects of PCs. Often used in configurations that are rarely changed, such as master/slave settings on IDE drives.

Kerberos   Authentication encryption developed by MIT to enable multiple brands of servers to authenticate multiple brands of clients.

kernel   Core portion of program that resides in memory and performs the most essential operating system tasks.

keyboard   Input device. Three common types of keyboards exist: those that use a mini-DIN (PS/2) connection, those that use a USB connection, and those that use wireless technology.

Keychain   The macOS password management and storage service that saves passwords for computer and non-computer environments. Also, the *iCloud Keychain* adds synchronization among any macOS and iOS devices connected to the Internet for a user account.

kilo-   Prefix that stands for the binary quantity 1,024 (2^{10}) or the decimal quantity of 1,000. One kilobyte is 1,024 bytes. One kilohertz, however, is a thousand hertz. Commonly used for KB (kilobyte), Kb (kilobit), and KHz (kilohertz).

Knowledge Base   Large collection of documents and FAQs that is maintained by Microsoft. Found on Microsoft's Web site, the Knowledge Base is an excellent place to search for assistance on most operating system problems.

KVM (keyboard, video, mouse) switch   Hardware device that enables multiple computers to be viewed and controlled by a single mouse, keyboard, and screen.

LAN (local area network)   Group of PCs connected via cabling, radio, or infrared that use this connectivity to share resources such as printers and mass storage.

laptop   Traditional clamshell portable computing device with built-in LCD monitor, keyboard, and trackpad.

laser   Single-wavelength, in-phase light source that is sometimes strapped to the head of sharks by bad guys. Note to henchmen: Lasers should never be used with sea bass, no matter how ill-tempered they might be.

laser printer Electro-photographic printer in which a laser is used as the light source.

Last Known Good Configuration Option on the Advanced Startup Options menu that enables your system to revert to a previous configuration to troubleshoot and repair any major system problems.

latency Amount of delay before a device may respond to a request; most commonly used in reference to RAM.

LBA (logical block addressing) Translation (algorithm) of IDE drives promoted by Western Digital as a standardized method for breaking the 504-MB limit in IDE drives. Subsequently universally adopted by the PC industry and standard on all EIDE drives.

LCD (liquid crystal display) Type of display commonly used on portable computers. LCDs have also replaced CRTs as the display of choice for desktop computer users. LCDs use liquid crystals and electricity to produce images on the screen.

LED (light-emitting diode) Solid-state device that vibrates at luminous frequencies when current is applied.

LED monitor LCD monitor that uses LEDs instead of CCFL tubes for backlighting, creating much higher contrast ratios and image quality.

Level 1 (L1) cache First RAM cache accessed by the CPU, which stores only the absolute most-accessed programming and data used by currently running threads. Always the smallest and fastest cache on the CPU.

Level 2 (L2) cache Second RAM cache accessed by the CPU. Much larger and often slower than the L1 cache, and accessed only if the requested program/data is not in the L1 cache.

Level 3 (L3) cache Third RAM cache accessed by the CPU. Much larger and slower than the L1 and L2 caches, and accessed only if the requested program/data is not in the L2 cache.

Li-Ion (Lithium-Ion) Battery commonly used in portable PCs. Li-Ion batteries don't suffer from the memory effects of Nickel-Cadmium (Ni-Cd) batteries and provide much more power for a greater length of time.

Library Feature in Windows 7 and later that aggregates folders from multiple locations and places them in a single, easy-to-find spot in Windows Explorer or File Explorer. Default libraries in Windows include Documents, Music, Pictures, and Videos.

Lightning An 8-pin connector, proprietary to Apple, that can be inserted without regard to orientation. Used to connect mobile devices to a power or data source.

Lightweight Directory Access Protocol (LDAP) Protocol used by many operating systems and applications to access directories.

line of sight   An unobstructed view between two devices. Required for IR communications.

link light   An LED on NICs, hubs, and switches that lights up to show good connection between the devices.

Linux   Open-source UNIX-clone operating system.

liquid cooling   A method of cooling a PC that works by running some liquid—usually water—through a metal block that sits on top of the CPU, absorbing heat. The liquid gets heated by the block, runs out of the block and into something that cools the liquid, and is then pumped through the block again.

Live DVD   The Windows installation media, which loads the Windows Preinstallation Environment (WinPE) directly from disc into memory and doesn't access or modify a hard drive or solid state drive.

Local Security Policy   Windows tool used to set local security policies on an individual system.

local user account   List of user names and their associated passwords with access to a system, contained in an encrypted database.

Local Users and Groups   Tool enabling creation and changing of group memberships and accounts for users.

location data   Information provided by a mobile device's GPS; used for mapping functions as well as for location-aware services, such as finding nearby restaurants or receiving coupons for nearby shops.

log files   Files created in Windows to track the progress of certain processes.

logical drives   Sections of an extended partition on a hard drive that are formatted and (usually) assigned a drive letter, each of which is presented to the user as if it were a separate drive.

logon screen   First screen of the Windows interface, used to log on to the computer system.

LoJack   Security feature included in some BIOS/UEFI that enables a user to track the location of a stolen PC, install a key logger, or remotely shut down the stolen computer.

loopback plug   Device used during loopback tests to check the female connector on a NIC.

Low-Speed USB   USB standard that runs at 1.5 Mbps. Also called USB 1.1.

LPT port   Commonly referred to as a printer port; usually associated with a local parallel port.

LPX   First slimline form factor; replaced by NLX form factor.

ls Linux equivalent of the dir command, which displays the contents of a directory.

lumens Unit of measure for amount of brightness on a projector or other light source.

Mac (Also **Macintosh**.) Common name for Apple Computers' flagship operating system. *See* macOS.

MAC (media access control) address Unique 48-bit address assigned to each network card. IEEE assigns blocks of possible addresses to various NIC manufacturers to help ensure that the address is always unique. The Data Link layer of the OSI model uses MAC addresses to locate machines.

MAC address filtering Method of limiting wireless network access based on the physical, hard-wired address of the wireless NIC of a computing device.

machine language Binary instruction code that is understood by the CPU.

macOS Apple's flagship operating system; runs on Intel-based hardware. CompTIA refers to the operating system as *Mac OS*. The OS has gone through many names: Macintosh, Mac, Mac OS X, OS X, and macOS.

maintenance kits Set of commonly replaced printer components provided by many manufacturers.

MAM (mobile application management) Software enabling a company's IT department to manage mobile apps on employees' mobile devices.

mass storage Hard drives, optical discs, removable media drives, etc.

matte Laptop screen finish that offers a good balance between richness of colors and reflections, but washes out in bright light.

MBR (master boot record) Tiny bit of code that takes control of the boot process from the system BIOS.

MCC (memory controller chip) Chip that handles memory requests from the CPU. Although once a special chip, it has been integrated into the chipset or CPU on modern PCs.

MCH (Memory Controller Hub) Intel-coined name for what is now commonly called the Northbridge.

md (mkdir) Command in the command-line interface used to create directories.

MDM (mobile device management) A formalized structure that enables an organization to account for all the different types of devices used to process, store, transmit, and receive organizational data.

mega- Prefix that stands for the binary quantity 1,048,576 (2^{20}) or the decimal quantity of 1,000,000. One megabyte is 1,048,576 bytes. One megahertz, however, is a million hertz. Sometimes shortened to *Meg*, as in "a 286 has an address space of 16 Megs." Commonly used for MB (megabyte), Mb (megabit), and MHz (megahertz).

megapixel   Term used typically in reference to digital cameras and their ability to capture data.

memory   Device or medium for temporary storage of programs and data during program execution. Synonymous with storage, although it most frequently refers to the internal storage of a computer that can be directly addressed by operating instructions. A computer's temporary storage capacity is measured in kilobytes (KB), megabytes (MB), or gigabytes (GB) of RAM (random-access memory). Long-term data storage on hard drives and solid-state drives is also measured in megabytes, gigabytes, and terabytes.

memory addressing   Taking memory address from system RAM and using it to address non-system RAM or ROM so the CPU can access it.

Memory Stick   Sony's flash memory card format; rarely seen outside of Sony devices.

mesh topology   Network topology where each computer has a dedicated line to every other computer, most often used in wireless networks.

Metro UI   The original name for the Windows 8 user interface. Due to legal concerns, it was rebranded the "Modern UI."

MFT (master file table)   Enhanced file allocation table used by NTFS. (*See also* FAT.)

Micro Secure Digital (MicroSD)   The smallest form factor of the SD flash memory standard. Often used in mobile devices.

micro USB   USB connector commonly found on Android phones.

microATX (µATX)   Variation of the ATX form factor, which uses the ATX power supply. MicroATX motherboards are generally smaller than their ATX counterparts but retain all the same functionality.

microBTX   Variation of the BTX form factor. MicroBTX motherboards are generally smaller than their BTX counterparts but retain all the same functionality.

microdrive   Tiny hard drives using the CompactFlash form factor. (*See also* CompactFlash (CF).)

microphone   An input device for recording audio.

microprocessor   "Brain" of a computer. Primary computer chip that determines relative speed and capabilities of the computer. Also called CPU.

Microsoft Certified IT Professional (MCITP)   An advanced IT certification specifically covering Microsoft products.

MIDI (musical instrument digital interface)   Interface between a computer and a device for simulating musical instruments. Rather than sending large sound samples, a computer can simply send "instructions" to the instrument describing pitch, tone, and duration of a sound. MIDI files are therefore very efficient. Because a MIDI file is made up of a set of instructions rather than a copy of the sound, modifying each component of the file is easy. Additionally, it is possible to program many channels, or "voices," of music to be played simultaneously, creating symphonic sound.

MIDI-enabled device   External device that enables you to input digital sound information in the MIDI format; for example, a MIDI keyboard (the piano kind).

migration   Moving users from one operating system or hard drive to another.

MIMO (multiple in/multiple out)   Feature of 802.11n devices that enables the simultaneous connection of up to four antennas, greatly increasing throughput. 802.11ac also uses MU-MIMO, which gives a WAP the capability to broadcast to multiple users simultaneously.

mini-audio connector   Very popular, 1/8-inch diameter connector used to transmit two audio signals; perfect for stereo sound.

mini connector   One type of power connector from a PC power supply unit. Supplies 5 and 12 volts to peripherals. Also known as a floppy connector.

mini-DIN   Small connection most commonly used for keyboards and mice. Many modern systems implement USB in place of mini-DIN connections. Also called *PS/2*.

Mini-ITX   The largest and the most popular of the three ITX form factors. At a miniscule 6.7 by 6.7 inches, Mini-ITX competes with microATX and proprietary small form factor (SFF) motherboards.

Mini-PCI   Specialized form of PCI designed for use in laptops.

Mini-PCIe   Specialized form of PCIe designed for use in laptops.

mini power connector   Connector used to provide power to floppy disk drives.

Mini Secure Digital (MiniSD)   The medium-size form factor of the SD flash memory standard.

mini USB   Smaller USB connector often found on digital cameras.

mirror set   A type of mirrored volume created with RAID 1. (*See also* mirroring.)

mirrored volume   Volume that is mirrored on another volume. (*See also* mirroring.)

mirroring   Reading and writing data at the same time to two drives for fault tolerance purposes. Considered RAID level 1. Also called *drive mirroring*.

Mission Control   A feature of macOS that enables switching between open applications, windows, and more.

mkdir   *See* md.

MMC (Microsoft Management Console)   Means of managing a system, introduced by Microsoft with Windows 2000. The MMC enables an administrator to customize management tools by picking and choosing from a list of snap-ins. Available snap-ins include Device Manager, Users and Groups, and Computer Management.

MMX (multimedia extensions)   Specific CPU instructions that enable a CPU to handle many multimedia functions, such as digital signal processing. Introduced with the Pentium CPU, these instructions are used on all ×86 CPUs.

mode   Any single combination of resolution and color depth set for a system.

modem (modulator/demodulator)   Device that converts a digital bit stream into an analog signal (modulation) and converts incoming analog signals back into digital signals (demodulation). An analog communications channel is typically a telephone line, and analog signals are typically sounds.

module   Small circuit board that DRAM chips are attached to. Also known as a "stick."

Molex connector   Computer power connector used by optical drives, hard drives, and case fans. Keyed to prevent it from being inserted into a power port improperly.

monaural   Describes recording tracks from one source (microphone) as opposed to stereo, which uses two sources.

monitor   Screen that displays data from a PC. Can use either a cathode ray tube (CRT) or a liquid crystal display (LCD) to display images.

motherboard   Flat piece of circuit board that resides inside your computer case and has a number of connectors on it. Every device in a PC connects directly or indirectly to the motherboard, including CPU, RAM, hard drives, optical drives, keyboard, mouse, and video cards.

motherboard book   Valuable resource when installing a new motherboard. Normally lists all the specifications about a motherboard, including the type of memory and type of CPU usable with the motherboard.

mount point   Drive that functions like a folder mounted into another drive.

mouse   Input device that enables users to manipulate a cursor on the screen to select items.

move   Command in the command-line interface used to move a file from one location to another.

MP3   Short for MPEG Audio Layer 3, a type of compression used specifically for turning high-quality digital audio files into much smaller, yet similar sounding, files.

MPA (Microsoft Product Activation)   The process of providing a valid Microsoft software key to prove the authenticity of your software.

MPEG-2   Moving Pictures Experts Group Layer 2 standard of video and audio compression offering resolutions up to 1280×720 at 60 frames per second.

MPEG-4   Moving Pictures Experts Group Layer 4 standard of video and audio compression offering improved compression over MPEG-2.

MS-CHAP   Microsoft's variation of the Challenge Handshake Authentication Protocol that uses a slightly more advanced encryption protocol. Windows Vista uses MS-CHAP v2 (version 2), and does not support MS-CHAP v1 (version 1).

msconfig (System Configuration utility)   Executable file that runs the Windows System Configuration utility, which enables users to configure a system's boot files and critical system files. Often used for the name of the utility, as in "just run msconfig."

MSDS (material safety data sheet)   Standardized form that provides detailed information about potential environmental hazards and proper disposal methods associated with various computing components.

msinfo32   Provides information about hardware resources, components, and the software environment. Also known as System Information.

multiboot installation   OS installation in which multiple operating systems are installed on a single machine.

multi rail   A power supply configuration where the current is split into multiple pathways, each with a maximum capacity and its own Over Current Protection circuitry. CompTIA calls two-rail versions of this technology "dual rail."

multicore processing   Using two or more execution cores on one CPU die to divide up work independently of the OS.

multifactor authentication   Authentication schema requiring more than one unique authentication method. For example, a password and a fingerprint.

multifunction device (MFD)   A printer with one or more other devices rolled in, such as scanner and copy machine. Also called a *multifunction printer (MFP)*.

multimedia extensions (MMX)   Originally an Intel CPU enhancement designed for graphics-intensive applications (such as games). It was never embraced but eventually led to improvements in how CPUs handle graphics.

multimeter   Device used to measure voltage, amperage, and resistance.

multiple Desktops   A GUI feature that enables a computer to have more than one Desktop, each with its own icons and background. The macOS supports multiple Desktops with Spaces. Most Linux distros use multiple Desktops, often called workspaces. Microsoft introduced the feature with Windows 10.

multisession drive   Recordable CD drive capable of burning multiple sessions onto a single recordable disc. A multisession drive also can close a CD-R so that no further tracks can be written to it.

multitasking   Process of running multiple programs or tasks on the same computer at the same time.

multi-touch   Input method on many smartphones and tablets that enables you to use multiple fingers to do all sorts of fun things, such as using two fingers to scroll or swipe to another screen or desktop.

music CD-R   CD using a special format for home recorders. Music CD-R makers pay a small royalty to avoid illegal music duplication.

mv   The move command in Linux and macOS.

My Computer   An applet that enables users to access a complete listing of all fixed and removable drives contained within a system and to view/manage configuration properties of the computer. Also, an aspect of Windows Explorer.

Nano-ITX   A 4.7 inch by 4.7 inch variation of the ITX form factor.

NAT (Network Address Translation)   A means of translating a system's IP address into another IP address before sending it out to a larger network. NAT manifests itself by a NAT program that runs on a system or a router. A network using NAT provides the systems on the network with private IP addresses. The system running the NAT software has two interfaces: one connected to the network and the other connected to the larger network.
    The NAT program takes packets from the client systems bound for the larger network and translates their internal private IP addresses to its own public IP address, enabling many systems to share a single IP address.

native resolution   Resolution on an LCD monitor that matches the physical pixels on the screen.

navigation pane   Windows 7's name for the Folders list in Windows Explorer.

net   Command in Windows that enables users to view a network without knowing the names of the other computers on that network.

NetBIOS (Network Basic Input/Output System)   Protocol that operates at the Session layer of the OSI seven-layer model. This protocol creates and manages connections based on the names of the computers involved.

NetBIOS Extended User Interface (NetBEUI)   The default networking protocol for early versions of Windows.

netbook   Small, low-power laptop used primarily for Web browsing.

network   Collection of two or more computers interconnected by telephone lines, coaxial cables, satellite links, radio, and/or some other communication technique. Group of computers that are connected and that communicate with one another for a common purpose.

Network   Interface in Windows Vista and Windows 7 for Windows Explorer; displays networked computers and other devices, such as network printers.

network attached storage (NAS)   A device that attaches to a network for the sole purpose of storing and sharing files.

network connection   A method for connecting two or more computers together. (*See also* network.)

network ID   Logical number that identifies the network on which a device or machine exists. This number exists in TCP/IP and other network protocol suites.

network printer   Printer that connects directly to a network.

network protocol   Software that takes the incoming data received by the network card, keeps it organized, sends it to the application that needs it, and then takes outgoing data from the application and hands it to the NIC to be sent out over the network.

network technology   A practical application of a topology and other critical standards to provide a method to get data from one computer to another on a network. It defines many aspects of a network, from the topology, to the frame type, to the cabling and connectors used.

NFC (near field communication)   Mobile technology that enables short-range wireless communication between mobile devices. Now used for mobile payment technology such as Apple Pay and Google Wallet.

NIC (network interface card or controller)   Expansion card or motherboard interface that enables a PC to connect to a network via a network cable. A *wireless NIC* enables connection via radio waves rather than a physical cable.

Ni-Cd (Nickel-Cadmium)   Battery used in the first portable PCs. Heavy and inefficient, these batteries also suffered from a memory effect that could drastically shorten the overall life of the battery. (*See also* Ni-MH, Li-Ion.)

Ni-MH (Nickel-Metal Hydride)   Battery used in early portable PCs. Ni-MH batteries had fewer issues with the memory effect than Ni-Cd batteries. Ni-MH batteries in computing devices have been replaced by Lithium-Ion batteries. (*See also* Ni-Cd, Li-Ion.)

nit   Value used to measure the brightness of an LCD display. A typical LCD display has a brightness of between 100 and 400 nits.

NLQ (near-letter quality)   Designation for dot-matrix printers that use 24-pin printheads.

NLX   Second form factor for slimline systems. Replaced the earlier LPX form factor. (NLX apparently stands for nothing; it's just a cool grouping of letters.)

NMI (non-maskable interrupt)   Interrupt code sent to the processor that cannot be ignored. Typically manifested as a BSoD.

NNTP (Network News Transfer Protocol)   Protocol run by news servers that enable newsgroups.

non-system disk or disk error   Error that occurs during the boot process. Common causes for this error are leaving a nonbootable floppy disk, CD, USB stick, or other media in the system while the computer is booting.

nonvolatile memory   Storage device that retains data even if power is removed; typically refers to a ROM or flash ROM chip, but also could be applied to hard drives, optical media, and other storage devices.

normal backup   Full backup of every selected file on a system. Turns off the archive bit after the backup.

Northbridge   Chip that connects a CPU to memory, the PCI bus, Level 2 cache, and high-speed graphics. Communicates with the CPU through the frontside bus. Newer CPUs feature an integrated Northbridge.

notebook   *See* laptop.

notification area   Contains icons representing background processes, the system clock, and volume control. Located by default at the right edge of the Windows taskbar. Many users call this area the system tray.

nslookup   Command-line program in Windows used to determine exactly what information the DNS server is providing about a specific host name.

ntdetect.com   One of the critical Windows NT/2000/XP startup files.

NTFS (New Technology File System)   Robust and secure file system introduced by Microsoft with Windows NT. NTFS provides an amazing array of configuration options for user access and security. Users can be granted access to data on a file-by-file basis. NTFS enables object-level security, long filename support, compression, and encryption.

NTFS permissions   Restrictions that determine the amount of access given to a particular user on a system using NTFS.

ntldr (NT Loader)   Windows NT/2000/XP boot file. Launched by the MBR or MFT, ntldr looks at the boot.ini configuration file for any installed operating systems.

NVIDIA Corporation   One of the foremost manufacturers of graphics cards and chipsets.

NVMe (Non Volatile Memory Express)   SSD technology that supports a communication connection between the operating system and the SSD directly through a PCIe bus lane, reducing latency and taking full advantage of the speeds of high-end SSDs. NVMe SSDs come in a couple of formats, such as an add-on expansion card and a 2.5-inch drive, like the SATA drives for portables. NVMe drives are a lot more expensive currently than other SSDs, but offer much higher speeds.

NX bit   Technology that enables the CPU to protect certain sections of memory. This feature, coupled with implementation by the operating system, stops malicious attacks from getting to essential operating system files. Microsoft calls the feature Data Execution Prevention (DEP).

object   System component that is given a set of characteristics and can be managed by the operating system as a single entity.

object access auditing   Feature of Event Viewer's Security section that creates an entry in the Security Log when certain objects are accessed, such as a file or folder.

ODBC Data Source Administrator   Programming tool for configuring the Open Database Connectivity (ODBC) coding standard. Data Source Administrator enables you to create and manage entries called Data Source Names (DSNs) that point OBDC to a database. DSNs are used by ODBC-aware applications to query ODBC to find their databases.

OEM (original equipment manufacturer)   Company that produces software or computer parts that other companies sell in their end products. Microsoft develops Windows OS, for example, that many companies sell with their PCs. Microsoft is the OEM for Windows. Alternatively, refers to companies that source parts from contract manufacturers but brand the end product as their own. Several Chinese companies make the circuit boards and screens used in Apple products, for example, but the final product is an Apple device. Apple is the OEM for the iPhone.

offline files   Windows 7/8/8.1/10 feature that enables storing a local, duplicate copy of files and folders on a hard drive. When the laptop connects to a network, Windows automatically syncs those offline files with the files and folders on a file server or other PC.

ohm(s)   Electronic measurement of a cable's impedance.

open source   Software environment that is not controlled by a central creator or distributer.

OLED (organic light-emitting diode)   Display technology where an organic compound provides the light for the screen, thus eliminating the need for a backlight or inverter.

OpenGL   One of two popular APIs used today for video cards. Originally written for UNIX systems but now ported to Windows and Apple systems. (*See also* DirectX.)

optical disc/media   Types of data discs (such as DVDs, CDs, BDs, etc.) that are read by a laser.

optical drive   Drive used to read/write to optical discs, such as CDs or DVDs.

optical mouse   Pointing device that uses light rather than electronic sensors to determine movement and direction the mouse is being moved.

optical resolution   Resolution a scanner can achieve mechanically. Most scanners use software to enhance this ability.

optical zoom   Mechanical ability of most cameras to "zoom" in as opposed to the digital ability.

option ROM   Alternative way of telling the system how to talk to a piece of hardware. Option ROM stores BIOS for the card in a chip on the card itself.

OS (operating system)   Series of programs and code that creates an interface so users can interact with a system's hardware; for example, Windows, macOS, and Linux.

OS X   Former name for the operating system on Apple Macintosh computers. *See* macOS.

OSI seven-layer model   Architecture model based on the OSI protocol suite that defines and standardizes the flow of data between computers. The seven layers are:

Layer 1, Physical layer   Defines hardware connections and turns binary into physical pulses (electrical or light). Repeaters and hubs operate at the Physical layer.

Layer 2, Data Link layer   Identifies devices on the Physical layer. MAC addresses are part of the Data Link layer. Bridges operate at the Data Link layer.

Layer 3, Network layer   Moves packets between computers on different networks. Routers operate at the Network layer. IP and IPX operate at the Network layer.

Layer 4, Transport layer   Breaks data down into manageable chunks. TCP, UDP, SPX, and NetBEUI operate at the Transport layer.

Layer 5, Session layer   Manages connections between machines. NetBIOS and Sockets operate at the Session layer.

Layer 6, Presentation layer   Can also manage data encryption; hides the differences between various types of computer systems.

Layer 7, Application layer   Provides tools for programs to use to access the network (and the lower layers). HTTP, FTP, SMTP, and POP3 are all examples of protocols that operate at the Application layer.

overclocking   To run a CPU or video processor faster than its rated speed.

P1 power connector Provides power to ATX motherboards; 20-pin with original ATX motherboards, 24-pin on current units.

P4 power connector Provides additional 12-volt power for the CPU to motherboards that support Pentium 4 and later processors.

P8 and P9 connectors Provide power to old, AT-style motherboards.

PaaS (Platform as a Service) Cloud-based virtual server(s). These virtualized platforms give programmers tools needed to deploy, administer, and maintain a Web application.

packet Basic component of communication over a network. Group of bits of fixed maximum size and well-defined format that is switched and transmitted as a single entity through a network. Contains source and destination address, data, and control information.

page fault Minor memory-addressing error.

page file Portion of the hard drive set aside by Windows to act like RAM. Also known as *virtual memory* or *swap file*.

PAN (personal area network) Small wireless network created with Bluetooth technology and intended to link PCs and other peripheral devices.

parallel execution When a multicore CPU processes more than one thread.

parallel port Connection for the synchronous, high-speed flow of data along parallel lines to a device, usually a printer.

Parental Controls Tool to allow monitoring and limiting of user activities; designed for parents to control the content their children can access.

parity Method of error detection where a small group of bits being transferred is compared to a single parity bit set to make the total bits odd or even. Receiving device reads the parity bit and determines if the data is valid, based on the oddness or evenness of the parity bit.

parity RAM Earliest form of error-detecting RAM; stored an extra bit (called the parity bit) to verify the data.

partition Section of the storage area of a hard disk. Created during initial preparation of the hard disk, before the disk is formatted.

partition boot table Sector of a partition that stores information important to its partition, such as the location of the OS boot files. Responsible for loading the OS on a partition.

partition table Table located in the boot sector of a hard drive that lists every partition on the disk that contains a valid operating system.

partitioning   Electronically subdividing a physical hard drive into groups called partitions (or volumes).

passcode lock   Mobile device security feature that requires you to type in a series of letters, numbers, or motion patterns to unlock the mobile device each time you press the power button.

passive cooling   System designed to remove heat from a processor without the use of power or mechanical parts; usually accomplished through a metal heat sink.

passive matrix   Technology for producing colors in LCD monitors by varying voltages across wire matrices to produce red, green, or blue dots.

passwd   Linux command for changing a user's password.

password   Key used to verify a user's identity on a secure computer or network.

Password Authentication Protocol (PAP)   Oldest and most basic form of authentication. Also the least safe, because it sends all passwords in clear text.

password reset disk   External storage media such as a floppy disk or USB flash drive with which users can recover a lost password without losing access to any encrypted, or password-protected, data. The password reset disk must be created proactively; if a user loses a password and did not already make a reset disk, it will be of no help to create one after the loss.

PATA (parallel ATA)   Implementation that integrates the controller on the disk drive itself. (*See also* ATA, IDE, SATA.)

patch   Small piece of software released by a software manufacturer to correct a flaw or problem with a particular piece of software.

patch cables   Short (2 to 5 feet) UTP cables that connect patch panels to a switch or router.

patch panel   A panel containing a row of female connectors (ports) that terminate the horizontal cabling in the equipment room. Patch panels facilitate cabling organization and provide protection to horizontal cabling.

path   Route the operating system must follow to find an executable program stored in a subfolder.

PC Card   Credit card–size adapter card that adds functionality in older laptops and other computer devices. PC Cards come in 16-bit and CardBus parallel format and ExpressCard serial format. (*See also* PCMCIA.)

PC tech   Someone with computer skills who works on computers.

PCI (Peripheral Component Interconnect)   Design architecture for the expansion bus on the computer motherboard that enables system components to be added to the computer. Local bus standard, meaning that devices added to a computer through this port will use the processor at the motherboard's full speed (up to 33 MHz) rather than at the slower 8-MHz speed of the regular bus. Moves data 32 or 64 bits at a time rather than the 8 or 16 bits the older ISA buses supported.

PCIe (PCI Express) Serialized successor to PCI and AGP that uses the concept of individual data paths called lanes. May use any number of lanes, although a single lane (×1) and 16 lanes (×16) are the most common on motherboards.

PCIe 6/8-pin power connector Connector on some power supplies for powering a dedicated graphics card.

PCI-X (PCI Extended) Enhanced version of PCI, 64 bits wide. Typically seen in servers and high-end systems.

PCL (printer control language) Printer control language created by Hewlett-Packard and used on a broad cross-section of printers.

PCM (pulse code modulation) Sound format developed in the 1960s to carry telephone calls over the first digital lines.

PCMCIA (Personal Computer Memory Card International Association) Consortium of computer manufacturers who devised the PC Card standard for credit card–size adapter cards that add functionality in older laptop computers and other computer devices. (*See also* PC Card.)

Pearson VUE Company that administers the CompTIA A+ exams.

peer-to-peer network Network in which each machine can act as both a client and a server.

pen-based computing Input method used by many PDAs that combines handwriting recognition with modified mouse functions, usually in the form of a pen-like stylus.

Pentium Name given to the fifth and later generations of Intel microprocessors; original had a 32-bit address bus, 64-bit external data bus, and dual pipelining. Also used for subsequent generations of Intel processors—the Pentium Pro, Pentium II, Pentium III, and Pentium 4. Currently used as a budget label for Intel CPUs.

Performance Tab in Task Manager that tracks PC performance.

Performance Information and Tools Applet that provides a relative feel for how your computer stacks up against other systems using the Windows Experience Index.

Performance Logs and Alerts Snap-in enabling the creation of a written record of most everything that happens on the system.

Performance Monitor Windows tool for observing a computer's performance.

Performance Options Tool enabling users to configure CPU, RAM, and virtual memory settings.

peripheral   Any device that connects to the system unit.

permission propagation   Term to describe what happens to permissions on an object when you move or copy it.

persistence   Phosphors used in CRT screens continuing to glow after being struck by electrons, long enough for the human eye to register the glowing effect. Glowing too long makes the images smeary, and too little makes them flicker.

personal safety   Keeping yourself away from harm.

Personalization applet   Windows Vista applet with which users can change display settings such as resolution, refresh rate, color depth, and desktop features. The Windows 7 version focuses on managing themes, desktop icons, mouse pointers, and account pictures. *For other options, see* Display applet.

PGA (pin grid array)   Arrangement of a large number of pins extending from the bottom of the CPU package. There are many variations on PGA.

phablet   Portmanteau of "phone" and "tablet." Colloquial term for a large phone. (And yes, I had to look up "portmanteau" as well. Love my editors!)

Phillips-head screwdriver   Most important part of a PC tech's toolkit.

phishing   The act of trying to get people to give their usernames, passwords, or other security information by pretending to be someone else electronically.

Phoenix Technologies   Major producer of BIOS software for motherboards.

phosphor   Electro-fluorescent material that coats the inside face of a cathode ray tube (CRT). After being hit with an electron, it glows for a fraction of a second.

photosensitive drum   Aluminum cylinder coated with particles of photosensitive compounds. Used in a laser printer and often contained within the toner cartridge.

Pico-ITX   A 3.8 by 2.8 inch version of the ITX form factor.

PII (personally identifiable information)   Any data or information that can identify a specific individual.

pin 1   Designator used to ensure proper alignment of floppy drive and hard drive connectors.

pinch   Multi-touch gesture that enables you to make an image bigger or smaller.

pinned application   Windows method of attaching programs to the taskbar. A pinned application gets a permanent icon displayed on the taskbar.

ping (packet Internet groper)   Slang term for a small network message (ICMP ECHO) sent by a computer to check for the presence and aliveness of another. Used to verify the presence of another system. Also, the command used at a prompt to ping a computer.

pinwheel of death   The macOS indicator that is the equivalent of a Windows unresponsive application; in this case, a spinning rainbow wheel.

PIO (programmed I/O) mode   Series of speed standards created by the Small Form Factor Committee for the use of PIO by hard drives. Modes range from PIO mode 0 to PIO mode 4.

pipeline   Processing methodology where multiple calculations take place simultaneously by being broken into a series of steps. Often used in CPUs and video processors.

pixel (picture element)   In computer graphics, smallest element of a display space that can be independently assigned color or intensity.

PKI (public key infrastructure)   Authentication schema where public keys are exchanged between all parties using digital certificates, enabling secure communication over public networks.

platform   The environment that supports a piece of software. One example is the hardware on which an operating system runs, such as the macOS platform. The mobile platform on which smartphone apps run is another example.

Play Store   Storefront where Android users can purchase and download apps and digital media.

plug   Hardware connection with some sort of projection that connects to a port.

plug and play (PnP)   Combination of smart PCs, smart devices, and smart operating systems that automatically configure all necessary system resources and ports when you install a new peripheral device.

polygons   Multisided shapes used in 3-D rendering of objects. In computers, video cards draw large numbers of triangles and connect them to form polygons.

polymorph virus   Virus that attempts to change its signature to prevent detection by antivirus programs, usually by continually scrambling a bit of useless code.

POP3 (Post Office Protocol 3)   One of the two protocols that receive e-mail from SMTP servers. POP3 uses TCP port 110. While historically most e-mail clients use this protocol, the IMAP4 e-mail protocol is now more common.

pop-up   Irritating browser window that appears automatically when you visit a Web site.

port (networking)   In networking, the number used to identify the requested service (such as SMTP or FTP) when connecting to a TCP/IP host. Examples: 80 (HTTP), 443, (HTTPS), 21 (FTP), 23 (Telnet), 25 (SMTP), 110 (POP3), 143 (IMAP), and 3389 (RDP).

port (physical connection) Part of a connector into which a plug is inserted. Physical ports are also referred to as jacks.

port forwarding Preventing the passage of any IP packets through any ports other than the ones prescribed by the system administrator.

port replicator Device that plugs into a USB port or other specialized port and offers common PC ports, such as serial, parallel, USB, network, and PS/2. Plugging a laptop into a port replicator can instantly connect the computer to nonportable components such as a printer, scanner, monitor, or full-size keyboard. Port replicators are typically used at home or in the office with the nonportable equipment already connected.

port triggering Router function that enables a computer to open an incoming connection to one computer automatically based on a specific outgoing connection.

positional audio Range of commands for a sound card to place a sound anywhere in 3-D space.

POST (power-on self test) Basic diagnostic routine completed by a system at the beginning of the boot process to make sure a display adapter and the system's memory are installed; it then searches for an operating system. If it finds one, it hands over control of the machine to the OS.

POST card Device installed into a motherboard expansion slot that assists in troubleshooting boot problems by providing a two-digit code indicating the stop of the boot process where the problem is occurring.

PostScript Language defined by Adobe Systems, Inc. for describing how to create an image on a page. The description is independent of the resolution of the device that will actually create the image. It includes a technology for defining the shape of a font and creating a raster image at many different resolutions and sizes.

POTS (plain old telephone system) Analog telephone service still used in many homes.

power conditioning Ensuring and adjusting incoming AC wall power to as close to standard as possible. Most UPS devices provide power conditioning.

power good wire Used to wake up the CPU after the power supply has tested for proper voltage.

Power over Ethernet (PoE) Technology that provides power and data transmission through a single network cable.

power options Windows feature that enables better control over power use by customizing a balanced, power saver, or high performance power plan.

power profile A collection of settings that determine how Windows manages power use. Adjust in the Control Panel.

power supply fan   Small fan located in a system power supply that draws warm air from inside the power supply and exhausts it to the outside.

power supply unit (PSU)   Provides the electrical power for a PC. Converts standard AC power into various voltages of DC electricity in a PC.

Power Users group   After Administrator/Administrators, the second most powerful account and group type in Windows. Power users have differing capabilities in different versions of Windows.

PowerShell   *See* Windows PowerShell.

ppm (pages per minute)   Speed of a printer.

PPP (Point-to-Point Protocol)   Enables a computer to connect to the Internet through a dial-in connection and enjoy most of the benefits of a direct connection.

preboot execution environment (PXE)   Technology that enables a PC to boot without any local storage by retrieving an OS from a server over a network.

primary corona   Wire that is located near the photosensitive drum in a laser printer and is charged with extremely high voltage to form an electric field, enabling voltage to pass to the photosensitive drum, thus charging the photosensitive particles on the surface of the drum. Also called the *primary charge roller*.

primary partition   Partition on a Windows hard drive that can store a bootable operating system.

print resolution   Quality of a print image.

print spooler   Area of memory that queues up print jobs that the printer will handle sequentially.

printed circuit board (PCB)   Copper etched onto a nonconductive material and then coated with some sort of epoxy for strength.

printer   Output device that can print text or illustrations on paper. Microsoft uses the term to refer to the software that controls the physical print device.

printhead   Case that holds the printwires in a dot-matrix printer.

printwires   Grid of tiny pins in a dot-matrix printer that strike an inked printer ribbon to produce images on paper.

PRL (Preferred Roaming List)   A list that is occasionally and automatically updated to a phone's firmware by the carrier so that the phone will be configured with a particular carrier's networks and frequencies, in a priority order, that it should search for when it can't locate its home carrier network.

Problem Reports and Solutions   Control Panel applet in Windows Vista that lists all Windows Error Reporting issues (plus a few easy-to-check items like firewall and antimalware status).

Processes   Tab in Task Manager that lists all running processes on a system. Frequently a handy tool for ending buggy or unresponsive processes.

processing   The second step of the computing process, where the CPU completes the tasks that the user's input has given it.

processor   Device that computes according to a computing device's programming.

product key   Code used during installation to verify legitimacy of the software.

profile   A list of settings that a calibration device creates when calibrating monitors and printers.

program/programming   Series of binary electronic commands sent to a CPU to get work done.

programmer   A person who writes applications or operating system software for computing devices.

Programs and Features   Windows Control Panel applet; enables uninstalling or changing program options and altering Windows features.

projector   Device for projecting video images from PCs or other video sources, usually for audience presentations. Available in front- and rearview displays.

prompt   A character or message provided by an operating system or program to indicate that it is ready to accept input.

proprietary   Technology unique to a particular vendor.

proprietary crash screen   A screen, differing between operating systems, that indicates an NMI.

protective cover   A case or sleeve that protects a mobile device from physical damage.

protocol   Agreement that governs the procedures used to exchange information between cooperating entities. Usually includes how much information is to be sent, how often it is to be sent, how to recover from transmission errors, and who is to receive the information.

proxy server   Device that fetches Internet resources for a client without exposing that client directly to the Internet. Usually accepts requests for HTTP, FTP, POP3, and SMTP resources. Often caches, or stores, a copy of the requested resource for later use. Common security feature in the corporate world.

ps   Linux command for listing all processes running on the computer.

Public folder   Folder that all users can access and share with all other users on the system or network.

punchdown tool   A specialized tool for connecting UTP wires to a punchdown block.

pwd   Linux command that displays the user's current path.

quad-channel architecture   Feature similar to dual-channel RAM, but requiring four sticks instead of two.

Quality of Service (QoS)   Policies that control how much bandwidth a protocol, PC, user, VLAN, or IP address may use.

queue   Area where objects wait their turn to be processed. Example: the print queue, where print jobs wait until it is their turn to be printed.

Quick Launch toolbar   Enables a user to launch commonly used programs with a single click in Windows.

QVGA   Video display mode of 320 × 240.

RAID (redundant array of independent [or inexpensive] disks)   Method for creating a fault-tolerant storage system. RAID uses multiple hard drives in various configurations to offer differing levels of speed/data redundancy.

RAID 0   Uses byte-level striping and provides no fault tolerance.

RAID 1   Uses mirroring or duplexing for increased data redundancy.

RAID 5   Uses block-level and parity data striping. Requires three or more drives.

RAID 6   Disk striping with extra parity. Like RAID 5, but with more parity data. Requires five or more drives, but you can lose up to two drives at once and your data is still protected.

RAID 0+1   A RAID 0 configuration created by combining two RAID 1s. Provides both speed and redundancy, but requires at least four disks.

RAID 10   The opposite of RAID 0+1, two mirrored RAID 0 configurations. Also provides both speed and redundancy, and also requires four disks.

rails   Separate DC voltage paths within an ATX power supply.

RAM (random access memory)   Memory that can be accessed at random; that is, memory which you can write to or read from without touching the preceding address. This term is often used to mean a computer's main memory.

RAMDAC (random access memory digital-to-analog converter)   Circuitry used on video cards that support analog monitors to convert the digital video data to analog.

Raspberry Pi   Latest generation of ultra-small, ARM-based computer motherboards with support for many operating systems and peripherals.

raster image   Pattern of dots representing what the final product should look like.

raster line   Horizontal pattern of lines that forms an image on the monitor screen.

rd (rmdir)   Command in the command-line interface used to remove directories.

read-only attribute   File attribute that does not allow a file to be altered or modified. Helpful when protecting system files that should not be edited.

ReadyBoost   Windows feature enabling the use of flash media as dedicated virtual memory.

rearview projector   Projector that shoots an image onto a screen from the rear. Rearview projectors are usually self-enclosed and very popular for TVs, but are virtually unheard of in the PC world.

reciprocity   *See* Ethic of Reciprocity.

Recovery Console   Command-line interface boot mode for Windows that is used to repair a Windows XP system suffering from massive OS corruption or other problems.

Recycle Bin   Location to which files are moved when they are deleted from a modern Windows system. To permanently remove files from a system, they must be emptied from the Recycle Bin.

Refresh your PC   Windows RE option to Refresh your PC in Windows 8 and later rebuilds the OS, but preserves all user files and settings and any applications purchased from the Windows Store. Note well: Refresh deletes every other application on your system.

regedit.exe   Program used to edit the Windows Registry.

region code   Encoding that restricts you from playing DVD or Blu-ray Disc movies on a player that doesn't share the same region code.

register   Storage area inside the CPU used by the onboard logic to perform calculations. CPUs have many registers to perform different functions.

registered RAM   *See* buffered RAM.

registration   Usually optional process that identifies the legal owner/user of the product to the supplier.

Registry   Complex binary file used to store configuration data about a particular Windows system. To edit the Registry, users can use the applets found in the Control Panel or regedit.exe or regedt32.exe.

regsvr32 In contrast with regedit.exe, the regsvr32 command can modify the Registry in only one way, adding (or *registering*) dynamic link library (DLL) files as command components in the Registry.

Reliability and Performance Monitor Windows Vista's extended Performance applet.

remediation Repairing damage caused by a virus.

remnant Potentially recoverable data on a hard drive that remains despite formatting or deleting.

Remote Assistance Feature of Windows that enables users to give anyone control of his or her desktop over the Internet.

Remote Desktop Windows tool used to enable a local system to graphically access the desktop of a remote system.

Remote Desktop Protocol Protocol used for Microsoft's Remote Desktop tool. Uses port 3389.

remote network installation A common method of OS installation where the source files are placed in a shared directory on a network server. Then, whenever a tech needs to install a new OS, he or she can boot the computer, connect to the source location on the network, and start the installation from there.

removable media Any storage on a computer that can be easily removed. For example, optical discs, flash drives, or memory cards.

ren (rename) Command in the command-line interface used to rename files and folders.

Reset your PC Windows RE option in Windows 8 and later that nukes the system—deleting all apps, programs, user files, and user settings—and presents a fresh installation of Windows. Use Reset as the last resort when troubleshooting a PC. And back up data first, if possible.

resistance Difficulty in making electricity flow through a material, measured in ohms.

resistive touchscreen Type of touchscreen that responds to the pressure applied to the screen.

resistor Any material or device that impedes the flow of electrons. Electronic resistors measure their resistance (impedance) in ohms. (*See* ohm(s).)

resolution Measurement for monitors and printers expressed in horizontal and vertical dots or pixels. Higher resolutions provide sharper details and thus display better-looking images.

resources Data and services of a PC.

respect   How all techs should treat their customers.

response rate   Time it takes for all of the sub-pixels on the panel to go from pure black to pure white and back again.

restore point   System snapshot created by the System Restore utility that is used to restore a malfunctioning system. (*See also* System Restore.)

RET (resolution enhancement technology)   Technology that uses small dots to smooth out jagged edges that are typical of printers without RET, producing a higher-quality print job.

RFI (radio frequency interference)   Another form of electrical interference caused by radio wave–emitting devices, such as cell phones, wireless network cards, and microwave ovens.

RG-6   Coaxial cabling used for cable television. It has a 75-ohm impedance and uses an F-type connector.

RG-58   Coaxial cabling used for 10Base2 networks.

ring   Network topology where the computers form a circle and all data flows in one direction only.

RIP (raster image processor)   Component in a printer that translates the raster image into commands for the printer.

riser card   Special adapter card, usually inserted into a special slot on a motherboard, that changes the orientation of expansion cards relative to the motherboard. Riser cards are used extensively in slimline computers to keep total depth and height of the system to a minimum. Sometimes called a daughterboard.

RJ (registered jack) connector   UTP cable connector, used for both telephone and network connections. RJ-11 is a connector for four-wire UTP; usually found in telephone connections. RJ-45 is a connector for eight-wire UTP; usually found in network connections.

RJ-11   *See* RJ (registered jack) connector.

RJ-45   *See* RJ (registered jack) connector.

rm   Linux command for deleting files.

rmdir   *See* rd (rmdir).

RoHS (Restriction of Hazardous Substances Directive)   A European Union (EU) standard that regulates toxic substances, such as lead, mercury, and cadmium; adopted by most computer part makers.

robocopy   Powerful command-line utility for copying files and directories, even over a network.

ROM (read-only memory)   Generic term for nonvolatile memory that can be read from but not written to. This means that code and data stored in ROM cannot be corrupted by accidental erasure. Additionally, ROM retains its data when power is removed, which makes it the perfect medium for storing BIOS data or information such as scientific constants.

root directory   Directory that contains all other directories.

root keys   Five main categories in the Windows Registry:
HKEY_CLASSES_ROOT
HKEY_CURRENT_USER
HKEY_USERS
HKEY_LOCAL_MACHINE
HKEY_CURRENT_CONFIG

router   Device connecting separate networks; forwards a packet from one network to another based on the network address for the protocol being used. For example, an IP router looks only at the IP network number. Routers operate at Layer 3 (Network) of the OSI seven-layer model.

RS-232   Standard port recommended by the Electronics Industry Association (EIA) for serial devices.

run   A single piece of installed horizontal cabling.

Run dialog box   Command box in which users can enter the name of a particular program to run; an alternative to locating the icon in older versions of Windows. *Run* opens a program, folder, document or Web site. Supplanted in Windows Vista and later with the Search box.

S.M.A.R.T. (Self-Monitoring, Analysis, and Reporting Technology)   Monitoring system built into hard drives.

S/PDIF (Sony/Philips Digital Interface Format)   Digital audio connector found on many sound cards. Users can connect their computers directly to a 5.1 speaker system or receiver. S/PDIF comes in both a coaxial and an optical version.

SaaS (Software as a Service)   Cloud-based service to store, distribute, and update programs and applications. The SaaS model provides access to necessary applications wherever you have an Internet connection, often without having to carry data with you or regularly update software. At the enterprise level, the subscription model of many SaaS providers makes it easier to budget and keep hundreds or thousands of computers up-to-date.

Safe mode   Important diagnostic boot mode for Windows that only runs very basic drivers and turns off virtual memory.

safety goggles   Protective glasses that keep stuff out of your eyes.

sampling   Capturing sound waves in electronic format.

SATA (serial ATA)   Serialized version of the ATA standard that offers many advantages over PATA (parallel ATA) technology, including thinner cabling, keyed connectors, and lower power requirements.

SATA bridge   Adapter that allows PATA devices to be connected to a SATA controller.

SATA Express (SATAe)   The newest version of SATA that ties capable drives directly into the PCI Express bus on motherboards. Each lane of PCIe 3.0 is capable of handling up to 8 Gbps data throughput. A SATAe drive grabbing two lanes, therefore, could move a whopping 16 Gbps through the bus.

SATA power connector   15-pin, L-shaped connector used by SATA devices that support the hot-swappable feature.

satellites   Two or more standard stereo speakers to be combined with a subwoofer for a speaker system (i.e., 2.1, 5.1, 7.1, etc.).

Scalable Link Interface (SLI)   Technology for connecting two or more NVIDIA GPUs together in a system.

scan code   Unique code corresponding to each key on the keyboard, sent from the keyboard controller to the CPU.

SCSI (small computer system interface)   Powerful and flexible peripheral interface popularized on the Macintosh and used to connect hard drives, optical drives, tape drives, scanners, and other devices to PCs of all kinds. Normal SCSI enables up to seven devices to be connected through a single bus connection, whereas Wide SCSI can handle 15 devices attached to a single controller.

SCSI chain   Series of SCSI devices working together through a host adapter.

SCSI ID   Unique identifier used by SCSI devices. No two SCSI devices may have the same SCSI ID.

SD (Secure Digital)   Very popular format for flash media cards, such as SD Card; also supports I/O devices.

SDK (software development kit)   Software that used to create custom applications or add features to existing applications on your mobile device.

SDRAM (synchronous DRAM)   DRAM that is synchronous, or tied to the system clock. This type of RAM is used in all modern systems.

sector   Segment of one of the concentric tracks encoded on the disk during a low-level format. A sector holds 512 bytes of data.

sector translation   Translation of logical geometry into physical geometry by the onboard circuitry of a hard drive.

sectors per track (sectors/track)   Combined with the number of cylinders and heads, defines the disk geometry.

secure boot   UEFI feature that secures the boot process by requiring properly signed software. This includes boot software and software that supports specific, essential components.

segment   The connection between a computer and a switch.

self-grounding   A less-than-ideal method for ridding yourself of static electricity by touching a metal object such as a computer case. Alternately, sending yourself to your own room as a form of punishment.

serial port   Common connector on older PC. Connects input devices (such as a mouse) or communications devices (such as a modem). Also referred to as a COM port.

server   Computer that shares its resources, such as printers and files, with other computers on a network. Example: network file system server that shares its disk space with a workstation that does not have a disk drive of its own.

service   A program that runs in the background of a PC but displays no icons anywhere. You can view a list of services in the Windows Task Manager. Also, a program stored in a ROM chip.

service pack   Collection of software patches released at one time by a software manufacturer.

Services   Tab in Windows Task Manager that lists all running services on a system.

set-top box   A device that adds "Smart TV" features, such as Internet streaming and show recording, to normal TVs.

Settings app   Windows 10 tool that combines a huge number of otherwise disparate utilities, apps, and tools traditionally spread out all over your computer into one fairly unified, handy Windows app.

setupapi.log   Log file that tracks the installation of all hardware on a system.

setuplog.txt   Log file that tracks the complete installation process, logging the success or failure of file copying, Registry updates, and reboots.

sfc (System File Checker)   Command-prompt program (sfc.exe) that scans, detects, and restores Windows system files, folders, and paths.

SFTP (Secure File Transfer Protocol)   A reliable protocol used for copying and moving files over a network. More secure than FTP.

shadow mask   CRT screen that allows only the proper electron gun to light the proper phosphors.

share-level security   Security system in which each resource has a password assigned to it; access to the resource is based on knowing the password.

Shared Documents   Windows premade folder that is accessible by all user accounts on the computer.

shared memory   Means of reducing the amount of memory needed on a video card by borrowing from the regular system RAM, which reduces costs but also decreases performance.

shareware   Program protected by copyright; holder allows (encourages!) you to make and distribute copies under the condition that those who adopt the software after preview pay a fee to the holder of the copyright. Derivative works are not allowed, although you may make an archival copy.

shunt   Tiny connector of metal enclosed in plastic that creates an electrical connection between two posts of a jumper.

shutdown   Windows and Linux command for shutting down the computer.

SID (security identifier)   Unique identifier for every PC that most techs change when cloning.

sidebanding   Second data bus for video cards; enables the video card to send more commands to the Northbridge while receiving other commands at the same time.

Sidebar   *See* Windows Sidebar.

signal-to-noise ratio   Measure that describes the relative quality of an input port.

signature   Code pattern of a known virus; used by antivirus software to detect viruses.

SIMM (single in-line memory module)   DRAM packaging distinguished by having a number of small tabs that install into a special connector. Each side of each tab is the same signal. SIMMs come in two common sizes: 30-pin and 72-pin.

simple file sharing   Allows users to share locally or across the network but gives no control over what others do with shared files.

simple volume   Volume created when setting up dynamic disks. Acts like a primary partition on a dynamic disk.

single rail   Power supply configuration where all power is supplied along a single pathway.

single-sided RAM   Has chips on only one side as opposed to double-sided RAM.

single source   *See* closed source.

sleep timers   A feature that enables you to put the computer into Standby after a set period of time, or to turn off the monitor or hard drive after a time, thus creating your own custom power scheme.

slimline   Motherboard form factor used to create PCs that were very thin. NLX and LPX were two examples of this form factor.

slot covers   Metal plates that cover up unused expansion slots on the back of a PC. Useful in maintaining proper airflow through a computer case.

smart battery   Portable PC battery that tells the computer when it needs to be charged, conditioned, or replaced.

smart camera   A digital camera incorporating the interface and computational features of a mobile device.

smart card   Hardware authentication involving a credit card–size card with circuitry that can be used to identify the bearer of that card.

SmartMedia   Format for flash media cards; no longer used with new devices.

smartphone   A cell phone enhanced to do things formerly reserved for fully grown PCs, such as Web browsing, document viewing, and media consumption.

smart TV   A television with network capabilities—both hardware and software—for use with streaming Internet video and audio.

smart watch   A watch incorporating features of and communicating with a mobile device.

S/MIME (Secure/Multipurpose Internet Mail Extensions)   Technology used to configure digital signature settings for e-mail, and contacts from a corporate address book, depending on how the corporate e-mail server is set up.

SMM (System Management Mode)   Special CPU mode that enables the CPU to reduce power consumption by selectively shutting down peripherals.

SMTP (Simple Mail Transport Protocol)   Main protocol used to send electronic mail on the Internet. Uses port 25.

snap-ins   Small utilities that can be used with the Microsoft Management Console.

snapshot   Virtualization feature that enables you to save an extra copy of the virtual machine as it is exactly at the moment the snapshot is taken.

SNMP (Simple Network Management Protocol)   A set of standards for communication with devices connected to a TCP/IP network. Examples of these devices include routers, hubs, and switches. Uses port 161.

social engineering   Using or manipulating people inside the networking environment to gain access to that network from the outside.

socket services   Device drivers that support the PC Card socket, enabling the system to detect when a PC Card has been inserted or removed, and providing the necessary I/O to the device.

SO-DIMM (small-outline DIMM)   Memory used in portable PCs because of its small size.

soft power   Characteristic of ATX motherboards, which can use software to turn the PC on and off. The physical manifestation of soft power is the power switch. Instead of the thick power cord used in AT systems, an ATX power switch is little more than a pair of small wires leading to the motherboard.

software   Single group of programs designed to do a particular job; always stored on mass storage devices.

SOHO (small office, home office)   Designation for devices for personal use or in small businesses.

solid core   A cable that uses a single solid (not hollow or stranded) wire to transmit signals.

solid ink printers   Printer that uses solid sticks of nontoxic "ink" that produce vibrant color documents with much less waste than color laser printers.

sound card   Expansion card that can produce audible tones when connected to a set of speakers.

Southbridge   Part of a motherboard chipset; handles all the inputs and outputs to the many devices in the PC.

Spaces   macOS feature enabling multiple desktops.

spam   Unsolicited e-mails from both legitimate businesses and scammers that account for a huge percentage of traffic on the Internet.

spanned volume   Volume that uses space on multiple dynamic disks.

SPD (serial presence detect)   Information stored on a RAM chip that describes the speed, capacity, and other aspects of the RAM chip.

speaker   Device that outputs sound by using magnetically driven diaphragm.

Spotify (spotify.com)   Internet streaming music site.

sprite   Bitmapped graphic, such as a BMP file, used by early 3-D games to create the 3-D world.

spyware   Software that runs in the background of a user's PC, sending information about browsing habits back to the company that installed it onto the system.

SRAM (static RAM)   RAM that uses a flip-flop circuit rather than the typical transistor/capacitor of DRAM to hold a bit of information. SRAM does not need to be refreshed and is faster than regular DRAM. Used primarily for cache.

SSD (solid-state drive)   Data storage device that uses flash memory to store data.

SSH (Secure Shell)   Terminal emulation program similar to Telnet, except that the entire connection is encrypted. Uses port 22.

SSID (service set identifier)   Parameter used to define a wireless network; otherwise known as the network name.

SSL (Secure Sockets Layer)   Security protocol used by a browser to connect to secure Web sites.

standard user account   User account in Windows that has limited access to a system. Accounts of this type cannot alter system files, cannot install new programs, and cannot edit some settings by using the Control Panel without supplying an administrator password.

standoffs   Small mechanical separators that screw into a computer case. A motherboard is then placed on top of the standoffs, and small screws are used to secure it to the standoffs.

star bus   A hybrid network topology where the computers all connect to a central bus—a switch—but otherwise take the form of a star topology.

star topology   Network topology where the computers on the network connect to a central wiring point, usually called a hub.

Start button   Button on the Windows taskbar that enables access to the Start menu.

Start menu   Menu that can be accessed by clicking the Start button on the Windows taskbar. Enables you to see all programs loaded on the system and to start them.

Start screen   Windows 10 version of the Start menu, which functions as a combination of the traditional Start menu and Windows 8/8.1 Modern UI.

Startup Repair   A one-stop, do-it-all troubleshooting option that performs a number of boot repairs automatically.

static charge eliminator   Device used to remove a static charge.

static IP address   Manually set IP address that will not change.

stealth virus   Virus that uses various methods to hide from antivirus software.

stepper motor   One of two methods used to move actuator arms in a hard drive. (*See also* voice coil motor.)

stereo   Describes recording tracks from two sources (microphones) as opposed to monaural, which uses one source.

stick   Generic name for a single physical SIMM or DIMM.

Storage Spaces   In Windows 8 and later, a software RAID solution that enables users to group multiple drives into a single storage pool.

STP (shielded twisted pair)   Cabling for networks, composed of pairs of wires twisted around each other at specific intervals. Twists serve to reduce interference (also called crosstalk)—the more twists, the less interference. Cable has metallic shielding to protect the wires from external interference.

stranded core   A cable that uses a bundle of tiny wire filaments to transmit signals. Stranded core is not quite as good a conductor as solid core, but it will stand up to substantial handling without breaking.

stream loading   Process a program uses to constantly download updated information.

streaming media   Broadcast of data that is played on your computer and immediately discarded.

stripe set   Two or more drives in a group that are used for a striped volume.

striped volume   RAID 0 volumes. Data is spread across two drives for increased speed.

strong password   Password containing at least eight characters, including letters, numbers, and non-alphanumeric symbols.

structured cabling   TIA/EIA standards that define methods of organizing the cables in a network for ease of repair and replacement.

stylus   Pen-like input device used for pen-based computing.

su   Older Linux command for gaining root access.

subnet mask   Value used in TCP/IP settings to divide the IP address of a host into its component parts: network ID and host ID.

sub-pixels   Tiny liquid crystal molecules arranged in rows and columns between polarizing filters used in LCDs.

subfolder   A folder located inside another folder.

subwoofer   Powerful speaker capable of producing extremely low-frequency sounds.

sudo   Linux command for gaining root access.

Super I/O chip   Chip specially designed to control low-speed, legacy devices such as the keyboard, mouse, and serial and parallel ports.

SuperSpeed USB   A fast form of USB, with speeds up to 5 Gbps. Also called USB 3.0.

SuperSpeed+ USB   Updated form of SuperSpeed USB providing speeds up to 10 Gbps. Also called USB 3.1.

surge suppressor   Inexpensive device that protects your computer from voltage spikes.

SVGA (super video graphics array)   Video display mode of 800 × 600.

swap file   *See* page file.

swipe   Gesture for mobile devices where you hold your finger on the screen and slide it across the screen, either right to left or top to bottom, depending on the type of application.

swipe lock   Mobile device feature that uses a swipe gesture to unlock the mobile device.

switch   Device that filters and forwards traffic based on some criteria. A bridge and a router are both examples of switches. In the command-line interface, a switch is a function that modifies the behavior of a command.

SXGA   Video display mode of 1280 × 1024.

SXGA+   Video display mode of 1400 × 1050.

sync   The process of keeping files on mobile devices up to date with the versions on desktop PCs or over the Internet.

synchronize   *See* sync.

syntax   The proper way to write a command-line command so that it functions and does what it's supposed to do.

Sysprep (System Preparation Tool)   Windows tool that makes cloning of systems easier by making it possible to undo portions of the installation.

system BIOS   Primary set of BIOS stored on an EPROM or flash ROM chip on the motherboard. Defines the BIOS for all the assumed hardware on the motherboard, such as keyboard controller, floppy drive, basic video, and RAM.

system bus speed   Speed at which the CPU and the rest of the PC operates; set by the system crystal.

system crystal   Crystal that provides the speed signals for the CPU and the rest of the system.

system disk   Any device with a functional operating system.

system fan   Any fan controlled by the motherboard but not directly attached to the CPU.

System File Checker   *See* sfc.

System Monitor   Utility that can evaluate and monitor system resources, such as CPU usage and memory usage.

System Preferences   The macOS tool containing many administrative functions.

System Protection   Feature in Windows that enables you to restore any previous version of a file or folder.

system resources   In classic terms, the I/O addresses, IRQs, DMA channels, and memory addresses. Also refers to other computer essentials such as hard drive space, system RAM, and processor speed.

System Restore   Utility in Windows that enables you to return your PC to a recent working configuration when something goes wrong. System Restore enables you to select a restore point and then returns the computer's system settings to the way they were at that restore point—all without affecting your personal files or e-mail.

system ROM   ROM chip that stores the system BIOS.

system setup utility   *See* CMOS setup program.

System Tools   Menu containing tools such as System Information and Disk Defragmenter, accessed by selecting Start | Programs or All Programs | Accessories | System Tools.

system tray   Contains icons representing background processes and the system clock. Located by default at the right edge of the Windows taskbar. Accurately called the notification area.

system unit   Main component of the PC, in which the CPU, RAM, optical drive, and hard drive reside. All other devices—the keyboard, mouse, and monitor—connect to the system unit.

T568A   Wiring standard for Ethernet cable.

T568B   Wiring standard for Ethernet cable.

tablet   A mobile device consisting of a large touchscreen, enabling the user to browse the Web, view media, or even play games.

Tablet PC   Small portable computer distinguished by the use of a touchscreen with stylus and handwriting recognition as the primary modes of input.

tailgating   Form of infiltration and social engineering that involves following someone else through a door as if you belong in the building.

Take Ownership   Special permission allowing users to seize control of a file or folder and potentially prevent others from accessing the file/folder.

tap   Touchscreen gesture where you press a spot on the screen to start an app or interact with a running app.

Task Manager Shows all running programs, including hidden ones, and is accessed by pressing CTRL-SHIFT-ESC. You can use the Task Manager to shut down an unresponsive application that refuses to close normally.

Task Scheduler Windows utility enabling users to set tasks to run automatically at certain times.

taskbar Contains the Start button, the notification area, the Quick Launch toolbar, and buttons for running applications. Located by default at the bottom of the desktop.

tasklist A command-line version of the Task Manager.

TCP (Transmission Control Protocol) Rules used for transporting data over a network; part of the TCP/IP protocol suite, the communications rules that enable the Internet to function.

TCP/IP (Transmission Control Protocol/Internet Protocol) Communication protocols developed by the U.S. Department of Defense to enable dissimilar computers to share information over a network; default networking rules in most networks.

tech toolkit Tools a PC tech should never be without, including a Phillips-head screwdriver, a pair of tweezers, a flat-head screwdriver, a hemostat, a Torx wrench, a parts retriever, and a nut driver or two.

telecommunications room Area where all the cabling from individual PCs in a network runs to.

teleconferencing Having a video-enabled remote business meeting.

telephone scams Social engineering attack in which the attacker makes a phone call to someone in an organization to gain information.

telepresence An immersive, interactive remote business meeting.

Telnet Terminal emulation program for TCP/IP networks that allows one machine to control another as if the user were sitting in front of it. Uses port 23.

tera- Prefix that usually stands for the binary number $1,099,511,627,776$ (2^{40}). When used for mass storage, it's often shorthand for 1 trillion bytes. Commonly used for TB (terabyte).

terminal Dumb device connected to a mainframe or computer network that acts as a point for entry or retrieval of information.

Terminal A command-line interface tool available in macOS and various Linux distros.

terminal emulation Software that enables a computer to communicate with another computer or network as if the computer were a specific type of hardware terminal.

termination   Using terminating resistors to prevent packet reflection on a network cable.

terminator   Resistor that is plugged into the end of a bus cable to absorb the excess electrical signal, preventing it from bouncing back when it reaches the end of the wire. Terminators are used with coaxial cable and on the ends of SCSI chains. RG-58 coaxial cable requires resistors with a 50-ohm impedance. Also, a humanoid robot from the future designed by Skynet to destroy all human life. He'll be back.

test the theory   Attempt to resolve the issue by either confirming the theory and learning what needs to be done to fix the problem, or by not confirming the theory and forming a new one or escalating. (Step 3 of 6 in the CompTIA troubleshooting theory.)

tethering   The act of using a cellular-network-connected mobile device as a mobile hotspot.

texture   Small picture that is tiled over and over again on walls, floors, and other surfaces to create the 3-D world.

TFT (thin film transistor)   Type of LCD screen. (*See also* active matrix.)

theory of probable cause   One possible reason why something is not working; a guess.

thermal compound   Paste-like material with very high heat-transfer properties. Applied between the CPU and the cooling device, it ensures the best possible dispersal of heat from the CPU. Also called heat dope or thermal paste.

thermal printer   Printer that uses heated printheads to create high-quality images on special or plain paper.

thick client   CompTIA's name for a standard desktop computer. Runs desktop applications and meets recommended requirements for selected OS.

thin client   A system designed to handle only very basic applications with an absolute minimum amount of hardware required by the operating system. Meets minimum requirements for selected OS.

thread   Smallest logical division of a single program.

throttling   Power reduction/thermal control capability allowing CPUs to slow down during low activity or high heat build-up situations. Intel's version is known as SpeedStep, AMD's as PowerNow!.

throw   Size of the image a projector displays at a certain distance from the screen. Alternately, what you do with a computer that you just can't seem to get working.

Thunderbolt   An open standards connector interface that is primarily used to connect peripherals to devices, including mobile devices, if they have a corresponding port.

TIA/EIA (Telecommunications Industry Association/Electronic Industries Alliance) Trade organization that provides standards for network cabling and other electronics.

tiers Levels of Internet providers, ranging from the Tier 1 backbones to Tier 3 regional networks.

Tiles The building blocks of Windows 8's Modern UI, as potentially "smart" app shortcuts, capable of displaying dynamic and changing information without even opening the app.

timbre Qualities that differentiate the same note played on different instruments.

Time Machine The macOS full backup tool that enables you to recover some or all files in the event of a crash; it also enables you to restore deleted files and recover previous versions of files.

TKIP (Temporal Key Integrity Protocol) Deprecated encryption standard that provided a new encryption key for every sent packet.

TN (twisted nematic) Older technology for LCD monitors. TN monitors produce a decent display for a modest price, but they have limited viewing angles and can't accurately reproduce all the color information sent by the video card.

tone generator *See* toner.

tone probe *See* toner.

toner A fine powder made up of plastic particles bonded to iron particles, used to create the text and images on a laser printer. Also, generic term for two devices used together—a tone generator and a tone locator (probe)—to trace cables by sending an electrical signal along a wire at a particular frequency. The tone locator then emits a sound when it distinguishes that frequency.

toner cartridge Object used to store the toner in a laser printer. (*See also* laser printer, toner.)

topology The way computers connect to each other in a network.

touch interface The primary user interface on modern mobile devices where keys are replaced with tactile interaction.

touchpad Flat, touch-sensitive pad that serves as a pointing device for most laptops.

touchscreen Monitor with a type of sensing device across its face that detects the location and duration of contact, usually by a finger or stylus.

tracert Windows command-line utility used to follow the path a packet takes between two hosts. Called traceroute in macOS and Linux.

traces Small electrical connections embedded in a circuit board.

track Area on a hard drive platter where data is stored. A group of tracks with the same diameter is called a cylinder.

trackball Pointing device distinguished by a ball that is rolled with the fingers.

TrackPoint IBM's pencil eraser–size joystick used in place of a mouse on laptops.

transfer corona Thin wire, usually protected by other thin wires, that applies a positive charge to the paper during the laser printing process, drawing the negatively charged toner particles off of the drum and onto the paper. Newer printers accomplish the same feat using a *transfer roller* that draws the toner onto the paper.

transfer rate Rate of data transferred between two devices, especially over the expansion bus.

transistor-transistor logic (TTL) A type of digital circuit found in early digital monitors.

transparency Effect in the Aero desktop environment (Windows Vista/7) that makes the edges of windows transparent.

triad Group of three phosphors—red, green, blue—in a CRT.

triple-channel architecture A chipset feature similar to dual-channel RAM, but requiring three matched sticks instead of two.

Trojan horse Program that does something other than what the user who runs the program thinks it will do. Used to disguise malicious code.

troubleshooting theory Steps a technician uses to solve a problem. CompTIA A+ defines six steps: identify the problem; establish a theory of probable cause; test the theory to determine cause; establish a plan of action to resolve the problem and implement a solution; verify full system functionality and if applicable implement preventive measures; and document findings, actions, and outcomes.

Trusted Platform Module (TPM) A hardware platform for the acceleration of cryptographic functions and the secure storage of associated information.

tunneling Creating an encrypted link between two programs on two separate computers.

TV tuner Typically an add-on device that allows users to watch television on a computer.

TWAIN (technology without an interesting name) Programming interface that enables a graphics application, such as a desktop publishing program, to activate a scanner, frame grabber, or other image-capturing device.

U (Units) The unique height measurement used with equipment racks; 1 U equals 1.75 inches.

UAC (User Account Control)   Windows feature that enables standard accounts to do common tasks and provides a permissions dialog box when standard and administrator accounts do certain things that could potentially harm the computer (such as attempt to install a program).

UART (universal asynchronous receiver/transmitter)   Device that turns parallel data into serial data and *vice versa*. The cornerstone of serial ports and modems.

UDF (universal data format)   Replaced the ISO-9660 formats, enabling any operating system and optical drive to read UDF formatted disks.

UEFI (Unified Extensible Firmware Interface)   Consortium of companies that established the UEFI standard that replaced the original EFI standard.

Ultra DMA   Hard drive technology that enables drives to use direct memory addressing. Ultra DMA mode 3 drives—called ATA/33—have data transfer speeds up to 33 MBps. Mode 4 and 5 drives—called ATA/66 and ATA/100, respectively—transfer data at up to 66 MBps for mode 4 and 100 MBps for mode 5. Mode 6 pushed the transfer rate to 133 MBps. Modes 4, 5, and 6 require an 80-wire cable and a compatible controller to achieve these data transfer rates.

Ultrabook   Thin, powerful laptop powered by Intel processors and built according to the Intel design specification. Competes directly with the Apple Mac Air.

unattended installation   A type of OS installation where special scripts perform all the OS setup duties without human intervention.

unauthorized access   Anytime a person accesses resources in an unauthorized way. This access may or may not be malicious.

unbuffered RAM   RAM without a buffer chip; in other words, normal, consumer-grade RAM.

UNC (Universal Naming Convention)   Describes any shared resource in a network using the convention \\\<server name>\\<name of shared resource>.

Unicode   16-bit code that covers every character of the most common languages, plus several thousand symbols.

unsigned driver   Driver that has not gone through the Windows Certification Program to ensure compatibility. The Windows Certification Program was formerly known as the Windows Hardware Quality Labs and the Microsoft Windows Logo Program.

UPC (Universal Product Code)   Bar code used to track inventory.

update   Individual fixes for Windows that come out fairly often, on the order of once a week or so.

Upgrade Advisor   Examines your hardware and installed software (in the case of an upgrade) and provides a list of devices and software that are known to have issues with it. The Upgrade Advisor is available for download at www.microsoft.com for Windows Vista and Windows 7. Windows 8/8.1 offers the Upgrade Assistant for similar purpose. The Get Windows 10 app generates a compatibility report that functions similarly.

upgrade installation   Installation of Windows on top of an earlier installed version, thus inheriting all previous hardware and software settings.

UPS (uninterruptible power supply)   Device that supplies continuous clean power to a computer system the whole time the computer is on. Protects against power outages and sags.

URL (uniform resource locator)   An address that defines the location of a resource on the Internet. URLs are used most often in conjunction with HTML and the World Wide Web.

USB (universal serial bus)   General-purpose serial interconnect for keyboards, printers, joysticks, and many other devices. Enables hot-swapping of devices.

USB host controller   Integrated circuit that is usually built into the chipset and controls every USB device that connects to it.

USB hub   Device that extends a single USB connection to two or more USB ports, almost always directly from one of the USB ports connected to the root hub.

USB root hub   Part of the host controller that makes the physical connection to the USB ports.

USB thumb drive   Flash memory device that uses the standard USB connection.

USB Type-C (connector)   Reversible USB type cable that supports USB Super-Speed+ USB 3.1 with a top speed of 10 Gbps.

user account   Container that identifies a user to an application, operating system, or network, including name, password, user name, groups to which the user belongs, and other information based on the user and the OS being used. Usually defines the rights and roles a user plays on a system.

User Accounts applet   Applet in Control Panel that enables you to make changes to current accounts (local or global), and gives you access to the Settings charm (or app in Windows 10) when you opt to add a new account.

user interface   Visual representation of the computer on the monitor that makes sense to the people using the computer, through which the user can interact with the computer. This can be a graphical user interface (GUI) like Windows 7 or a command-line interface like the Windows PowerShell or the Recovery Console.

user profiles   Settings that correspond to a specific user account and may follow users regardless of the computers where they log on. These settings enable the user to have customized environment and security settings.

User's Files   Windows default location for content specific to each user account on a computer. It is divided into several folders such as Documents, Pictures, Music, and Video.

Users group   List of local users not allowed, among other things, to edit the Registry or access critical system files. They can create groups, but can only manage the groups they create.

USMT (User State Migration Tool)   Advanced application for file and settings transfer of multiple users.

Utilities   The macOS folder that contains tools for performing services on a Mac beyond what's included in System Preferences, including Activity Monitor and Terminal.

UTP (unshielded twisted pair)   Popular type of cabling for telephone and networks, composed of pairs of wires twisted around each other at specific intervals. The twists serve to reduce interference (also called crosstalk). The more twists, the less interference. Unlike its cousin, STP, UTP cable has no metallic shielding to protect the wires from external interference. 1000BaseT uses UTP, as do many other networking technologies. UTP is available in a variety of grades, called categories, as follows:

CAT 1 UTP   Regular analog phone lines—not used for data communications.

CAT 2 UTP   Supports speeds up to 4 Mbps.

CAT 3 UTP   Supports speeds up to 16 Mbps.

CAT 4 UTP   Supports speeds up to 20 Mbps.

CAT 5 UTP   Supports speeds up to 100 Mbps.

CAT 5e UTP   Supports speeds up to 1000 Mbps.

CAT 6 UTP   Supports speeds up to 10 Gbps.

CAT 6a UTP   Supports speeds up to 10 Gbps.

CAT 7 UTP   Supports 10-Gbps networks at 100-meter segments; shielding for individual wire pairs reduces crosstalk and noise problems. CAT 7 is not a TIA/EIA standard.

V standards   Standards established by CCITT for modem manufacturers to follow (voluntarily) to ensure compatible speeds, compression, and error correction.

vendor specific   Stores that only sell products from one manufacturer, like the Apple store.

verify full system functionality   Making sure that a problem has been resolved and will not return. (Step 5 of 6 in the CompTIA troubleshooting theory.)

vertices   Used in the second generation of 3-D rendering; have a defined X, Y, and Z position in a 3-D world.

VESA (Video Electronics Standards Association)   Consortium of computer manufacturers that standardizes improvements to common IBM PC components. VESA is responsible for the Super VGA video standard and the VLB bus architecture.

VGA (video graphics array)   Standard for the video graphics adapter that was built into IBM's PS/2 computer. It supports 16 colors in a 640 × 480 pixel video display.

vi   Linux and macOS command-line tool for editing text files.

video capture   Computer jargon for the recording of video information, such as TV shows or movies.

video card   Expansion card that works with the CPU to produce the images displayed on your computer's display.

video display   *See* monitor.

virtual assistant   Voice-activated technology that responds to user requests for information. Virtual assistants can be used to search the Internet, make reminders, do calculations, and launch apps.

virtual machine (VM)   A complete environment for a guest operating system to function as though that operating system were installed on its own computer.

virtual machine manager (VMM)   *See* hypervisor.

virtual memory   *See* page file.

virus   Program that can make a copy of itself without your necessarily being aware of it. Some viruses can destroy or damage files. The best protection is to back up files regularly.

virus definition or data file   Files that enable the virus protection software to recognize the viruses on your system and clean them. These files should be updated often. They are also called signature files, depending on the virus protection software in use.

virus shield   Passive monitoring of a computer's activity, checking for viruses only when certain events occur.

VIS (viewable image size)   Measurement of the viewable image that is displayed by a CRT rather than a measurement of the CRT itself.

VMM (virtual machine manager)   *See* hypervisor.

voice coil motor   One of two methods used to move actuator arms in a hard drive. (*See also* stepper motor.)

VoIP (Voice over Internet Protocol)   Collection of protocols that makes voice calls over a data network possible.

volatile   Memory that must have constant electricity to retain data. Alternatively, any programmer six hours before deadline after a nonstop, 48-hour coding session, running on nothing but caffeine and sugar.

volts (V)   Measurement of the pressure of the electrons passing through a wire, or voltage.

volume   Physical unit of a storage medium, such as tape reel or disk pack, that is capable of having data recorded on it and subsequently read. Also, a contiguous collection of cylinders or blocks on a disk that are treated as a separate unit.

volume boot sector   First sector of the first cylinder of each partition; stores information important to its partition, such as the location of the operating system boot files.

voucher   Means of getting a discount on the CompTIA A+ exams.

VPN (Virtual Private Network)   Encrypted connection over the Internet between a computer or remote network and a private network.

VRM (voltage regulator module)   Small card supplied with some CPUs to ensure that the CPU gets correct voltage. This type of card, which must be used with a motherboard specially designed to accept it, is not commonly seen today.

VRR (vertical refresh rate)   The amount of time it takes for a CRT to draw a complete screen. This value is measured in hertz, or cycles per second. Most modern CRTs have a VRR of 60 Hz or better.

wait state   Occurs when the CPU has to wait for RAM to provide code. Also known as pipeline stall.

WAP (wireless access point)   Device that centrally connects wireless network nodes.

wattage (watts or W)   Measurement of the amps and volts needed for a particular device to function.

wave table synthesis   Technique that supplanted FM synthesis, wherein recordings of actual instruments or other sounds are embedded in the sound card as WAV files. When a particular note from a particular instrument or voice is requested, the sound processor grabs the appropriate prerecorded WAV file from its memory and adjusts it to match the specific sound and timing requested.

Web browser   Program designed to retrieve, interpret, and display Web pages.

Web server   A computer that stores and shares the files that make up Web sites.

webcam   PC camera most commonly used for Internet video.

Welcome screen   Logon screen for Windows. Enables users to select their particular user account by clicking on their user picture.

WEP (Wired Equivalent Privacy)   Wireless security protocol that uses a standard 40-bit encryption to scramble data packets. Does not provide complete end-to-end encryption and is vulnerable to attack.

Wi-Fi   Common name for the IEEE 802.11 wireless Ethernet standard.

Wi-Fi calling   Mobile device feature that enables users to make voice calls over a Wi-Fi network, rather than a cellular network.

Wi-Fi Protected Setup (WPS)   A standard included on many WAPs and clients to make secure connections easier to configure.

wide area network (WAN)   A widespread group of computers connected using long-distance technologies.

wildcard   Character used during a search to represent search criteria. For instance, searching for *.docx will return a list of all files with a .docx extension, regardless of the filename. The * is the wildcard in that search.

WiMAX   Defunct wireless telecommunications technology.

Windows 7   Version of Windows; comes in many different editions for home and office use, but does not have a Server edition.

Windows 7 Compatibility Center   Microsoft Web page that lists the hardware and software that work with Windows 7.

Windows 8   Version of Windows noted for the Metro/Modern interface. Used for desktop and portable PCs and for mobile devices.

Windows 10   Version of Windows that blends the sleek interface of Windows 8 with the solid functionality of Windows 7. Used for desktop and portable PCs and for mobile devices.

Windows Easy Transfer   Windows method of transferring files and settings to a new PC.

Windows Explorer   Windows utility that enables you to manipulate files and folders stored on the drives in your computer. Rebranded as File Explorer in Windows 8, 8.1, and 10.

Windows Hardware Certification Program   Microsoft's rigorous testing program for hardware manufacturers, which hardware devices must pass before their drivers can be digitally signed.

Windows logo key   Key on a keyboard bearing the Windows logo that traditionally brings up the Start menu, but is also used in some keyboard shortcuts.

Windows Memory Diagnostic   Tool found in Windows 7 and later that can automatically scan a computer's RAM when encountering a problem.

Windows PowerShell   Command-line tool included with Windows. Offers a number of powerful scripting tools for automating changes both on local machines and over networks.

Windows Preinstallation Environment (WinPE)   The installation program for Windows.

Windows Recovery Environment (WinRE)   A special set of tools in the Windows setup that enables you to access troubleshooting and repair features.

Windows Sidebar   User interface feature in Windows Vista that enables users to place various gadgets, such as clocks, calendars, and other utilities, on the right side of their desktop.

Windows Update   Microsoft application used to keep Windows operating systems up to date with the latest patches or enhancements. (*See* Automatic Updates.)

Windows Vista   Version of Windows; comes in many different editions for home and office use, but does not have a Server edition.

Windows XP   Version of Windows that replaced both the entire Windows 9*x* line and Windows 2000; does not have a Server version. No longer supported by Microsoft.

Windows XP Mode   A Windows XP virtual machine that ships with Professional, Enterprise, and Ultimate editions of Windows 7 to enable users to run programs that don't work on Windows 7.

Wired (wired.com)   Hip Internet news site.

wireless local area network (WLAN)   Small group of computers that connect via Wi-Fi.

wireless security   A system of authentication for wireless clients that connect to a SOHO router. *See also* WEP, WPA, *and* WPA2.

work area   In a basic structured cabling network, often simply an office or cubicle that potentially contains a PC attached to the network.

workgroup   A simple, decentralized network that Windows PCs are configured to use by default.

worm   Very special form of virus. Unlike other viruses, a worm does not infect other files on the computer. Instead, it replicates by making copies of itself on other systems on a network by taking advantage of security weaknesses in networking protocols.

WPA (Wi-Fi Protected Access)   Wireless security protocol that uses encryption key integrity-checking/TKIP and EAP and is designed to improve on WEP's weaknesses. Supplanted by WPA 2.

WPA 2 (Wi-Fi Protected Access 2)   Wireless security protocol, also known as IEEE 802.11i. Uses the Advanced Encryption Standard (AES) and replaces WPA.

WQUXGA   Video display mode of 2560 × 1600.

wrapper   *See* container file.

WSXGA   Video display mode of 1440 × 900.

WSXGA+   Video display mode of 1680 × 1050.

WUXGA   Video display mode of 1920 × 1200.

WVGA   Video display mode of 800 × 480.

WWW (World Wide Web)   System of Internet servers that supports documents formatted in HTML and related protocols. Can be accessed by applications that use HTTP and HTTPS, such as Web browsers.

www.comptia.org   CompTIA's Web site.

WXGA   Video display mode of 1280 × 800.

x64   Describes 64-bit operating systems and software.

x86   Describes 32-bit operating systems and software.

xcopy   Command in the command-line interface used to copy multiple directories at once, which the copy command could not do.

xD (Extreme Digital) picture card   Very small flash media card format.

Xeon   Line of Intel CPUs designed for servers.

XGA (extended graphics array)   Video display mode of 1024 × 768.

XPS (XML Paper Specification) print path   Printing subsystem in Windows. Has enhanced color management and good print layout fidelity.

ZIF (zero insertion force) socket   Socket for CPUs that enables insertion of a chip without the need to apply pressure. Intel promoted this socket with its overdrive upgrades. The chip drops effortlessly into the socket's holes, and a small lever locks it in.

INDEX

O

octa-core architecture, CPUs, 42
OLED (organic light-emitting diode)
    in LCD displays, 68
    physical damage, 335
one-time passwords, 281
OneDrive
    as backup media, 205
    for data storage, 30
online data storage
    as backup media, 205
    data storage locations, 99
online peer-to-peer networks, 242
online security
    adjusting browser settings, 308
    adware, 290–292
    anti-malware programs, 299–300
    clearing cookies, 308–310
    clearing history and temporary Internet
      files, 311
    disabling autofill forms and passwords,
      312–313
    disabling unneeded plug-ins, toolbars, and
      extensions, 312
    e-mail phishing, 295–296
    fake vs. real alerts, 296
    firewalls and, 312
    infiltration, 294–295
    limiting use of personally identifiable
      information, 307
    malicious software, 289–290
    malware prevention and recovery, 300–301
    overview of, 289
    protective measures, 298
    Q&A, 314–316
    ransomware, 297–298
    recognizing suspicious banner ads, 306–307
    recognizing suspicious links, 304–306
    review, 314
    risks of public workstations, 302–303
    secure/trusted Web sites, 303–304
    smart use of Web, 301
    social engineering, 294
    spam, 293–294
    spyware, 292–293
    telephone scams, 295
    Trojan horses and worms, 297
    updates and patches, 298–299
    updating browers and plug-ins, 307–308
    viruses, 296
online store, installing applications from,
    162–163
open source
    licensing and, 179
    Linux OS, 127
operating systems (OSs)
    accessibility options, 148–149
    Chrome interface, 139–143
    complexity, 127–128
    connecting to hardware, 145–146
    connecting to Internet, 146
    executing programs, 143–145
    functions of, 125–126
    hotkeys, 146–147
    licensing, 127
    Linux interface, 139
    macOS interface, 138
    managing files, 145
    multiboot systems, 32
    overview of, 125
    programming, 7
    Q&A, 150–152
    review, 149
    screen captures, 147–148
    setting up PCs, 116–117
    software, 8
    software compatibility, 127–128
    Windows 8/8.1, 131–136
    Windows 10, 136–138
    Windows interface generally, 128–129
    Windows Vista/7, 129–131
operating systems (OSs), for desktops
  and laptops
    Chrome OS, 18
    GUI vs. command line operation, 13–14
    hardware platforms, 13
    Linux OS, 15–18
    macOS, 15, 17
    overview of, 13
    Windows OS, 14–15
operating systems (OSs), for mobile devices
    Android OS, 22–23
    Apple iOS, 22
    BlackBerry OS, 25
    mobile computing devices, 21–22
    Windows Phone OS, 23–24

platforms
application platforms, 169
hardware platforms, 13
Plug and Play, 146
plug-ins
disabling unneeded, 312
updating, 307–308
pointing devices
as input device, 76–77
Windows 8/8.1, 133
policies, password management, 282
pop-ups, adware and, 290–291
ports and connectors
audio (sound) cards, 60
for monitors, 69–74
motherboard, 50
for peripherals, 63–66
peripherals will not work, 338
troubleshooting loose connections, 335
PoS (point-of-sales) terminals
processing purchase transactions, 34
types of printer technologies, 81
possession factors, authenticating users, 280
power conditioners, ensuring reliable AC
power, 113
power management. *See also* heat management
choosing energy efficient devices, 317–318
ensuring reliable AC power, 112–113
overview of, 317
power profiles (plans), 320–322
power saving modes, 318–319
troubleshooting lack of power, 333–334
power outages, 112
power profiles (plans), 320–322
power sags, 113
power supply units (PSUs), 52–54
pre-sear license, licensing options, 180
Preview pane, 202
print servers, 27
printers
consumables, 83
disposing of, 328
enabling file and printer sharing, 259–260
installing and sharing, 267–269
overview of, 80
peripherals will not work, 338
resource sharing, 28
setting up, 84–85
types of, 81–83

printhead, on impact printers, 81
printwires, on impact printers, 81
privacy
configuring/adjusting browser settings, 308
limiting use of personally identifiable
information, 307
problem solving. *See* troubleshooting
processing, in data flow process, 39
processors. *See* CPUs (central processing units)
product keys, installing applications and,
180–181
product manuals, documentation, 339–340
productivity software, 169–170
Program and Features applet (Windows OS)
locating/removing adware, 292
uninstalling unneeded software, 120–121
Program Compatibility Troubleshooter, 337
programs/programming. *See also* applications
(apps); software
executables for running, 173
executing with operating systems, 143–145
operating systems and applications, 7
vs. applications, 153
projectors, 69
properties (attributes)
adding new from Details tab, 194
file attributes, 191–192
viewing and modifying, 192–193
proprietary software, licensing and, 180
PS/2, 65–66
PSUs (power supply units), 52–54
public domain software, licensing and, 180
push-button configuration (PBC), setting up
router security, 254

Q

quad-core architecture, CPUs, 42
quarantine, malware recovery steps, 301
Quit (Exit) commands, exiting applications, 159
QWERTY layout, keyboards, 74–75

R

radio frequency (RF)
wireless connectivity, 243
wireless keyboards, 75
RAM (random access memory)
cache, 43
capacity of, 48
identifying, 47–48

software as a service (SaaS), 164
software foundation, operating systems as, 13
SOHO (small office/home office)
   accessing router configuration utility, 247–248
   changing router SSID, 250–252
   checking Internet connectivity, 246–247
   choosing and setting up routers, 245–246
   connecting wireless clients to router, 254–255
   encryption options for routers, 251–253
   logging in and setting password for router, 247–248
   maintaining PCs, 108
   network connectivity devices, 244
   routers in, 25
   setting up router security, 253–254
   setting up wireless security, 251
   types of networks, 243
   updating router firmware, 248–250
   wired router connections, 246
solder, shifting from lead-based to tin-based, 328
solid state drives (SSDs), 93
solid state memory, RAM options, 47
solid-state storage, 93–94
sorting files, 202–203
sound (audio). *See* audio (sound)
spam, 293–294
speakers
   setting up PCs, 114
   sound cards connecting to, 60
   sound output and, 78
specialized computer systems
   ATMs (automated teller machines), 34
   GPS (global positioning system), 34–35
   overview of, 33–34
   PoS (point-of-sales) terminals, 34
   telepresence (VoIP), 35
specialized software, 171–172
specialty mobile devices, 20–21
spikes, ensuring reliable AC power, 112
spyware, 292–293
SSDs (solid state drives), 93
SSH (Secure Shell), 100
SSID (service set identifier), 250–252, 254

SSL (Secure Sockets Layer), 101, 303
Standard accounts. *See also* user accounts, 279–280
Start button
   running applications, 154–155
   Windows 8/8.1, 133–135
   Windows 10, 137
   Windows Vista/7, 129
Start menu
   executing programs, 144
   running applications, 154–155
   Windows 10, 136–137
Start screen, Windows 8/8.1, 131–133
start-up, troubleshooting, 335–336
status tray, Chrome interface, 140–142
sticks, of RAM, 47
storage. *See* data storage
streaming media, 29, 173
stylus pens, 76–77
subnotebook computers, 12
supercomputers, 8–9
Surface/Surface Pro, 20
surge suppressors, 112
switches
   network, 25
   in network connectivity, 243–244
   in SOHO LANs, 244
system attribute, files, 191
system bus, 43
system hardware
   64-bit CPUs, 42
   cache levels of CPUs, 43
   codebook or instruction set of CPUs, 43
   CPUs, 40
   motherboards, 50–51
   multicore CPUs, 42
   overview of, 39
   power and heat management, 43–46
   PSUs (power supply units), 52–54
   Q&A, 55–57
   RAM, 47–49
   review, 54–55
   speed of CPUs, 40–42
system health, monitoring, 126
system RAM, 47
System Restore, 335–336

workgroups, in network organization, 259–261
workstations
    as networking client, 240
    risks of public workstations, 302–303
    in SOHO LANs, 244
worms, 297
WPA (Wireless Protected Access), 252–253
WPA2-PSK (WPA2-pre-shared key), 253–254
WPS (Wi-Fi Protected Setup), 254

Y

Yahoo!
    adwareness, 291
    disabling unneeded plug-ins, toolbars, and
      extensions, 312

Z

zip archive files, 173

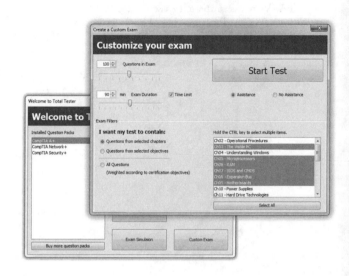